# Brands and Branding Geographies

For my parents, Michelle, Ella and Connell

# Brands and Branding Geographies

*Edited by*

Andy Pike

*Centre for Urban and Regional Development Studies (CURDS), Newcastle University, UK*

**Edward Elgar**

Cheltenham, UK • Northampton, MA, USA

© Andy Pike 2011

All rights reserved. No part of this publication may be reproduced, stored in a retrieval system or transmitted in any form or by any means, electronic, mechanical or photocopying, recording, or otherwise without the prior permission of the publisher.

Published by
Edward Elgar Publishing Limited
The Lypiatts
15 Lansdown Road
Cheltenham
Glos GL50 2JA
UK

Edward Elgar Publishing, Inc.
William Pratt House
9 Dewey Court
Northampton
Massachusetts 01060
USA

A catalogue record for this book
is available from the British Library

Library of Congress Control Number: 2011925747

MIX
Paper from
responsible sources
FSC
www.fsc.org    FSC® C018575

ISBN 978 1 84980 159 1 (cased)

Typeset by Servis Filmsetting Ltd, Stockport, Cheshire
Printed and bound by MPG Books Group, UK

# Contents

# Figures

# Tables

# Contributors

**Simon Anholt** is a leading authority on managing and measuring national identity and reputation, and the creator of the field of nation and place branding. He is a member of the UK Foreign Office's Public Diplomacy Board, and has advised the governments of some 30 other countries from Chile to Botswana, Korea to Jamaica, and Bhutan to the Faroe Islands. He is founding editor of the quarterly journal *Place Branding and Public Diplomacy,* and author of *Another One Bites the Grass; Brand New Justice; Brand America; Competitive Identity: The New Brand Management for Nations, Cities and Regions;* and *Places: Identity, Image and Reputation.* He publishes two major annual surveys, the Anholt Nation Brands Index and State Brands Index. He was awarded the 2009 Nobel Colloquia Prize for Leadership in Economics and Management and is a Parliamentarian of the European Cultural Parliament. For further information, please see www.simonanholt.com.

**Adam Arvidsson** is Associate Professor of Sociology in the Department of Social and Political Sciences, University of Milano, Italy. He also lectures on creative industries at the Copenhagen Business School, Denmark. He has written on brands, the information economy, and cities and creativity. He is author of *Brands: Value and Meaning in Media Culture* (Routledge, 2006) and co-author of *The Ethical Economy* (Columbia University Press, forthcoming, with Nicolai Peitersen). His research interest concerns information economy and new economy forms, creative industries and the economic value of reputation. He works with actics.com, a London-based company that develops peer-based measurement systems for the social impact of companies and organisations and sometimes blogs at the P2P Foundation.

**David Bennison** is Professor of Retailing and Research Coordinator in the Marketing and Retail Division, Manchester Metropolitan University Business School, UK. His research and teaching interests have focused on retail location and planning issues, and more recently on place marketing. Although primarily concerned with the UK scene, he has continued a life-long specialist interest in retail change in Greece and other Mediterranean and Middle Eastern countries. He has published widely, and has been actively involved in work which seeks to inform both public policy and corporate strategies. He has undertaken research for a diverse range of organisations, including B&Q, Tesco Stores, the National Retail Planning Forum, Accessible Retail, the Countryside Agency, P&O Shopping Centres, and Bolton MBC. He is a Senior Fellow of the Institute of Place Management.

**Ulrich Ermann** is a Researcher at the Leibniz Institute for Regional Geography in Leipzig, Germany. He also lectures at the University of Leipzig. His research interest is located in the intersection of economic and cultural geography, particularly in geographies of consumption and production, commodities and brands. He has written on regional economic circuits and local food labels in Germany, and on fashion markets in Bulgaria.

**Henrik Halkier** is Professor of Regional and Tourism Studies at the Department of Culture and Global Studies, Aalborg University, Denmark. His main area of research is public policy, including place branding, tourism policy, and knowledge processes in regional economic development. He has published with international editors and journals on regional policy, place branding, and tourism policy, and is currently working on a project on knowledge processes and policies for regional and tourism development and on a comparative study of city branding.

**Andrew Harris** is a Lecturer in Geography and Urban Studies at University College London, UK. His research focuses on the role of art and artists in processes of urban transformation and the three-dimensional geographies of contemporary cities. He is currently undertaking ESRC-funded research on the construction and maintenance of flyovers and skywalks in Mumbai.

**Atle Hauge** is a Senior Researcher at the Eastern Norway Research Centre. He has a Ph.D. from the Department of Social and Economic Geography at Uppsala University, and held a postdoctoral position at the University of Toronto from 2007 to 2008. He has worked on several projects on the cultural industries, and his Ph.D. thesis was on the Swedish fashion industry. His research has mainly focused on the interface between the material and the immaterial dimensions of products, with a particular focus on the production of immaterial and symbolic value. In addition, he is interested in regional development and talent attraction and retention.

**Peter Jackson** is Professor of Human Geography at the University of Sheffield, UK. He is co-author of *Making Sense of Men's Magazines* (Polity Press, 2001) and editor of *Changing Families, Changing Food*

(Palgrave Macmillan, 2009). His current work focuses on consumer anxieties about food, funded by the European Research Council (for further details, see www.sheffield.ac.uk/conanx).

**Johan Jansson** is a Lecturer in the Department of Social and Economic Geography at Uppsala University, Sweden. His main research interest is within economic geography, with a theoretical focus on agglomerations, local–global linkages, knowledge flows, creative (urban) milieus, entrepreneurship and branding. These theoretical approaches are employed in research on cultural industries (e.g. design, music, arts), the internet industry, urban milieus and urban branding. He has published books, chapters and articles in international journals within these research areas. He is also engaged as a cultural industries policy adviser and consultant.

**Guy Julier** is the University of Brighton Principal Research Fellow in Contemporary Design at the Victoria and Albert Museum, London. He was formerly a Director of 'Leeds. Love It. Share It', a community interest company dedicated to developing new approaches to regeneration, as well as Professor of Design at Leeds Metropolitan University, UK. He is the author of *The Culture of Design* (Sage, 2008) and co-editor, with Liz Moor, of *Design and Management: Policy, Management and Practice* (Berg, 2009). His research ranges across design activism, public policy and economies of design.

**Bodo Kubartz** is a Consultant and Trend Researcher with interest in the fragrance and cosmetics industry. He holds a Ph.D. in Economic Geography from the University of Oklahoma, US, where he has been an Instructor since 2006. His research interests are brands and branding; socioeconomic geographies of knowledge, learning and innovation; practice-based studies in economic geography; and spaces of creativity. He has published in journals such as *Urban Geography*, *Regional Studies* and *European Planning Studies* and co-authored (with Frank J. Schnitzler) *Das grosse Buch vom Parfum* (Collection Rolf Heyne, 2011).

**Nick Lewis** is an economic and political geographer at the University of Auckland. He is interested in the relationships among geographical imaginaries, claims about geographical provenance, and the construction of economic value. He has studied the wine, international education and fashion industries. More widely his interests extend to ideas of 'post-development' and post-structural approaches to political economy, especially as they pertain to the work of economic development agencies and initiatives in New Zealand and the Pacific. Nick is heavily involved in projects to promote the social sciences in New Zealand, and is Co-Director of the national Building Research Capability in the Social Sciences network.

**Celia Lury** is Professor of Sociology at Goldsmiths, University of London, UK. She teaches on the MA in Brand Development with Liz Moor at Goldsmiths. She is author of *Brands: The Logos of the Global Economy* (Routledge, 2004) and *Global Culture Industry: The Mediation of Things* (with Scott Lash, Polity, 2007) and a new edition of *Consumer Culture* (Polity and Rutgers Press, 2011). Her research interests include feminism, culture industry, authorship and intellectual property, and topology.

**Dominic Medway** is a Senior Lecturer and Head of the Marketing Group at Manchester Business School, UK. His research interests bring together his academic roots in geography and marketing, with a particular focus on place marketing and management. The findings of this research have been published in a variety of marketing and geography journals, including *European Journal of Marketing*, *Environment and Planning A*, *Area* and *Cities*. He welcomes discussion and debate about place marketing research and can be contacted at dominic.medway@mbs.ac.uk. He is also working on a number of other projects, including a study on the development of farm-based business ventures, and an ongoing investigation into the practicalities of undertaking carbon-neutral research.

**Liz Moor** is Senior Lecturer in Media and Communications at Goldsmiths, University of London, UK. Her research interests are in the area of consumer culture, material culture, design and branding. She is the author of *The Rise of Brands* (Berg, 2007) and the co-editor (with Guy Julier) of *Design and Creativity: Policy, Management and Practice* (Berg, 2009).

**Nicolas Papadopoulos** is Chancellor's Professor and Professor of Marketing and International Business at the Sprott School of Business of Carleton University in Ottawa, Canada. His research focuses on international strategy and buyer responses to it and includes place images and branding, the role of culture, expansion strategy, and international market systems. He has over 200 publications, including the edited books *Product and Country Images* (1993) and *Marketing from the Trenches* (2006), the textbook *International Marketing* (with Cateora, Gilly and Graham, 3rd edition, McGraw-Hill, 2011), and recent articles in *International Business Review*, *Journal of International Business Studies* and *Journal of International Marketing*. He lectures and consults in North America and Europe, and is a member of six journal editorial boards including the *Journal of the Academy of Marketing Science*, *International Marketing Review* and *Place Branding and Public Diplomacy*.

**Cecilia Pasquinelli** is a Ph.D. student in management, competitiveness and development at Scuola Superiore Sant'Anna in Pisa, Italy. Her research is on place brand and branding processes and it focuses on socio-economic and political conditions favouring the development of brand networks. She is research assistant at Management and Innovation Lab, Scuola Sant'Anna, where she works on innovation policies for local and regional development, and place marketing. She graduated in economics from Pisa University, Italy, and holds an MA in local and regional development from the Centre for Urban and Regional Development Studies (CURDS), Newcastle University, UK.

**Andy Pike** is Professor of Local and Regional Development in the Centre for Urban and Regional Development Studies (CURDS), Newcastle University, UK. His research interests are in the geographical political economy of local and regional development. He is widely published in international journals, co-author of *Local and Regional Development* (Routledge, 2006) and co-editor of *Handbook of Local and Regional Development* (Routledge, 2011) (both with Andrés Rodríguez-Pose and John Tomaney). He has undertaken research projects for the OECD, European Commission and national, regional and local organisations. He is currently working on brands and branding geographies, evolution in economic geography and spatial inequalities, spatial economic policy and decentralisation. He is an editor of *Regional Studies* and leads the postgraduate local and regional development programmes in CURDS.

**Dominic Power** is Professor of Economic Geography at Uppsala University, Sweden. His research is concerned with clustering, regional and industrial competitiveness, and innovation dynamics. His chief focus has been the workings of the cultural economy and industries: in particular the music, design and fashion industries. Most recently he is working on geographies and spaces of positionality and differentiation as competitive strategies within the cultural economy. He has published extensively within these areas. He has worked as a cultural policy adviser and consultant to various Nordic government ministries and authorities in the areas of cultural, innovation and industrial policy.

**Polly Russell** received her Ph.D. from the University of Sheffield in 2003, funded by an ESRC-CASE award. She is co-author of *Kitchen Revolution* (Ebury Press, 2008) and currently works as a content specialist in the social science division of the British Library, responsible for their wide range of food-related resources.

**Ngai-Ling Sum** is Senior Lecturer in Politics and International Relations and Co-Director (with Bob Jessop) of the Cultural Political Economy

Research Centre in Lancaster University, UK. She has research and teaching interests in international political economy, Gramsci and Foucault; globalisation and competitiveness knowledge; and the Pearl River Delta region. She was awarded (with Bob Jessop) the Gunnar Myrdal Prize by the European Association of Evolutionary Political Economy for their co-authored book *Beyond the Regulation Approach* (2006). She publishes in journals including *New Political Economy, Capital and Class, Urban Studies* and *Economy and Society*, as well as edited collections. She was awarded the British Academy BARDA Award for the project Changing Cultures of Competitiveness: China and India between 2008 and 2010.

**Anette Therkelsen** is Associate Professor of Tourism Studies at the Department of Culture and Global Studies, Aalborg University, Denmark. Her research interests are place branding, tourists' consumer behaviour, image formation processes and tourism market communication, and she has published internationally on these topics. She is currently working on a project on storytelling and destination branding and on a comparative study of city branding.

**Neil Ward** is Dean of the Faculty of Social Sciences at the University of East Anglia, UK, and was previously Director of the Centre for Rural Economy at Newcastle University, UK. He is a human geographer by training and is a specialist in agriculture, environmental management and rural development. He is co-author of *The Differentiated Countryside* (Routledge, 2003), and his recent publications on food and branding include 'Moral economies of food and geographies of responsibility' in *Transactions of the Institute of British Geographers* (2009, with Peter Jackson and Polly Russell).

**Gary Warnaby** is a Senior Lecturer in Marketing at the University of Liverpool Management School, UK, where he is the Director of Studies for the M.Sc. in consumer marketing. His research interests include the marketing of places (in particular the marketing of towns and cities as retail destinations), town centre management and retailing more generally. Results of this research have been published in academic journals including *Environment and Planning A, Journal of Marketing Management, European Journal of Marketing* and *Local Economy*, as well as a variety of professional and trade publications. He is currently working on research projects including the role of architecture in creating differentiation in urban shopping destinations, the role of maps in place marketing, and the co-creation of value from a consumer perspective.

# Acknowledgements

The assembly of this collection has been a collective effort. I would like to thank Matthew Pitman for encouraging the development of the volume and supporting its production. Many thanks are due to all the contributors for their commitment and delivery of insightful and thought-provoking chapters. Thanks to all the contributors and participants in the original sessions on 'Brand and Branding Geographies' at the Association of American Geographers Annual Meeting in Boston, 2008. Thanks to colleagues at the Centre for Urban and Regional Development Studies (CURDS), Newcastle University, UK, which continues to provide a distinctive and stimulating research culture and outlook that have inspired and inflected this collection. The insights and questions of the Ph.D. and MA postgraduates in the local and regional development programmes in CURDS and undergraduates on the geography programmes at Newcastle University have further contributed to sharpening the understanding and communication of brands and branding geographies. Thanks to Emma Wilson in CURDS for helping to sort out the manuscript and Michelle Wood for the cover art. Thanks also to Joan Fitzgerald at the Centre for Urban and Regional Studies, Northeastern University, and the Boston Public Library for the space to conclude it. The usual disclaimers apply.

The publishers wish to thank the following, who have kindly given permission for the use of copyright material:

- Photo: Ulrich Ermann; Battibaleno Rila Style for the advertising billboard image in Chapter 7.
- Photo: Ulrich Ermann; Advertisement photo: Peter Lindbergh for the Hugo Boss billboard image in Chapter 7.
- Aalborg and Aarhus local authorities for the city brand images in Chapter 12.
- Marketing Leeds and Leeds Love It Share It CIC for the city brand images in Chapter 13.
- Tourism New Zealand for the Brand New Zealand images in Chapter 16.

Every effort has been made to trace all the copyright holders, but if any have been inadvertently overlooked the publishers will be pleased to make the necessary arrangements at the first opportunity.

PART I

Introduction – conceptualising and theorising
brands and branding geographies

# 1. Introduction: Brands and branding geographies

**Andy Pike**

## INTRODUCTION

Blundstone boots are an archetypal Australian product, produced by a '100% Australian family-owned' business since 1870 in Hobart, Tasmania. The brand's differentiation and value are based upon its hard-working, tough and sturdy attributes situated in its particularly Australian national context (Blundstone 2010:1). Going by the slogan of 'Australian for boot' and using Australian rock legend Angry Anderson as 'the face of Blundstone', 'Blunnies' are marketed as tough, sporty and comfortable, and provide 'hard working footwear for "Hard Working Men"' (Blundstone 2010:1). In the early 2000s, Blundstone employed 500 people in Hobart, and the company was considered 'the last major full footwear manufacturer in Australia' with '80% of their product . . . fully manufactured in Australia, 15% have uppers made overseas and 5% . . . fully imported' (Colbeck 2003: 4).

By 2007, the brand owner's Australian manufacturing operation faced acute cost and viability pressures. These resulted from trade liberalisation and increased competition for consumers demanding increasingly differentiated products requiring extra labour content and 'en masse . . . not willing to pay more dollars for product that is of comparable quality and features just because it is Australian made' (Blundstone 2010:1). Exhausting its potential to further improve productivity and innovation in its Australian factory, the company concluded that 'all we can see is our costs going up, the market forcing our prices to either drop or stay the same' (Blundstone 2010:1). Blundstone decided to relocate most of its production overseas to India and Thailand, where labour costs were one-fifteenth to one-twentieth of local Australian costs, resulting in the loss of 360 jobs in Hobart (Darby 2007). Amidst public outcry that such iconic goods were no longer being 'Made in Australia' and talk of product boycotts, Blundstone argued that:

> Long after the rest of our industry had relocated most, if not all, of its manufacturing offshore, we have been trying our darnedest to make a fist of local manufacturing – at the expense of profitability. Blundstone is privately owned by people who are committed to the Australian community. Had we been publicly owned, the pressure to make a return for shareholders year on year would have seen us make the same decision many years ago. We share the disappointment many people are feeling. We are proud of our 137 year heritage, the iconic nature of our brand, our workforce and products. Moving some of our manufacturing offshore has been a very difficult decision for us. (Blundstone 2010:1)

Particular constructions of the 'Made in Australia' attribute that created meaning and value for its brand owner were thrown into question by the shifting geographies of consumer demand and Blundstone's material production in an international context. And this episode in the life of a brand and its branding is important because it illustrates not just symbolic but material effects on the livelihoods and prosperity of people and places. Trading on its local origins, Blundstone will continue to be 'Australian owned and passionate about Australia' (Blundstone 2010:1), but the shift in production was expected to leave only a 'skeleton Australian workforce in sales, customer service and head office' employing about 100 by the end of the 2007 (Darby 2007: 1). While 'The brands live on and the company lives on' (Chief Executive quoted in Darby 2007: 1), Blundstone faces intense competition for consumers who appear to be ambiguous about, if not disinterested in, the provenance of the boots in their purchasing decisions.

The experience of Blundstone's boots demonstrates the importance and significance of the value and meaning of the inescapable geographical associations and connections wrapped up in the brands and branding of goods and services. Brands and branding can sometimes seem pervasive, especially when brands are claimed to be a 'central feature of contemporary economic life' (Lury 2004: 27) and branding is interpreted as a 'core activity of capitalism' (Holt 2006: 300), and when some interpret a 'well nigh all-encompassing brand-space' (Arvidsson 2005: 236) in which it can appear 'as if there is hardly any market arena, not even a niche, that has been left uncolonized by branding processes' (Goldman and Papson 2006: 328). Brands and branding geographies matter in this context because the spatial and multi-faceted nature of brands intersects economic, social, cultural and political worlds; they are simultaneously 'economic' as goods and services in markets, 'social' as collectively produced, circulated and consumed objects, 'cultural' as entities providing meanings and identities, and 'political' as regulated intellectual properties, traded financial assets and contested symbols (Pike 2009).

Yet the ways in which the geographies of space and place are inescapably intertwined with brands and branding have been unevenly recognised

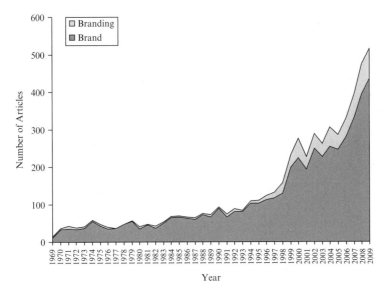

*Source:*   Author's calculation from ISI Web of Knowledge databases.

*Figure 1.1*   *Number of articles with 'brand' and/or 'branding' in their title, 1969–2009*

and under-researched. Important reasons are, first, that brands and branding are a longstanding, crowded and periodically fashionable field in the academic and popular literature. Notwithstanding some differences in usage and meaning, a crude tally of articles with 'brand' and/or 'branding' in their title published between 1969 and 2009 demonstrates the increase in academic attention across disciplines in this area and its dramatic growth since the late 1990s (Figure 1.1). Work spans across numerous disciplines (including Architecture, Business Studies, Economics, Economic History, Geography, International Relations, Marketing, Media Studies, Planning, Political Science, Tourism Studies, Sociology and Urban Studies) and is reflective of a burgeoning industry spawning a multitude of prescriptive guides and analytical frameworks from gurus and practitioners (e.g. Anholt 2006; Hart and Murphy 1998; Olins 2003; Roberts 2004), academics (e.g. de Chernatony 2001; Kapferer 2008) and international consultancies (e.g. Interbrand, Saffron). A political sociology of the production of this literature would reveal a sometimes sharp, but often blurred, distinction between work focused on how to do brands and branding better and other studies concerned with questioning its purpose, value and effects. Such diversity and variety in the approaches, aims and ways of thinking about brands and branding have fostered only partial and fragmented engagement with their spatial aspects. Second, brands and branding have drastically extended their reach beyond just goods and services in the economy and culture more deeply into society and polity by encompassing knowledge, people, places, charities, campaigns, universities, political parties, states and supranational institutions (Moor 2007; van Ham 2008). This dramatic growth and pervasiveness have made it difficult to keep pace for the tasks of conceptualising, theorising and studying empirically the geographies of brands and branding. Even within the more spatial disciplines, despite their apparent reach and relevance for geographical inquiry, economic geography in particular has 'consistently undervalued brands as an area of study' (Power and Hauge 2008: 21).

While a literature is emerging (see, for example, Cook and Harrison 2003; Edensor and Kothari 2006; Jackson *et al.* 2007; Lewis *et al.* 2008; Pike 2009; Power and Hauge 2008), there has been little examination or formulation of conceptual and theoretical frameworks to understand brands and branding geographies and to inform empirical work. Contributing to addressing this gap, the origins of this collection lie in an effort to focus and further develop our understandings of the geographies of brands and branding. The overarching aim is to provide a reference point for the emergent topic of brands and branding geographies in a multi-disciplinary and international context. Specifically, the collection aims:

1.  to engage critically with and establish the emergent conceptual and theoretical literature and empirical analyses on brands and branding geographies;
2.  to connect and relate the leading edge multi-disciplinary and international work on the spatial dimensions of brands and branding, especially exploring links between the hitherto separate strands of studies of goods and services and space and place brands and branding;
3.  to engage with and reflect upon the contribution of geographical understandings in considering the politics and limits of brands and branding;
4.  to map out potential future research directions for the geographies of brands and branding.

To fulfil such aims, the process began with an open call for contributions which filled a set of four themed sessions at the Association of American Geographers Conference in Boston in 2008 and, second, the commissioning of further contributions from leading voices in disciplines beyond geography internationally. No claim is made to any exhaustive comprehensiveness – no doubt other authors, disciplines, empirical studies and/or geographies might have been included – but the collection has sought to identify and incorporate the most important and resonant concerns for brands and branding geographies. To frame what follows, this introduction seeks to establish the geographical nature of brands and branding by explaining their inescapable spatial associations and connotations, spatially differentiated manifestations and circulation, and uneven development. The organisation of the collection is then outlined.

## ESTABLISHING THE GEOGRAPHIES OF BRANDS AND BRANDING

The pervasiveness of brands and branding underlines the need to establish their geographical nature and to develop conceptual and theoretical ways to interpret and explain their spatial aspects. This collection seeks to establish and further develop the following arguments: i) brands and branding are geographical because they are situated in and/or associated with spaces and places; ii) brands and branding travel and are experienced differently across time and space; and iii) richer people in prosperous places have different roles than relatively poorer people in less prosperous places in relation to the spatial circuits of value and meaning in the production, circulation, consumption and regulation of brands and branding.

### Inescapable Geographical Associations and Connotations

As an identifiable kind of good or service, a brand is constituted of values or 'equity' (Aaker 1996) – such as associations, awareness, loyalty, perceived quality and, crucially, origin – that are imbued to varying degrees and in differing ways by spatial connections and connotations. As a process that works to articulate, connect, enhance and represent the facets and cues embodied in brands in meaningful ways (Moor 2007), branding too is enmeshed in and cannot rid itself of geographical associations and contexts. What values and meanings people ascribe to specific brands and how they respond to branding, for example, are entangled in their own socio-spatial relations and identities and their perceptions of the brand and branding's spatial associations and connotations. Echoing marketing's longstanding 'country of origin' effect (Bilkey and Nes 1982), where brands are perceived to have come from or the 'place of the brand' is a longstanding and discernible influence in purchasing decisions (Papadopoulos, this volume, Chapter 2). As Bernstein (1984: 133) argues, 'Brands are born somewhere. Companies are born somewhere

. . . international brands are creations of their homelands.' Over time, branded objects and branding processes accumulate histories that are social *and* spatial and matter to their evolution. In diverse ways and to variable extents, space and place are written through branded objects and the social practices of branding. It might even be said that brands and branding embody an 'inherent spatiality' (Power and Hauge 2008: 21).

One way to further develop our conceptualisation of the inescapable geographies of brands and branding is by drawing upon the interdisciplinary debates about entanglement in economic anthropology and economic sociology. This work focuses upon the ways in which commercial imperatives in markets are compelling the ever more inclusive entanglement of – typically branded – goods and services in the lives of consumers. Such 'transactable objects' are being made meaningful across a 'diversity of values and value systems by the agency of sellers – often through branding processes – across a range of registers (e.g. rationally, aesthetically, culturally, morally)' (Barry and Slater 2002: 183). Competition is driving innovation and differentiation in the 'qualification' and 'singularisation' of goods and services and their closer attachment to consumers (Callon 2005: 6). Examples include the ways in which certain brands offer heightened customisation of products, the configuration of bespoke packages of services for individuals and the creation of retail experiences through 'brandspace' outlets in particular places (see, for example, Klingman 2007). Through market transactions, Callon (2005) sees a necessary moment of framing and disentanglement that frees the protagonists in exchange from further ties that would prevent the inalienable transfer of property rights. In contrast, Miller (2002: 227) interprets a process of increasing entanglement because:

> most industries have to engage in highly qualitative and entangled judgements about looks and style and image and 'feel' out of which they may, if they have the right sense of the 'street', make a profit. The way to profitability is not through disentanglement, but through further entanglement.

Amidst a broader understanding of the entanglements of space, place and politics (Massey 2005), Lee (2006: 422) sees that such:

> Entangled economic geographies . . . remain unframed – or rather multiply framed – in the senses both that the agents, objects, goods and merchandise involved in them remain more, or less, imperfectly distinguished and associated with one another and that multiple social relations are at play between them.

For Lee (2006: 414), Callon's economism and desire for a 'purification of economic relations' risks missing 'the inherent complexity of ordinary economies and thereby places limits on the economic geographical imagination'. Reflecting Miller's reading of increasing entanglements in the commercial sphere and Lee's interpretation of the complexity of entangled economic geographies, the notion of *geographical* entanglements can be distinguished to mean the spatial associations and connotations that inescapably intertwine brands and the meaning-making of branding for goods, services, knowledges, spaces and places (Pike, 2011b).

Such a spatially sensitive approach provides a way of understanding how brands and their branding are inescapably entangled in 'geographical knowledges – based in the cultural meanings of places and spaces . . . deployed in order to 're-enchant' . . . commodities and to differentiate them from the devalued functionality and homogeneity of standardised products and places' (Cook and Crang 1996: 132). Accounts in other disciplines recognise such geographical entanglement too, including 'spatial identifications' (Miller 1998: 185) in economic anthropology, 'country and cultural signifiers' (Phau and Prendergast 2000: 164) in marketing, and how 'place gets into goods by the way its elements manage to combine' (Molotch 2002: 686) in sociology. Indeed, sociologist Arvidsson (2005: 239) argues that 'Building brand equity is about fostering a number of possible attachments around the brand . . . experiences, emotions, attitudes, lifestyles or, most importantly perhaps, loyalty.' Many of such attachments have inescapable geographical associations that ensnare brands and branding, some of which attributes and connections may be emphasised, such as the heritage, quality and reputation connoted by particular places, while other markers, such as the characteristics of cheap, tacky and poor value linked to specific places, may be hidden. Distinguishing between different types of goods and services and demonstrating the connections to the brands and branding of spaces and places, Ermann (this volume, Chapter 7) refers to 'value-adding places' and 'value-reducing places' to capture this spatial differentiation in the value and meaning of the geographical associations enmeshing brands and branding (see also Molotch 2005; Power and Jansson, this volume, Chapter 9).

Geographical entanglements are more than just the material connections of brands and branding in fixed relationships to certain spaces and places. Capable of changing over time, geographical entanglements can be of different kinds (e.g. material, symbolic, discursive, visual, aural), varying in their extent (e.g. strong, weak) and nature (e.g. authentic, fictitious) (Pike 2009). Interpreting a brand's geographical entanglements, then, may reveal strong and authentic material linkages to particular origins represented in the branding of its advertising, packaging, retailing and trademark protection – as Hauge (this volume, Chapter 6) illustrates in the association of extreme sports equipment with Nordic producers,

Power and Jansson (this volume, Chapter 9) demonstrate with their analysis of Scandanavian design, and Lewis (this volume, Chapter 16) reveals in the analysis of Brand NZ. Another brand might embody weaker and entirely constructed geographical associations to an entirely fictitious or aspirational place assembled and branded to appeal to particular market segments – as Jackson *et al.* (this volume, Chapter 4) show in their examples of the 'manufacture of meaning' in the construction of Oakham chicken and Lochmuir salmon, and Arvidsson (this volume, Chapter 18) and Harris (this volume, Chapter 11) demonstrate in their dissection of the use of 'creative class' narratives in city branding.

## Geographically Differentiated Manifestation and Circulation

> The world's needs and desires have been irrevocably homogenized . . . Commercially, nothing confirms this as much as the success of McDonald's from the Champs Elysées to the Ginza, of Coca-Cola in Bahrain and Pepsi-Cola in Moscow, and of rock music, Greek salad, Hollywood movies, Revlon cosmetics, Sony televisions, and Levi jeans everywhere. 'High touch' products are as ubiquitous as high-tech. (Levitt 1983: 93)

As Lury (this volume, Chapter 3) notes, Levitt's (1983: 92–93) seminal arguments about 'the globalisation of markets', in which 'Global competition spells the end of domestic territoriality' and 'The global corporation operates with resolute constancy – at low relative cost – as if the entire world (or major regions of it) were a single entity; it sells the same things in the same way everywhere', have resonated deeply in the world of brands and branding. For some, especially 'global' brands and branding are seen as vehicles in the vanguard of such kinds of globalisation, crossing borders as a 'global fluid' that is 'super-territorial and super-organic, floating free' (Urry 2003: 60, 68). Echoing the 'earth is flat' (Levitt 1983: 100) and 'end of geography' (O'Brien 1992) arguments, in this reading the picture of brands and branding geographies is marked by homogenisation and sameness, as their ubiquity and mobility serve to lessen spatial differences in a flat and slippery world (e.g. Friedman 2005). As Levitt (1983: 93) foresaw it, 'No one is exempt and nothing can stop the process. Everywhere everything gets more and more like everything else as the world's preference structure is relentlessly homogenized.' Here, the sheer pervasiveness of brands and branding is turning the public realm into uniform commercial 'brandscapes' dominated by the same global brands and their branding of images, logos and signs (Klingman 2007). This kind of relational view of space and place emphasises an unbounded spatiality for branding and brands because through media pluralisation 'The interface of the brand is not . . . to be located in a single place, at a single time. Rather . . . it is distributed across a number of surfaces (. . . products and packaging), screens (television, computers, cinemas) or sites (retail outlets, advertising hoardings)' (Lury 2004: 50; see also Lury, this volume, Chapter 3).

Counterposed against this view is a more spatially sensitive interpretation of brands and branding geographies that sees heterogeneity and much diversity and variety in the ways in which brands and branding heighten geographical differentiation in a spiky and sticky world (Pike 2009; see also Christopherson *et al*. 2008; Markusen 1996). This analysis sees branded objects and branding processes as geographically differentiated and spatially uneven in, for example, their manifestation, representation, visibility, fixity and mobility throughout the spaces, places and temporalities of economy, society, culture and polity. Taking a more territorial view, this approach emphasises the delineated, even jurisdictional, entities in establishing, representing and regulating the spatial origins of brands and branding. Moving beyond marketing's *nationally* focused approach to '*Country* of Origin', space and place as territory can frame geographical entanglements of brands and branding through spatial connections and connotations forged by producers, circulators, consumers and regulators drawing upon and/or delimiting territories at specific spatial levels. These scales include the supranational (e.g. European, Latin American), sub-national administrative (e.g. Bavarian, Californian), 'national' (e.g. Catalan, Scottish), pan-regional (e.g. Northern, Southern), regional (e.g. North-Eastern, South-Western), sub-regional or local (e.g. Bay Area, Downtown), urban (e.g. Milanese, Parisian) or even neighbourhood (e.g. Upper East Side, Knightsbridge) (Pike 2009).

In a more geographically differentiated conceptualisation of their manifestation and circulation, branded objects find changing kinds and degrees of commercial, social, cultural and political resonance and become sticky in specific spaces and particular places over time. The spatial circuits of the production, circulation, consumption and regulation of specific brands may be highly geographically uneven. In seeking to shape and respond to the particularities of different geographical market contexts, branding practices may similarly be spatially attenuated and heterogeneous – even for the same brand in different places. More geographically sensitive marketing analysts, for example, have demonstrated the importance of managing the global attributes of brands in their adaptation to particular marketplaces (Holt *et al*. 2004). Geographical differentiation, then, is integral to the different ways in which different people in different places see, interpret and act in response to branded objects and branding processes. Moving beyond the dualistic positions between territorial or relational views in recent geographical debates about space and place (Hudson 2007), considering the geographical entanglements of brands and branding can more usefully address their spatialities as relational *and* territorial, bounded *and* unbounded, fluid *and* fixed, territorialising *and* de-territorialising (Pike 2009). It is argued that openness to the tensions involved and contingency of such contrary and overlapping tendencies is helpful in empirical examination of the complex and unfolding geographical entanglements and socio-spatial histories of particular brands and branding.

In thinking about causation and how to explain the geographical differentiation inscribed in brands and branding geographies it is important to distinguish how the geographical notion of entanglements renders the object of the brand and the process of branding inescapably spatial but not in a linear or simplistic way. Geographical entanglements are seldom inherent, except in specific cases such as agro-foods with intrinsic ties to particular places (Morgan *et al.* 2006) and in some versions of space and place brands and their branding. In the main, geographical entanglements in brands and branding shape and are shaped by the social construction of agents. Related and animated in spatial circuits of value and meaning, producers (e.g. manufacturers, 'place-makers', residents), circulators (e.g. advertisers, marketers, media), consumers (e.g. shoppers, residents, tourists) and regulators (e.g. trademark authorities, local councils, export agencies) attempt to construct and are conditioned by the spatial associations of brands and branding in market contexts (Pike 2011a).

Brands and branding histories accumulate geographically entangled characteristics, identities, meanings and values from which extrication or reworking can be difficult. Such 'geographical lore' can be sticky and slow changing and adhere to particular commodities (Jackson 2004) and spaces and places. These socio-spatial histories impart degrees of path dependence upon brands' subsequent evolution, trajectories and branding. For some brands these associations can be negative and difficult to shake off, for example McDonald's reputation for poor-quality fast food and its links to American economic and cultural imperialism have proved resilient despite its recent brand makeover and attempts to improve the dietary quality of its products in the UK and elsewhere (Ritzer 1998). For other brands, the close associations between products and places resonate, for example in the lasting effect of the boycott of Danish products in Islamic countries following the religious cartoons controversy in 2006, while for some brands the geographical associations can be positive and demonstrate the commercially beneficial effects of rebranding. South Korean electronics group Samsung, for example, has rid itself of a reputation for poor quality, unreliability and low prices associated with new entrant producers from East Asia during the 1970s and 1980s through high levels of investment in new product ranges, quality and brand building and promotion including high-profile celebrity endorsement and sponsorship deals (Wilmott 2007).

Commodity geographies in particular have recognised the wider webs of brands and branding agents in building upon Thrift's (2005) 'cultural circuit of capital' and moving beyond linear 'commodity chain' studies (Hudson 2005; Jackson 2002). The emphasis upon producer–consumer relations in shaping commodity value and meaning has been broadened more fully to incorporate circulation and regulation (Bridge and Smith 2003; Castree 2001; Smith *et al.* 2002; Watts 2005). Commodity 'following' work, for example, has enrolled a diverse mix of concepts, actors and processes to map 'a constellation of people, plants, bugs, diseases, recipes, politics, trade agreements, and histories, whose multiple, complex entanglements and disjunctures animate this "thing" and its travels' (Cook and Harrison 2007: 40). Other studies have interpreted spatial circuits of agents engaged in value production, enhancement, extraction, exchange and appropriation (Castree 2004; Henderson *et al.* 2002; Jackson 2002; Lee 2006; Smith *et al.* 2002; Watts 2005). While the exploration of the 'brand architectures' (Lewis, this volume, Chapter 16) or webs of agents involved in the brands and branding of spaces and places is beginning (see, for example, Therkelsen and Halkier, this volume, Chapter 12; Pike 2011a), this social construction by such agents underlines the importance of empirical study because it imparts contingency in brands and branding geographies, making them diverse and variable across time and space.

**Uneven Development**

The spatial associations of brands and branding matter because of their uneven geographies and their relationship with spatially uneven development through the orchestration and reinforcement of economic and social inequalities and the articulation of unequal and competitive socio-spatial relations and divisions of labour. Not only are the entanglements of brands and branding geographically differentiated but they intertwine with spatially uneven development because their underlying dynamic of differentiation is predicated on the search for, exploitation and (re) production of economic and social inequalities over space and through time. Producers, circulators, consumers and regulators with differing commercial and other interests work selectively to reveal and obscure the meaning and value of spatial associations in brands and branding (Pike 2011a). Accumulation and the differentiation imperatives of branding drive brand owners' market segmentation efforts in carving out, defending and exploiting profitable parts of goods and services markets. In spaces and places, local agents attempt to render their place distinctive relative to other places in territorial competition for investment, jobs, residents and visitors (Turok 2009). As Richard Sennett (2006: 143) describes for goods and services, 'branding seeks to make a basic product sold globally seem distinctive, seeks to obscure homogeneity'. Brand owners, then, expend much time, effort and resources developing differentiation strategies. These include platform systems to integrate the infrastructures behind brands that generate unseen scale economies and cost savings while premium prices are maintained, cycles of fashion and season are introduced to quicken capital circulation and profitable premium niches are constructed to stimulate consumers to trade up to perhaps less affordable but higher margin offerings (Frank 2000).

For goods and services, branding seeks to de-stabilise existing markets and re-institutionalise them around new, strategically calculated brand definitions such that the 'aesthetic and cultural meanings of brands and sub-brands then become ways of segmenting markets by ability to make the premium payments required to possess the desired brand' (Hudson 2005: 69). Spatial manifestations of economic and social inequalities then fuel such market segmentation because 'Wide disparities between rich and poor . . . bring into being more luxurious types of goods than would otherwise exist' (Molotch 2002: 682). Brands' and branding's differentiation imperative (re)produces such inequalities and fosters social polarisation since 'The new poor, without the right labels and brands, are not just excluded but invisible' (Lawson 2006: 31). The identification, reflection and orchestration of socio-spatial disparities are central to brand owner strategy. The Global Brand Director for Mars sweets, for example, claims that 'the age of the average is dead' (Murray 1998: 140) and seeks sub-national 'pockets of affluence' as a branding priority. Geographically entangled brands and branding perpetuate uneven development by heightening the spatial and:

> hierarchical division of labour . . . with design-intensive producers located at the top . . . and many of those actually involved in manufacturing the products or delivering the service at the bottom . . . only a few pennies of the price of a Starbucks cappuccino goes to pay for the labour of those who harvest and roast coffee beans, and not many more are paid to those who serve the drinks. The remainder accrues to those able to assert the value of their contribution to the brand in terms of creativity, product innovation or design activity. (Lury 2004: 37)

The unequal socio-spatial division of labour is (re)produced by the geographical organisation of brand owners' activities, seeking out particular places and labour pools that provide appropriate and cost-effective skills to support the web of producers, circulators, consumers and regulators of spatial circuits of value and meaning in brands and branding.

The geographical entanglements of brands and branding further contribute to uneven development through creating, embodying, reinforcing and even amplifying the competitive socio-spatial relations between spaces and places and sometimes intersecting branded goods and services markets. As the contributions in Part III, 'Brands and branding geographies – spaces and places' (this volume), demonstrate, especially recently competition in goods and services markets has connected and overlapped with the emergent industry of 'place branding' in the territorial competition for investment, jobs, residents and visitors (Greenberg 2008; Hannigan 2004; Hollands and Chatterton 2003; Julier 2005; Molotch 2005). This has occurred, for example, through brand owners' outsourcing and exploitation through playing off marginal labour pools against each other internationally for investments and contracts, competition between rival producers and circulators of competing brands from particular places, and regulatory agencies in specific jurisdictional territories seeking to define market standards capable of excluding specific goods or services brands. Indeed, it is now claimed that branding has extended beyond the world of goods and services to become 'one of the core strategic and commercial competences driving firms, clusters, regions, and nations in the contemporary economy' (Power and Hauge 2008: 3).

'Place branding' has explored the geographical extension of goods and services branding to spaces and places, building on studies of the 'commodification [of the] traditional multi-dimensional meanings of place' (Gold and Ward 1994: 295) that revealed its economic and social logics and the attempts of entrepreneurial institutions to transform the competitiveness of spaces in the 'place market' (see Harvey 1989; Kearns and Philo 1993). Some of this work tends toward the prescriptive and uncritically elides the 'national' and the 'brand' in seeking to conceptualise a notion of 'brand equity' for states. Van Ham (2001: 2, 6), for example, claims that:

> brands and states often merge in the minds of the global consumer . . . strong brands are important in attracting foreign direct investment, recruiting the best and the brightest and wielding political influence . . . In this crowded arena, states that lack relevant brand equity will not survive. (See also Anholt 2002.)

More reflective research explores the overlap of place and goods/services marketing within streamlined national brands such as Brand NZ (Lewis, this volume, Chapter 16) and others including Brand Canada, Belgium's .be and Cool Britannia (Papadopoulos 2004; see also Jaffe and Nebenzahl 2001), and questions whether the mass public citizenry rather than elite 'ownership' of place renders product/service branding principles inappropriate (Papadopoulos and Heslop 2002). Recognising the geographical entanglements in brands and branding illustrates the ways in which they can contribute to uneven development by (re)producing competitive socio-spatial relations and geographically differentiated outcomes between unequally endowed spaces and places.

This relationship between brands and branding geographies and uneven development is central to their politics. It connects to Harvey's (1990: 422, 432) call to 'get behind the veil, the fetishism of the market and the commodity, in order to tell the full story of social reproduction' by 'tracing back' the relationships between commodities and 'uneven geographical development'. The 'hidden life to commodities' can 'reveal profound insights into the entire edifice – the society, the culture, the political economy – of commodity producing systems' (Watts 2005: 533). Moreover, it can begin to make connections between the uneven development of brands and branding geographies in relation to goods and services *as well as* spaces and places (see Lewis, this volume, Chapter 16). The 'de-fetishisation' project has been subject to critique, however. Issues concern: the 'double fetish' of the thing-like quality of social relations embodied in commodities and the geographical imaginaries constructed by commercial interests (Cook and Crang 1996); the complexity of imaginative geographies in the social lives of commodities (Castree 2001); the privileging of academic over popular, increasingly sophisticated consumer knowledges (Jackson 1999); the imagining of alternative geographies by 'working with the fetish' (Bridge and Smith 2003: 262); and the questioning of commodity fetishism's relevance and whether 'reconnecting' will 'restore to view a previously hidden chain of commitments and responsibilities' (Barnett *et al.* 2005: 24).

Despite the prominence of brands and branding for goods, services, spaces and places, the explanations and politics of how their geographies are involved in any reconnecting (Hartwick 2000) or 'getting with' (Castree 2001: 1521) the commodity fetish remain underdeveloped. If 'an effect of branding is to distance the commodity from the social relations and conditions involved in its production by layering it with myths and symbols' (Edensor and Kothari 2006: 332), then conceiving of the geographical entanglements of brands and branding provides a 'non-abstract starting point' (Klein 2000: 356) to analyse their uneven development and politics. This is an important but difficult task because:

> Branding in its current form takes this process [fetishization] a step further, promoting, in a sense, a fetishization of the fetish: that is, the commodification of the reified image of the commodity itself. Effectively, branding not only makes the 'mystical veil' which hides the social origins of the commodity that much thicker, but creates a veritable industry for the production and circulation of mystical veils, and devises methods for knitting these veils together to give the illusion of totality. (Greenberg 2008: 31)

In the uneven geographical development of branded commodities, spaces and places and their branding, Castree's (2001: 1520) 'important critical work' of de-fetishisation remains unfinished. In relation to commodities, piercing the mystical veils of brands and branding constructed by agents 'requires us to go beyond polarised debates about authenticity, "unveiling" the commodity fetish and revealing the exploitative social relations that are concealed beneath the commodity form' to instead articulate 'a more complex argument about the discursive process of appropriation . . . to understand the cultural processes through which meanings are manufactured *as much as* the political-economic processes through which alienation and exploitation occur' (Jackson *et al.* 2007: 328–329, emphasis added). The notion of geographical entanglements in brands and branding can contribute in several ways. First, it can capture the material *as well as* the discursive and the symbolic in the diversity and variety revealed in cultural economy approaches (e.g. Cook and Harrison 2003; Lewis, this volume, Chapter 16). Second, it can connect cultural construction with the systematising rationales and processes of contemporary capitalism (i.e. accumulation, commodification) emphasised (but not reducible to any singular outcome) by more culturally sensitive political economies (e.g. Castree 2001, 2004; Watts 2005). Third, it can begin to elucidate the connections between uneven development and its politics in the geographies of brands and branding of goods, services, spaces and places.

## ORGANISATION OF THE BOOK

In situating brands and branding geographically in an international and multi-disciplinary frame, the contributions are organised into four connected parts. Part I, 'Introduction – conceptualising and theorising brands and branding geographies', introduces and reflects the current state of conceptual and theoretical approaches to brands and branding geographies from across key disciplines internationally. Reviewing the longstanding work in international marketing, Nicolas Papadopoulos demonstrates the centrality and growing importance of place. He distinguishes between place image and place branding to underline the increasing importance of affective factors associated with places, such as affinity or animosity, in strongly shaping buying behaviours. Second, he explains the pivotal role of the co-ordination of the different general, product, tourism, or other place images in place branding efforts as they interplay and influence different kinds of 'buyers' ranging from consumers and industrial purchasers to investors, tourists or students. From a sociological perspective, Celia Lury uses the notion of the performativity of the brand's interface to explain the 'space-making' capacities of brands and branding. She suggests that brands occupy and organise 'multiple spaces' through acting as boundary objects, operating spatial boundaries rather than extending or deflecting them.

Part II, 'Brands and branding geographies – goods, services and knowledges', demonstrates the different conceptual approaches in drawing together empirical work on the brands and branding geographies of goods, services and – introducing a new analytical category – knowledges. Bringing novel insights into studying and branding food, Peter Jackson, Polly Russell and Neil Ward examine the 'manufacture of meaning' through branding and how its purpose for organisations is both external, for consumers in buying goods and services, and internal, in configuring and articulating the values and aspirations of staff. Using oral life history methodology, they argue that the process of brand development involves the interweaving of personal and corporate narratives and demonstrates the importance of space and place in the geographical and historical constitution of brands, articulated at a variety of spatial scales. Liz Moor focuses on 'place-affiliated' brands in consumption and addresses the extent to which consumers are involved in the making of such places. Drawing upon the examples of travel, politics and co-production in considering the place of brands, she demonstrates the importance of addressing the relative autonomy people experience in consumption in the context of the place-making power of larger-scale institutions such as brand owners and regulatory bodies such as the World Trade Organization. Atle Hauge makes a distinctive connection between innovation and branding in his study of the role of consumers in the development and marketing of high-specification sports equipment. He shows how the role of users in stimulating new ideas and shaping branding strategies is critical in explaining commercial performance because it links the technical and functional value of products with their immaterial and symbolic worth.

Ulrich Ermann explores the extent to which economic value has become detached from physical use value in the 'new brand economy' and its tendencies towards 'placelessness' in the 'spaces of brand economies'. Drawing upon a study of the launch of new fashion brands in post-socialist Bulgaria, he demonstrates the centrality of brands in constructing and performing discourses of economic modernisation and privileging the role of symbolic values in configuring consumers and raising their brand literacy in a transition economy. Bodo Kubartz makes fresh links between the role of proximity and distanciation in knowledge and knowing in the creation and branding of perfumes in the fragrance industry. He demonstrates how knowing takes place around brands and distinguishes an initial process of 'sensing a brand' (formulating and testing a concept for a market niche) and 'branding a scent' (inter-relating the scent with all its other material and metaphysical product components).

Situating their analysis in the context of global circuits and cyclical clusters, Dominic Power and Johan Jansson explore the emergence and persistence of 'place-based brands', drawing from empirical work on Scandinavian design. Developing the notion of 'brand channels' that connect spatial circuits of value and meaning across and between geographical scales, they illustrate how the origins of products can be considered as powerful 'collective brands' built upon and fostered by symbiotic relationships between industries and places. In the context of the increasing commodification and branding of knowledge for marketing and sale through consultancy in business strategy and public policy, Ngai-Ling Sum develops the notion of the 'knowledge brand' to explain how 'competitiveness' is constructed and contextualised across different sites and scales. Exploring the example of the Harvard-Porterian brand of 'competitive advantage', she illustrates how this knowledge brand circulates and is reconstructed and negotiated in particular contexts by regional and local actors through sites and relays of translation and persuasion.

Part III, 'Brands and branding geographies – spaces and places', addresses the brands and branding geographies of spaces and places, focusing upon cities, localities, districts, neighbourhoods, nations and other constructed geographical imaginaries. Analysing the experience of Hoxton in London, Andrew Harris investigates the complex and geographically specific social and cultural worlds in which the 'brandscapes' of post-industrial city branding have been forged. He argues that a distinctive group of creative entrepreneurs and artists fashioned a successful brand but it proved unsustainable and ultimately undermined the basis of its own construction in the face of powerful gentrification and property development interests. In this way, he concludes that particular forms of urban branding promote new kinds of economic activities but, often unwittingly, construct new forms of spatial capture and control.

Anette Therkelsen and Henrik Halkier explore the politics of branding provincial cities by comparing the experiences of Aarhus and Aalborg in Denmark. Developing the concepts of inclusion, strategy and commitment to analyse the dynamics of agents involved in place branding projects, they demonstrate how inclusion does not necessarily secure long-term stakeholder commitment with or without the presence of shared strategy making. Guy Julier engages the intersection of design activism with place branding to review how it contests and disrupts its assumed and inherent spatialities. Through a critical analysis of the subversion and contestation of the branding of the city of Leeds in West Yorkshire, northern England, he challenges the dominant spatial ideology of cities and city branding concerned with attractiveness and competition as post-industrial sites of consumption in neo-liberal global networks. Against this, he argues that financial meltdown and climate change have opened up a space for political engagement and dialogue about alternatives and change in the tempo and focus of local governance.

Drawing upon the experience of Val di Cornia in southern Tuscany, Italy, Cecilia Pasquinelli deploys the notion of relational branding to explore whether and how cooperation rather than competition amongst a spatially discontinuous network of places can constitute a brand. She develops a dynamic model of place brands capable of identifying the formative actors involved and concludes that this network brand has provided a viable rebranding strategy for a locality struggling with the effects of de-industrialisation. Gary Warnaby, David Bennison and Dominic Medway explore the construction of branded spaces in their examination of the rebranding of Hadrian's Wall as a Roman frontier spanning northern England. Demonstrating the fluid and evolving relationships between territorial and the more 'fuzzy' relational spatialities of the brand, they demonstrate how its meaning and extent have been negotiated by the actors involved and are likely to change over time.

Nick Lewis interprets the rise of nation branding as part of the wide-ranging and globalising strategies, rhetorics and practices deployed by nation states in the context of international inter-territorial competition. Engaging with the interconnecting architecture of various agents involved in branding New Zealand, he discerns a political project focused upon reinforcing the global orientation of the nation state in economic practice and social identity, and questions what and who are represented in the brand and to what ends. Reflecting from his position as a leading practitioner in the world of place branding, Simon Anholt addresses critically the idea of the 'nation brand' and situates it in global geopolitical context. Contrasting the experiences of South Korea and Italy, he emphasises the role of image, identity and reputation and how strategy, substance and symbolic actions are critical in their management.

Part IV, 'Conclusions', ends the collection. Focusing upon the nature of the current mature paradigm of city branding, Adam Arvidsson argues that the 'creative city' model centres upon a direct connection between the biopolitical interventions in individual and social practices and the financial valorisation of their results. Drawing upon international experiences, he explores how 'creative city' branding has been highly conducive to the gentrification strategies inflating inner city property and housing prices. He concludes by ruminating on the kinds of self-organisation and social production that may lie beyond the branded version of the 'creative city' and its branding. The final chapter draws together and reflects upon the key contributions in the book to understanding the geographies of brands and branding, offers some reflections on methods and researching this topic, considers the contribution of geographical readings to the politics and limits of brands and branding and, finally, outlines potential future research directions. In sum, this collection intends to provide a focal point for the beginning of a fruitful and worthwhile engagement with the geographies of brands and branding in a multi-disciplinary and international context.

## ACKNOWLEDGEMENTS

Thanks to all the authors for their contributions and commitments to this collection. Thanks also to Joan Fitzgerald at the Centre for Urban and Regional Studies, Northeastern University, and the Boston Public Library for the space to conclude it. The usual disclaimers apply.

## REFERENCES

Aaker, D.A. (1996) *Building Strong Brands*, New York: Free Press.

Anholt, S. (2002) 'Foreword', *Brand Management*, 9, 4–5, 229–239.

Anholt, S. (2006) *Competitive Identity: The New Brand Management for Nations, Cities and Regions*, Basingstoke: Palgrave Macmillan.

Arvidsson, A. (2005) 'Brands: A critical perspective', *Journal of Consumer Culture*, 5, 2, 235–258.

Barnett, C., Cloke, P., Clarke, N. and Malpass, A. (2005) 'Consuming ethics: Articulating the subjects and spaces of ethical consumption', *Antipode*, 37, 23–45.

Barry, A. and Slater, D. (2002) 'Introduction: The technological economy', *Economy and Society*, 31, 2, 175–193.

Bernstein, D. (1984) *Company Image and Reality: A Critique of Corporate Communications*, Eastbourne: Holt, Rinehart and Winston.

Bilkey, W.J. and Nes, E. (1982) 'Country-of-origin effects on product evaluations', *Journal of International Business Studies*, 8, 1, 89–99.

Blundstone (2010) *Blundstone: An Australian Tradition*, http://www.blundstone.com/index.cgi, accessed 26 July 2010.

Bridge, G. and Smith, A. (2003) 'Intimate encounters: Culture-economy-commodity', *Environment and Planning D: Society and Space*, 21, 257–268.

Callon, M. (2005) 'Why virtualism paves the way to political impotence: A reply to Daniel Miller's critique of *The Laws of the Markets*', *Economic Sociology – European Electronic Newsletter*, 6, 2, February, 3–20.

Castree, N. (2001) 'Commodity fetishism, geographical imaginations and imaginative geographies', *Environment and Planning A*, 33, 1519–1525.

Castree, N. (2004) 'The geographical lives of commodities: Problems of analysis and critique', *Social and Cultural Geography*, 5, 1, 21–35.

Christopherson, S., Garretsen, H. and Martin, R. (2008) 'The world is not flat: Putting globalization in its place', *Cambridge Journal of Regions, Economy and Society*, 1, 3, 343–349.

Colbeck, R. (2003) *Submission to the Productivity Commission Inquiry into Post-2005 Textile, Clothing and Footwear Assistance Arrangements*, Liberal Senator for Tasmania, Tasmania, 7 March, www.pc.gov.au/__data/assets/file/0003/27966/sub061.rtf, accessed 26 July 2010.

Cook, I. and Crang, P. (1996) 'The world on a plate: Culinary culture, displacement and geographical knowledges', *Journal of Material Culture*, 1, 131–153.

Cook, I. and Harrison, M. (2003) 'Cross over food: Re-materializing postcolonial geographies', *Transactions of the Institute of British Geographers*, NS, 28, 296–317.

Cook, I. and Harrison, M. (2007) 'Follow the thing: "West Indian hot pepper sauce"', *Space and Culture*, 10, 1, 40–63.

Darby, A. (2007) 'These boots were made for walking: Blundstone strides off to Asia', *The Age*, 17 January, Melbourne, http://www.theage.com.au/news/national/these-boots-were-made-for-walking-blundstone-strides-off-to-asia/2007/01/16/1168709752862.html, accessed 26 July 2010.

de Chernatony, L. (2001) *From Brand Vision to Brand Evaluation*, Amsterdam: Elsevier.

Edensor, T. and Kothari, U. (2006) 'Extending networks and mediating brands: Stallholder strategies in a Mauritian market', *Transactions of the Institute of British Geographers*, 31, 323–336.

Frank, R.H. (2000) *Luxury Fever: Why Money Fails to Satisfy in an Era of Excess*, Princeton, NJ: Princeton University Press.

Friedman, T. (2005) *The World Is Flat: A Brief History of the Twenty-first Century*, New York: Farrar, Straus and Giroux.

Gold, J.R. and Ward, S.V. (eds) (1994) *Place Promotion*, Chichester: John Wiley & Sons.

Goldman, R. and Papson, S. (2006) 'Capital's brandscapes', *Journal of Consumer Culture*, 6, 3, 327–353.

Greenberg, M. (2008) *Branding New York: How a City in Crisis Was Sold to the World*, New York: Routledge.

Hannigan, J. (2004) '*Boom towns and cool cities: The perils and prospects of developing a distinctive urban brand in a global economy*', Unpublished paper from Leverhulme International Symposium: The Resurgent City, 19–21 April, LSE, London.

Hart, S. and Murphy, J. (eds) (1998) *Brands*, Basingstoke: Macmillan.

Hartwick, E. (2000) 'Towards a geographical politics of consumption', *Environment and Planning A*, 32, 1177–1192.

Harvey, D. (1989) *The Condition of Postmodernity*, Oxford: Blackwell.

Harvey, D. (1990) 'Between space and time: Reflections on the geographical imagination', *Annals of the Association of American Geographers*, 80, 3, 418–434.

Henderson, J., Dicken, P., Hess, M., Coe, N. and Yeung, H.W.C. (2002) 'Global production networks and the analysis of economic development', *Review of International Political Economy*, 9, 436–464.

Hollands, R. and Chatterton, P. (2003) 'Producing nightlife in the new urban entertainment economy', *International Journal of Urban and Regional Research*, 27, 2, 361–385.

Holt, D. (2006) 'Toward a sociology of branding', *Journal of Consumer Culture*, 6, 3, 299–302.

Holt, D.B., Quelch, J.A. and Taylor, E.L. (2004) 'How global brands compete', *Harvard Business Review*, September, 68–75.

Hudson, R. (2005) *Economic Geographies*, London: Sage.

Hudson, R. (2007) 'Regions and regional uneven development forever? Some reflective comments upon theory and practice', *Regional Studies*, 41, 1149–1160.

Jackson, P. (1999) 'Commodity cultures: the traffic in things', *Transactions of the Institute of British Geographers*, 24, 95–108.

Jackson, P. (2002) 'Commercial cultures: Transcending the cultural and the economic', *Progress in Human Geography*, 26, 3–18.

Jackson, P. (2004) 'Local consumption cultures in a globalizing world', *Transactions of the Institute of British Geographers*, 29, 165–178.

Jackson, P., Russell, P. and Ward, N. (2007) 'The appropriation of "alternative" discourses by "mainstream" food retailers', in D. Maye, L. Holloway and M. Kneafsey (eds), *Alternative Food Geographies: Representation and Practice*, Amsterdam: Elsevier, 309–330.

Jaffe, I.D. and Nebenzahl, E.D. (2001) *National Image and Competitive Advantage*, Copenhagen: Copenhagen Business School Press.

Julier, G. (2005) 'Urban designscapes and the production of aesthetic consent', *Urban Studies*, 42, 5/6, 869–887.

Kapferer, J.N. (2008) *The New Strategic Brand Management: Creating and Sustaining Brand Equity Long Term*, 4th edition, London: Kogan Page.

Kearns, G. and Philo, C. (eds) (1993) *Selling Places*, Oxford: Pergamon Press.

Klein, N. (2000) *No Logo*, London: Flamingo.

Klingman, A. (2007) *Brandscapes: Architecture in the Experience Economy*, Cambridge, MA: MIT Press.

Lawson, N. (2006) 'Turbo-consumerism is the driving force behind crime', *Guardian*, 29 June, 31.

Lee, R. (2006) 'The ordinary economy: Tangled up in values and geography', *Transactions of the Institute of British Geographers*, NS, 31, 413–432.

Levitt, T. (1983) 'The globalization of markets', *Harvard Business Review*, May–June, 92–102.

Lewis, N., Larner, W. and Le Heron, R. (2008) 'The New Zealand designer fashion industry: Making industries and co-constituting political projects', *Transactions of the Institute of British Geographers*, NS, 33, 42–59.

Lury, C. (2004) *Brands: The Logos of the Global Economy*, London: Routledge.

Markusen, A. (1996) 'Sticky places in slippery space: A typology of industrial districts', *Economic Geography*, 72, 3, 293–313.

Massey, D. (2005) *For Space*, London: Sage.

Miller, D. (1998) 'Coca-Cola: A black sweet drink from Trinidad', in D. Miller (ed.), *Material Culture*, London: Routledge, 169–187.

Miller, D. (2002) 'Turning Callon the right way up', *Economy and Society*, 31, 2, 218–233.

Molotch, H. (2002) 'Place in product', *International Journal of Urban and Regional Research*, 26, 4, 665–688.

Molotch, H. (2005) *Where Stuff Comes From: How Toasters, Toilets, Cars, Computers and Many Other Things Come to Be as They Are*, New York: Routledge.

Moor, L. (2007) *The Rise of Brands*, London: Berg.

Morgan, K., Marsden, T. and Murdoch, J. (2006) *Worlds of Food*, Oxford: Oxford University Press.

Murray, J. (1998) 'Branding in the European Union', in S. Hart and J. Murphy (eds), *Brands: The New Wealth Creators*, Basingstoke: Macmillan, 135–151.

O'Brien, R. (1992) *Global Financial Integration: The End of Geography*, London: Pinter.

Olins, W. (2003) *On Brand*, New York: Thames and Hudson.

Papadopoulos, N. (2004) 'The rise of country branding: Implications for business in developed and developing countries', Paper for New Frontiers in Marketing Strategy: Brand Value and Business Success, 6 May, Budapest, Hungary.

Papadopoulos, N. and Heslop, L.A. (2002) 'Country equity and country branding: Problems and prospects', *Brand Management*, 9, 4–5, 294–314.

Phau, I. and Prendergast, G. (2000) 'Conceptualizing the country of origin of brand', *Journal of Marketing Communications*, 6, 159–170.

Pike, A. (2009) 'Geographies of brands and branding', *Progress in Human Geography*, 33, 619–645.

Pike, A. (2011a) 'Economic geographies of brands and branding: "Britishness" and Burberry in the luxury fashion business', Unpublished paper, CURDS, Newcastle University, Newcastle upon Tyne.

Pike, A. (2011b) 'Placing brands and branding: A socio-spatial biography of "Newcastle Brown Ale"', *Transactions of the Institute of British Geographers*, 36, 2, 206–222.

Power, D. and Hauge, A. (2008) 'No man's brand – brands, institutions, fashion and the economy', *Growth and Change*, 39, 1, 123–143.

Ritzer, G. (1998) *The McDonaldization Thesis: Explorations and Extensions*, London: Sage.

Roberts, K. (2004) *Lovemarks: The Future beyond Brands*, Brooklyn, NY: power-House Books.

Sennett, R. (2006) *The Culture of the New Capitalism*, New Haven, CT: Yale University Press.

Smith, A., Rainnie, A., Dunford, M., Hardy, J., Hudson, R. and Sadler, D. (2002) 'Networks of value, commodities and regions: Reworking divisions of labour in macro-regional economies', *Progress in Human Geography*, 26, 1, 41–63.

Thrift, N. (2005) *Knowing Capitalism*, London: Sage.

Turok, I. (2009) 'The distinctive city: Pitfalls in the pursuit of differential advantage', *Environment and Planning A*, 41, 1, 13–30.

Urry, J. (2003) *Global Complexity*, Cambridge: Polity.

van Ham, P. (2001) 'The rise of the brand state', *Foreign Affairs*, 80, 5, 2–6.

van Ham, P. (2008) 'Place branding: The state of the art', *Annals of the American Academy of Political and Social Science*, March, 1–24.

Watts, M. (2005) 'Commodities', in P. Cloke, P. Crang and M. Goodwin (eds), *Introducing Human Geographies*, 2nd edition, Abingdon: Hodder Arnold, 527–546.

Wilmott, H. (2007) 'Political cultural economy and the financialisation of brand equity', Paper for the Centre for Research on Socio-Cultural Change Annual Conference 'Re-thinking Cultural Economy', 5–7 September, University of Manchester, Manchester.

# 2. Of places and brands

## Nicolas Papadopoulos

## INTRODUCTION

'Place' is central to human life. From 'Joseph of Arimathea' and 'Mexican standoff' to 'French joie de vivre' and 'British stiff upper lip', place designators, whether emphasizing the place itself or the people who live in it or its other characteristics, have been used commonly as a form of shorthand to convey large amounts of both simple and complex information in human communication. Since 'place' can refer to a room, building, home, neighbourhood, community, city, subnational region, country, supranational region, or the entire world, we experience it when buying a new home, growing up or working in a city, travelling to a destination, buying services at or products from it, and so on. It would not be an exaggeration to say, by paraphrasing the title of a popular movie, that 'There's Something [Very, Very Special] about Place'.

Considering its centrality, it is not surprising that place has been studied in a range of disciplines including geography, anthropology, sociology, and environmental psychology (e.g. respectively Brown and Raymond 2007; Low and Lawrence-Zúñiga 2003; Gieryn 2000; Lewicka 2010). In all these fields, interest has been shifting (Cresswell 2004) from studying and describing place in the traditional narrow sense of 'region' or 'location' to viewing it as a socially constructed experience (Low and Lawrence-Zúñiga 2003) – leading Kearney and Bradley (2009: 79) to conclude that 'place . . . cannot be separated from people'. As a result, there has recently been growing recognition that place matters considerably more than previously thought (Trentelman 2009). While each field considers place from its own perspective, they share a common interest in viewing it mostly as 'home' and examine such issues as its role in evoking feelings of attachment and rootedness (Brown and Raymond 2007) or as a symbol that communicates personal and social identities (Cuba and Hummon 1993).

This chapter considers place from the perspective of international marketing (Roth and Diamantopoulos 2009) or, more specifically, international buyer behaviour. This discipline has brought its own distinct perspective to the study of the core construct, through extensive research that spans nearly five decades, by focusing on the nature and effects of place image (PI; also referred to as made-in, country-of-origin, or product-country image). Interest in this field has been rekindled recently as a result of the rise of country, nation, or, more generally, place branding (PB; the correct term would actually be place marketing, since it most often refers to much more than branding, but for this discussion we can stay with the more commonly used 'PB'). PB evolved from the confluence of various factors since the early 1990s, including globalization and growing international competition in many sectors, the fall of communism, specific events that served to exacerbate the intensity of competition, and demographic pressures and changing migratory patterns (Papadopoulos 2004). To address this new environment, governments and trade groups began to develop systematic campaigns intended to safeguard or promote their constituents' interests, such as protecting domestic industries against imports (Crafted with Pride in America), attracting tourism, investment, skilled labour, and/or foreign students (I Luv NY, Invest in Austria), promoting domestic products abroad (100% Colombian Coffee), or reassuring consumers after major health scares such as BSE and avian flu (e.g. Australia's Gate to Plate agri-food certification programme). Coupled with a drastically different international political landscape after 1990, which underscored the need for systematic 'public diplomacy' in international affairs in general, these developments gave rise to what van Ham (2001) called 'the rise of the brand state' and made PB a central issue of our time (Anholt 2007).

PI and PB can be considered as two sides of the same coin, since (1) PI deals primarily with the demand side of the place image equation, that is, with the effects of place images on buyers; (2) PB deals with the supply side of the same equation, that is, with the management of these images; and (3) both are interested in how place images affect buyers and how they can be used constructively in marketing places and/or the products that are associated with them. In this light, this chapter deals with how PIs work in the product sphere, the types of images that appear to prevail in buyers' minds, and their implications for PB.

The discussion draws on findings from a number of studies led by the author, and some by others in which he participated, as part of his long-term international programme of research on PI and PB. To date, the programme comprises well over 80 field studies in more than 25 countries, with an aggregate sample of some 25 000 consumers, investors, tourists, and others, and has resulted in over 100 publications reporting on conceptual and field research on the topic. The chapter draws selectively on this research and earlier reports to emphasize selected PI-related issues that have not been investigated extensively in this field before, rather than attempting to 'catalogue' the entire potential set of related issues and studies. To prevent clutter, the methodologies and statistical procedures used are presented here only in summary form, and only statistically significant results are discussed, since details on the various studies can be found through the original sources that are cited when necessary (regrettably but unavoidably, this leads to many citations to the chapter's author and his associates).

## BY WAY OF BRIEF BACKGROUND: WHAT PLACE IMAGES ARE AND HOW THEY WORK

The construct of interest here refers to the place-based image with which a product is associated by buyers and/or sellers. In line with basic marketing precepts, in this definition (1) 'product' is anything that can be offered by someone to someone else (from toothpaste to a political platform during an election); (2) 'association' is broadly defined and can be the product's actual location of manufacture, its place of assembly or design, the origin of its principal ingredients or parts, the producer's headquarters location, or simply an unrelated place whose image is used to enhance the product's appeal (e.g. an Australian wine with a French name); (3) the 'buyer' may be a consumer or organization considering a purchase, a government considering a political proposition by another, or any company, tourist, worker, or student looking for a place to invest, visit, work, or study; and (4) the 'seller' may be any organization using 'place' to help market its offering – such as 'Swiss Made' in watches or 'Viva Mexico!' in tourism promotion.

Following the first known reference to the potential importance of the 'little phrase made-in' on product labels (Dichter 1962), the first study that confirmed this hypothesis empirically (Schooler 1965), and the first literature review (Bilkey and Nes 1982), research in this field took off. A comprehensive database maintained by this author shows that academic output to date in the PI and PB fields amounts to well over 1400 publications, including over 800 refereed journal articles in addition to books, book chapters, and papers in conference proceedings, and several scholars have called this the 'most researched' issue in international buyer behaviour and marketing (Tan and Farley 1987; Peterson and Jolibert 1995; Jaffe and Nebenzahl 2006).

Perhaps a key reason why the subject attracts so much attention is that it combines three elements that are of paramount importance to international marketing researchers and, indeed, to academics, practitioners, and people in general: culture, which largely defines who we are; place, which says where we come from; and perception, which is how we understand the world around us. Marketing is founded largely on the premise that perception matters. Buyers' attitudes and behaviour are shaped by how they perceive information cues about a product's intrinsic and extrinsic characteristics such as, respectively, its technical features and its price or brand name. Intrinsic cues are hard to assess, and so buyers more often than not turn to extrinsic cues, such as PI, for help, since these act as summary information carriers that encapsulate and reflect product features.

Cognitive psychology tells us that such information is stored in the brain in the form of mental schemata. These are the sets of hierarchically structured constructs, generalizations, objects, events, or feelings which form complex 'webs of associations' of nodes and their links that help us to structure our understanding of our environment (Hawkins *et al.* 2001). Dominant associative networks lead to stereotyping, a process that helps us cope with cognitive overload and information processing (Yarhouse 2000).

Place images are complex mental schemata that can be activated by extrinsic place cues we experience in the marketplace, and typically represent strong stereotypes. As we go through life, we learn a lot about places from school, the media, our exposure to products, and other sources. We learn to speak of such things as 'Italian fashion', the 'Russian steppe', or the 'friendly Aussies', and over time we stereotype PIs and use them as shorthand for making purchase decisions: 'If it's German, it must be well engineered' (so Volkswagen advertises its 'German engineering' for cars made in Brazil), and 'Japanese electronics are the best' (which explains the brand origin of the TV, CD player, or camera most of us likely own). This is why in the context of international marketing, as in others, 'place matters'.

## SELECTED FINDINGS ON PLACE IMAGE AND ITS EFFECTS

### The Images of Places and Their Products around the World

The role of culture in human behaviour, and in buyer behaviour in particular, is pervasive. In our context, culture influences the views of people about places and their products. Culture matters, in other words, and accordingly our research has focused heavily on cross-national and/or cross-cultural comparative studies.

A cross-national study we carried out in 15 countries offers a good overview of how countries are perceived (Papadopoulos, Heslop, and

*Table 2.1    Aggregate assessment of 18 origins by 15 samples\* (n=4627)*

| Level of develop-ment | Countries assessed | Composite index | | Rank by variable \*\* | | | |
|---|---|---|---|---|---|---|---|
| | | Mean (7-point scale) | Rank | Products overall | Willing to buy | Ideal country | Want closer ties with – |
| **Higher** | Germany | 5.3 | 1 | 1 | 1 | 9 | 3 |
| | Japan | 5.2 | 2 | 2 | 2 | 12 | 3 |
| | U.S. | 5.1 | 3 | 3 | 3 | 9 | 8 |
| | Holland | 5.1 | 4 | 5 | 4 | 3 | 3 |
| | Australia | 5.1 | 5 | 9 | 4 | 1 | 1 |
| | Canada | 5.1 | 6 | 9 | 8 | 1 | 1 |
| | France | 5.0 | 7 | 3 | 7 | 5 | 8 |
| | Britain | 5.0 | 8 | 5 | 4 | 7 | 7 |
| | Sweden | 5.0 | 9 | 7 | 9 | 4 | 3 |
| | Norway | 4.9 | 10 | 8 | 9 | 5 | 10 |
| | Spain | 4.8 | 11 | 11 | 9 | 7 | 11 |
| **Lower** | Hong Kong | 4.3 | 12 | 12 | 12 | 13 | 12 |
| | Greece | 4.3 | 13 | 14 | 13 | 11 | 13 |
| | Hungary | 3.9 | 14 | 15 | 14 | 14 | 14 |
| | Israel | 3.8 | 15 | 13 | 14 | 17 | 18 |
| | Mexico | 3.8 | 16 | 16 | 14 | 15 | 15 |
| | Indonesia | 3.7 | 17 | 16 | 17 | 16 | 17 |
| | India | 3.5 | 18 | 18 | 18 | 18 | 15 |

*Notes:*
\*    The sampled countries were the same as those assessed except for Japan, Sweden, and India.
\*\*    The rankings are based on the unrounded means. Inter-scale differences of 0.2 or higher generally are statistically significant at 0.01. Equal ranks signal non-significant differences in the means.

*Source:*    Author's research.

IKON Research Group 2000). Table 2.1 shows the rank ordering of 18 origins based on a composite index comprising four image variables, of which the first two deal with a country's products and the other two with the country itself. The variables were measured on 7-point scales (7=good), and within each type one was a cognitive assessment ('products overall', 'ideal country') and the other a conative measure ('willing to buy', 'want closer ties with –'). The 18 origins evaluated follow more or less an expected rank ordering from most to least developed – but also portray discrepancies between the 'product' and 'country' images in some cases. In what is perhaps the most strikingly lopsided set of findings, Germany, Japan, and the U.S. score highly on 'product' but quite a bit lower as 'ideal' countries, whereas Canada and Australia are near the bottom of the more developed countries on 'product', but are tied for first place on the 'country' dimensions.

We have found almost identical results in a number of other studies, suggesting that some countries benefit from a very positive 'country' image even though their products are not well known or appreciated, while others have strong product images that may weaken over the long term because of less positive country images. For example, one study done in Seoul, South Korea (Elliot and Papadopoulos 2006), which dealt with a broader set of variables also measured on 7-point scales, found that respondents rated Canadian and Australian products lower on a variety of 'product' variables, at about 4.4, compared to the U.S. (5.0) and Japan (5.4), but gave Canada and Australia significantly higher scores as countries (5.1) compared to the two major industrial powers (4.3 for the U.S. and 4.1 for Japan).

## Subnational Differences in Place Images

Most PI studies deal with images at the national level, but subnational differences also matter. Ethnicity is of particular interest in the PI context: on the one hand, it influences behaviour significantly (Laroche *et al.* 1997); on the other, PI essentially reflects the ethnicity of a product. Therefore, ethnic identity may lead to varying consumer reactions depending on a brand's perceived nationality and the consumer's like or dislike of it – the so-called 'affinity' (Papadopoulos *et al.* 2008; Oberecker *et al.* 2008) or 'animosity' (Klein *et al.* 1998) effects.

We were able to test and confirm this hypothesis in two studies which assessed the views of English- and French-speaking Canadians toward ethnically affiliated origins and their products (with additional 'neutral' countries used as controls) (Heslop *et al.* 1998, Papadopoulos *et al.* 2008). The findings were that ethnic affiliation does indeed influence English Canadians' ratings of Ontario, Great Britain, the U.S., and Canada positively, and French Canadians' ratings of Quebec but, interestingly, not of France. In fact, evaluations by French-speakers of products from most countries tended to be significantly lower than the norm. The data generally suggested a sense of disenfranchisement on the part of French Canadians, confirming the widely noted suggestions that they feel 'as an island in a North American sea' and focus their emotional attachment on their home province, rather than France, unlike their English-speaking counterparts – and also providing strong support for the hypothesis that *sub*-culture matters.

Similarly intriguing findings emerged in a subnational study carried out in two regions in Spain that are purported to be at odds with each other, the 'separatist' Basque Country and the more 'mainstream' Navarra, and a neighbouring one in France, Bordeaux (Orbaiz and Papadopoulos 2003). Using a combination of 'product', 'country', and 'animosity' scales, we found that, surprisingly, there was greater affect and less or non-existent animosity between the two Spanish regions than between either of them and France, toward which affect in the Spanish regions was low and animosity high. For instance, in Navarra the mean for the 'affect' construct on the 7-point scale was 5.4 for the Basque Country and 4.6 for Argentina, a far-away country included to test the 'affinity' construct, versus only 4.0 for France (the differences are both substantive and statistically significant at 0.001). This matches findings from another study (Papadopoulos *et al.* 2000), where the image of France was tested in Madrid and was also found to be quite negative. It would appear that, in spite of common membership in the European Union, neighbour status, and shared Latin culture, Spanish consumers harbour antipathy toward France perhaps for historical reasons or because of intra-EU trade disputes or other factors.

Such findings have led us to suggest that the structure and content of place images may be even more intricate and complex than we and other observers previously thought. This view is supported by preliminary findings from another study on animosity, which we recently completed in India (Delhi) and Pakistan (Lahore). While the results are still being analysed, the data suggest that such factors as consumer cosmopolitanism and world-mindedness, which are attracting growing interest in international marketing research and had rarely been included as moderators in earlier studies, may help to explain variations in PIs and reactions to them across and within countries.

**The Content of Place Images**

While hundreds of studies have examined how consumers evaluate products from various origins, a basic question has not yet been researched systematically: what products and brands do respondents have in mind when doing the evaluation? The question appears simple, but the answer is hard to come by because it involves a very substantive and hard-to-manage effort in coding, processing, and analysis. Yet the issue is important, since the objects that comprise a country's image are germane to what this image will be – and one's awareness of items in memory, and ability to

*Table 2.2     Well-known versus less well-known product origins*

| Completion rates* | Study | | | |
|---|---|---|---|---|
| Sample: | (a) Multinational study (15 countries, *n*=4627) | | | |
| Target countries: | Japan | U.S. | Sweden | Canada |
|   Left blank | 22% | 23% | 53% | 65% |
|   Brand mentions | 50% | 56% | 46% | 17% |
| Sample: | (b) South Korea study (*n*=349) | | | |
| Target countries: | Japan | U.S. | Australia | Canada |
|   Left blank | 52% | 45% | 77% | 80% |
|   Brand mentions | 59% | 67% | 34% | 33% |

*Note:*    * The maximum possible number of mentions was 92 540 in the multinational study (n=4627 × 5 countries assessed × 4 blanks each) and 12 564 in South Korea (n=349 × 4 countries × 9 blanks [3 each for country overall, products, and tourism features]).

*Source:*   Author's research.

recall them, depends largely on how effectively they have been encoded and whether memory traces are available to enable their retrieval (Grusec *et al.* 1990). Research of this type can use aided recall techniques (akin to a multiple choice test), which are easier to manage but weaker in result since they suggest response options which the respondent may not have considered on his or her own, or unaided recall, in which the respondent is asked to note whatever comes to mind at the mention of a cue. The latter technique is strongly recommended as more effective, since it helps to reveal stronger nodes and associations in memory (Solso 1995).

We have used unaided recall in various studies by asking respondents to name the products, companies, brands, or other characteristics that come to mind when a known or less well-known country name is mentioned. Table 2.2 shows summary findings for two of these studies, which were mentioned above: the multinational project, which focused on products only, and the South Korean study, which also tried to evoke tourism-related and general country characteristics. Respondents in each case had a few 'blanks' to fill for each target country, and expert coders recorded each item mentioned and noted whether it referred to a specific brand name or a generic product category (e.g. 'Ford' versus 'cars', or 'the Outback' versus 'wide open spaces'). We received, coded, and processed over 58 000 responses in the multinational study and 4300 in South Korea.

As shown in Table 2.2, the completion rates were significantly lower for Canada, Australia, and Sweden than for Japan and the U.S. (the completion rate was lower overall in South Korea because of response time constraints due to the 'consumer intercept' sampling technique used, but the pattern was identical to that of the multinational study). As well, the incidence of specific brand-name mentions was much higher for Japan and the U.S. than for Canada and Australia. Interestingly, while the overall completion rate for Sweden was fairly low (53%), the proportion of brand mentions rivalled that of Japan and the U.S., suggesting that even a small handful of well-known brands (Volvo, Saab, IKEA, Electrolux), which Australia and Canada generally lack, can have a significant effect on a country's overall image.

Table 2.3 shows a summary of the top-of-mind awareness data for two key countries, the U.S. and Japan, from the multinational study (Papadopoulos 2007). In line with schema theory, sectors that attract 10 per cent or more of the total response are 'nodal', i.e. the most important sectors associated with each country. The image of the 'bundle of goods' that respondents associated with these countries is rather fascinating. There are five nodal sectors for the U.S., with none exceeding 20 per cent of the response, while only two sectors account for fully 77 per cent of all mentions for Japan, with entertainment and leisure at 41 per cent and transportation at 36 per cent. Further analysis at the level of product categories and specific brands suggests similarly interesting findings; for example, there were 16 nodal brands for Japan, 14 for the U.S., and only 4 for Canada (detailed data are not shown here because of lack of space; the cut-off for individual brands was set at 1 per cent). Toyota is a typical case of a brand that 'defines' its home country: 22 per cent of the respondents worldwide mentioned it (and, it can be assumed, many more had it in mind when mentioning the category 'cars' without naming any brands). Such findings go beyond simple name recognition: when we rank-ordered the sector mentions based on their degree of technological advancement and correlated them to the product evaluations for the country, the findings were significantly superior for Japan (a 'sector-based advancement score' of 7.4 out of 10 and a 'product evaluation score' of 5.6 on the 7-point scale, compared to Canada's 4.1 and 4.8, respectively).

In an earlier study (Papadopoulos 1997), we asked a similar top-of-mind awareness question of technology investors in the U.S. and Canada ($n$=164). Partial results are in Table 2.4. It is interesting to note the correspondence between the frequency of mentions and the known features of the target regions (e.g. generally higher frequency of 'high tech' for the three U.S. regions, 'government' for Ottawa), but it is even more interesting to note that Kitchener-Waterloo outscores Boston on the number of 'university' mentions: the former has only one institution globally known in high tech, the University of Waterloo, whereas the latter has the largest number of universities of any city, including MIT and Harvard. As with

Table 2.3  Nodal sectors in the images of the U.S. and Japan (percentage of response)

| Sectors \ Samples | Overall average | USA | Canada | Mexico | Britain | France | Germany | Norway | Holland | Hungary | Greece | Spain | Israel | Australia | Indonesia | Hong Kong |
|---|---|---|---|---|---|---|---|---|---|---|---|---|---|---|---|---|
| Agriculture, fishing | 3 | 5 | 5 | 2 | 4 | 1 | 1 | 2 | 4 | 1 | 4 | 6 | 0 | 3 | 1 | 4 |
| Natural resources | 1 | 2 | 1 | 1 | 1 | 0 | 1 | 3 | 1 | 1 | 4 | 3 | 0 | 1 | 1 | 0 |
| **Food, beverages, tobacco, pharma** | **16** | **10** | **9** | **15** | **21** | **25** | **20** | **19** | **15** | **19** | **18** | **23** | **13** | **13** | **13** | **11** |
| **Clothing** | **14** | **9** | **12** | **18** | **11** | **11** | **12** | **13** | **13** | **13** | **12** | **9** | **30** | **12** | **15** | **24** |
| Other household | 5 | 4 | 5 | 10 | 2 | 2 | 1 | 2 | 1 | 5 | 9 | 1 | 12 | 3 | 10 | 6 |
| Other industrial | 2 | 3 | 3 | 4 | 0 | 1 | – | 2 | 1 | 1 | 3 | 2 | 1 | 2 | 2 | 1 |
| **Services, miscellaneous** | **20** | **12** | **19** | **17** | **33** | **24** | **23** | **19** | **24** | **14** | **12** | **25** | **14** | **26** | **20** | **18** |
| Entertainment and leisure | 4 | 4 | 4 | 6 | 3 | 7 | 2 | 4 | 4 | 5 | 4 | 6 | 3 | 5 | 2 | 3 |
| **Transportation** | **19** | **33** | **26** | **14** | **15** | **15** | **22** | **23** | **20** | **23** | **22** | **14** | **16** | **20** | **19** | **6** |
| **Advanced technology** | **16** | **21** | **16** | **13** | **10** | **14** | **16** | **13** | **17** | **17** | **12** | **11** | **11** | **15** | **17** | **28** |

Origin country: United States

*Table 2.3* (continued)

| Origin country | Sectors \ Samples | Overall average | USA | Canada | Mexico | Britain | France | Germany | Norway | Holland | Hungary | Greece | Spain | Israel | Australia | Indonesia | Hong Kong |
|---|---|---|---|---|---|---|---|---|---|---|---|---|---|---|---|---|---|
| Japan | Agriculture, fishing | 4 | 2 | 4 | 2 | 5 | 5 | 3 | 4 | 8 | – | 4 | 7 | 1 | 5 | – | 2 |
| | Natural resources | – | – | – | – | – | – | – | – | – | – | – | 1 | – | 1 | – | – |
| | Food, beverages, tobacco, pharma | 2 | 2 | 2 | 2 | 3 | 3 | 2 | 1 | 6 | 1 | 1 | 2 | 1 | 3 | 3 | 4 |
| | Clothing | 3 | 2 | 2 | 4 | 1 | 3 | 1 | 3 | 2 | 5 | 3 | 6 | 4 | 3 | 4 | 5 |
| | Other household | 3 | 2 | 2 | 3 | 2 | 2 | 1 | – | 2 | – | 8 | 3 | 1 | 3 | 4 | 17 |
| | Other industrial | 2 | 1 | 2 | 3 | 1 | 1 | – | 1 | 2 | 1 | 3 | 3 | – | 1 | 2 | – |
| | Services, miscellaneous | 2 | 1 | 1 | 2 | 1 | 1 | – | 1 | 2 | 1 | 1 | 2 | 1 | 2 | 2 | 6 |
| | **Entertainment and leisure** | **41** | **42** | **45** | **52** | **47** | **44** | **44** | **37** | **37** | **40** | **31** | **35** | **42** | **39** | **41** | **45** |
| | **Transportation** | **36** | **42** | **37** | **23** | **31** | **34** | **42** | **45** | **33** | **41** | **42** | **28** | **44** | **35** | **41** | **19** |
| | Advanced technology | 7 | 6 | 5 | 9 | 9 | 6 | 7 | 8 | 8 | 11 | 6 | 13 | 5 | 8 | 3 | 2 |

*Source:* Author's research.

35

*Brands and branding geographies*

*Table 2.4   Top-of-mind awareness for five main technology cluster regions in North America (percentage of responses to question 'First thing that comes to mind' for each place name)*

| Mentions | Palo Alto U.S. | Raleigh U.S. | Boston U.S. | Kitchener-Waterloo Canada | Ottawa Canada |
|---|---|---|---|---|---|
| High technology | 33 | 16 | 25 | 8 | 18 |
| Nickname* | 15 | 15 | 2 | 1 | 1 |
| Climate | 11 | 5 | 2 | 7 | 18 |
| Lifestyle | 6 | 7 | 6 | 4 | 2 |
| A university(ies) | 6 | 3 | 15 | 21 | 0 |
| Government | 0 | 1 | 0 | 0 | 29 |

*Note:*   * Most common nicknames mentioned: Palo Alto = Silicon Valley; Raleigh = Research Technology Triangle; Boston = Route 128; Kitchener-Waterloo = Canada's Technology Triangle; Ottawa = Silicon Valley North.

Toyota for Japan, the University of Waterloo is a defining characteristic of Canada's Technology Triangle.

## Comparing Country, Product, and Tourism Images

The availability of large amounts of data from various different studies has enabled us to examine how PIs work in a number of ways. For example, using the South Korean data we recently developed 'image schemata maps' (ISM) through which we can portray, compare, and analyse the content of images in detail (Elliot *et al.* 2008). While space does not permit a display of the actual maps here, Table 2.5 shows the coded and classified responses on the 'general country' and 'tourism destination' images of three countries and serves to illustrate the usefulness of ISMs. Note the greatly different strong points of each country (in bold). For instance, the 'built' environment of Canada hardly received any mentions, whereas it presents itself as a strength for Australia (in particular, the city of Sydney, its harbour, and the Sydney Opera House received numerous mentions, illustrating once again the power of symbols in perception). Japan received significantly more mentions in the 'sports and leisure' (19 per cent) and 'industry' (18 per cent) categories than either of the other two countries – but it also received substantive proportions of negative mentions on the 'people and culture' (28 per cent) and 'politics and military' (12 per cent) dimensions, reflecting long-standing animosities given the turbulent history between the countries.

*Table 2.5   Summary ISM for Canada, Australia, and Japan (percentage responses)*

| General country image | | | Response categories | Tourism destination image | | |
|---|---|---|---|---|---|---|
| Canada | Australia | Japan | | Canada | Australia | Japan |
| 47 | 60 | 7 | Natural environment | 35 | 17 | 11 |
| 0 | 6 | 8 | Built environment | 1 | 22 | 9 |
| 8 | 4 | 13 | Sports and leisure | 7 | 3 | 19 |
| 16 | 14 | 14 | Country characteristics | 56 | 56 | 55 |
| 13 | 7(+) | 28(−) | People and culture | 0 | 0 | 1 |
| 4 | 3 | 12(−) | Politics and military | 0 | 0 | 3 |
| 12 | 6 | 18 | Industry | 0 | 1 | 1 |

*Source:*   Author's research.

Another interesting way for exploring images is through models that look at the causal relationships among the constructs that comprise buyers' mental schemata. For example, using data from South Korea and Canada for four countries (eight applications in total), we developed a complex model which (1) relates the cognitive and affective components of a place's image and, more importantly, (2) examines the potential cross-over relationships between its product and tourism images (Elliot *et al.* 2010). The model examines a total of 21 relationships, and, while some did not work, most did and provided strong or partial support for the posited hypotheses – specifically that cognitive elements influence both product and tourism beliefs; that 'affect' influences receptivity (willingness to buy from or travel to a country) directly rather than through 'beliefs'; and that there is a variety of interactions between the 'product' and 'tourism' image of a place, including one of potentially great interest to place market-ers, namely that consumer beliefs about a country's products affect their evaluation of the country as a tourism destination.

We can shed further light on the above relationships by looking at the concept of 'cultural distance' between countries. While many observers have noted that cultural boundaries between nations may become fuzzier as economic integration grows, this has rarely been tested empirically. Overall, cultural distance tends to be shorter amongst nations that are highly developed and have significant trade flows with one another. For example, using Hofstede's (1980) dimensions of culture, the distance from the U.S. to Australia, Britain, and Canada, all of which are countries with high Gross National Income (GNI), is only 11, 22, and 24 respectively. By comparison, the distance from Sweden to Mexico is 208, to Greece 200, and to Indonesia 164. Against this background, in one study (Nes and Papadopoulos 2007) we tested the relationship between cultural distance, GNI, and two key product variables, product evaluation and willingness to buy. The results showed that, on the one hand, consumers in less developed countries evaluate products from high-GNI countries more positively, and vice versa, while, on the other hand, cultural distance had no effect on product evaluation but did have a significant effect on willingness to buy. In other words, the higher the producer's GNI is, the more positively its products are evaluated; but the greater the cultural distance between seller and buyer is, the lower the latter's willingness to buy is.

Considering the difference between cognitive, affective, and normative information processing (where the origin cue is used, respectively, as a signal for product quality, or as a link to symbolic and emotional associations, or in relation to the buyer's social and personal norms), it appears that cultural distance may play only a small role in cognitive processing, but a critical one in affective and normative processing. This is in line with the structural model mentioned above, which showed that affective factors impact 'willingness to buy' directly rather than through 'product beliefs' (a cognitive measure), and 'willingness to visit' both directly and indirectly. This means that business firms, and the governments and trade associations that support and represent them, need to do much more than simply put forth 'good' products. Consumers may appreciate a product's quality, but still be reluctant actually to buy and use it if it comes from a culturally dissimilar place.

### What Kinds of Place Cues Are Out There?

While there has been much research on buyers' perceptions of the images of places and their products, there have been no studies on the extent to which businesses and other organizations use PI in their promotion. Yet knowing this can be very important, partly to help us understand the inputs that form the product and brand schemata in consumers' minds (the question asked in 'The content of place images' section above) and partly to indicate whether practising marketers consider place images as a useful component in their strategies. In a recent study we used the 'content analysis' technique to identify and catalogue in detail the place

*Table 2.6   Use of 'place' in U.S. and Canadian magazine advertisements*

| Place cues in advertising | Main | | Secondary | | Total | |
|---|---|---|---|---|---|---|
| | **n** | **%** | **n** | **%** | **n** | **%** |
| Cues in ad copy/art | 5 238 | 26.8 | 949 | 4.9 | 6 187 | 31.7 |
| Cues in brand/company name | 9 549 | 48.9 | 3 801 | 19.5 | 13 350 | 68.3 |
| Total place cues | 14 787 | 75.7 | 4 750 | 24.4 | 19 537 | 100.0 |
| Average cues per ad | 4.9 | | 1.6 | | 6.5 | |

*Source:*   Author's research.

cues appearing in 3008 ads from eight U.S. and Canadian magazines in the news, business, fashion, and lifestyle areas. First results indicate that business firms, governments, and NGOs use PI extensively indeed and much more so than we could ever have expected. Specifically, place-based executions ranked seventh in usage rate out of 27 execution styles catalogued, well above 'consumer testimonial', 'problem-solution', and other such techniques that are generally considered common, and, as indicated in the summary data in Table 2.6, in total there were 19 537 place-related cues in the ads studied. In other words, there was an average of 6.5 place cues per ad, as either a main or secondary (copyright, etc.) component. These cues ranged from direct references to a product's place of manufacture to the use of national symbols, such as flags or signature animals (e.g. kangaroos for Australian products), and place-defined brands, such as Rimmel London or Deutsche Telekom. Interestingly, place designators or images were used more commonly in ads addressed to business buyers than consumers, and they were most often embedded in the seller's brand or corporate name instead of appearing as part of the ad's copy or art. This research confirms the omnipresence of place-related cues, and indicates that places are seen as important not only by buyers, as we already knew from demand-side studies, but also by the marketing managers who use their images extensively in executing their promotional strategies.

## IMPLICATIONS AND CONCLUSIONS

The intricacies of how product-country image works, and the reason why it is important, can be illustrated by using the following brief exchange from the movie *Back to the Future III*, a comedy about time travel. It occurs in 'real time' 1955 between Doc, the scientist, and Marty, the young hero who has been to 1985 and back, and helps to portray many of the elements that are the focus of this report:

> *Doc*    No wonder this circuit failed . . . it says 'Made in Japan'.
> *Marty*  What do you mean, Doc? All the best things are made in Japan.
> *Doc*    Unbelievable!

In this vignette, Doc attributes the product's (poor) performance to its provenance, given his time-frame in the mid-1950s, while Marty, from his vantage point of the mid-1980s, clearly has a very positive view of Japanese products. The two time points roughly correspond to a 'bottom' and 'high' of Japan's image as a producer, and together they show that place images can change through focused strategies. Given their respective mindframes prior to this incident, Doc would be highly unlikely to choose, while Marty would probably seek out, a Japanese circuit – showing that perceptions and beliefs guide consumer choices. Interestingly, Marty's line was '*All* the best things are made in Japan', not just 'circuits', that is, the country images of individual product classes may differ from one another but all are likely to be congruent with its overall image as a producer, which is shaped by various factors including its flagship products, as revealed by the 'Toyota' and 'Sydney' examples in the above discussion. Lastly, the concluding line indicates that Doc will likely change his views of Japanese products, illustrating how place images 'travel'.

In a nutshell, place image matters, and this is especially so in the contemporary era where the systematic branding (or, better, marketing) of places has become a must-do for governments and trade groups, at both national and subnational levels, worldwide. Two general conclusions can be drawn from the preceding discussion. First is the importance of 'affect', which was mentioned several times in the preceding sections and cannot be over-emphasized. If one were to draw a hypothetical all-inclusive model of PI effects, the 'traditional path' would be shown as well tested and confirmed: we know that cognitive country images influence product beliefs, which influence purchase predispositions; but there would be significant scope for new research to examine in more depth the role of affective factors, such as affinity or animosity, which appear to have a strong and often direct effect on final outcomes. The second conclusion was also alluded to above, especially when outlining the product–tourism interactions in the South Korean study: inter-sectoral coordination of PB efforts is critical, and the interplay between the general, product, tourism, or other images of places, as these affect various types of 'buyers' ranging from consumers and industrial purchasers to investors, tourists, or students, must be carefully studied in order to enable place marketers to optimize the results of such efforts through synergy.

It is well understood that a favourable image for a place can bestow on it a competitive advantage, and therefore that there can be merit to both places and the business firms that are associated with them in 'flying the flag'. The recent evolution of PB is rapidly turning governments into active participants in the international competitive arena, helping to fuel the rush to systematic place marketing as a *sine qua non* to global competitiveness. This presents significant challenges to all places and firms, which stand to lose from the avalanche of aggressive 'flag waving' unless they join and best it by capitalizing on their niche strengths. It is hoped that this chapter has helped to portray the scope and complexity of place images and their effects, and that readers may consider in their future work some of the issues that were discussed.

## ACKNOWLEDGEMENTS

I gratefully acknowledge the contributions of over 30 colleagues and 300 students at universities worldwide who participated in these studies, and of more than 20 granting agencies, government departments, and universities in Canada, the U.S., and Europe which helped to fund this research.

## REFERENCES

Anholt, S. (2007) *Competitive Identity: The New Brand Management for Nations, Cities and Regions*, Basingstoke: Palgrave Macmillan.

Bilkey, W.J. and Nes, E. (1982) 'Country-of-origin effects on product evaluations', *Journal of International Business Studies*, 8, Spring/Summer, 89–99.

Brown, G. and Raymond, C. (2007) 'The relationship between place attachment and landscape values: Toward mapping place attachment', *Applied Geography*, 27, 2, 89–111.

Cresswell, T. (2004) *Place: A Short Introduction*, Oxford: Blackwell Publishing.

Cuba, L. and Hummon, D.M. (1993) 'A place to call home: Identification with dwelling, community, and region', *Sociological Quarterly*, 34, 1, 111–131.

Dichter, E. (1962) 'The world customer', *Harvard Business Review*, 40, 4, 113–122.

Elliot, S. and Papadopoulos, N. (2006) 'Toward a comprehensive place brand: Expanding the measurement of tourism destination image', in *Proceedings, Annual Conference of the Travel and Tourism Research Association* (Canada Chapter, Montebello, QC, 15–17 October).

Elliot, S., Papadopoulos, N. and Chen, C. (2008) 'An integrated schema of place image for the U.S.', *Proceedings, Travel and Tourism Research Association International Conference*, Philadelphia, PA, 15–17 June.

Elliot, S., Papadopoulos, N. and Kim, S.S. (2010) 'An integrative model of place image: Exploring relationships between destination, product, and country images', *Journal of Travel Research*, 22 September.

Gieryn, T.F. (2000) 'A space for place in sociology', *Annual Review of Sociology*, 26, 1, 463–496.

Grusec, J.E., Lockhart, R.S. and Walters, G.C. (1990) *Foundations of Psychology*, Toronto, ON: Copp Clark Pitman.

Hawkins, D.I., Best, R.J. and Coney, K.A. (2001) *Consumer Behavior: Building Marketing Strategy*, 8th edition, Columbus, OH: McGraw-Hill Higher Education.

Heslop, L.A., Papadopoulos, N. and Bourk, M. (1998) 'An inter-regional and inter-cultural perspective on subcultural differences in product evaluations', *Canadian Journal of Administrative Sciences*, 15, 2, 113–127.

Hofstede, G. (1980) *Cultures Consequences: International Differences in Work-Related Values*, Beverly Hills, CA: Sage Publications.

Jaffe, E. and Nebenzahl, I. (2006) *National Image & Competitive Advantage: The Theory and Practice of Place Branding*, 2nd edition, Copenhagen: Copenhagen Business School Press.

Kearney, A. and Bradley, J.J. (2009) '"Too strong to ever not be there": Place names and emotional geographies', *Social & Cultural Geography*, 10, 1, 77–94.

Klein, J.G., Ettenson, R. and Morris, M.D. (1998) 'The animosity model of foreign product purchase: An empirical test in the People's Republic of China', *Journal of Marketing*, 62, 1, 89–101.

Laroche, M., Kim, C. and Clarke, T.E. (1997) 'The effects of ethnicity factors on consumer deal interests: An empirical study of French and English Canadians', *Journal of Marketing Theory and Practice*, 5, 1, 100–111.

Lewicka, M. (2010) 'What makes neighborhood different from home and city? Effects of place scale on place attachment', *Journal of Environmental Psychology*, 30, 1, 35–51.

Low, S.M. and Lawrence-Zúñiga, D. (2003) *The Anthropology of Space and Place: Locating Culture*, Malden, MA: Blackwell Publishers.

Nes, Erik B. and Papadopoulos, N. (2007), 'The role of national cultural distance on country image-based product evaluations', in K. Al-Sulaiti (ed.), *Country of Origin Effects*, Qatar: Institute for Administrative Development, 281–299.

Oberecker, E.M., Riefler, P. and Diamantopoulos, A. (2008) 'The consumer affinity construct: Conceptualization, qualitative investigation, and research agenda', *Journal of International Marketing*, 16, 3, 23–56.

Orbaiz, L.V. and Papadopoulos, N. (2003) 'Toward a model of consumer receptivity of foreign and domestic products', *Journal of International Consumer Marketing*, 15, 3, 101–126.

Papadopoulos, N. (1997) *Competitive Profile of a World City: Ottawa-Carleton Compared to Leading Technology Centres in North America*, Ottawa, ON: IKON Research Group and Ottawa-Carleton Board of Trade.

Papadopoulos, N. (2004) 'Place branding: Evolution, meaning, and implications', *Place Branding*, 1, 1, 36–49.

Papadopoulos, N. (2007) 'What "made-in" images are made of: An in-depth examination of the content behind product-country evaluations', in *Developments in Marketing Science*, vol. XXX, Coral Gables, FL: Academy of Marketing Science, 23–26 May.

Papadopoulos, N., Heslop, L.A. and Graby, F. (2000) 'Une étude comparative et longitudinale sur l'image des produits français en France et à l'étranger', *16ᵉ Congrès International, Association Française du Marketing*, Montréal, Québec, 18–20 May, 681–695.

Papadopoulos, N., Heslop, L.A. and IKON Research Group (2000) *A Cross-National and Longitudinal Study of Product-Country Images with a Focus on the U.S. and Japan*, Report 00-106, Cambridge, MA: Marketing Science Institute.

Papadopoulos, N., Laroche, M., Elliot, S. and Rojas-Mendez, José I. (2008) 'Subcultural effects of product origins: Consumer ethnicity and product nationality', in *Proceedings, 37th Annual Conference, European Marketing Academy*, Brighton, UK, 27–30 May.

Peterson, R.A. and Jolibert, A.J.P. (1995) 'A meta-analysis of country-of-origin effects', *Journal of International Business Studies*, 26, 4, 883–900.

Roth, K.P. and Diamantopoulos, A. (2009) 'Advancing the country image construct', *Journal of Business Research*, 62, 7, 726–740.

Schooler, R.D. (1965) 'Product bias in the Central American Common Market', *Journal of Marketing Research*, II, 394–397.

Solso, R.L. (1995) *Cognitive Psychology*, 4th edition, Boston, MA: Allyn and Bacon.

Tan, C.T. and Farley, J.U. (1987) 'The impact of cultural patterns on cognition and intention in Singapore', *Journal of Consumer Research*, 13, March, 540–544.

Trentelman, C.K. (2009) 'Place attachment and community attachment: A primer grounded in the lived experience of a community sociologist', *Society and Natural Resources*, 22, 3, 191–210.

van Ham, P. (2001) 'The rise of the brand state: The postmodern politics of image and reputation', *Foreign Affairs*, 80, 5, 2–6.

Yarhouse, M.A. (2000) 'Review of social cognition research on stereotyping: Application to psychologists working with older adults', *Journal of Clinical Psychology*, 6, 2, 121–131.

# 3.  Brands: Boundary method objects and media space

## Celia Lury

## INTRODUCTION

> When I coined the term 'nation brand' in 1996, it was in recognition of the fact that the reputation of places had become as important to their progress as the brand images of products and companies. I didn't mean that any country from Azerbaijan to Zimbabwe could build a Nike-sized brand if it could only raise a Nike-sized marketing budget: I was talking about brand image as a way of understanding the challenges faced by countries and cities, not proposing brand marketing as a way of fixing them. (Anholt 2007: 57)

How can it be that the challenges that countries and cities face might be understood by considering brand image? Certainly brand managers have been concerned with the challenges of globalization for some time. In what has come to be considered a classic article, Theodore Levitt identified in 1983 the arrival of a 'new commercial reality – the emergence of global markets'. Levitt argued that 'Global competition spells the end of domestic territoriality, no matter how diminutive the territory may be' and proposed that differences in national and regional customer preferences were disappearing: 'The global corporation operates with resolute constancy – at low relative cost – as if the entire world (or major regions of it) were a single entity; it sells the same things in the same way everywhere (1983: 92–93).' He continued, 'The earth is round, but for most purposes it's sensible to treat it as flat. Space is curved, but not much for everyday life here on earth (1983: 100).' Since then brand managers have developed a huge number of global-local brand development strategies, very few of which treat the earth as flat in the sense predicted by Levitt. In most cases, while brand names are global, brand campaigns and products remain limited to specific, sometimes 'diminutive' domestic territories. Indeed, a very large number of diverse strategies have been developed (see the contributions in this collection), most of which seek to acknowledge, in some way or other, that it is not possible to sell the same thing in the same way everywhere. Indeed, as Pike puts it, brands and branding inevitably intertwine with geography, because 'their underlying dynamic of differentiation is predi-cated on the search for, exploitation and (re)production of economic and social inequalities over space and through time' (2009: 11). He goes on, 'Inescapably geographical brands and branding can further contribute to uneven development by forging and even amplifying competitive socio-spatial relations between spaces and places involved in their spatial cir-cuits of production, circulation, consumption and regulation' (2009: 12). In short, the reliance of branding upon processes of differentiation is one of the reasons that globalization does not mean that the entire world – or even large parts of it – is a single market entity.

In what follows, some of the many ways in which brands acknowledge more complex processes of globalization are described. These responses are not easy to put in the same space; they do not add up to or occupy a single three-dimensional space, and so they are listed here, one after the other, without any attempt to synthesize them or give them intersecting coordinates. Indeed, the suggestion is that it is precisely because brands simultaneously inhabit multiple spaces – or, perhaps better, organize spaces of multiplicity – that they provide an indication of the challenges faced by countries and cities today. In each of these responses, however, the space-making capacities of brands and branding are understood in terms of the performativity of the brand's interface (Lury 2004), and its capacity to make space not by extending or pushing back boundaries, but by *operating* them.

## EVERYDAY LIFE HERE ON EARTH

Consider a scene at the beach in Los Angeles. It is late afternoon: the shadows are lengthening. Two boys are playing in the waves. Both are wearing Nike shorts, the letters NI and KE on each leg of their match-ing shorts. One is bigger, and one is smaller: the shorts are what unite them; the boys are larger and smaller versions of each other. The shorts give a flickering message as the boys run in and out of the water. This is a visual message, but it also has a rhythmic accompaniment: a bit like a football chant, a crowd chant. NI-KE, NI-KE. The eye focuses, pinpoints, abstracts, locating the object and viewer in physical space, organizing depth through the lens of perspective, but the ear is attuned to sound from any direction. In the wearing of Nike shorts, the brothers are lifted out of their background, the pictorial space of the beach, and relocated in a dynamic, acoustic space, 'always in flux, creating its own dimensions moment by moment' (McLuhan 1997: 41).

Consider another scene. As you sit by the boulevard, as you fail to notice the sun going down until you suddenly feel the chill, you can watch people going by, some cycling, some roller-skating, some roller-blading; the insignia on their clothes are usually too small to see until they have passed. You too would have to be on the move to see whether it was Adidas or Nike. If you were on blades, you could move up behind people, overtake, hang back, or turn around to get a second look. Then you would be able to see that insignia are communication in movement, moving communication: not turn-taking, but turn and turn about, as fronts and backs of people move past and around each other. In this movement, the placing of insignia on the back of clothing makes sense: you still have a face, even when your back is turned. Look also at how, as you leave the beach, in shopping malls, in movements up and down escalators, in hesitations outside windows, the careful positioning of Nike logos situates the wearer's body in space. The marks or logos mark out movement in three-dimensional space, as is clear observing a woman sitting down, with one leg at a right angle to the other, the ankle of one leg resting on the top of the knee of the other. There is a Swoosh in a contrasting colour on the sole of the shoe, looking out, as it were, watching you. This proper, perpendicular space is also apparent watching people walking by, wearing shorts and socks, the Swoosh riding high on the outside of their ankles. Yet, although their legs move in sequential time, while the roller-bladers are clearly in three-dimensional space they are simultaneously re-positioned by the logos or marks. The mark of the brand collapses the foreground into the background, and slides now into then, bringing the future into the present. It offers an opening into a flow, a multiply mediated field, a dynamic, curved space in which window-shoppers and roller-bladers are moving into and out of multiple planes in space and multiple frames of time.

In this and other cases the logo not only integrates its surroundings the way a lens focuses and intensifies light, but it also integrates the differential events in the ambient environment which function as a kind of motor for it, a potential to be tapped (Kwinter 1998). In the organization of the editing of seeing that creates brand image, logos may not only be active and flexible, but also in ongoing communication with their everyday environment. On the one hand, logos may constitute within themselves such a dense system of self-referencing, co-relations and exchanges that they can throw up a boundary of order, a frame or a discontinuity between themselves and the world that surrounds them. On the other, the discontinuity introduced by the framing effect of the logo enables it to open on to a series of non-present spaces, a series of products, placements, promotions and events elsewhere, from the window display to the cinema screen to the baseball field. The logo operates a boundary in such a way that the environment is not only a space in which foreground and background can be brought into and out of focus but a space which we can be at a distance from and still be near by.

Alternatively put, these examples show how the logo makes connections, builds continuity, organizes one frame so as to succeed another, linking across products, packaging, publicity, and screens, inserting the overflow of everyday movements into the depth of brand image. In this and other ways, the brand interface introduces everyday movements and meanings into brand space. This is achieved, not by rendering the earth flat and homogeneous, extending the boundaries of a market by including more and rendering it homogeneous, but by making more out of what is already inside, and turning the inside out, by framing movement and marking difference.

## PLACE OF ORIGIN

A second kind of relation to space established in branding practices is that of connecting (or not) to a place of origin. Consider Swatch. A key component of the logo of this brand is its insistent self-identification in relation to Switzerland. Swatch watches display not only the name Swatch (itself a contraction of Swiss and watch) and the Swiss flag, but also the description 'Swiss' on their faces. In addition, much of the promotional literature accompanying Swatch products makes reference to the Swissness of the Swatch ethos. Such references are widely held to have the effect of strengthening consumer perceptions of trust in the quality of Swatch products in what is perceived to be a risky global commercial environment. Thus Nicolas Hayek, one-time Swatch CEO, has gone so far as to claim that the buyers of Swatch are 'sympathetic' to the Swiss: 'We're nice people from a small country. We have nice mountains and clear water', he says. Indeed, he attributes the company's success to the fact that:

> We are not just offering people a style. We are offering them a message . . . Emotional products are about message – a strong, exciting, distinct, authentic message that tells people who you are and why you do what you do. There are many elements that make up the Swatch message. High quality. Low cost. Provocative. Joy of life. But the most important element of the Swatch message is the hardest for others to copy. Ultimately, we are not just offering watches. We are offering our personal culture. (Quoted in Taylor 1993)

Here Hayek describes the way in which a place of origin may be deliberately designed into the interface of a brand. This design activity enables Swatch products to sell in many local markets by securing the trust of (some) consumers, providing a guarantee of quality, by tying the brand to an origin (a 'personal culture'). This guarantee is indirectly linked to the use of Swiss labour in the manufacture of Swatch products. The action of the Swatch interface may thus be seen to assert its significance as a territorial brand, but perhaps it might be more accurate to say that Swatch is part of a reterritorialization of global flows in the context of a competitive global economy.

So too may PGIs, or Protected Geographical Indications, be seen, for example the official recognition given to Welsh Lamb by the European Commission as a premium protected brand in July 2003. At the time this was announced, the Welsh Minister for Environment, Planning and Countryside, Carwyn Jones, said: 'We want to promote Welsh Lamb as a known quality brand and this is excellent news for Welsh lamb producers.' The character of Welsh Lamb is said to arise from the influence of the traditional hardy Welsh breeds from the mountains providing quality breeding stock which form the basis of the lowland flocks. Hybu Cig Cymru Chairman Rees Roberts added: 'Welsh Lamb is already much sought after and has some well-established markets; with PGI it will now clearly stand out in butchers' displays and supermarket shelves across the UK and further afield.' In contrast to the action asserted by the Swatch logo, a privileged status is given to the product rather than to the producer by PGIs, so anyone producing the product to the registered specification can use the name. Thus they are an example of the creation of 'collective competition goods' (Crouch 2007) by local and regional institutions. In this particular case, this means that all Welsh Lamb producers may qualify to use the registered name if they can demonstrate that the animals are bred, born, and reared in Wales and slaughtered in approved abattoirs (http://wales. gov.uk/news/archivepress/environmentpress/enviropress2003/714299/?lang =en). What both the Swatch logo and PGIs authorize, however, is the operation of a border or boundary to enclose a territory – defined in relation to the location of labour, a genealogy of stock, and/or a physical geography (Parry 2008) – as a protected, originary space for the creation of value.

Importantly, however, there are other examples of origin stories for brands, where an origin is not necessarily tied to a single, fixed place. An example is the slogan for the Starbucks sub-brand Fairtrade coffee: 'Coffee that cares: commitment to origins'. As the publicity leaflet puts it, '"Commitment to origins" means we're committed to paying and treating suppliers fairly, to respecting and sustaining the global environment, to contributing to local communities, and most of all, to being a partner rather than just a purchaser of coffee.' Indeed, other brands – including for example Nike – may be even less clearly tied to a territorialized place of origin or, indeed, to an origin at all. To some extent, the physical location of the Nike company itself, dedicated retail outlets such as Niketowns and sports events sponsored by the company may serve as such an origin. Certainly this perception of the flagship retail outlets, Niketowns, as origins is encouraged not only by the highly charged design of the stores, but also by the range of stock available, typically including all the most recent models of shoes, clothes, and accessories. Alongside such dedicated sites, however, Nike presents itself as original in relation to the almost endless multiplicity of the sites of its products' uses through the brand's elevation (and ownership) of an ethos of competition, determination, and individuality. Just Do It is the brand injunction, and in this 'doing' multiple origins for the brand are brought into being. Of course, it is possible to argue that a culture of competition, determination, and individuality is the national culture of the USA, and in this sense there is a parallel between the interfaces of the Nike and Swatch brands. But what makes the interface of the Nike brand so distinctive is that it appears as if there is no need to locate this ethos within territorial boundaries in order to secure its ownership or claim its effects. Through the workings of its interface the Nike brand is not tied to any specific organization or distribution of the production process; it is deterritorializing.

Comparing Swatch to Welsh Lamb to Starbucks Fairtrade to Nike, what becomes clear is that all rely upon the same process. In each case, the operation of a brand interface has the effect of differentially including (and excluding) sources of value in such a way as to frame the space(-time) of markets in terms of a dynamic of flows, an indefinite, ongoing series of products, placements, services, and experiences. In doing so, it connects and separates places of production from spaces of consumption within an increasingly globalized world.

## GREY AREAS

A further – third – relation to space is produced in the use of trademark law by companies in relation to what are called grey markets, that is, to markets created by the parallel imports of trademarked goods through indirect purchase from the trademark holders. For example, in the late 1990s, the supermarket chain Tesco obtained genuine Levi 501 jeans from suppliers outside the European Economic Area (EEA) and sold them, without the explicit permission of the trademark holders, Levi Strauss, in their UK stores at almost half the price of jeans sold in authorized Levi stores. Levi Strauss had always refused to sell jeans to Tesco, in part because the sale of Levi jeans alongside groceries was held to undermine the image of the brand. Levi Strauss therefore began proceedings in the UK High Court of Justice claiming that the import into and subsequent sale of jeans within the EEA constituted an infringement of its trademark rights. The 2001 judgement was that the mark holder – Levi Strauss in this case – must give explicit consent to importation before it could be considered that it had renounced its rights. Implied consent, it was argued, could not be inferred merely from silence of a trademark proprietor. The judgement was a refusal of the possibility of a parallelism that threatened to undermine the integrity of the protected space; it was an attempt to assert the primacy of a flat earth in which parallel lines must never meet.

In the USA, the legal response to parallel imports of trademarked products is rather different. In an early decision permitting the unauthorized importation and sale of genuine branded bottled water from Europe, it was held that, once a trademarked product is placed on the market, trademark rights may not be used to control the product's further destination. Thus US laws have long considered that the nature of trademark rights, at least with respect to parallel imports, is what is described as universal, that is, once a genuine trademarked product is placed on the global marketplace anywhere in the world, by or with the consent of the trademark owner, the trademark owner may not control the further distribution of that product under a theory of trademark infringement. This theory – of universal, or international, exhaustion – might at first sight be thought to allow unrestricted parallel imports, but it does so only by asserting the importance of a linear consequentiality that denies the very possibility of parallelism, by insisting that it is possible to establish a single originary moment. In this 'flat' legal environment, trademark owners have developed a number of strategies which allow parallel movements but curve space so as to make sure that these movements do not meet. So, for example, because a trademark owner can stop the importation of grey market items that are 'materially different' from trademarked goods marketed in the US with the mark owner's approval, some companies have used a variety of means to differentiate products intended for the US and non-US markets. They have argued that grey market goods are materially different from authorized US goods because they have, for instance, different warranties, different packaging, or different inserts contained in the packaging (written in different languages) (www.ip-watch.org/weblog/2009/12/23/us-weighs-copyright-as-barrier-to-grey-market-imports/).

## PLACE BRANDS AND THE SPACE OF MEASUREMENT

A fourth kind of relation to space is established in place branding, the application to cities and countries of techniques similar to those applied to products and services. Indeed, many agencies do not offer their services simply to establish places as brands, but also to measure the value of place brands. Consider the 'European City Brand Barometer' produced by Saffron, a British branding consultancy specializing in place branding. Saffron has developed a brand valuation exercise to 'compare and contrast place brand strengths', using metrics that compare the strength of cities' 'natural' assets – that is, their relatively fixed practical and cultural amenities – with their current 'brand strength', that is, the extent to which those 'assets' were recognized by outsiders and exploited by the city itself. It is an example of the way in which new forms of systematization and measurement have promotional, as well as descriptive, functions (Julier and Moor 2009; Lury and Moor, 2010), and of how brand valuation and measurement are directly linked to the use of brands and branding in value creation. For the argument being developed here, what makes such a case especially interesting is that, by explicitly focusing on the gap between where a city 'is at' and where it 'could be', the exercise locates new opportunities for value creation and positions branding itself as an enterprise 'focused on identifying, measuring and exploiting sources of value' (see Power 2007: 133).

In Saffron's brand valuation exercise, city asset strength refers to 'a city's baseline potential', determined by scoring cities out of 100 in key areas found by a survey of UK citizens to reflect the practical amenities and cultural qualities that were most important to people in choosing a city break. These included sightseeing and historical attractions, cuisine and restaurants, friendly and helpful locals, and good shopping facilities, as well as practical factors such as low cost, good weather, and ease of getting around. A city's 'brand strength', by contrast, was calculated using factors chosen by Saffron itself: 'pictorial recognition' of a place, 'quality and strength of attractive qualities', 'conversational value', and 'media recognition'. Again, cities were scored up to a maximum of 100. Perhaps unsurprisingly, the survey found that, while in general a high score for 'asset strength' was accompanied by a high score for 'brand strength', there were also cases where a city's 'assets' were stronger than its recognition or brand value, or where a city's 'brand strength' outperformed its apparently more fixed and objective 'assets'. In fact, Saffron went so far as to produce a 'brand utilization' score, by calculating brand strength as a percentage of asset strength. Cities such as Sofia in Bulgaria, Lisbon in Portugal, Wroclaw in Poland and Vilnius in Lithuania all emerged as 'hidden gems', which, 'much like undervalued stocks, seem to have a reality (city asset strength) that is more attractive and of higher quality than is currently accounted for in their brand (city brand strength)' (Hildreth n.d.: 10). In these cases, Saffron suggests, 'active branding' could help cities to push their 'brand utilization' score close to, or even above, 100 per cent.

This example is interesting here however insofar as it illustrates not only the branding of places but also how places produced in this way are simultaneously located in an abstract representational space (Rheinberger 1997), the finite but unlimited space of the measurement of brand value. This co-existence of brand place and brand representational space is productive in a number of ways. As described above, place brands are identified in relation to multiple dimensions of value, most of which lack any kind of external standard or metric. The 'brand strength score', for example, includes 'conversational value' as a key variable, which is determined using the hypothetical question 'How interesting would it be at a cocktail party to say, "Hey, I just got back from _____"?' (Hildreth n.d.: 8). This variable in turn is combined with other measures derived from surveys, content analysis, and prompted and unprompted consumer 'associations'. Such heterogeneity, along with the lack of external metrics, is indicative of not only the inventiveness of contemporary valuation systems but also the fact that there is no single, fixed space of measurement that can contain the differences of one brand from another. Indeed, it is as a consequence of their use of such a representational space that Saffron's 'Brand Barometer' is able to serve a promotional function for the consultancy; by highlighting the gap between a brand's current and potential value, it creates the opportunity for Saffron to be employed to narrow or even exceed that gap or, rather, gaps. Here then, place branding does not just describe places in an already given territory but introduces potential by inserting the brand's own dimensions into the representational space between where a place is and where it might be.

## BOUNDARY OBJECTS

In each of these four cases (and there are more), the performativity of the brand can be understood in terms of the brand's organization as an object of the artificial sciences, an artefact in the sense outlined by the economist Herbert Simon (1981). Simon argues that an artefact can be thought of as a meeting point – an interface – 'between an "inner" environment, the substance and organisation of the artefact itself, and an "outer" environment, the surroundings in which it operates'. For Simon design is understood as the organization of an (artificial) entity in terms of an intended purpose, that is, it is the organization of an interface or surface of communication between inner and outer environments. As he says, the 'description of an artifice in terms of its organisation and functioning – its interface between inner and outer environments – is a major objective of invention and design activity' (1981: 13). In the examples above, the interface of the brand is a meeting point for the exchange and communication of information between 'producers' and 'consumers', the economy and society. But what putting the examples alongside each other makes clear is that this interface does not (only) produce a single, homogeneous space, a flat earth: it does not (only) function as the marker of the edge of a territory. Instead, its operation is such that it appears as if the border between economy and society need not only be at the edge of a territorially defined economy but may also be in the middle(s), that is, it may be in the curves of mediation (see Balibar 2004 for a related analysis of migration, and Mezzadra and Neilson 2008 for the development of the idea of the operation of the border as method).

To try to understand what is at issue here let me add to the description of the brand as an artefact as described by Simon by introducing the notion of the boundary object, as described by Leigh Star and Griesemer (1989) and Bowker and Leigh Star (1999). In the latter's striking definition:

> Boundary objects are those objects that both inhabit several communities of practice and satisfy the informational requirement of each of them. Boundary objects are thus both plastic enough to adapt to local needs and constraints of several parties employing them, yet robust enough to maintain a common identity across sites. They are weakly structured in common use and become strongly structured in individual site-use. These objects may be abstract or concrete. (1999: 297)

In many respects, brands may be seen as boundary objects as defined here: they inhabit several communities at once, are plastic yet robust, and may be abstract or concrete. However, the definition of boundary objects given here presents them, somewhat surprisingly, as inert, dependent for their internal structuring on the space of their use. Brands in contrast are boundary objects in the sense that they variously – and not always consistently – multiply relations with a series of environments while still preserving the internal organization of the brand so that it may be identified and owned. That is, to propose a hybrid term, they are *boundary method objects*, and the space that is brought into being by such objects is not only the extensive, flat earth described by Levitt but also a dynamic, curved, multi-dimensional space.

In another respect too, brands breach the characteristics assigned to boundary objects by Bowker and Leigh Star, who, in their definition, consider such objects to 'arise over time from durable cooperation among communities of practice. They are working arrangements that resolve anomalies' (1999: 297). In Bowker and Leigh Star's terms, boundary objects are 'most useful' in analysing cooperative and relatively equal situations. Indeed, they suggest that 'issues of imperialist imposition of standards, force and deception have a somewhat different structure'. As boundary method objects, however, brands do not only or necessarily operate by means of cooperation; indeed, they may sometimes depend on one or all of standards, force, or deception. But, equally importantly, brands often need to satisfy the informational requirements of each of the several communities of practice they inhabit. Such requirements may be distinguished from both the relations of symbolic exchange (and violence) *and* the dense discursive frameworks of representation, deliberation, and cooperation common among communities of practice. The informational requirements of branding – organized by the brand interface – arise from its implication in an increasingly mixed spatio-temporal sign-system in which the power of the iconic to intensify values and of the indexical to introduce movement has been substantially enhanced by new data management and transaction technologies. It is this enhanced sign-system that makes it possible, I suggest, for the brand to act as a model of and for the multiplicity of space of possible states which a physical system can have, some real, some virtual, some concrete, some abstract, some curved and some flat.

More particularly, it has been suggested here that it is the operation of the interface of the brand as a boundary method object that not only introduces excess into its space of representation but also enables a strategic appropriation of the constantly shifting excess of inclusion over belonging (Badiou 2008). It does so by enabling multiple spatial strategies of market-making, sometimes reinforcing the alignment of markets with territorial boundaries, defining the edges of homogenized, standardized regions, nations, and localities, while at other times affording the possibility of selective openness, and differential inclusion. The resulting co-present composite of market-spaces can overlap one another, be added to, combined, composited with, juxtaposed, superimposed, interpenetrated, and merged with each other. This, perhaps, is the reason why brands offer strategies for countries and cities wishing to respond to the challenges of globalization: no matter how large or small their territory, no matter the size of their marketing budget, they need to manage the excess of belonging over inclusion, and to do so requires a multiplicity of spaces. The world is no longer (only) flat.

# BIBLIOGRAPHY

Anholt, S. (2007) 'Africa needs brand aid', *Monocle*, 1, 6, September, 56–57, p. 57.
Appadurai, A. (1993) 'Disjuncture and difference in the global cultural economy',

in B. Robbins (ed.), *The Phantom Public Sphere*, Minneapolis: University of Minnesota Press, 269–297.

Arvidsson, A. (2006) *Brands: Meaning and Value in Media Culture*, London and New York: Routledge.

Badiou, A. (2008) *Number and Numbers*, trans. A. Mackay, Cambridge: Polity.

Balibar, E. (2004) *We, the People of Europe? Reflections on Transnational Citizenship*, Princeton, NJ: Princeton University Press.

Bowker, C. and Leigh Star, S. (1999) *Sorting Things Out: Classification and Its Consequences*, Cambridge, MA and London: MIT Press.

Crouch, C. (2007) 'Trade unions and local development networks', *Transfer*, 13, 2, 211–224.

Hildreth, J. (n.d.) *The Saffron European City Brand Barometer*, www.saffron-consultants.com/news-views/publications, accessed 14 July 2009.

Julier, G. and Moor, L. (eds) (2009) *Design and Creativity: Policy, Management and Practice*, Oxford and New York: Berg.

Kwinter, S. (1998) 'The hammer and the song', *Tijdschrift voor architecteur OASE Architectural Journal*, 48, 31–43.

Leigh Star, S. and Griesemer, J. (1989) 'Institutional ecology, "translations" and boundary objects: Amateurs and professionals in Berkeley's Museum of Vertebrate Zoology, 1907–39', *Social Studies of Science*, 19, 387–420.

Levitt, T. (1983) 'The globalisation of markets', *Harvard Business Review*, May–June, 39–49.

Lury, C. (2004) *Brands: The Logos of the Global Economy*, London: Routledge.

Lury, C. and Moor, L. (2010) 'Brand valuation and topological culture', in M. Aronczyk and D. Powers (eds), *Blowing Up the Brand: Critical Perspectives on Promotional Culture*, New York: Peter Lang Publishing.

McLuhan, M. (1997) *Understanding Media: The Extensions of Man*, London: Routledge.

Mezzadra, S. and Neilson, B. (2008) 'Border as Method, or, the Multiplication of Labor', *Transversal*, 06-08, http://eipcp.net/transversal/0608/mezzadraneilson/en.

Moor, L. (2007) *The Rise of Brands*, London and New York: Berg.

Parry, B.C. (2008) 'Geographical indications: Not all "champagne and roses"', in L. Bently, J. Davis and J. Ginsberg (eds), *Trademarks and Brands*, Cambridge: Cambridge University Press.

Pike, A. (2009) 'Brand and branding geographies', *Geography Compass*, 2, 1, 1–24.

Power, M. (2007) *The Audit Society: Rituals of Verification*, Oxford: Oxford University Press.

Rheinberger, H.-J. (1997) *Toward a History of Epistemic Things: Synthesizing Proteins in the Test Tube*, Stanford, CA: Stanford University Press.

Shields, R. (1997) 'Flow', *Space and Culture*, 1, 1–5.

Simon, H.A. (1981) *The Sciences of the Artificial*, Cambridge, MA: MIT Press.

Taylor, W. (1993) 'Message and muscle: An interview with Swatch titan Nicolas Hayek', *Harvard Business Review*, March–April, 98–110.

# PART II

# Brands and branding geographies – goods, services and knowledges

# 4. Brands in the making: A life history approach

## Peter Jackson, Polly Russell and Neil Ward

## INTRODUCTION: BRANDS AND BRANDING

Taking British retailer Marks & Spencer's food business as a case study, this chapter examines the development and marketing of the Oakham brand of chicken, arguing that branding can be understood as a narrative process where brands are developed and 'storied' in ways that are consistent with the commercial positioning of the firm and with the personal investments of the brand developers. Our focus is on the interweaving of corporate and personal narratives in the branding of a contemporary food product, reinforcing Susanne Freidberg's argument that, 'especially in the advertising-saturated countries of the global North, most food is sold with a story' (2003: 4). Our research examines the way retailers are engaged in the process of making and managing the meaning of food products. We refer to this as a process of manufacturing meaning, arguing that these cultural constructions help shape the economic fortunes of food retailers such as Marks & Spencer's.

Our emphasis on brands as narrative constructions, telling stories that are designed to encourage consumer loyalty, is not new. The symbolic role of brands in the construction of cultural meaning is a well-established theme from Levy's pioneering work (1959) on 'selling symbols' to Lury's argument (2004) about how brands make the meaning of goods manageable for producers and consumers. According to Muniz and O'Guinn (2001), successful brands enable the construction of 'brand communities' involving a consciousness of kind among consumers, together with shared rituals and traditions and a sense of moral responsibility. Most of this work has focused on what Holt (2004) refers to as 'iconic brands' – brands which are rich in what McAlexander *et al.* (2002) call 'expressive, experiential, or hedonic qualities' such as Coca-Cola and Nike. We focus instead on a more mundane product (chicken) and its role in reviving the commercial fortunes of a high-street retailer (Marks & Spencer).

According to de Chernatony, successful brands involve a judicious balance between the functional and emotional values associated with them: 'brands help people perpetuate their particular beliefs' and 'consumers choose brands on the basis of the way these values fit their lifestyles and enable them to satisfy their needs' (2006: 5–6). As well as focusing on their external function in communicating brand values to consumers, increasing attention is being paid to the internal role of brands for employees within the firm. De Chernatony describes this dual process in terms of an almost circular logic where senior managers, staff and customers all play a role in defining the brand:

> Every brand exists by virtue of a continuous process whereby *senior managers* specify core values that are enacted by the organisation's *staff* and interpreted and re-defined by *customers* whose changing behaviour influences managers' views about more appropriate ways for staff to live the brand's values. (2006: 7–8, emphasis added)

We develop these ideas by looking at the internal and external functions of the Oakham brand as they emerged in the process of brand development. In the course of our research, we had access to many of the key actors involved in the process of brand development, including those who worked on product development, category management and marketing. Our interviews occurred only a short time after the events described, allowing us almost 'real-time' access to the process of brand development. Our research suggests that the development of the Oakham brand served a dual function in meeting the external needs of Marks & Spencer's consumers who were searching for a slower-growing bird, with greater concern for animal welfare and a nostalgic yearning for 'chicken as it used to be' (Jackson *et al.* 2010), while also addressing many of the current concerns of brand managers within the firm regarding the need for improved animal welfare, product innovation and quality, reconnecting producers and consumers, and differentiating Marks & Spencer's from its high-street competitors. The Oakham brand was consistent with the message that the firm sought to convey, particularly at a time when the company was struggling commercially and trying to reposition itself within a highly competitive marketplace (for details, see Mellahi *et al.* 2002). We argue, in particular, that the success of the Oakham brand was rooted in a series of interconnected personal and corporate narratives where the 'storying' of the brand was consistent with the personal investments of the brand developers as well as being consistent with the firm's corporate identity (see Russell 2008). We demonstrate this process of active negotiation between personal and corporate narratives through an analysis of the life history interviews we undertook with some of the key players involved in the development of the Oakham brand.

The life history approach aims to record change within living memory and to set the individual life story within wider narratives of social and economic change (Perks and Thomson 2006). The method records personal testimony and subjective experience and is particularly suited to uncovering the role of memory in accounts of the recent past. While life history interviewing was developed as a method for recording the experience of 'ordinary' people whose lives might otherwise be hidden from history, there has been a growing interest in taking a similar approach to commercial enterprise and big business. For example, the National Life Stories archive at the British Library now includes life histories of people who work in the City of London and the wine trade as well as in the food industry. This chapter draws on a series of life history interviews with brand developers at Marks and Spencer. Interviews lasted from 4 to 12 hours, usually recorded over several sessions, and they were transcribed in full. The tapes, tape summaries and transcripts are deposited with the British Library Sound Archive as part of the National Life Stories' 'Food: From source to salespoint' collection. (Subject to any restrictions imposed by the interviewees, they can be accessed via the Library's on-line catalogue at http://www.bl.uk.collections/sound-archive/cat.html.) In referring to branding as a 'narrative process', we draw on the strand of oral history research that focuses on the narrative construction of life histories (Chamberlain & Thompson 1998), sensitive to the connections between narrative process and personal identity (Somers 1994).

## THE DEVELOPMENT OF MARKS & SPENCER'S OAKHAM CHICKEN

During the post-war decades, Marks & Spencer (M&S) was one of the UK's most successful retailers, but its fortunes changed dramatically in the late 1990s. Its share price collapsed from a high of £6.60 in October 1997 to a low of £1.70 in October 2000 (Burt *et al.* 2002: 192). Its profits fell from more than a billion pounds in 1997–98 to £145 million in the year ending 31 March 2001. M&S was judged to be over-reliant on its own brand (St. Michael). Compared to other retailers, M&S had been late in accepting credit and debit cards in its stores and had a low profile in the rapidly developing out-of-town retail parks. The company tended not to advertise and was facing increasing competition from other supermarkets' premium brands (such as Tesco's Finest and Sainsbury's Taste the Difference ranges). By 2004, M&S was in the throes of an attempted takeover by the Arcadia Group and the owner of British Home Stores, Philip Green. A new wave of innovation in its food lines became a key part of the company's strategy for commercial revival. The development of the Oakham brand must therefore be seen in this specific historical and geographical context, as a response by a revered British retailer to particularly challenging financial circumstances.

M&S had pioneered the development of the refrigerated 'cold-chain' in the late 1960s and early 1970s, which enabled the widespread consumption of fresh as opposed to frozen poultry. This not only involved comprehensive changes to distribution, transportation, refrigeration and hygiene, but also helped transform chicken from a relatively rare, luxury product to the most popular form of meat consumption in the UK. Following this tradition of constant innovation, M&S undertook a major review of all its poultry lines before developing the Oakham brand (launched in 2003). According to M&S's agricultural technologist Mark Ranson (interviewed by Polly Russell, January 2004), the development of the Oakham brand took 18 months and was 'a joint team effort' involving the company's chicken buyer, product technologist and himself, working with the breeder company, a nutritionist from the processing firm Buxted and their suppliers.

Oakham chickens are a relatively standard breed (the Ross 508), owned by the international poultry breeding company Aviagen, from which M&S obtained exclusive rights to the breed. The Ross 508 is a slower-growing bird than other breeds, with a higher proportion of breast to leg meat. What distinguishes Oakham chicken from standard broilers, however, is less to do with the breed and more about how the birds are reared. As an M&S press release promoting Oakham explained, the chickens are fed on 'a nutritious feed ration which is non-GM, cereal-based and free from antibiotic growth promoters and encourages health and welfare too'. Besides the specifications for the feed regime, Oakham chickens are housed at lower stocking densities (34 kilograms per square metre compared to the industry standard of 38 kilograms per square metre) and have a slower growing cycle (living on average four to five days longer than the typical 39–40 days of conventionally produced broiler chickens). The birds also have access to 'natural behaviour enablers' (such as bales of straw that the chickens can pick, claw and peck at). Thus Oakham chickens can be marketed as slower growing and reared under more welfare-friendly conditions (though still not to free-range or organic standards). Indeed, as we have argued elsewhere, the development of the Oakham brand can be seen as an attempt by a 'mainstream' food retailer to appropriate the discourse of 'alternative' (free-range and organic) farming (see Jackson *et al.* 2007).

Oakham chicken featured as one of three products in the first of a new series of television advertisements which sought to distinguish the quality of Marks & Spencer's food from that of its high-street competitors. The advert featured slow-motion, close-up footage of M&S foods, with a sultry voice-over by Irish actress Dervla Kirwan and a soundtrack of Fleetwood Mac's 'Albatross'. The ad began with the words 'This is not just a chicken, it's a naturally reared, farm assured, extra succulent Oakham chicken' before going on to make similar claims about the quality of other M&S food products. The advert became iconic, endlessly parodied and shamelessly copied by other food retailers.

The acceleration and intensification of chicken production have been a commercial success story throughout the world, but have given rise to increasing consumer concern in recent years (Boyd and Watts 1997; Dixon 2002; Ellis 2007). M&S developed Oakham chicken precisely to allay consumer fears about the pace and direction of change in chicken production and to address changing customer tastes and perceptions. Retail competitors, such as Tesco and Sainsbury, sell chicken at a cheaper year-round price, while M&S has tended to emphasise quality over price. The Oakham brand was therefore designed to address this market and to offer what M&S poultry buyer Catherine Lee (interviewed by Polly Russell, May 2004) described as 'a unique proposition on the high street'. Unlike its commercial rivals, Catherine explained, M&S is not about economy fillets or buy-one-get-one-free special offers, as such strategies 'don't fit with anything else in our proposition'. They are not 'what an M&S customer expects'. In contrast to its competitors' emphasis on everyday low prices and cost-cutting promotions, M&S's proposition emphasises quality and value.

Articulating Oakham's points of difference, M&S's agricultural technologist Mark Ranson, responsible for animal welfare, explained how the product development process had to start with what customers wanted:

> This intensively produced chicken is a commodity, or was a commodity, and what we needed to do was to differentiate our chicken offer compared to the rest of the high street. So it was about looking at what our customers [wanted] . . . starting off at the other end, whereas normally we go at the farm end and work upwards towards the customer, speaking to customers about what they wanted. So they wanted chickens to taste like chicken used to taste years ago. So we looked at various different factors: we've got a named, a bespoke breed of bird, or strain of bird which is exclusive to Marks & Spencer; we've got a bespoke diet which we've formulated with nutritionists . . . It's a slower-growing breed . . . we've set certain husbandry standards . . . And then probably the other thing is that we put the name of the farmer on the pack . . . So that in itself, rather than saying as a point of difference and a key selling [point] 'we have 100% traceability', just by saying we are so proud of our farmers we put the name of the farmer on the pack.

The labelling is actually more complicated than this. Each label has the name of the farmer stamped on it. But it also quotes 'a typical Marks &

Spencer farmer', who gives a further endorsement. The label bears the photograph of this 'typical' farmer, not that of the actual farmer who reared this particular chicken.

The brand was introduced in 2003 as part of the company's commitment to bringing customers 'the best tasting, freshest products' (press release, 4 November 2003). In the press release, Mark Ranson is quoted as saying that:

> The introduction of the Oakham chicken is based around listening to our customers and their concerns about issues such as the welfare of animals and what they are fed . . . Our customers told us they wanted chicken to 'taste like it used to taste'. So, responding to this, we've introduced birds that are grown in enriched environments, with the Oakham White grown in barns with straw bales enabling the birds to perch and rest, and as a result, the Oakham is a slower growing bird.

Oakham chicken were originally called Oakham White, with a different designation, Oakham Gold, reserved for the free-range variety. According to Catherine Lee, the difference between Oakham and rival brands is 'essentially a marketing message' for what M&S specify agriculturally and in terms of processing and packaging.

Coming up with a name for the Oakham brand was not straightforward. Market research with M&S customers highlighted how they wanted to be reassured that 'from the M&S perspective everything's OK, but they don't want to know the details. So saying it's from Marks and Spencer is great, reassuring. Saying it's exclusive to M&S is even better.' The company originally planned to call the brand 'Suffolk White', because the processing plant was located in the county of Suffolk. However, subsequent market research suggested that such a brand name might work in southern England but would have less appeal in other parts of the UK. What was needed was a more generic name with 'some provenance-type imagery'. Oakham is, in fact, a small market town in Rutland in the East Midlands of England. Oakham chicken has no direct association with the town, but the name was chosen because of its positive association with 'countryside imagery and nice places'. A similar approach was taken to the naming of M&S's Lochmuir salmon brand, chosen because of its 'Scottish resonance' and generating adverse media commentary because of its lack of specific provenance ('M&S fakes loch to launch salmon', *Sunday Times*, 20 August 2006). As Catherine Lee explained:

> It's more about an image than it is a place and provenance. I suppose it does sound British, there's a Britishness to it . . . and there's a provenance feel, a bit

like Aberdeen Angus. Because that's effectively what we were looking for . . . the Aberdeen Angus of the poultry world.

As these comments suggest, the branding process involves key distinctions of space and place, even where symbolic locations are alluded to rather than actual places or precise provenance.

The growth of its food business has been critical in M&S's commercial revival since 2003, and the success of Oakham chicken contributed strongly to that process. According to Mark Ranson and Andrew Mackenzie, interviewed at Marks & Spencer headquarters (29 November 2006), the Oakham brand generated 30 per cent sales growth, well ahead of the rest of the market. Since June 2005 the company's share price went from £3.19 a share to a high of £7.66 in May 2007. The company won an award in 2005 for the development of the Oakham brand from the animal welfare group Compassion in World Farming and a commendation from the RSPCA for its commitment to improving farm animal welfare. Competitors have sought to copy the success of the Oakham brand with, for example, Tesco's Willow chicken and Sainsbury's Devonshire Red being similar branding exercises. Unlike its competitors, however, which have reserved these labels for their premium brands, M&S applied the Oakham label throughout its entire range of fresh chicken products, including whole birds, chicken portions and certain processed chicken products including sandwiches. M&S are now 'Oakhamising' other protein species (including duck, turkey, salmon, pork and lamb), raising interesting questions about whether the process is sufficiently sophisticated and supple to support market differentiation within each sector while being generalised across different product categories.

## PERSONAL AND CORPORATE NARRATIVES

In the course of our interviews with M&S employees involved in developing and implementing the Oakham strategy, it became apparent that there was a strong correspondence between individuals' personal invest-ments in the brand and the way they understood and narrated the brand in commercial terms. In this section, we examine the intersection between these personal and corporate narratives. For all of our interviewees, the telling of their life story and the 'storying' of the brand coincided in sig-nificant ways. We draw on interviews with three of our key informants: an agricultural technologist, a category manager and a protein manager, showing how, in each case, the development of the Oakham brand corresponded with their own personal investments and subjectivities.

### Agricultural Technologist Mark Ranson

A prominent feature of the Oakham brand is the improved welfare of Oakham chickens compared with standard broilers. This improvement centres on the adoption of lower stocking densities than the industry norm, providing 'natural behaviour enablers' such as straw bales, and a slower growing cycle, argued to cause less strain to the birds' legs and to decrease the incidence of animal health problems such as hock burn. M&S agricultural technologist Mark Ranson was central to implementing these policies and to determining the degree of welfare improvements that were possible without undermining the commercial viability of the Oakham brand.

Mark is responsible for ensuring the safety and welfare of all animals produced for M&S up to the point of slaughter. Born in 1967, Mark has an expertise and interest in animal welfare that evolved gradually during his university education. Reflecting on the origins of his interest in welfare, Mark recalled that, while studying biology and rural science at Leeds University, welfare was not studied and did not enter students' consciousness. His theoretical understanding and practical awareness of animal welfare developed later while studying for an M.Sc. in applied animal behaviour and animal welfare. During his Master's course, Mark visited an abattoir, an event which left a lasting impression on him.

A kind of ethical pragmatism allows Mark to continue to do his job despite his awareness of the strange and violent character of meat production. As he explained, 'I think where animals are used for whatever purpose . . . we have a moral obligation to use them humanely and properly.' He is, for example, strongly critical of the amount of waste that the industry creates in the preparation and tasting of food products. When thinking about the Oakham brand, Mark spent a good deal of time describing, explaining and reflecting on the ethics and practicalities of animal welfare. He was involved from the start in delivering the Oakham project in conjunction with M&S suppliers. The brand offered a vehicle for applying welfare improvements to a product that was previously sold as a loss leader.

Where Mark's personal convictions and M&S's commercial strategy most strongly coincided was in his ability to make an impact on the welfare of large quantities of animals. Mark initially worked for the RSPCA as a scientific officer. In this role he implemented the Society's Farm Welfare Scheme, a project which was aimed at influencing policy makers and industry to improve welfare standards and regulations. Mark commented on the limited reach of the RSPCA's influence:

For me it [the RSPCA] was about improving animal welfare, so it was a very good job going to the RSPCA. But how much direct positive change did I do? Probably, you know, minimal, minimal really. Then look at what I do with Marks & Spencer in terms of setting the standards. So, if tomorrow I went in and wrote new standards, they're implemented. So it's back to, are you influencing 1 per cent of the animals or 90 per cent? With M&S, if it's done, it's done across the whole board. So I would probably say I've got more sense of achievement with what I've done with Marks & Spencer than at the RSPCA.

Where farmers and processors had previously given him little time as a representative of the RSPCA, once Mark had joined M&S as an agricultural technologist he found doors opened and people listened. Oakham 'worked' for Mark because of the coincidence between his commercial responsibilities for improved animal welfare and his personal commitment to extending his influence over as large a volume of livestock as possible.

### Category Manager Andrew Mackenzie

Our second example is Andrew Mackenzie, who works as a category manager at Marks & Spencer, with responsibility for meat and poultry, dairy and juice. Born in 1957, Andrew joined M&S as a junior management trainee in 1977 and has worked for the company ever since. The Oakham brand worked for him as a commercial proposition – the latest in a long line of product innovations – and in terms of his personal commitment to the company's values and its reputation for innovation and quality merchandise. Recounting his working life at M&S, Andrew recalled the firm's long-standing role in product development, being 'first to market' with a series of innovations from pre-packed sandwiches to recipe dishes. The development of the Oakham brand represented another innovation which helped differentiate M&S from its competitors.

Andrew talked about his pride in working for M&S, selling high-quality products and sharing the company's commitment to principles of honesty and integrity: 'I love the culture of Marks & Spencer. I like what it stands for. I like the integrity. I like the honesty and the trust of the business.' In this context, then, the Oakham brand provided a commercial opportunity to re-establish the difference between M&S and its competitors, building on the company's reputation for quality and innovation. In Andrew's narrative, the Oakham brand was a logical development of the company's legacy, extending its principles to an ordinary 'everyday' commodity like chicken:

I felt that our chicken business could be more . . . I didn't feel we were different enough, I didn't feel we were special enough, although we had a good and loyal following with chicken, I didn't think we were where we needed to be . . . so we wrote a blueprint which was about a three-page document, which was: what brand values do we want, what visual appearances do we want and what are the main things that we want to achieve? And it was about visual appearance to the customer; it was about leading standards in terms of growing the bird; it was about great standards in terms of slaughter. So basically, the whole thing, right the way through, and how could we actually derive a point of difference? 'Clear blue water' is the expression that we use: how could we be different with our chicken business?

Oakham provided a commercial opportunity to get away from the 'everyday low prices' that the competition favoured and to re-emphasise M&S's reputation for quality and value. Establishing the difference involved a radically different 'blueprint', including changes to the breed, improvements in animal welfare and husbandry, new processing facilities and commercial incentives. Andrew recognises that, in the poultry industry, the differences can be quite small but that the end result is a less intensively reared chicken. He reflects on possible future developments, including a move to free-range and organic production:

Because I think, having established a point of difference, albeit that the points of difference in the chicken industry are relatively slim, you know, this bird grows for about 10 per cent more in terms of time, so it's a slower-growing bird, that is correct, but it's only about three or four days in the life of a chicken. It has a different ration, which is what it eats. It has a slightly better environment. But they are incremental rather than step-changing, and of course, if you want to go step-changing, then you're into your free range, and if you want to go step-changing again you're into organic, so that's how you actually achieve in this area, the differences.

In this case, then, the development of the Oakham brand provided Andrew Mackenzie with an opportunity to reinvest in Marks & Spencer's core values in terms of its commitment to product innovation and quality merchandise, focusing on a commodity where it was relatively difficult to distinguish its product from that of its principal competitors. To some extent, of course, Andrew is simply speaking in the language of a typical category manager (brand values, blueprints, points of difference). But there is evidence here, too, of a personal commitment to product quality and brand values that suggests that he would have struggled to be as enthusiastic about marketing, say, spicy chicken nuggets.

## Technical Manager Paul Wilgos

Our final example concerns M&S's technical manager for protein categories including poultry, where the development of Oakham chicken
provided an opportunity to reconnect food producers and consumers and
to re-assert the company's core values of quality and integrity. Born in
1964, Paul Wilgos studied horticulture at Reading University and worked
for the Agricultural Advisory Service at the Ministry of Agriculture,
Fisheries and Food before moving to M&S. Like many other observers of
the contemporary farming scene, Paul commented on the need for farmers
to become more integrated with other elements in the food supply chain:

> I think a lot of farmers still think they're just, they're just farming because that's
> what they do and that's what their fathers did and so on, and I think . . . you're
> producing food and it's as important for the farmer to integrate themselves
> into the food chain and be part of it and play a responsible role as it is for the
> customer to try and understand what the issues are in the way food's produced
> today.

Paul reflects nostalgically on the origins of his own commitment to less
intensive farming methods:

> I still think that at the end of the day maybe it's something that goes right back
> to my childhood of walking round farms and friends and whatever, who had
> free-range . . . chickens just scrabbling around for eggs, production, you know,
> not commercially but . . . And chickens roam around and they roost and they go
> and you know, that's how chickens are. Now that might be just me being mad,
> but that's what I think, you know. I don't know, I think the animal's just, it's
> more interesting, and I think the meat's got more character as a consequence.

For Paul Wilgos, the development of Oakham chicken provided a commercial opportunity to produce a less intensively reared chicken, consistent with his nostalgic memories of how chicken was produced during his
own childhood.

Paul comments on the possibility of extending Oakham principles
across the whole business:

> Do I want us to have Oakham White across our business as a minimum stand-
> ard? Yes, I do, because I actually think that that's what, that's who we are,
> that's what we should do, and as a principle I personally believe that's where
> we should be. Would I like us to be all free range? Yes. And, but I'm being
> very personal now and I don't think, we may do it on our fresh chicken at
> some point in the future, but I wouldn't be surprised if it takes us five years. I
> wouldn't be surprised if it was 20 years before we saw it across the whole of our
> chicken business.

Like the previous extracts, this interview demonstrates the value of a life history approach where personal reflections are interwoven with more straightforward 'on the record' accounts of people's working lives. Phrases like 'that might be just me being mad' and 'I'm being very personal now' (from Paul Wilgos) indicate the points at which interviewees depart from the standard interview script and where a blending of personal and corporate narratives can be seen at work There is a further example of this transition in the interview with Andrew Mackenzie. Asked if he had any misgivings about intensive chicken production, he replied:

> No, not really, because they're sort of strange things really, chickens, aren't they? I mean when you see large amounts of them, no it . . . doesn't bother me. [*Interviewer:* Because there's such huge amounts of them?] Yeah, there are vast amounts. No, it doesn't particularly bother me, and some of the things around, if you start to stop and think about it, you know, you would question and really perhaps – I say question, you would think about it a bit more . . . It is a production line, and with chicken even more than anything else, because it works on volume, 9000 an hour or whatever, then that is quite, it's a production, but it's a production where something dies. And I suppose sometimes you do get a bit of a thought around that, but if I'm honest with you, Polly, I don't really dwell on that. I don't really dwell on that at all, because I don't think you can. I mean, if you did, then you'd probably struggle to do the job.

Here, as in the previous examples from Paul Wilgos, an intensely personal moment breaks through the public narrative ('if I'm honest with you, Polly'), demonstrating the value of a life history approach in probing beyond the corporate narrative to one where the 'official' public narrative is combined with moments of more personal self-reflection.

There are, of course, also some limitations to the life history approach. Although we interviewed more than a dozen people at Marks & Spencer plus several of their suppliers, the method is an intensive one, focusing in detail on the lives of a relatively small number of people. We did not originally set out to trace the Oakham story, and we would probably have interviewed a different range of people if this had been our specific focus from the outset. While we are convinced that we have identified the key dynamics in the development of the Oakham story and have corroborated this with some of the key players, our project would have been shaped somewhat differently if Oakham had been our initial focus. We could, for example, have traced more directly how the Oakham 'blueprint' was derived, how dissenting voices were accommodated and how different interests were resolved into a common branding strategy. A life history approach is, arguably, better placed to reflect on the interweaving of personal and corporate narratives, as we have done here, than to trace the articulation of power within the firm in terms of who led the branding process and who made the key decisions. We do not, therefore, suggest that there is a direct or causal relationship between the kind of personal investments that are revealed in the individual life stories and the specific commercial decisions that were involved in 'storying' the brand. Our evidence suggests a strong correspondence between personal narratives and corporate investments, but we are happy to acknowledge the limitations imposed by our choice of method. Future research might, for example, focus on how competing narratives are articulated and resolved, provided that access to sufficient of the key players can be achieved.

Our argument about the consistency of corporate and personal narratives can also be questioned in cases where commercial imperatives conflict with the personal convictions of those involved in the process of brand development. We have discussed this possibility with our interviewees, and two such instances were raised. The first concerned the commercial opportunity of retailing roast potatoes that had been cooked in goose fat (considered desirable in terms of taste but raising animal welfare concerns because of the controversy surrounding the forced feeding of geese). In this case, M&S did not pursue this opportunity, while several of its competitors did. The second example also concerns a potential conflict between animal welfare and economic opportunity where it would have been possible for M&S to rear guinea fowl on a commercial scale but only by using caged livestock, raising concerns about animal cruelty. These examples of commercial opportunities that were not exploited for ethical reasons demonstrate the existence of conflicting corporate values as well as potential conflicts between personal and commercial values. They indicate some of the ways that our argument might be extended in future work.

## CONCLUSION

In this chapter we have presented the case of Oakham chicken as an example of a brand in the making, arguing that the process of brand development involved an interweaving of personal and corporate narratives. In our account of this process, Oakham emerges as a partial reversal of the long-term and relentless intensification of chicken production. Driven by consumer demand for 'chicken as it used to be', Marks & Spencer invested in a slower-growing product with increased animal welfare and improved husbandry standards. We have argued that a life history approach provides a valuable way of observing this process of product development and branding, illustrating both the internal and the external functions of brands and a strong degree of consistency between corporate and personal narratives.

Analysing a series of life history interviews with food retailers who were intimately involved in the development of the Oakham brand, we have demonstrated how the process of branding worked both externally, communicating key commercial messages to Marks & Spencer's customers, and internally, serving the personal interests of brand managers within the firm. The process of brand development was central to the revival of the company's commercial fortunes, repositioning its food lines with a renewed emphasis on quality and value. But it also addressed the personal commitments and biographical investments of those who were closely involved in developing and marketing the brand. The Oakham story is an example of what Gail Hollander (2003) has called 'supermarket narratives' – stories about place and production that appear on food packaging, designed to appeal to consumers' sense of social justice, environmental consciousness and moral virtue. Besides these external messages, however, we have also shown how the process of branding works internally within the firm. In this case, we argue, the development of the Oakham brand was successful because the commercial narrative about quality and innovation, animal welfare and product differentiation coincided closely with the personal investments of the key players involved in the process of brand-making.

Our analysis of the Oakham story also demonstrates the importance of space and place in the articulation of the brand development process. This applies at a variety of geographical scales, including the national level, where the 'Britishness' of Oakham chicken was a critical marker of its reputed quality. It also applies at the level of the firm, where Marks & Spencer's reputation for quality and reliability is legendary among certain sections of the British public and where the company's economic revival required exactly the kind of product innovation that was epitomised in the development of the Oakham brand. It is equally true of the regional and rural imagery implied by the Oakham label, and at the individual level, where key actors in the process of brand development were able to invest their personal and emotional energies to ensure the brand's success. In each of these respects, we argue, brands are geographically and historically constituted, their development inseparable from the particular places and times of their conception.

## ACKNOWLEDGEMENTS

The project on which this chapter is based was entitled 'Manufacturing meaning along the food commodity chain' and was funded via the AHRC-ESRC's Cultures of Consumption research programme (award number RES-143-25-0026). Previous versions of the chapter were presented at Queen Mary, University of London, Newcastle University and the Association of American Geographers' Annual Conference in San Francisco. We are grateful to Andy Pike for his comments on a draft of the chapter.

# REFERENCES

Boyd, W. and Watts, M. (1997) 'Agro-industrial just-in-time: The chicken industry and postwar American capitalism', in D. Goodman and M. Watts (eds), *Globalising Food: Agrarian Questions and Global Restructuring*, London: Routledge, 139–164.

Burt, S.L., Mellahi, K., Jackson, T.P. and Sparks, L. (2002) 'Retail internationalization and retail failure: Issues from the case of Marks and Spencer', *International Review of Retail, Distribution and Consumer Research*, 12, 191–219.

Chamberlain, M. and Thompson, P. (eds) (1998) *Narrative and Genre*, London: Routledge.

de Chernatony, L. (2006) *From Brand Vision to Brand Evaluation*, 2nd edition, Oxford: Butterworth-Heinemann.

Dixon, J. (2002) *The Changing Chicken: Chooks, Cooks and Culinary Culture*, Sydney: University of New South Wales Press.

Ellis, H. (2007) *Planet Chicken: The Shameful Story of the Bird on Your Plate*, London: Hodder & Stoughton.

Freidberg, S. (2003) 'Editorial: Not all sweetness and light: New cultural geographies of food', *Social and Cultural Geography*, 4, 3–6.

Hollander, G. (2003) 'Re-naturalizing sugar: Narratives of place, production and consumption', *Social and Cultural Geography*, 4, 59–74.

Holt, D.S. (2004) *How Brands Become Icons: The Principles of Cultural Branding*, Cambridge, MA: Harvard Business School Press.

Jackson, P., Russell, P. and Ward, N. (2007) 'The appropriation of "alternative" discourses by "mainstream" food retailers', in D. Maye, L. Holloway and M. Kneafsey (eds), *Alternative Food Geographies: Representation and Practice*, Amsterdam: Elsevier, 309–330.

Jackson, P., Ward, N. and Russell, R. (2010) 'Manufacturing meaning along the chicken supply chain: Consumer anxiety and the spaces of production', in M. Goodman, D. Goodman and M. Redclift (eds), *Consuming Space: Placing Consumption in Perspective*, Aldershot: Ashgate, 163–188.

Levy, S.J. (1959) 'Symbols for sale', *Harvard Business Review*, 37, 117–124.

Lury, C. (2004) *Brands: The Logos of the Global Economy*, London: Routledge.

McAlexander, J., Schouten, J. and Koenig, H. (2002) 'Building brand community', *Journal of Marketing*, 66, 38–54.

Mellahi, K., Jackson, P. and Sparks, L. (2002) 'An exploratory study into failure in successful organizations: The case of Marks & Spencer', *British Journal of Management*, 13, 15–29.

Muniz, A.M. and O' Guinn, T. (2001) 'Brand community', *Journal of Consumer Research*, 27, March, 412–432.

Perks, R. and Thomson, A. (eds) (2006) *The Oral History Reader*, 2nd edition, London: Routledge.

Russell, P. (2008) 'Manufacturing memories: Commercial, team and individual narratives in poultry production', *Oral History*, 36, 1.

Somers, M. (1994) 'The narrative constitution of identity: A relational and network approach', *Theory and Society*, 23, 605–649.

# 5. The making of place: Consumers and place-affiliated brands

## Liz Moor

### INTRODUCTION: CONSUMPTION AS A SPACE OF PROBLEMS

If one of the tasks of the social scientist is to sort and state problems (Mills 2000 [1959]), then the sphere of consumption ought to be a particularly fertile area for academic enquiry. Within both public and academic spheres, consumer culture is frequently regarded as problematic terrain – both in its own right and in its relation to issues of value, ethics and labour, to name just a few. As Daniel Miller (1998a) has noted, commentaries on consumption since Marx's time have often been marked by a fear of 'object domination' and a concern that objects, and relations with objects, will supplant people. Such fears, he notes, have frequently been exaggerated, and often lack either historical or anthropological substantiation (see also Trentmann 2009); nonetheless, there is a continuing concern that societies are more 'consumerist' than they used to be, and that an exaggerated orientation towards objects – and especially objects accessed via the market – causes alienation, exclusion and feelings of inadequacy or even humiliation, which in turn are dangerous for the polity and the planet (e.g. Bauman 1990, 2007; see also Lury 1996).

There are, however, a variety of perspectives on consumption. Anthropologists, for example, have tended to approach it in terms of a more general interest in the uses of material culture and in terms of the extent to which the activities of powerful institutions (whether private or public) are able to limit the ways in which people can use material culture autonomously for their own projects (Miller 1987; Lury 1996). Elsewhere, a number of authors have explored the question of how far, and in what ways, consumption either is or ought to be a sphere of ethical action (e.g. Barnett *et al.* 2004; Littler 2008), while consumer culture has also become central to an important set of debates about contemporary governance, as many governments try to impose markets, market logics and a discourse of consumer choice in areas that are formally or historically outside of the sphere of commercial exchange.

In what follows, two particular sets of problems frame a discussion of the ways in which consumption practices and the activities of brands are tied to the making of place. Firstly, I take seriously the question of how far practices of consumption in any given society or culture work to deepen actual exclusion or feelings of alienation. This possibility, it should be noted, may exist within a variety of political and economic structures, and one does not need to believe that societies are more consumerist than they used to be, or to resolve questions of how or why this might be so, to express concern at the possibility that the kinds of relationships made or expressed through consumption might deepen existing divisions or bring new ones into being. This question is particularly pressing if such divisions, and the feelings to which they give rise, can be argued to have wider ramifications for democracy or public wellbeing. Secondly, I see as legitimate concerns about the extent to which the activities of powerful institutions are able to shape the uses to which material culture may be put by ordinary people. Again, one does not need to accept that material cultures have become standardized or homogenized – and there is plenty of evidence that they have not – to see these questions of institutional power as important. In fact, as I shall suggest later in the chapter, the relationship between the power of large institutions and the projects of smaller-scale (individual or collective) actors is perhaps *the* central question for contemporary studies of consumption, although it extends well beyond issues of standardization and homogenization.

Clearly questions of place and geography represent only a fraction of the ways in which consumption is framed as problematic, while the relationship between place and consumption is itself highly variegated and may be approached from a range of perspectives. Partly for the sake of brevity, this chapter focuses on just two sets of issues, which follow from the problematics outlined above: that is, in what ways the 'placed-ness' of brands contributes to the narrowing or widening of social divisions and, secondly, how far powerful institutions are able to shape the uses of place by ordinary consumers. In focusing on brands and branding, the emphasis in this chapter is also primarily on the symbolic manipulation of *ideas* about place rather than on specific geographical sites and the ways in which these may be invested with meaning and significance through consumption (but see Miller *et al.* 1998), or on how consumption is framed by where and how it 'takes place'. My understanding of the concept of 'place' is correspondingly loose, referring at different points both to a relatively fixed, bounded, geographical sense of place and to a more open sense of place as 'an ever-shifting *social* geometry of power and signification' (Massey 1994: 3, my emphasis). Indeed the tension between these two – territorial and relational – conceptions of place is, I argue, part of what is at stake in debates about consumers and place-affiliated brands (see also Pike 2009): while consumers may draw upon relatively fixed and even exclusivist notions of place in their consumption activities, they also invoke a rather fluid, relational and imaginative 'sense of place'. Conversely, while some institutions seek to appeal to such a fluid and malleable sense of place, they very often appeal to – and seek to formalize – a more limited, and limiting, sense of place as bounded and territorial.

## CONSUMPTION AND INSTITUTIONS

The incorporation of information about place of origin into the fabric of goods has a long history. Early brand-like marks such as monograms, earmarks and hallmarks frequently included information about place of origin (Mollerup 1997), and European trade in the early modern period is argued to have been characterized by a growing consumer knowledge of place-based reputations and an effort by producers to appeal to that knowledge (Mukerji 1983: 31). Yet the development of a more fully international trading system seems to have fostered a more ambivalent approach to the use of place in the design and manufacture of goods. On the one hand, the opening up of new markets appeared to necessitate the removal of place-specific qualities that might appear alien in new contexts. On the other hand, there were many cases in which the cultural value of place seemed central to the way in which economic value was constituted (Mukerji 1983) and in which objects were made meaningful. The removal of place markers could also be risky; as branding consultant Wally Olins noted in 1978, 'people don't like it when their roots are torn up . . . in the interest of some central homogenising force for neatness' (1978: 50).

This ambivalence about the value of place in the design and market-ing of goods has continued to the present day. In many ways it reflects a perception that consumers themselves are split with regard to the value of place: place may be part of what makes objects intelligible and meaning-ful, but it is not the only thing that makes them so, and in some cases it may inhibit the 'domestication' of goods in new markets. This complexity of place is part of what motivates the continued use of 'country of origin' surveys by manufacturers (Lury 1997), the use of multinational teams in global or trans-national advertising and marketing campaigns (Moor 2007: 119) and the use of external consultants to develop and manage a place's identity and reputation (e.g. Julier 2000; Leonard 1997; Moor 2007). Some contemporary place branding initiatives have even tried to quantify the economic value of place, combining measures of a place's amenities or infrastructure with consumer research into perceptions (Lury and Moor 2010). But brand owners are not only responding to signals from consumers; there are wider institutional forces at work in the making and remaking of place and its significance. The World Trade Organization (WTO), in particular, influences the ways in which place may be used in the promotion of goods through its mediation of discussions about geographical indications and protected designations of origin (see Rangnekar 2004). National governments have frequently sought to direct consumers' interests in place, through patriotic consumption initiatives and the promotion of trade within protected markets. Trade unions have often joined these campaigns for 'patriotic' consumption, although they have also led boycotts of goods from particular countries or regions in order to express solidarity with workers in those countries (Littler 2008). Finally, the meaning of place for consumers is mediated through international trading and investment rules, whose impact upon consumption is outlined in later sections of the chapter.

The meaning of place and place-affiliated brands is, therefore, highly mediated through institutional activities, but this does not mean that these exhaust or determine the ways in which brands may become meaningful for consumers. If consumption may be said to be a purposive activity, these purposes do not necessarily overlap fully with those of producers, or the institutional interests controlling circulation. One way to understand this partial or potential autonomy of consumption is through Daniel Miller's (1987) analysis of mass consumption as a practical effort to counter alienation. In Miller's approach, processes and rituals of consumption – in which goods are presented and re-presented in new contexts, and woven into broader social and stylistic frameworks – are also, at least potentially, processes of objectification in which 'mass' goods are transformed in the service of personal, and often highly idiosyncratic, ends. Here, objects whose production and point of origin express 'the very abstraction of the market and the state' are put to work in the creation of worlds 'that strive to be specific and diverse precisely because we wish to escape our sense of alienation from the[se] vast institutions' (Miller 1998b: 192–194). In this process, goods and services that may be 'alien' in origin are transformed into '*in*alienable cultural material' that may be put to work in the development of the human subject (1987: 17, my emphasis).

Miller's approach raises a number of further questions, to do with the extent to which processes of mass consumption *actually* generate close social ties and groupings, and the extent to which, by contrast, they inhibit the formation of such ties or the development of human subjects (1987: 16). Miller himself acknowledges that the study of consumption must consider the ways in which the use of goods in the formation of social groupings is influenced by the activities of design, marketing and other institutions (such as the state), which may seek in various ways to act upon the relationship between 'social difference' and 'commodity difference' (1987: 9–10). These interventions may, presumably, contribute to the consolidation or even extension of forms of differentiation that are divisive and exclusionary as well as sociable or generative. But the value of Miller's approach is that these questions are left empirically open, with consumption presented as a set of processes in which close social groupings, the development of inalienable cultural materials, and the development of the human subject are immanent possibilities.

## TRAVEL, TOURISM AND MIGRATION

Miller's work sits alongside a range of anthropological approaches to material culture and consumption that see material goods as ways of giving form, substance and meaning to social relationships (e.g. Douglas and Isherwood 1979; Sahlins 1976). Such approaches often see considerable continuity between the place of material goods in 'traditional' societies and their role in contemporary consumer cultures (Lury 1996). Yet clearly the factors underpinning ritual uses of goods may vary. Perhaps most pertinently in relationship to the place connotations of brands, practices of travel, tourism and migration have had significant implications for the study of the relationship between consumer culture and geographical place. Arjun Appadurai (1996), for example, has argued that changing patterns of migration have had a significant impact upon what consumption is called upon to do; the 'deterritorialization' brought about by the movement of populations, he argues, creates new markets for a range of products and services that 'thrive on the need of the deterritorialized population for contact with its homeland' (1996: 38). Yet the 'places' consumed through such objects do not map on to specific geographical territories in a straightforward way; the mediating forces are those of imagination, memory and nostalgia (Appadurai 1996: 77), as well as the media themselves. These forces are set to work on and through objects to construct 'invented homelands' that accompany migrants as they travel. In this way, processes of consumption (in which, as Miller suggests, alienable commodities are imaginatively transformed into inalienable cultural materials) are part of the way in which place itself is constituted, remembered and made, literally and figuratively, to *matter*. An example of this more imaginative elaboration of 'place of origin' can be seen in Miller's account of the soft drinks industry in Trinidad (Miller 1998a). Thus although Coca-Cola, for example, is 'really' an American product, it can be read as a 'black sweet drink from Trinidad' through an emphasis on its production process (local bottling factories owned and staffed by Trinidadians) and through the superimposition of local ethnic categories that distinguish different types of 'sweet drinks' and their relative popularity among different sections of the population. In this way, Miller suggests, far from representing a force of 'Americanization', Coca-Cola and other soft drinks are drawn into the remaking of a specifically Trinidadian consumer culture.

Taking a slightly different approach, Lury (1997) considers the way in which possible relations of travelling and dwelling might themselves be encoded into objects, such that these relations may be seen, at least in part, as 'the outcome of a set of object-people practices' (1997: 81). Objects, she suggests, embody to varying degrees a preferred mode or context of use (1997: 82). Thus 'traveller objects' (or images of objects) such as artworks, handicrafts and items with 'historical, political or religious significance in relation to national or folk cultures' may be able to travel smoothly because their meaning and significance are secured through a clear or indexical relation to a place of origin. 'Tripper' objects, on the other hand, are those objects whose ability to travel well is secured precisely by their *lack* of obvious relation to a place of origin; this category might include 'found objects' such as tickets or pebbles from a beach, but also many contemporary consumer goods. The (place-based) meaning and significance of such objects are not immanent or juridically fixed but arbitrary, 'imposed from outside the object by external context or final dwelling place' (and, we might add, through the practices of consumers). Finally, Lury notes the existence of a category of 'tourist objects' whose meaning is neither entirely fixed nor entirely open; these are objects whose significance comes from movement *between* places. These objects have a 'self-conscious location in mobility' (1997: 80), even if that 'mobility' is one that is virtual or imagined (through the activities of marketing, for example) rather than real. Thus this category might include, for Lury, items of clothing that are marked with reference to a place, or other consumer goods that make a feature of the distance between here and there (Lury describes a 'Global Collection' of bath products, including 'Desert Rain' shampoo and 'West Coast Surf' bubble bath).

In making these distinctions between different relations of travelling and dwelling, Lury makes two key observations about contemporary consumption and its relation to place, geography and, in particular, debates about cosmopolitanism. Firstly she suggests that if cosmopolitanism is a 'capacity' – of openness to others, for example – then it is one that may belong to objects as well as people. Here she draws attention once again to the ways in which large-scale institutions – in this case those of design, marketing and branding – may intervene in processes of consumption, delimiting, to different degrees, the ways in which objects may be used, and in some cases *determining* the possibilities of making place through objects. In the second, she notes that, in so far as cosmopolitanism is also a human propensity, it is one that is unevenly distributed. It is bound up with the lifestyle of the new middle class, and is typically an individualized affair, in which the (middle-class) person is enabled to move not just between places, but also 'backwards and forwards between immersion in and distance from objects through the acquisition of a specific set of cultural competences' (1997: 90).

The 'discrepant cosmopolitanisms' (Clifford, cited in Lury 1997: 81) at work in these object-people practices can be seen more clearly if we return to Appadurai's argument about the role of material culture and commodities in constructing the migrant's sense of place. While the consumption of goods from a place of origin may be experienced as a necessity for deterritorialized groups (because it is familiar or because it maintains a desired connection to people and places elsewhere), it may also, he suggests, rub up against a further need – sometimes experienced as a demand – to 'fit in' to one's new place of residence, to demonstrate one's viability as a citizen (to avoid being too obviously 'different' or foreign) and to show one's commitment to the new nation. This is a rather different project, concerned above all with the 'politics of *representing a family as normal . . .* to neighbors and peers in the new locale' (Appadurai 1996: 44, my emphasis). The consumption of place-affiliated goods and brands in this context becomes a careful balancing act, which might be contrasted with the more freely chosen movements towards and away from certain types of goods expressed in middle-class consumption practices. Here questions about the potential of consumption practices to either deepen feelings of exclusion or generate close social ties are closely related to concerns about the extent to which the activities of powerful institutions serve to circumscribe in advance what consumption can or cannot be made to do (or to mean). But clearly it is not only the activities of design and advertising that shape what consumption can mean in this context (and which, as Lury notes, may vary a great deal), but also a wider set of social forces that compel deterritorialized groups to demonstrate their legitimacy as subjects in the first place. While the particular medium for expressing belonging – goods accessed primarily via the market – may be linked to broader ideologies of possessive individualism or 'consumer citizenship', the need itself may not (see Berlant 1999).

## PLACE, IDENTITY AND RELATIONSHIP

With this in mind, we might push a little further the question of the ways in which consumption practices within a given society or culture work to deepen or extend forms of social division, by attending not only to those forces or institutions that act directly on consumption, but also those that act more indirectly upon the contexts in which it takes place. This in turn means that understanding the significance of place for consumption cannot involve treating it separately as an independent dimension. As Doreen Massey has pointed out, while social relations have always had a spatial form and content, so too is space itself constituted through a multiplicity of social relations (Massey 1994: 2–4). Thus one may find that apparently abstract sets of social relations turn out to have important spatial dimensions, but also that activities that are ostensibly 'about' place turn out, upon closer inspection, to reflect quite different sets of concerns.

In the sphere of second-hand consumption, for example, Gregson and Crewe (2003) have shown that, while 'retail geographies' are an important part of how value is constituted (a pair of jeans that might sell for £5–7 at a car boot sale may be worth far more in an obviously 'alternative' or 'bohemian' location such as a vintage store), the spatial significance of brand names often has less to do with geographical place and more to do with their symbolic connection to a point of origin. This is particularly important in clothes shopping, they suggest, because clothes shopping is closely intertwined with discourses of the body, and the unknowability of 'other' bodies that may have owned an item previously. In this context, brand names may come to 'stand in' for knowledge of place of origin, with the known associations of particular brands helping to offset the risks associated with *un*known others. In their study, brands such as Marks & Spencer, Paul Smith and Principles did not necessarily gain their significance from being British, but rather from what they could be taken to indicate about the class, taste or even age of previous owners (Gregson and Crewe 2003: 112–113). However, Gregson and Crewe point out that the risks associated with second-hand shopping, and therefore the need to identify the origins of goods, are felt more keenly by some people than others. In more middle-class spheres, for example, brands from distant or unknown locations may in fact be highly valued, while the safety of 'familiar' brands may be derided as an 'unrisky form of prescribed taste' for 'lazy shoppers' (Gregson and Crewe 2003: 101). Thus even when they do *not* obviously indicate a place of origin, brands can nonetheless be part of a symbolic ordering of space that is bound up with a wider set of projects of marking social sameness and distance.

Another example of this tension between social closeness and distance can be seen in the subcultural consumption practices of British football fans in the 1980s (see Armstrong 1998; Moor 2006). This 'Casual' sub-culture – a predominantly white, male and working-class grouping – was marked aesthetically by a preference for 'designer' goods and brand names, many of which were associated by consumers with either middle-class sports activities (Pringle, Aquascutum) or 'continental' (European) taste (Tacchini, Ellesse, Lacoste). Like Lury's 'tourist objects', these goods often had a 'self-conscious location in mobility' – whether the geographi-cal mobility of travelling to Europe for football matches and bringing home 'exotic' foreign clothes, or the social mobility of associating oneself with middle- and upper-class activities. However, while the adoption of such goods often involved the generation of close social ties between groups of fans – a way, in Miller's terms, to 'express their [collective] interests' – and has been read by some as a refusal of those forces attempt-ing to 'fix' the meaning of working-class masculinity (Armstrong 1998), these group relations could also be marked by hostility and violence. This hostility was expressed both within and between groups of fans, but was also aimed at other, often minoritized, social groups. Hierarchies and distinctions based on the display of clothing brands could complement, or even substitute for, physical violence and competition; as one fan put it, 'the buzz of dressing was as good as the buzz of a football riot' (cited in Moor 2006: 333).

As these examples illustrate, separating projects that build close social ties from those that reinforce divisions and exclusions is not always easy. Nor is it necessarily helpful to assert that certain types of consumption are 'about' relationships while others are not. For it is of course possible to argue that *all* consumption practices are involved in making or sustaining relationships to some degree; the point, perhaps, is that some relation-ships are based on quite rigid markers of inclusion and exclusion, while others are more fluid and potentially open (Massey 1994). Yet, as Lury's argument indicates, the more fluid and open qualities of 'cosmopolitan' consumption may themselves be linked to particular class formations and dispositions. This suggests that the capacity of consumption practices to either reinforce divisions or generate close social ties (which are not, in any case, mutually exclusive alternatives) cannot, in practice, be sepa-rated from questions about the capacity of more powerful institutions to frame or direct the uses of material culture. To understand consumers' micro-level judgements and assertions of inclusion or exclusion as having any wider significance – as a *politics* of consumption, for example – it is necessary, in other words, to relate them to those broader institutional for-mations that make consumption a plausible site for material or symbolic struggle in the first place.

## PLACE AND POLITICS

To do this, let us consider an example in which political concerns are foregrounded as explicit components of consumption, and in which place emerges as a significant component of those political claims. In her history of 'Buy American' campaigns, Dana Frank (1999) shows that union-led nationalist shopping campaigns in the United States in the 1970s and 1980s – which were aimed initially at lessening the impact of trade liberalization – often switched from a collective effort to save communities (i.e. an effort to build close social ties) into a generalized anti-Asian sentiment that drew heavily upon pre-war racist imagery and sentiment (i.e. a set of practices that deepened divisions and exclusions). Hostility to Japanese car imports, for example, 'quickly spilled over into a more generic fury at Japan' (1999: 162), and fury at Japan, in turn, spilled over into hostility towards all Asian nations and towards Asian-Americans. The politics of such campaigns are complex, but, while they clearly tapped into a reserve of racist sentiment and mobilized 'exclusivist' claims to place (Massey 1994), they were also clearly related to – and activated by – the activities of more powerful institutions (such as the state) and their failure to ameliorate the consequences of trade liberalization for workers.

The impact of national-level orderings of space and relationships on a more 'local' politics of consumption can be seen in other ways too. Principal among these are those institutions that determine household income – which in turn has an impact upon the level of income available for basic household provisioning, and the proportion left for 'discretionary' spending – and those that regulate time spent at work, which has an impact upon the need to access goods via the market rather than some other method (Lodziak 2002). Fiscal policy, by determining degrees of income inequality as well as the extent of state provision of goods and services, also has an impact indirectly upon how far consumption emerges as a practice oriented towards the 'making up' of social distance (so-called 'competitive' consumption) and also – by determining which goods must be paid for directly and which are provided by the state as public goods – on the spheres in which one must see oneself as a consumer in the first place.

At the international level, the WTO regulates not only the terms under which goods can flow from one country to another, but also the extent to which those goods may bear different kinds of place markers. Geographical indications and, in the EU, 'protected designations of origin' are legal artefacts that ensure that only certain types of goods emanating from particular regions and territories can carry place-based signifiers such as 'champagne', 'Parma ham' or 'Parmesan' (see e.g. Rangnekar

2004). Although this has an impact upon producers more than consumers – determining the ability of both individual manufacturers and, often, entire national economies to compete in global markets for certain types of goods – it also has an impact upon consumption in so far as it insists, in effect, that entire populations must exist *only* as consumers, rather than producers, of particular goods. Such rules are also notable for their attempts to fix relations of place in particular ways, prohibiting the formation of new relationships between place, people and goods, and insisting on a narrowly geographic definition of place (Parry 2008). Of course, WTO rules also determine the extent to which other objects with a high degree of 'objective' signifying potential – such as cultural or knowledge-based goods – can travel and the terms under which they can do so (Yúdice 2003). In both cases powerful institutions are able to determine the terms under which objects circulate *as* commodities, and therefore the range of materials that are available via the market for meaning-making purposes, even if they cannot determine the full range of uses to which such commodities will ultimately be put.

## BRANDS AND CO-PRODUCTION

There are also a number of 'mid-range' institutions that attempt to shape relations between production, consumption and place. Fair trade marks are one way in which relations between place, and the terms of those relations, are made to matter in the sphere of consumption. Similarly 'green' consumption movements attempt to act directly upon consumption by making place of origin (or 'provenance') a salient factor in household purchasing decisions, while a number of brands now try to recoup these ethical dimensions of consumption as elements of the brand (Moor and Littler 2008). In fact, brands occupy an interesting position in relation to the making of place, since they must abide by national and international laws that determine how goods can travel and what kinds of place signifiers they may contain, while also experiencing considerable freedom to frame the spatial or place-based qualities of goods for consumers. They also, increasingly, seek to draw *from* consumers in the production of brand value. As Lury notes, one of the key operations of branding is the effort to link subject and object together in ways that make it possible to appropriate aspects of the consumption experience as though they were aspects of the brand (Lury 2000). This is also what Adam Arvidsson (2006: 93) is getting at when he argues that the point of brand management is to ensure that the 'becoming of subjects and the becoming of value coincide'. This effort partly explains attempts to fix positive place-based associations in particular brands and to remove negative ones. Thus Apple is keen to show consumers that its range of iPods is not only 'Made in China' but also 'Designed in California', and to appropriate positive associations with California as dimensions of the brand's value. Similarly, the clothing retailer American Apparel has developed its business in part by targeting a transnational group of educated middle-class consumers and inviting them to use their own knowledge to compare the (moral) value of something 'Made in America' with the 'sweatshop' methods associated with 'foreign' manufacturers (Moor and Littler 2008). Turning these ethical impulses and forms of knowledge into a source of brand value has also involved an effort to encode notions of transparency and 'fairness' in the very materiality of stores, products and promotional materials (Moor and Littler 2008).

Clearly it is not always easy to ensure that those aspects of consumption that are significant and meaningful for consumers also represent qualities that are desirable from the point of view of the brand. However, there are a number of ways in which brands try to circumvent this problem. One of the most recent is the effort to recruit consumers as 'co-producers' of brands. As marketing academics Cova and Dalli (2009) point out, consumers already 'work' in the sense that they are active in the process of value creation, whether through imbuing brands with sentiment, meaning and significance, innovating in modes and contexts of use, or acting as collaborators in the production of a paid-for experience. But the development of new technologies allows this agency to be used in a more systematic way. Consumers are increasingly recruited into processes of innovation and testing, and (for example through websites) into the development and circulation of marketing campaigns. The advantage for producers is that such forms of involvement may increase the perceived value of the good or service, and instil greater loyalty and feelings of satisfaction. For critics, however, such efforts are to be understood in terms of the exploitation of labour, and more specifically in terms of the 'immaterial' labour (Lazzarato 1996) of consumption and its 'double exploitation' of consumers – who work for the brand for nothing, and then pay a premium for the goods and services thus produced (Zwick *et al.* 2008).

However, it is also useful to return to the questions posed at the beginning of the chapter, about the role of powerful institutions in shaping the uses to which material culture can be put, and about the relationships of proximity and distance that are enacted or reproduced through consumption activities. Contemporary marketing efforts force us to consider another dimension of institutional power, to do with the ways that institutions may not *prescribe* particular uses of goods but instead may, as in Arvidsson's (2006) account, draw upon a more freely generated set of consumption practices as a way of consolidating their economic power. It follows from this that relations of inclusion and exclusion, and of proximity and distance, are not only possible *outcomes* of particular arrangements of consumption and material culture, but also *resources* that may be tapped into by commercial (and other) organizations as potential dimensions of brand value. Branding and marketing, in other words, are concerned not only with the prescription of uses and contexts for goods, but with the ongoing management of the relationships and feelings that emerge around them. The significance of place and geography to these co-production initiatives may vary a great deal. Forms of consumer involvement such as testing, collaborating, customizing, innovating or sharing may help producers to understand modes or contexts of use that are specific to particular geographical sites (and indeed may be designed with that end in mind), but they may also throw up highly personal or idiosyncratic understandings of brands or create new branded spaces that have little if anything to do with a geographical place of origin. The relevance of such activities does not lie primarily in their relation to a place of origin or, necessarily, to a context of consumption, but rather in their capacity to add value to the brand.

## CONCLUSION

In briefly reviewing some contemporary perspectives on place and consumption, this chapter has suggested that, to address the question of how far consumers are involved in the making of place, it is necessary to consider the degrees of freedom experienced by ordinary people in their day-to-day consumption activities, and to weigh this against the place-making power of larger-scale institutions. While it is important to acknowledge that consumers may be inventive, creative and even elusive in their use of material culture, it is equally important to acknowledge that such inventiveness takes place under quite variable conditions. Powerful institutions shape consumption, and the uses to which consumer culture can be put, in a number of ways. These include the 'macro' level of national fiscal policy, and its impact upon relative income levels, as well as the areas in which people are asked to think and act as 'consumers' in the first place. They also include those international mechanisms (such as the WTO) for determining who may use particular place associations in their marketing activities. The ongoing debates about the legitimacy of 'geographical indications' are, I would suggest, one of the most significant ways in which the power to 'make place' is taken away from individuals, groups and small-scale producers and put into the hands of more powerful institutions – whose understandings of place are often much more narrow, exclusionary and instrumental.

At a more mid-range level, institutions such as design, marketing and branding agencies may attempt to encode and fix, with various degrees of success, the place connotations (or lack of them) in goods. It is at this level that it is possible to argue, following Lury, that place-making is the outcome of 'object-people practices', and that objects may make people as well as the other way around. It is also at this level, however, that we can see how the 'objective' properties of goods may interact with wider social forces and structures such as class, ethnicity or nationhood to produce uneven patterns of constraint that bear upon the uses to which the potential signifying properties of goods may be put. Brands very often seek to act upon these social forces and structures, providing goods and services that promise to narrow or redress inequality, or conversely to mark forms of difference (which, it should be noted, is not necessarily the same as being divisive). Yet, as I have suggested in the preceding section, brands' activities do not only involve 'framing' or fixing such meanings in advance, but may also include the effort to incorporate more freely generated associations as sources of brand value in an ongoing way. Here, a more fluid set of understandings of place may be permitted, but only in so far as they 'reproduce . . . brand image and strengthen brand equity' (Arvidsson 2006: 74).

From here, we can reconsider the question of the extent to which consumption practices generate close social ties or, by contrast, reinforce existing social divisions. As I have noted above, it is possible to argue that *all* consumption practices are involved in the making of relationships to some degree. The point, rather, is whether those relationships are open and fluid – and thus oriented, potentially, to the development of greater social solidarity – or more bounded and exclusionary. Consumers' uses of place-affiliated brands exhibit both sets of possibilities: while they may be drawn into projects that assert a narrowly geographical or exclusivist definition of place, they may also disrupt such ideas and reconfigure relationships between place in unexpected new ways. Yet these uses are themselves often framed by broader structures or forces – of class, income inequality, citizenship and so on – and may, as we have seen, be selectively exploited by brands as sources of value. If consumers' uses of place-affiliated brands have any wider significance for the making of place it must, then, emerge through their relationship to the interests of these more powerful institutions. Analysing this relationship means attending to the more general potential of material culture, outlined in the discussion of Miller's work at the start of the chapter, to act as a countervailing force to institutional processes of abstraction and alienation. It also involves being wary of some of the more generalized fears surrounding consumption – fears of object domination, of homogenization, and of a particular understanding of consumerism as 'greed' or selfishness – and focusing instead on the power of those large institutions to direct consumption in particular ways.

## REFERENCES

Appadurai, A. (1996) *Modernity at Large: Cultural Dimensions of Globalization*, Minneapolis and London: University of Minnesota Press.

Armstrong, G. (1998) *Football Hooligans: Knowing the Score*, Oxford: Berg.

Arvidsson, A. (2006) *Brands: Meaning and Value in Media Culture*, London: Routledge.

Barnett, C., Cloke, P., Clarke, N. and Malpass, A. (2004) 'Articulating ethics and consumption', Cultures of Consumption Working Paper Series, No. 17, available at www.bbk.ac.uk/publications.html.

Bauman, Z. (1990) *Thinking Sociologically*, Oxford: Blackwell.

Bauman, Z. (2007) *Consuming Life*, Cambridge: Polity.

Berlant, L. (1999) 'The compulsion to repeat femininity', in J. Copjec and M. Sorkin (eds), *Giving Ground: The Politics of Propinquity*, London and New York: Verso.

Cova, B. and Dalli, D. (2009) 'Working consumers: The next step in marketing theory?', *Marketing Theory*, 9, 3, 315–339.

Douglas, M. and Isherwood, B. (1979) *The World of Goods*, London: Allen Lane.

Frank, D. (1999) *Buy American: The Untold Story of Economic Nationalism*, Boston, MA: Beacon Press.

Gregson, N. and Crewe, L. (2003) *Second-Hand Cultures*, Oxford and New York: Berg.

Julier, G. (2000) *The Culture of Design*, London: Sage.

Lazzarato, M. (1996) 'Immaterial labour', in P. Virno and M. Hardt (eds), *Radical Thought in Italy: A Potential Politics*, Minneapolis: University of Minnesota Press.

Leonard, M. (1997) *Britain™: Renewing Our Identity*, London: Demos.

Littler, J. (2008) *Radical Consumption: Shopping for Change in Contemporary Culture*, Maidenhead: Open University Press.

Lodziak, C. (2002) *The Myth of Consumerism*, London: Pluto.

Lury, C. (1996) *Consumer Culture*, New Brunswick, NJ: Rutgers University Press.

Lury, C. (1997) 'The objects of travel', in C. Rojek and J. Urry (eds), *Touring Cultures: Transformations of Travel and Theory*, London: Routledge.

Lury, C. (2000) 'The united colors of diversity: Essential and inessential culture', in S. Franklin, C. Lury and J. Stacey (eds), *Global Nature, Global Culture*, London: Sage.

Lury, C. and Moor, L. (2010) 'Brand valuation and topological culture', in M. Aronczyk and D. Powers (eds), *Blowing Up the Brand*, New York: Peter Lang.

Massey, D. (1994) *Space, Place and Gender*, Cambridge: Polity Press.

Miller, D. (1987) *Material Culture and Mass Consumption*, Oxford: Blackwell.

Miller, D. (1998a) 'Coca-Cola: A black sweet drink from Trinidad', in D. Miller (ed.), *Material Cultures: Why Some Things Matter*, London: UCL Press.

Miller, D. (1998b) 'Conclusion: A theory of virtualism', in J. Carrier and D. Miller (eds), *Virtualism: A New Political Economy*, Oxford and New York: Berg.

Miller, D., Jackson, P., Thrift, N., Holbrook, B. and Rowlands, M. (1998) *Shopping, Place and Identity*, London and New York: Routledge.

Mills, C. Wright (2000 [1959]) *The Sociological Imagination*, New York: Oxford University Press.

Mollerup, P. (1997) *Marks of Excellence: The History and Taxonomy of Trademarks*, London: Phaidon.

Moor, L. (2006) '"The buzz of dressing": Commodity culture, fraternity and football fandom', *South Atlantic Quarterly*, 105, 2, 327–347.

Moor, L. (2007) *The Rise of Brands*, Oxford: Berg.

Moor, L. and Littler, J. (2008) 'Fourth worlds and neo-Fordism: American apparel and the cultural economy of consumer anxiety', *Cultural Studies*, 22, 5, 700–723.

Mukerji, C. (1983) *From Graven Images: Patterns of Modern Materialism*, New York: Columbia University Press.

Olins, W. (1978) *The Corporate Personality: An Inquiry into the Nature of Corporate Identity*, London: Design Council.

Parry, B. (2008) 'Geographical indications: Not all "champagne and roses"', in L. Bently, J. Davis and J.C. Ginsburg (eds), *Trade Marks and Brands: An Interdisciplinary Critique*, Cambridge: Cambridge University Press.

Pike, A. (2009) 'Geographies of brands and branding', *Progress in Human Geography*, 33, 5, 619–645.

Rangnekar, D. (2004) 'The socio-economics of geographical indications: A review of empirical evidence from Europe', UNCTAD-ICTSD Project on IPRs and Sustainable Development, Issue Paper No. 8, Geneva: UNCTAD.

Sahlins, M. (1976) *Culture and Practical Reason*, Chicago: Chicago University Press.

Trentmann, F. (2009) 'Crossing divides: Consumption and globalization in history', *Journal of Consumer Culture*, 9, 2, 187–220.

Yúdice, G. (2003) *The Expediency of Culture: Uses of Culture in the Global Era*, Durham, NC and London: Duke University Press.

Zwick, D., Bonsu, S.K. and Darmody, A. (2008) 'Putting consumers to work: "Co-creation" and new marketing governmentality', *Journal of Consumer Culture*, 8, 2, 163–196.

# 6. Sports equipment: Mixing performance with brands – the role of the consumers

## Atle Hauge

## INTRODUCTION

> We provide high quality, protective technical gear for work survival and sport. We work and play in the harshest environments on the planet to learn what's needed to create the best performance gear possible. We work closely with people who work and/or play outdoors more days than they are indoors to continuously optimize the technology and design of our products. (Norwegian sports and outdoor equipment manufacturer Helly Hansen's homepage, http://www.hellyhansen.com/about-us, accessed 25 November 2009)

Most theorists, literature and studies on how to survive in today's highly competitive and global economy seem to agree on one thing – innovation is the key to success (Porter 1990; Scott 1995; Storper 1997; Maskell and Malmberg 1999; Florida 2002). This mirrors the widespread belief that continual improvements are the basic elements required to maintain dynamic competitive advantages. The innovation literature is broad and abundant (Malmberg and Power 2006), but a common feature is the notion that few good ideas develop in a vacuum; innovation is a collective process and involves different kinds of social interaction (Asheim 1999). Innovations are in most cases less the product of individual firms than of the assembled resources, knowledge, and other inputs and capabilities that concentrate in specific places. However, most of the innovation literature has had a bias towards the firm and/or groups of firms. Less has been said about how these superior products find their way to the consumers. When it comes to consumer preferences, there is often an implicit assumption that the individual has perfect information about the innovative level that different products embody (Power and Hauge 2008). In reality, our consumer choices are often slanted, and rarely is there perfect information behind our decisions.

Accordingly, the innovation literature focuses on the first stages of the value chain. At the other end of the chain, we find theories on market communication, marketing and branding. This strand of literature has an explicit focus on how to convince consumers that the product or firm in question should be the chosen one. Here, relatively little attention is paid to the functionality and the quality of the product. This is often taken for granted, and the focus is on storytelling and how to charge the finished product (or the company behind it) with symbolic value (see for example Olins 2003; Roberts 2004).

In this chapter, I argue that there is a need for a more comprehensive approach to the development of new products and the innovation process. If we want to understand why some products and companies succeed in the marketplace, we need to take into account both the technical/ functional and the immaterial value of products. This calls for a more ample consideration and analysis of the users' role: how they affect and influence both the innovation and the production process, as well as how users' influence is employed in marketing and branding. Until recently, there has been relatively little interest in how consumers are involved in this ongoing process of upgrading the innovative and performative assets. Notable exceptions include von Hippel (1978, 2005) and his ground-breaking work on lead users' role in the innovation process. However, by and large user involvement has been confined to business-to-business environments with traditionally tight-knit user–producer interactions, for example Porter's (1990) 'demanding consumers'. Notwithstanding, innovation policies and support systems have tended to concentrate on research- or technology-driven innovation, and have left little room for the user or consumer. This is almost ironic, as innovation theory for many years has been arguing for 'the interactive innovation model' where the interaction between users, producers and other actors is seen as essential. Despite this, the consumer is more or less viewed as a black box, if consumers are taken into consideration at all. As Grabher *et al.* (2008) argue, despite the universal mantra that 'The customer is king', the role of the customer so far seems limited to being a passive recipient of products at the end of the value chain. Innovation in particular has largely been seen as an affair within and between firms, and the most important concern has been with the producer side. The customer, the alleged king, is largely absent from the portrayals of innovation and production. More recently, however, this traditional view has been confronted, and studies have shown that even more traditional business-to-consumer products are more open to direct innovative feedback from the demand side than was long assumed (see for example Lüthje 2004; Franke and Shah 2003). The new and active role consumers are playing presents companies with certain challenges. Microsoft's Mich Matthews, for example, claims that there is a shift in its corporate strategy from 'informing, persuading, and reminding' to 'demonstrating, involving and empowering' (Jaffe 2007: XV). The sports and outdoor equipment industry is an interesting case because it makes up an arena where technical innovation and symbolic innovation are performed, and the users are deeply involved in both these processes. The products are often meant for use in harsh and demanding conditions, so there is a need for high performance. At the same time, sportswear and related products are often lifestyle expressions; they say something about who we are or, rather, who we want to be.

## HOW TO COMBINE INNOVATION AND BRANDING THEORIES?

One challenge is to fit the technical and functional biased innovation theories with the more immaterial and symbolic approach of branding literature, within the same conceptual framework. One way to do this is to start with the ultimate judge of products' functionality and symbolic value – the consumer. Our consumer choices are on one hand determined by the utility of the product, but also by the symbolic value of the product or the company behind it.

At the same time, as we will see later in this chapter, more and more businesses take advantage of users, customers and amateurs. They see them as valuable sources of knowledge when it comes to both innovation and market communication. The group of consumers loosely labelled as lead users is seen as especially important. At this point, I want to stress that not all users are consumers. Children's and teenagers' sporting equipment is an example. Often parents buy safety equipment for their children, and it is therefore not just the users' interests and concerns that suppliers must address.

The lead user concept has been employed by both marketing and innovation literature. The underpinning idea behind both these theoretical slants is that there are certain individuals who play a key role in diffusing ideas or products. Lead users face needs that will be general in the marketplace, but, because they often test these products to the limits, they face them much earlier than the majority of consumers. In addition, lead users are positioned to benefit significantly by obtaining a solution to those needs (von Hippel 1986). At the same time the lead users can function as gatekeepers in the dispersal of products. They adopt new products more quickly and with more ease than ordinary users. They also lead in the diffusion of new products, as they have a tendency to pick up on the latest first. In that sense they serve as opinion leaders (Schreier *et al.* 2007).

Sport companies draw on lead users to test and develop new equipment, and lead users are also employed as ambassadors for marketing or branding purposes. This is because they use and test equipment under arduous situations. In addition, many of them have a high media profile and often enjoy credibility among more ordinary users (Bråtå *et al.* 2009). Lately, the industry has turned its focus towards manufacturing and selling on the basis of intangibles such as style, fashion, trends and symbolic values. This is not to say that consumers do not highly value functional, safe and well-made products, or that traditional product innovation is not fundamental. Rather, in a marketplace where safe and high-performance equipment is now almost standard, intangibles help firms differentiate themselves and create loyal customers.

## WHAT IS BRANDING AND HOW IS IT DIFFERENT FROM MARKETING?

The relationship between product marketing and branding is close, but they are not the same. There is no common definition of 'brands' or 'branding'. However, most commentators agree that any definition should include both tangible and intangible attributes of a product, e.g. both functional and emotional characteristics (see for example Olins 2003; Lury 2004). These qualities primarily function as marketing arguments, but branding is not just an add-on in the marketing process. Branding is an attempt to encapsulate a balance between different economic values: quality, utility, and symbolic and cultural worth. Lury (2004: 27) argues that branding 'is an abstract machine for the reconfiguration of production'. Branding should thus be viewed as a holistic strategy which if implemented well ought to saturate the production process on all levels from innovation, through design, via retail to marketing. Successful brand strategies tap into socially founded and embedded movements, rather than creating a brand for one single product. The aim of branding is to produce an interchangeable link between the character of an object and its branded image or form (Power and Hauge 2008).

Essentially, the branding literature can be seen as divided into two extremes. On one hand there is a group that is very sceptical and critical about the power of brands and marketing (see for example Klein 2000; Quart 2003). Often branding is presented as a process whereby a brand image is invented by experts and foisted on to the masses, which swallow it whole. On the other hand there is the view that consumers engage in a reciprocal relationship with brands, based on dialogue and negotiations (see for example Fournier 1998; Atkin 2004; Roberts 2004). This view is based on a strong belief in consumers as a self-aware and reflexive group. The consumers 'are involved in relationships with a collectivity of brands so as to benefit from the meanings they add into their lives' (Fournier 1998: 361). How these reflexive relationships between consumers and their brands of choice are conceptualised differs. Fournier (1998) goes as far as to compare these relationships to those that people form with other people. She claims, for example, that one of her informants' 'experiments with potential brand partners resemble a series of trial courtships' (Fournier 1998: 344). The consumers interact with the brands without waiting for corporate permission. Forging brand meaning is no longer a matter of top-down control (Walker 2008). However, advertising and branding might best be conceptualised as a form of seduction: making use of our already established needs and desires (Heath and Potter 2005: 208). Consumers are not being brainwashed, but we are obviously not indifferent to the marketing and branding process. In the end, it is up to the consumer if he or she will take the offer despite all the seduction techniques of the firm.

## SPORTS AND OUTDOOR BRANDS

We see logos everywhere, and we are exposed to brands to the degree that Sherry (1998) suggests the ubiquity of branding messages has transformed the economic landscape into a 'brandscape'. Athletes embody this development through the way they dress and expose products. Puma's global campaign featuring the world's fastest man, Usain Bolt, Alpine skiers taking off their skies seconds after they cross the finish line so they will be covered on television, and athletes with their clothes covered with company logos are all examples of the close relationships between branding and the current sports industry. Indeed, the sports industry as we know it today would not be possible without heavy sponsorship. The reason for this symbiotic relationship is that athletes are seen as powerful carriers of cultural meaning (Kennedy and Hills 2009). Athletes are viewed as the embodiment of the lifestyle and values many companies so desperately want to be associated with. There is a transfer of the qualities of the athlete to the consumer goods. However, this must be a person with qualities that the brand wants to be associated with. This athlete is not always the best at what he or she does, but media appeal and other more intangible qualities are just as important.

Nike has been a forerunner in marketing sports goods, and it was early in its use of high-profile athletes in branding. It gave the tennis player John McEnroe a personal sponsor contract when this was not common. McEnroe was in addition to his dazzling game known for his tantrums on the court. Nike co-founder Phil Knight decided that McEnroe's 'bad boy' image would fit well with the 'Rebel with a Cause' ad campaign in 1978 (Adams 2005). This campaign went on to be a big success, and paved the way for numerous similar campaigns. This powerful branding tool can however backfire. When athletes do not live up to being model citizens, this reflects back upon the sponsors.

## WHO ARE THE LEAD USERS AND WHY ARE THEY IMPORTANT IN THE SPORTS AND OUTDOOR INDUSTRY?

Lead users are those in a given domain who are ahead of an important marketplace trend and experience high benefits from innovating (von Hippel 1986). These users sometimes come up with attractive inventions themselves in order to meet their own leading-edge requirements which cannot be satisfied by commercially available products. As the concept 'lead users' hints at, these innovations might be of commercial value to broader parts of the market tomorrow (von Hippel 1986). The sports equipment sector proves an interesting sector in which to study user involvement (Bråtå *et al.* 2009). First, the industry is forced to focus on user-driven innovation since it supplies highly demanding and competent customers. Firms provide users with facilities, services, equipment and so on, but equally they rely heavily on users' acceptance of firm innovations: at the end of the day it is the users who will be risking themselves skating, skiing or sliding around on 'innovative' products, and they are therefore very motivated to make sure their equipment is something they can understand and trust.

In addition, users are involved in production of immaterial facets of the product. As mentioned, consumers do not buy products only because of their utilitarian value, but also because of the image, brand or symbolic value. However, this is not produced by corporate forces alone, because symbolic value cannot be dictated, but is always a social construction (Bourdieu 1984). In this process, other users and/or consumers play a central role. In particular, communities of consumers are contributors to the construction of social identities. They can provide brands and products with part of the symbolic and communicative elements underpinning product value (Di Maria and Finotto 2008). As a result we see firms increasingly seeking to tap into marketing through person-to-person communication, and marketing is thus driven by a select group of empowered users. Jaffe (2007) argues that, with today's information overload, the most trusted source of information is our peers.

A number of studies of user involvement in the sports equipment

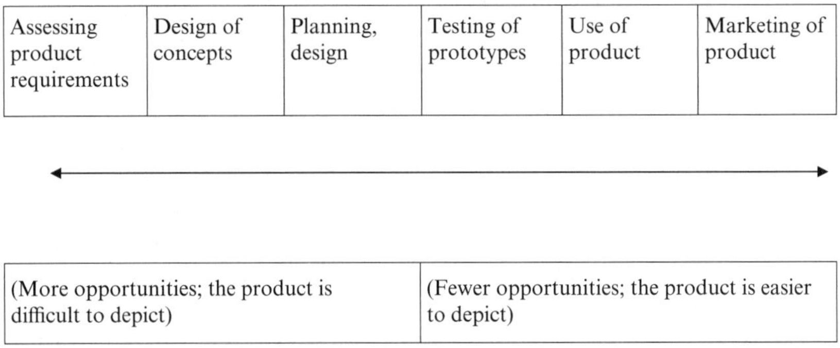

| Assessing product requirements | Design of concepts | Planning, design | Testing of prototypes | Use of product | Marketing of product |
|---|---|---|---|---|---|

| (More opportunities; the product is difficult to depict) | (Fewer opportunities; the product is easier to depict) |
|---|---|

*Source:* Adapted from Bråtå *et al.* (2009).

*Figure 6.1   Users' opportunities to affect the innovation process*

industry have been conducted. Shah (2000) shows for example in her study of snowboarding, skateboarding and windsurfing that innovations often happen outside the big firms. Instead, they are developed by a few early adopters. This is explained by the stickiness of information – it is problematic to transfer from the user to the manufacturer. The bigger firms can also have problems with realising both the functional and the commercial potential of the product. Schreier *et al.* (2007) conclude from a study of extreme sports that lead users push the limits of performance, and are the first to be subjected to leading-edge needs. They expect high benefits from new solutions, and show a strong interest in new developments in the field. They are aware of new products and technologies at a very early stage, perceive new technologies as less 'complex', and might therefore be more prepared to adopt them. In addition, lead users show strong opinion leadership. If this group of users pick up and adopt specific products or brands, less demanding consumers are inclined to follow suit. These and other studies of user involvement in the sports and outdoor industry (von Hippel 2005; Lüthje 2004; Lüthje *et al.* 2005) point in the same direction: users are important for the development of competitive strategies when it comes to both technical innovation and brand development. However, the opportunity for user involvement changes in the course of a product's development. Figure 6.1 shows a schematic overview of the different stages in the innovation and production processes and user involvement. The model calls for a consideration and analysis of how users affect and influence both innovation and production processes as well as how users influence and are employed in marketing and branding. The next section will illustrate this through some empirical findings.

# USERS' INVOLVEMENT THROUGHOUT THE VALUE CHAIN – EXAMPLES FROM THE SPORTS AND OUTDOOR INDUSTRY

Many sports and outdoor equipment producers try to implement their brand values all through the production process. A message we hear from many companies is that they cater for users with particular needs. More than one company claims that the products are made by users for users. A way to ensure this is to involve users at all stages. A main reason for this is that lead users give the products they are involved in authenticity. The idea is that the products' symbolic value is grounded in empirical proven reality: if you dig behind the symbol you will find what the products represent (Walker 2008). This is crucial currency for the sports and outdoor industry, and is one of the main reasons lead users are involved throughout the whole value chain.

Even though there are variations, most of the sports and outdoor producers' business strategies are in reality quite similar. The actual manufacturing of the products is typically outsourced to countries with low labour costs, while high-cost and high-value-added activities are normally performed at the company's home base. Through strong connections to their suppliers, the firms take high-quality products more or less for granted. The business strategies focus mainly on linking to consumers and retailers, and innovative, well-designed and good-quality products are contributing to this. In the following section I will go through some examples of how users are involved in product development in the different phases of the innovation process and how this reflects back to the brand value of a product.

# CANNOT FIND WHAT YOU NEED – MAKE IT YOURSELF! USERS AS ENTREPRENEURS

We have several examples from the sports and outdoor industry where demanding customers could not find what they were after in the commercial market, and decided to develop it themselves. The most prominent examples might be Gary Fisher and the leading role he played in developing mountain biking, and Tom Sims and Jake Burton, who developed what would be known as the snowboard at about the same time in two different places in North America.

These are examples of so-called user entrepreneurs. They seek to develop and design equipment for their own personal use. They often come up with attractive innovations in order to meet their own leading-edge requirements which cannot be satisfied by commercially available products. Whilst they primarily work to solve their own problems and challenges, solutions they develop might be of future commercial value to broader parts of the market. Lüthje (2004) and Shah (2000) have looked at recently developed sports (snowboarding, skateboarding), and the users were always the first developers of the first version of the products.

One example of a firm started by an innovative enthusiast that became a thriving firm is Klättermusen, a Swedish firm located in the winter sports destination Åre. The founder is active in outdoor sports, amongst others climbing. He started to make his own outerwear and backpack because he was not satisfied with existing products for winter use, and turned this into a successful company. Based on his direct sporting experience, he and his designers develop products they are sure will work and be demanded by consumers. Klättermusen makes a priority of technical function: 'Klättermusen's innovation is always driven by function' (CEO and founder of the company, personal interview, January 2008). When functional requirements are satisfied, the team start to work on the visual design.

However, we found little evidence that established firms systematically exploited users' ideas for entirely new products or radical innovations. Instead they used them for feedback on prototypes and/or refinement of existing products. Most of the ideas for new products come from their own employees and their outdoor activity. These employees can be labelled 'passionate insiders', and they internalise expert know-how. They are especially engaged in or fervent about sports activities that are relevant for the products or goods produced by the firm (Bråtå *et al.* 2009). Often they want to work in such firms because they are practitioners of a sport for which the firm produces equipment. There is a growing emphasis on the importance of passionate insiders, and firms are increasingly prioritising these types of employees. A CEO claimed: 'If you are not active, interested in sports and the outdoors, you will not get a job here' (CEO and founder of the company, personal interview, January 2008). As a designer of 'base layer' (underwear) said, 'I am a lead user myself. I am wearing our products 200 days a year' (Helly Hansen designer, personal interview, October 2007).

## WALK A MILE IN MY SHOES – USERS AS TESTERS OF EQUIPMENT

Sports and outdoor equipment manufacturers employ users to test new and refine already existing products. For this purpose firms bring into play users on different levels. Professional users are mainly top athletes or people making their living from being sponsored when they are on expeditions, climbing, sailing and so on. Through the media we hear of multimillion-dollar sponsor contracts, but we find sponsoring on most levels – from the global megastars to the local talents. Sponsorship for athletes may involve both free equipment and payment. The wages may be fixed or dependent on success in the sport. In some cases athletes consider it even more important to get the best equipment than the fixed wages, because if they win a race or get another good result this is a reward in itself (in addition to possible prize bonuses). In return some of them have to take part in development of the equipment, whereas others primarily are used for PR purposes in market communication. Although athletes can be important to developing equipment it is also important to see their limits. There are examples of products tested by highly trained professionals, probably under good supervision and with assistance, and launched on the market. However, when the products were used by ordinary users problems emerged because the products were used in more variable conditions, for example in places with excessive snow and on trails of varying quality. The lesson is that equipment has to be tested in different conditions and by ordinary users in order to capture the variety of conditions for use.

Fjällräven (a part of the larger company Fenix) is an outdoor equipment producer. Its product line includes backpacks, tents, sleeping bags and clothing. It claims that it is 'not a technical company, but we are an innovative company' (company representative, personal interview, January 2008). It focuses more on being innovative when it comes to design and function. The customers require high technical and functional material in their outdoor clothes and equipment and take this for granted. Instead, they look for products with an interesting design or smart solutions. One novel way the company gets in touch with lead users is through organising Fjällräven Classic – a trekking event and competition. It is a team contest, even though the competitive elements are of minor importance. The track is 110 kilometres in Kungsleden, North Sweden. The whole Fjällräven office and product development team attend this event. They talk to the participants, both formally and informally. The company informant thinks this is a very good channel to get in touch with the 'ordinary users' and to get direct feedback from the consumers. It is a way to see the end users in their right environment. In addition, this creates good relations with the consumers – it helps build brand loyalty.

# THE USERS AS BRAND AMBASSADORS

Athletes are powerful vehicles in the transfer of cultural meaning (Kennedy and Hills 2009), and the most visible way users are involved with brands, companies and products is through sponsorship. Companies pay athletes and users to use their products in different forms of marketing processes and events. There is a myriad of ways and levels this can be done, from using global megastars for worldwide campaigns to sponsoring local events. Bennett *et al.* (2009) show that there is a link between sport sponsorship and actual consumption of the sponsor's marketed product. Most of the companies interviewed for this project had one or more athletes or users they sponsored, who were featured on different forms of marketing like brochures, flyers, web pages and so on. In reality, these users are seldom used in development of new products from scratch. They are more likely to give feedback on prototypes, on both functionality and fashion features like cuts, trimmings and colours. However, there seems to be a certain reluctance to label the relationship between firms and athletes as sponsorship. Instead athletes are referred to as partners, ambassadors, friends of the company and so on. The relationships are presented as being built on mutual respect, trust and reciprocal benefit rather than being commercial exchanges.

One example of how athletes can be used in a branding strategy is the Swedish company J. Lindeberg's use of skier Jon Olsson. J. Lindeberg started out as a golf wear producer, but quickly extended its product line to fashion wear. Olsson is one of the biggest stars in the so-called new school of skiing or jibbing. This sport features big jumps with acrobatic effort and spectacular tricks. This is a field of skiing that has seen a remarkable growth in the last few years, in terms both of participants and of media exposure. It is inspired more by snowboarding than traditional freestyle skiing. J. Lindeberg had experience of working closely with golfers in its golf collection. It wanted to see if this could be transferred to ski wear. The ideas for new collections were interactive through the whole design process. Ideas for products could come both from Olsson and from the company designers. He gave feedback on functionality when he used the products. He gave a personal touch to his design, both in the design and in the colours. Among other things he had pink trousers in a season when most collections were based on earth colours. This fitted well with Olsson's own somewhat flamboyant image, and made the collection stand out. There was an undeniable 'buzz' around the collection. In addition, Olsson was used for cross-branding. He wore the company's suits, leisure wear and golf clothes as well. Because of a high media profile, good results and close interaction with the company, Lindeberg's representative thought the co-operation was a success (sales manager, personal interview, October 2007).

## DISCUSSION

There are without a doubt quite a few good examples on user involvement and ideas that turn into big commercialised successes. The core competence of innovation is, however, still to be found within the firms' borders. Users are in a position where they face needs that have to be solved through innovations, and experience any possible shortcomings of existing products. However, it is rare that they have the skills to transfer these good ideas to functioning products. It can prove difficult to turn prototypes into commercial products. To do this one needs: know-how, i.e. knowledge on how to produce; know-who, i.e. who to get to produce; and know-where, i.e. where to sell it and which channels can be used for distribution. This is probably the reason why we see user entrepreneurs most often at the early stages of a product's life cycle. As soon as they have proven that there is a market for the products, the ideas are picked up by larger companies with the ability to produce in larger batches and for a more widespread market. This can be done by copying the ideas or buying the smaller company. This does not mean that the users do not have valuable knowledge and information that could prove valuable for the producers, but few of the innovation processes can be defined as user led. A more correct description might be user influenced.

When employing professionals or other experts to test new products, one has to bear in mind that testing has to reflect how and when ordinary users really use the products. While this involves the user in developing the brand, the strategies are generally carefully managed and developed by the firm rather than the user. There are multiple examples where the products used by professional athletes in competition are different from the ones that are being sold commercially, even though the design is identical. As a former Canadian Olympic snowboarder told us: 'The "normal" rider would find the board I used in competition disgusting – it is way too stiff and hard to handle for them' (Anonymous, personal interview, March 2008). This points to the fact that athletes are powerful agents for sparking and cultivating a groundswell of desire within desired target markets. They help create a certain level of authenticity and credibility that is important for many customers. This does not mean that athletes function only as billboards for products, without any form of contribution to the creation. Many are deeply involved in both the technical and the aesthetic development of the products they promote. However, the level of involvement differs, and there seems to be a tendency to exaggerate the participation of certain athletes in the product development.

Enthusiastic amateurs, both 'friends of the firm' (i.e. sponsored users) and other engaged users, are valuable because they give both positive and negative feedback on products and equipment. However, their comments have to be filtered and considered relative to other comments and activities in the firm. This group is important for another reason as well; it takes part in defining the symbolic value of products. We see a tendency towards ordinary, engaged users becoming an important advertising channel for firms. The major reason for this is that intangibles, such as brand value, grow in importance when equipment has reached a certain level of sophistication. The technical differences may be quite marginal; what matters for sale is intangible values. One fact that is almost totally neglected in the literature is that employees are often lead users. They are drawn to the industry and their passion is demanded. These passionate insiders can be useful and reliable links between the product development/manufacturing side of the business and the firm's customers and fans.

## CONCLUSION

In many ways there is a gap, both conceptual and empirical, between much of the technical and functionally biased innovation literature, and the branding literature's focus on intangibles and storytelling. This chapter is an attempt to bridge that gap, employing users in sports and outdoor markets as a point of departure. Sports and outdoor products are, like most products, sold through a combination of their symbolic value and a promise of technical performance. User involvement in the innovation and production process reflects this. On one hand, users' first-hand knowledge is used as a source of information and inspiration for new products or to improve already existing products. On the other, users are valuable resources for credibility and authenticity. Through their results and position in the field, and the fact that they endorse and use the product, they are functioning as a guarantee of performance.

However, in this project we have found few examples of innovation processes that can be defined as user led. A more correct description might be user influenced; users are more likely to give feedback and input to processes controlled by the firms. The people working in sports and outdoor firms are often keen and skilled users themselves, and can as such use their own experiences in the innovation and design process. In this chapter they have been labelled 'passionate insiders'; they combine the passion of the enthusiast with the skill and competence of a professional.

Users beside these passionate insiders are seldom brought into play when it comes to development of new products from scratch. They are more likely to give feedback on prototypes and developed products. On the other hand, all companies interviewed had so-called 'team riders'. These are athletes or users being sponsored with both goods and money. Some of these give feedback on the equipment, but as this is rarely systematised they seem more important as branding 'tools'. The experience and in-depth understanding of the cultures (and sub-cultures) of different sports and activities and average users can be a very useful supplement to the skills of professionals. Users provide a valuable knowledge source both for firms and for other consumers.

However, a certain level of scepticism is advised. The firm needs to sort the information, and decide what kind of knowledge it is after. Is it on a product's functionality? At which consumer groups are the products targeted? Will the information help the firm to cater for certain markets? The consumers must bear in mind that athletes are sponsored by the firm, and they are paid to sell the products. As such they are not the unbiased sources of information they may often appear to be.

## ACKNOWLEDGEMENTS

This chapter is based on the studies undertaken in the project 'Users' role in innovation processes in the sports equipment industry', financed by Nordic Innovation Centre (NICe). The author is very much in debt to the other project participants: Hans Olav Bråtå, Svein Erik Hagen, Tanja Kotro, Dominic Power, Mikko Orrenmaa and Petteri Repo (see Bråtå *et al.* 2009).

## REFERENCES

Adams, T. (2005) *On Being John McEnroe*, New York: Crown.
Asheim, B. (1999) 'Interactive learning and localised knowledge in globalising learning economies', *GeoJournal*, 49, 345–352.
Atkin, D. (2004) *The Culting of Brands: When Customers Become True Believers*, New York: Portfolio.
Bennett, G., Ferreira, M., Lee, J. and Polite, F. (2009) 'The role of involvement in sports and sport spectatorship in sponsor's brand use: The case of Mountain Dew and action sports sponsorship', *Sport Marketing Quarterly* [serial online], 18, 1, March, 14–24.
Bourdieu, P. (1984) *Distinction: A Social Critique of the Judgement of Taste*, London: Routledge & Kegan Paul.

Bråtå, H.O., Hagen, S.E., Hauge, A., Kotro, T., Orrenmaa, M., Power, D. and Repo, P. (2009) 'Users' role in innovation processes in the sports equipment industry – experiences and lessons', NICe report, http://www.nordicinnovation.net/_img/07028_users_role_in_innovation_processes_in_the_sports_equipment_industry_final_report_web.pdf.

Di Maria, E. and Finotto, V. (2008) 'Communities of consumption and made in Italy', *Industry and Innovation*, 15, 2, April, 179–197.

Florida, R. (2002) 'The economic geography of talent', *Annals of the Association of American Geographers*, 92, 4, 743–755.

Fournier, S. (1998) 'Consumers and their brands: Developing relationship theory in consumer research', *Journal of Consumer Research*, 24, 4, 343–373.

Franke, N. and Shah, S. (2003) 'How communities support innovative activities: An exploration of assistance and sharing among end-users', *Research Policy*, 32, 157–178.

Grabher, G., Ibert, O. and Flohr, S. (2008) 'The neglected king: The customer in the new knowledge ecology of innovation', *Economic Geography*, 84, 3, 253–280.

Heath, J. and Potter, A. (2005) *The Rebel Sell: How the Counterculture Became Consumer Culture*, London: Capstone Publishing.

Jaffe, J. (2007) *Join the Conversation: How to Engage Marketing-Weary Consumers with the Power of Community, Dialogue, and Partnership*, Hoboken, NJ: John Wiley & Sons.

Kennedy, E. and Hills, L. (2009) *Sport, Media and Society*, New York: Berg Publishers.

Klein, N. (2000) *No Logo: Taking Aim at the Brand Bullies*, Toronto: Knopf Canada.

Lury, C. (2004) *Brands: The Logos of the Global Economy*, New York: Routledge.

Lüthje, C. (2004) 'Characteristics of innovating users in a consumer goods field: An empirical study of sport-related product consumers', *Technovation*, 24, 9, 683–695.

Lüthje, C., Herstatt, C. and von Hippel, E. (2005) 'User-innovators and "local" information: The case of mountain biking', *Research Policy*, 34, 6, August, 951–965.

Malmberg, A. and Power, D. (2006) 'True clusters: A severe case of conceptual headache', in B. Asheim, P. Cooke and R. Martin (eds), *Clusters in Regional Development*, Regional Development and Public Policy Series, London: Routledge.

Maskell, P. and Malmberg, A. (1999) 'Localised learning and industrial competitiveness', *Cambridge Journal of Economics*, 23, 167–185.

Olins, W. (2003) *On Brand*, London: Thames and Hudson.

Porter, M. (1990) *The Competitive Advantage of Nations*, New York: Free Press.

Power, D. and Hauge, A. (2008) 'No man's brand: Brands, institutions, fashion and the economy', *Growth and Change*, 39, 1, 123–143.

Quart, A. (2003) *Branded: The Buying and Selling of Teenagers*, Cambridge, MA: Perseus.

Roberts, K. (2004) *Lovemarks: The Future beyond Brands*, New York: power-House Books.

Schreier, M., Oberhauser, S. and Prügl, R. (2007): 'Lead users and the adoption and diffusion of new products: Insights from two extreme sports communities', *Marketing Letters*, 18, 15–30.

Scott, A. (1995) 'The geographic foundations of industrial performance', *Competition and Change: The Journal of Global Business and Political Economy*, 1, 51–66.

Shah, S.K. (2000) 'Sources and patterns of innovation in a consumer products field: Innovations in sporting equipment', Working Paper 4105, MIT Sloan School of Management, Cambridge, MA.

Sherry, J.F.J. (1998) 'The soul of the company store: Nike Town Chicago and the emplaced brandscape', in J.F.J. Sherry (ed.), *ServiceScapes: The Concept of Place in Contemporary Markets*, Lincolnwood, IL: NTC Business Books.

Storper, M. (1997) *The Regional World*, New York: Guilford.

von Hippel, E. (1978) 'Successful industrial products from customer ideas', *Journal of Marketing*, 42, 1, 39–49.

von Hippel, Eric (1986) 'Lead users: A source of novel product concepts', *Management Science*, 32, 7, July, 791–805.

von Hippel, Eric (2005) *Democratizing Innovation*, Cambridge, MA: MIT Press.

Walker, R. (2008) *Buying In: The Secret Dialogue between What We Buy and Who We Are*, New York: Random House.

# 7. Consumer capitalism and brand fetishism: The case of fashion brands in Bulgaria

## Ulrich Ermann

## INTRODUCTION

In her bestseller *No Logo*, Naomi Klein (2000) described a new mode of capitalist economy, in which consumption plays a fundamental role. Brands are seen as the central element of such 'consumer capitalism'. This term has been used in popular criticism of globalization and capitalism, and also in academic publications, since the 1990s, for example in Lash and Urry's *Economies of Signs and Space* (1994: 2). But what is new about this new capitalism? Klein says that the management motto 'Brands, not products!' has caused radical changes in the economy. She cites Phil Knight, the former CEO of Nike:

> For years we thought of ourselves as a production-oriented company, meaning we put all our emphasis on designing and manufacturing the product. We've come around to saying that Nike is a marketing-oriented company, and the product is our most important marketing tool. (Klein 2000: 44)

The main function of brands is no longer to protect from imitation by marking origin, but to invent and render identities and lifestyles. Brands reflect an economy of signs, in which 'the greater part of consumption is the consumption of signs' (Slater 1987: 157) and consumption 'must not be understood as the consumption of use-values, as material utility, but primarily as the consumption of signs' (Featherstone 2007 [1991]: 83).

However, the new mode of consumer capitalism dated by Klein to the early 1990s is seen much more in the reflexivity of consumer–producer relations, as Nigel Thrift (1997) stresses with the notions of 'soft capitalism' and 'knowledge capitalism', as well as Daniel Miller with the notion of 'virtualism' (Miller 2000; see Thrift 1998). Thrift (2006: 302) argues that there is a change in the relation of production and consumption, in which consumers are playing a very active role. In his view this reflexivity goes along with new concepts of value: '[W]hat is now going on in business is intended to [. . .] gain through a general redefinition of what counts as value.'

What is new is not that economic values are now seen as symbolically mediated and created by the exchange of commodities (see Appadurai 1986: 3). The crucial point is that companies quite purposefully adapt this observation in a reflexive way in their practices. Sign values are no longer regarded as side effects of production but as the main object of business activity itself. Following Joanne Entwistle (2002: 321), such an 'aesthetic economy' is not just a general '"aestheticization" of economics and every-day life. Rather it is an economy in which aesthetic values are generated as part of the calculation of economic markets.' Thus the motto 'brands, not products' can be understood as a performative act of brand building, as Celia Lury (2004) emphasizes. Branding can be analysed as 'a mechanism – or medium – for the co-construction of supply and demand' (Lury 2004: 27, with reference to Callon *et al.* 2002; see Moor 2003, 2007; Arvidsson 2005; Holt 2006; Ermann 2007; Pike 2009).

In post-socialist economies in Central and Eastern Europe brands are performative media of modernization. Brands are one of the most visible symbols of the new market economy and consumer society. They connect identities and dreams of (potential) consumers with business objectives of producers and retailers. Consumer patterns and marketing strategies reflect the imaginations and expectations of how individuals should act in a functioning market economy and consumer society (see e.g. Humphrey 1995; Veenis 1999; Fehérváry 2002; Patico and Caldwell 2002; Stitziel 2005).

In what follows I analyse some contradictions emerging from a branding-oriented way of doing business. A major claim of the new brand economy is that economic value becomes increasingly detached from a 'physical' use value. Secondly, focusing on the notion of fetishism, I will show that criticizing fetishism of the modern capitalist economy does not combat the contradictions between material values and immaterial values, but rather strengthens them. Then, based on empirical research, I will demonstrate how the slogan 'brands, not products' has been adapted by the fashion business in Bulgaria. I will raise the question how, in the economic everyday life of a post-socialist society, different concepts of value are being reproduced, perpetuated or re-interpreted. Subsequently some thoughts on how brand economies and consumer capitalism are related to place and space in a geographical sense will follow. In the conclusion, I will outline research perspectives stemming from these considerations.

# DIVESTMENT OF THE WORLD OF THINGS?

When signs and symbols are sold, instead of physical products, this has many implications: it confirms the rather trivial statement that the economic value of products is mediated symbolically and that economic value is only weakly related both to material exchange value (more precisely, the value of labour invested in material production) and material use value (more precisely, the value of the satisfaction of physical needs). However, the crucial point is that an economy which follows the slogan 'brands, not products' transforms the mere statement into a principle of its economic activity. Companies that follow this slogan concentrate their activities on the creation of symbolic meaning rather than on the production of goods. They do this because they believe that producing brands creates more value than producing goods. If this principle is to work, the brand must not only 'seem to the consumers more than the thing itself' (Sennett 2006: 144); the brand must be more important also for those selling it.

Klein (2000: 27) names the move of economic strategies from the production of goods to the production of signs, images and lifestyles by marketing and branding the 'divestment of the world of things'. For characterizing the function of brands she uses religious vocabulary: 'the selling of the brand acquired an extra component that can only be described as spiritual . . . Branding, in its truest and most advanced incarnations, is about corporate transcendence' (2000: 43). (Ironically, Naomi Klein is often called 'the icon of anti-capitalism' and 'the icon of anti-globalization campaigners'.) In this regard, the way anti-globalization activists describe brands as metaphysical figures is very similar to the vocabulary used by marketing gurus. Marketing specialists speak about the 'myths' and the 'aura' of brands, and they see 'subliminal' and 'transcendental' effects of brands.

Hence it appears that both marketers and people engaged in anti-globalization campaigns unanimously see brands as playing a central role in the present economy. They entirely agree that the creation of value through branding is no longer bound to the production of goods and their physical characteristics (see Holt 2002). They only disagree on how to ethically assess this issue. While brand enthusiasts hail the idea that creating economic values has finally liberated itself from the constraints of the material world, brand opponents worry about the lack of morality in an economy which aims at disguising the 'real' (material) value of goods and seeks to train consumers to adore images, signs and stories, rather than to base their consumptive decisions on the physical characteristics of the goods they buy.

Both attitudes assume that there was an 'old capitalism' where the value of goods was bound to their materiality. Depending on one's standpoint, this either means that in former times it was 'real value' that counted, whereas nowadays economic values are created out of illusory worlds and phantasmagorias, or it means that in former days economic values were bound to the burdensome material world including the burden of corporeality and physical production, whereas today economic values are first of all the result and the nucleus of human sociality and individuality.

However, believing that non-material, quasi-religious aspects of economic value have only just recently become important would be a mistake. Karl Marx, almost one and a half centuries ago, was concerned about the transcendental characteristics of consumer goods. 'A commodity appears, at first sight, a very trivial thing, and easily understood. Its analysis shows that it is, in reality, a very queer thing, abounding in metaphysical subtleties and theological niceties' (Marx 1906 [1867]: 81). He criticizes the fetishism of commodities, which he characterizes as mistaking the material for the immaterial.

The function of brands developed from origin- and quality-marking making uniform industrial products more distinct (see Sennett 2006: 148); later, brands were used for reflexive production of symbolic values and lifestyles. This culminated in brands being turned into a management concept. The economy which is shaped according to this concept does not only aim at filling and generating consumptive needs. Rather, the task is to invent consumers and to invent their lifestyles. Producing brands as well as market research, therefore, also means producing 'virtual consumers'. As Miller (2000: 197) puts it: 'Models which are thought to be descriptive of economic relations have become so powerful that they become in and of themselves the forces that determine economic relations' (see Thrift 2000: 694; and Slater 2002).

Unlike the perspective of 'virtualism', Michel Callon's performativity programme (Callon 2007) stresses not the influence of theories on the economic reality – how the 'model of the world becomes the world of the model' (Thrift 2000: 694) – but rather how the economy is 'performed': how producers, marketers and consumers are concerned with framing commodities, values, firms and themselves as economic players, without a clear distinction between theories and practices. In this manner, the slogan 'brands, not products' can be seen as a performative speech act (see Austin 1973 [1955]) in which the producers and sellers of branded products redefine themselves, and marketing could be seen as a 'performative discipline' (Lury 2004: 18; see Cochoy 1998). Some scholars called this the '*give-them-what-they-want* school of marketing theory and practice' (Shankar *et al.* 2006: 490) to denote the performative effects of marketing.

# FETISHISM AND THE SELF-DECEPTION OF THE MODERN ECONOMY

Brands are related to phenomena of materialization as well as of demate-rialization. Where products, by being branded, offer lifestyles and identi-ties to their buyers, immaterial values become material. At the same time, however, the process of the physical production of goods takes on a more immaterial quality, because the product's brand replaces the product's origin. Karl Marx describes this dialectic relationship of materialization and dematerialization of commodities with his notion of fetishism based on concepts of ethnology and religious studies. In Marx's interpretation, there is 'a definite social relation between men, that assumes, in their eyes, the fantastic form of a relation between things', similar to the 'mist-enveloped regions of the religious world' (Marx 1906 [1867]: 83). Hartmut Böhme (2006) shows that Marx, when accusing fetishism, always takes an attitude of enlightenment, similar to that of Sigmund Freud when speak-ing about fetishism in sexuality. Marx remarks: 'The whole mystery of commodities, all the magic and necromancy that surrounds the products of labour as long as they take the form of commodities, vanishes therefore, so soon as we come to other forms of production' (Marx 1906 [1867]: 87).

Along the lines of Marx, David Harvey demands to 'get behind the veil, the fetishism of the market and the commodity, in order to tell the full story of social reproduction' (Harvey 1990: 423). Notably, this Marxist concep-tion of commodity fetishism criticizes the reversal of subject and object in capitalism, or, in other words, both the personification (or spiritualization) of material objects and the objectification of (immaterial) ideas. Hence the criticism is directed towards worshipping mere things, as well as the reifica-tion of human subjects in the industrialized process of work.

Like Böhme, Bruno Latour provides a very different reading of fet-ishism to that of Marx. He suggests that discerning facts and fetishes is not possible, since 'it is obvious that the two have a common element of fabrication' (Latour 1999: 306). For Latour, the 'moderns', when criticiz-ing fetishism, deceive themselves. Modern society is convinced that it has reified and disenchanted the world and that it has purified things of any magic features. In believing so, the moderns do not realize that exactly this produces new contaminations and enchantments. According to Böhme (2006: 30) fetishism is the 'glue' of social life, characterized by an ecstatic relationship between individuals and things.

Thus, in an attempt to exorcize fetishism the modern exorcists become fetishists themselves (Böhme 2006: 92). Demonizing the fetish and denouncing fetishists mean proving that the fetish is dangerous and pow-erful and that it is capable of its own action. This is the paradox of modern anti-fetishism. Modern anti-fetishism reproaches fetishists for their pre-modern belief in things having a power to act. It is modern society itself which – through its attempt to purify the world and to draw a line of demarcation between a world of meaning and a world of materiality – populates the world with monsters and 'hybrids' resisting all attempts to locate them in either of the two worlds (Latour 1993). According to Böhme, for Marx and his successors it is similarly true that persecuting the fetishism of others strengthens the fetishism in oneself. 'Other people's fetishism most usually is a projection of one's own' (Böhme 2006: 330, transl. U.E.).

From the perspective of political economy, unveiling the real conditions of production means unmasking the supposed placelessness of the capitalist – respectively neoliberal – world of commodities by giving a clear view of the 'real' and concrete origin of the products. I believe that it is indeed an important task of geographical research to unveil the material conditions of production. However, we should look more closely at the veil itself and its production. The fetishes themselves are to be taken seriously both in the context of where they are created and in the context of where they are utilized (see Castree 2001: 1521; Cook and Crang 1996: 134; and critically Guthman 2009: 198ff.).

Analysing brands not as unreal projections but as real objects of economic practice could shed light on manifold interdependencies and blurred division lines between utility value and symbolic value, between contexts of manufacturing products physically and the world of marketing, as well as between the 'reality' of material exchange of commodities and the supposed 'illusion' of exchanging symbolic meanings, dreams and narrations. Instead it should be taken into account that all of these 'illusions' are products with real local labour and material inputs.

In this view the first step 'to demystify the demand side of economic life' (Appadurai 1986: 58) paradoxically is accepting the 'magic' of the world of commodities. Therefore understanding fetishism as being 'not environment, but inland of the economy' (Böhme 2006: 287) could help conceptualize geographies of production and consumption in the light of consumer capitalism. Instead of denunciating all aspects of lust, fantasy, emotions and so on as illusions and phantasmagorias and separating them from the purified and sober world of 'economic reality', it is important to focus on such phenomena, which are considered to be non-economic in their economic context of production and in their commercial effect. Of course, this should not lead to the reverse mistake: dismissing the material conditions under which commodities are produced. However, in my view, one important objective of doing geographical research on brands and branding is to re-connect worlds of production and consumption (Hartwick 2000: 1190). This does not mean denying the borderlines between economy and non-economy, between rationality and passion. Much more, it is about facing the practices of making and dealing with such demarcations in everyday life and in the (academic and practical) production of knowledge, reproducing neither naive affirmation nor naive critique.

## LAUNCHING FASHION BRANDS IN POST-SOCIALIST BULGARIA

### The Apparel and Fashion Business in Bulgaria

The aim of my empirical research on fashion brands in Bulgaria is to analyse brands as an interface between producers and consumers in an emerging market economy in post-socialist Europe. The Bulgarian apparel and fashion business can be characterized by increasing labour costs as a result of economic growth and EU accession in 2007, with many new regulations. This led to a reduction in offshore assembly production (see Begg *et al.* 2003; Pickles *et al.* 2006) and to moving production to other low-wage countries. A number of manufacturers have attempted to upgrade their share in the value chain with their own designs and brands, which has led to an increase of original brand manufacturers (see Gereffi 1999; Hassler 2003). Another tendency is the adaptation of (west) European standards regarding the quality of products and the promotion of brands. Therefore the brand building strategies are dominated by efforts of 'Europeanization', 'Westernization' and 'globalization' of brands. One problem is the high barriers to entry of global brand building markets owing to limited access to 'performative resources' (e.g. sponsoring of Western celebrities), as Tokatli (2007) pointed out. The upgrading strategy, as it is recommended especially by 'Western' business consultants, seems not to be appropriate for all the apparel and fashion companies. Many firms cannot afford large investments in design, branding and marketing. Furthermore, the domestic market as well as the export market are able to absorb only a limited number of new Bulgarian brands.

The manager of a Bulgarian fashion house told me in an interview:

> In the socialist period we just produced fashionable clothes. In the last 15 years we learned a lot . . . Specialists from Europe helped us to learn . . . Now we produce ideas of how you can dress yourself and how to distinguish yourself from other people . . . Without high quality you could not create value . . . Only the symbolic value is important for the clients today. (April 2008)

He reproduces exactly what the consultants and marketing specialists have told them about how the 'modern economy' must work. Unlike the

*Source:*   Photo: Ulrich Ermann.

*Figure 7.1    Battibaleno billboard, central Sofia*

credo of apparel production under the former centrally planned economy, the credo of production is no longer focused on the output of a certain amount of certain products, but on the production of ideas, images and lifestyles.

### Example: Battibaleno, Rila Style

In the street scenery of Sofia, fashion brands are omnipresent. The brand Battibaleno (Figure 7.1) was created for the company Rila Style, which has existed since 1972. In the socialist era the state-owned company was the biggest fashion producer in Bulgaria. After privatization in the early 1990s, the company produced apparel chiefly for 'Western' brands. Ten years later, the management decided to launch its own brand to keep a higher share of the value added.

As the sales manager said, the Italian brand name had been chosen according to consumer preference. She explained: 'marketing specialists found out that there is no other way to succeed on the Bulgarian market

*Source:*   Photo: Ulrich Ermann; Advertisement Photo: Peter Undbergh.

*Figure 7.2   Boss billboard, residential district in Sofia*

than to copy Western brands. The Bulgarians love Italian fashion and the Italian way of life' (April 2008). Most of the young consumers whom I talked to knew the brand, and indeed the majority believed it to be an Italian brand. Thus the company attempts to separate the brand image from the production taking place in a factory in central Sofia and other locations. In respect of the 'Western' image it was consequent to register the brand in the UK. A brand manager told me: 'If you want to increase the value of a brand, you just have to invest in the right place. Only when the customers see that a brand is present in the new malls or in Vitoshka [Vitosha Boulevard, the most expensive shopping street in the city] do they accept the brand as a valuable brand' (April 2008).

### Example: Hugo Boss

For several years, there have been numerous large billboard campaigns for the Hugo Boss brand in the city of Sofia (Figure 7.2). The owner of the German brand Boss, an Italian enterprise group, today spends much more money on its brand building activities than on the physical production of the clothes. For its brand building, Boss runs partnerships with music, art and sports events and celebrity testimonials. A significant portion of the brand's fashion is manufactured in South-West Bulgaria. In the small town of Gotse Delchev the company Pirintex, a German–Bulgarian joint venture, produces menswear for Boss and other brands such as Joop and Tommy Hilfiger. However, the owner also tries to reduce his dependency on 'global' brands. One of the strategies to achieve this is launching a 'local' brand, starting in the Bulgarian market.

While the costs of producing the clothes as they leave the factory are only 6 per cent of the retail price, for an original brand the main part of the value added could be realized within the company. For the 'global brands' – the entrepreneur told me – it is common practice not to let customers know where the products are manufactured. But for his local brand he likes to make the origin 'Made in Bulgaria' known:

> The value at the point of sale is at most 50 per cent of a high value brand . . . The quality is the same . . . Without producing for the high-value brands we could not launch our own brand because nobody would trust in the high quality our products actually have. (March 2007, transl. U.E.)

The entrepreneur explained that it is only because the customers know that he has the capacity to produce for well-known global brands that he is able to sell products under his own brand. This means a kind of free-rider situation, in which the production of global brands such as Boss is important for the value of the own brand.

### Conflicts and Negotiations of 'Value(s)'

Both examples show several contradictions of value creation by branding. In analysing these contradictions some distinctions between various understandings of 'value' are helpful (see Lee 2006: 415). Firstly, a distinction can be drawn between theories in academic economics, in applied economy and the 'ordinary economy'. Secondly, there are distinctions between different concepts of value (especially between objectivist and subjectivist concepts) within these theories. And thirdly, there are distinctions between economic values (in neoclassical mainstream economics value is defined as marginal utility) on the one hand and ethical values (opinions and certainties of what is good and what is bad) on the other hand.

In the post-socialist situation these considerations imply the change of value concepts across time and space:

1. value(s) in the past to value(s) in the present (and in the future); and
2. value(s) here to value(s) there (local–global; East–West; periphery–core).

As the examples show, theories of value are very pragmatically adapted by the companies in Bulgaria from their partner firms and consultants in Western Europe and transformed into business practices. Another finding from my case studies is that the value of places and spaces has its performative elements. If, in common opinion, 'Bulgaria' means low quality and low value and 'Italy' stands for high quality and high value, it would be difficult to break these rules. In this case 'value' is not just economic value, but is strongly intertwined with a bunch of social and moral notions of values.

Talking about fashion brands and branding strategies in Bulgaria reflects many general problems concerning the distinction between different concepts of value in the economy. Some complain about the fetishism of the fashion brands; others perceive the fetish of brands in a very positive way. Producers, marketers and consumers do not often share the same notions of value(s), but nearly all of them share a fatalistic attitude and accept the existing ('modern') rules of value adding and value perception.

Fashion brands typically are detached from the products' manufacturing sites. Unlike the situation in many other markets, branding is usually connected with deterritorialization. Even the marking of origin as in the case of 'Italian fashion' is mostly understood as the marking of a certain kind of style or quality; the consumers do not expect the production to be located in Italy. With a few exceptions fashion brands are perceived to be successful if they are recognized as 'global brands'. Owing to the small and medium size of all Bulgarian apparel and fashion companies, the Bulgarian fashion brands are not able to achieve the state of global brands. As 'local brands' the only opportunity for high economic performance is finding or creating special niche markets.

Consumers often connect the brand performance with the product's quality. For instance, one interviewed consumer said: 'When a brand asserts itself on the market, you know that this brand offers high-quality products' (June 2008, transl. T. Köster/U.E.). However, many consumers also reflect the questionability of the performative valuation of brands. The same interviewee added: 'I am against brand slavery: that you say I wear a certain brand only because it is the most expensive one. This is terrible. This is the negative effect of brands.' This example shows that brand literacy plays an important role in the valuation of products by consumers, even if the brand literacy itself is criticized. Consumers reflect not only the message of brands but also the branding strategies of companies in everyday discourses about shopping, fashion and style.

## SPACES OF BRAND ECONOMIES

Economic geography typically focuses on places and spaces of material (industrial) production, the trade of physical goods and to a lesser extent the business locations of the service sector. Marketing, advertising and branding mostly do not appear at all, or at best as negligible transaction costs with no 'real' productive value. However, they are not only an important factor of adding value; they influence the connections between producers and consumers on a global scale.

The most decided views on branding are provided by the global commodity chain (GCC), the global value chain (GVC) analysis and the approach of global production networks (GPN) (see Bair 2009). The GCC and GVC approaches (Gereffi and Korzeniewicz 1994; Gereffi *et al.* 2005) provide not only a temporal dimension but also a spatial dimension of the biographies and exchanges of commodities. The apparel and fashion commodity chains are used to being typical examples for buyer-driven commodity chains. As Gereffi writes, the shaping of consumer habits by brands characterizes this kind of chain: 'the main leverage in buyer-driven chains is exercised by retailers, marketers, and manufacturers through their ability to shape mass consumption via strong brand names and their reliance on global sourcing strategies to meet this demand' (Gereffi 1999: 43). The global apparel and fashion business – according to this approach and the underlying Wallerstein's world-system theory – consists of a division of labour between the processes of designing, marketing, branding and retailing in the West European and North American core regions and the fabrication of the clothes in low-wage countries in Latin America and Asia ('periphery') or parts of Central and Eastern Europe ('semi-periphery'). Especially in the semi-periphery many firms try to seize the chance of industrial upgrading. The idea of upgrading reflects the distinction between the physical production of goods in factories – work intensive and resource intensive – on the one hand and the intellectual development of designs, signs, brands and lifestyle patterns on the other hand. One problem of this kind of mapping is the implying congruence of spatial definition and economic-hegemonic definition of cores and (semi-) peripheries. Another problem is the one-dimensional and productivist perspective on brands.

The GPN approach emphasizes the creation, enhancement and capture of value (Coe *et al.* 2004: 473), among others by realizing 'brand rents' (Henderson *et al.* 2002: 21), and highlights, much more than other concepts of economic geography, the possibility of adding value by marketing and branding. However, there are some of the same deficits as in the approaches of global commodity/value chains in respect of the analysis of brand economies. Firstly, as the GPN proponents admit themselves, the global production network approach is overwhelmingly productivist, ignores consumption, and needs 'to find ways of integrating the role of consumption more fully' (Coe *et al.* 2008: 286). Secondly, these conceptions of adding value are based on a straight objectivistic notion of value, in particular 'a combination of the Marxian notion of surplus value with more orthodox notions of economic rent' (Henderson *et al.* 2002: 20). In my opinion a subjectivist notion of value could help to obtain a better understanding of the interrelations between the creation of value by producers and marketers on the one hand and the perception (and creation!) of value by consumers on the other. Only such a subjectivist view could allow the conceptualizing of phenomena like 'fashion', 'trends' and 'cultism' for consumer goods. This could be fruitful for the continuation of important contributions in connecting perspectives of economic and cultural geography at the interface of commodities and consumption (e.g. Jackson 2002; Barnes 2005), respectively commodity chains, circuits or networks (Leslie and Reimer 1999; Hughes and Reimer 2004).

An analysis of how brands are embedded in time and space focuses on places and spaces where signs are produced, transformed and used for communicative ends, and thus will unveil asymmetries of power and of access to semiotic resources (for the analysis of fashion brands in an exemplary manner, see Crewe 2004). However, situations of post-colonialism, as they have been described for the relationship between Eastern and Western Europe (Kuus 2004; Timár 2004; Pickles 2005; Stenning 2005), cannot be described following a core–periphery model with clear (national) borders. The power over economically relevant symbols is not in the hands of colonizing nation states. It is in the hands of globally active enterprises. What once was the core has become flexible, mobile and network-like.

There are two ideas at hand now: the idea of discerning use value (often regarded as the 'real' value) from symbolical value (often regarded as merely 'virtual' value); and the idea of discerning – spatially – core regions from (semi-)peripheral regions. Combining both ideas leads to a picture where we see use value being added in the semi-periphery at a very low price, and symbolic value being added in the core regions at high prices.

However, looking at the Bulgarian fashion business makes the picture appear more complex. Producers attempt to upgrade their position in the value chain by launching original brands and by participating actively, in various ways, in the production of signs. They are often inspired to do so by consultants, in projects which on their parts are financed by the European Union or the German development organization GTZ (see for Bulgaria Evgeniev 2008; Evgeniev and Gereffi 2008; or for Turkey Tokatli 2007; Tokatli and Kızılgün 2009). Adding value by branding takes place locally, but always needs strong connections to networks of communication formed by the media. From an outside position it could be very difficult to enter the circuits of symbolic value, not least because of situations of exclusion by powerful gatekeepers. However, the core–periphery dichotomy is not very suitable for analysing such flows and networks of signs and values between production, marketing and consumption, even if economic practices as well as academic discourses often reproduce and perpetuate such dichotomies and spatially fixed hegemonic structures. Therefore a geographical analysis of brands such as I propose should focus predominantly on the question of how producers, marketers and consumers as well as political institutions are concerned with the construction and deconstruction of such spatial formations.

## CONCLUSIONS

In writings of popular and academic management literature as well as in writings of popular and academic critiques of capitalism the contemporary economy is characterized by the increased importance of consumer orientation and an economy of signs. Brands are regarded as one central manifestation of this consumer capitalism. The common understanding of the economies and economic geographies of branding is based on several cultural binaries (see Berndt and Boeckler 2009: 536): the dichotomy between use value and symbolic value, between material value (quality, utility) and immaterial value (signs, sense, ideas and imaginations), between modernity and backwardness, often connected with the dichotomy between core and periphery or West and East, between the present and the past, between socialism and capitalism and, last but not least, between the good and the bad. These dichotomies are consequently reproduced by the knowledge of 'economists in the wild' (Callon 2007) (producers and consumers), as well as by academic knowledge and the applied knowledge of business players.

The empirical findings in the Bulgarian fashion business show how discourses of economic modernization are performative. The production of sign values is separated from the production of use values because of a belief that the modern economy must work in this manner. Consumers reproduce this concept of value, too, by valuing brands in respect of the quality of the symbolic values and their performance. In the post-socialist context this performance is driven by a strong discourse of modernization. Producers, marketers and consumers in Bulgaria strive to adapt concepts of value adding and value perception in regard to economic success and individual welfare. Investors, consultants and politicians from abroad try to implement their concepts in the new markets of the 'New Europe'.

The self-perpetuation of binaries such as between material values and non-material values or between core and periphery is not reduced, but even enhanced, by anti-fetishist critiques which imply the same dichotomies. Treating the immaterial values as about the non-real, illusive values underestimates the material reality of producing and cherishing these values and confirms the validity of this dichotomy. At the same time, the relation between core and periphery runs into the danger of implying a container-like spatiality with a lock-in position of the included economic subjects.

Branding as a main feature of consumer capitalism has strong effects on economic values and spaces. In order to analyse the proliferation of such a consumer-oriented and sign-oriented economy, the seemingly placeless and non-material business activities of marketing and branding have to be taken seriously. Deconstructing the discourses of fetishism and anti-fetishism in economic practice does not mean defetishizing the economy, but examining how distinctions between the 'real' and the 'virtual' economy as well as between 'real' and 'virtual' spaces perform economic geographies.

## ACKNOWLEDGEMENTS

The project 'Marken(t)räume' is sponsored by the Deutsche Forschungs Gemeinschaft (DFG) – code ER 475/3-1.

## REFERENCES

Appadurai, A. (1986) 'Introduction: Commodities and the politics of value', in A. Appadurai (ed.), *The Social Life of Things: Commodities in Cultural Perspective*, Cambridge: Cambridge University Press, 3–63.

Arvidsson, A. (2005) 'Brands: A critical perspective', *Journal of Consumer Culture*, 5, 2, 235–258.

Austin, J. (1973 [1955]) *How to Do Things with Words*, New York: Oxford University Press.

Bair, J. (2009) 'Global commodity chains: Genealogy and review', in J. Bair, *Frontiers of Commodity Chain Research*, Stanford, CA: Stanford University Press, 1–34.

Barnes, T. (2005) 'Culture: Economy', in P. Cloke and R. Johnston (eds), *Spaces of Geographical Thought*, London: Sage, 61–80.

Begg, R., Pickles, J. and Smith, A. (2003) 'Cutting it: European integration, trade regimes, and the reconfiguration of East-Central European apparel production', *Environment and Planning A*, 35, 2191–2207.

Berndt, C. and Boeckler, M. (2009) 'Geographies of circulation and exchange: Constructions of markets', *Progress in Human Geography*, 33, 4, 535–551.

Böhme, H. (2006) *Fetischismus und Kultur: Eine andere Theorie der Moderne*, Hamburg: Rohwolt.

Callon, M. (2007) 'What does it mean to say that economics is performative?', in D. MacKenzie, F. Muniesa and L. Siu (eds), *Do Economists Make Markets? On the Performativity of Economics*, Princeton, NJ: Princeton University Press, 311–357.

Callon, M., Méadel, C. and Rabeharisoa, V. (2002) 'The economy of qualities', *Economy and Society*, 31, 2, 194–217.

Castree, N. (2001) 'Commodity fetishism, geographical imaginations and imaginative geographies', *Environment and Planning A*, 33, 1519–1525.

Cochoy, F. (1998) 'Another discipline for the market economy: Marketing as a performative knowledge and know-how for capitalism', in M. Callon (ed.), *The Laws of the Markets*, Oxford and Malden, MA: Blackwell, 194–221.

Coe, N.M., Dicken, P. and Hess, M. (2008) 'Global production networks: Realizing the potential', *Journal of Economic Geography*, 8, 271–295.

Coe, N.M., Hess, M., Yeung, H. Wai-chung, Dicken, P. and Henderson, J. (2004) '"Globalizing" regional development: A global production networks perspective', *Transactions of the Institute of British Geographers*, 29, 468–484.

Cook, I. and Crang, P. (1996) 'The world on a plate: Culinary culture, displacement and geographical knowledges', *Journal of Material Culture*, 1, 2, 131–153.

Crewe, L. (2004) 'Unravelling fashion's commodity chains', in A. Hughes and S. Reimer (eds), *Geographies of Commodity Chains*, Routledge Studies in Human Geography 10, London: Routledge, 195–214.

Entwistle, J. (2002) 'The aesthetic economy: The production of value in the field of fashion modelling', *Journal of Consumer Culture*, 2, 3, 317–339.

Ermann, U. (2007) 'Magische Marken: Eine Fusion von Ökonomie und Kultur im globalen Konsumkapitalismus?', in C. Berndt and R. Pütz (eds), *Kulturelle Geographien: Zur Beschäftigung mit Ort und Raum nach dem Cultural Turn*, Bielefeld: Transcript, 317–347.

Evgeniev, E. (2008) *Industrial and Firm Upgrading in the European Periphery: The Textile and Clothing Industry in Turkey and Bulgaria*, Sofia: Professor Marin Drinov Academic Publishing House.

Evgeniev, E. and Gereffi, G. (2008) 'Textile and apparel firms in Turkey and Bulgaria: Exports, local upgrading and dependency', Икономически Изследвания [Economic Studies], 17, 3, 148–179.

Featherstone, M. (2007 [1991]) *Consumer Culture and Postmodernism*, Los Angeles: Sage.

Fehérváry, K. (2002) 'American kitchens, luxury bathroorns, and the search for a "normal" life in postsocialist Hungary', *Ethnos*, 67, 3, 369–400.

Gereffi, G. (1999) 'International trade and industrial upgrading in the apparel commodity chain', *Journal of International Economics*, 48, 37–70.

Gereffi, G. and Korzeniewicz, M. (eds) (1994) *Commodity Chains and Global Capitalism*, Contributions in Economics and Economic History 149, Westport, CT: Greenwood.

Gereffi, G., Humphrey, J. and Sturgeon, T. (2005) 'The governance of global value chains', *Review of International Political Economy*, 12, 78–104.

Guthman, J. (2009) 'Unveiling the unveiling: Commodity chains, commodity fetishism, and the "value" of voluntary, ethical food labels', in J. Bair,

*Frontiers of Commodity Chain Research*, Stanford, CA: Stanford University Press, 190–206.

Hartwick, E. (2000) 'Towards a geographical politics of consumption', *Environment and Planning A*, 32, 1177–1192.

Harvey, D. (1990) 'Between space and time: Reflections on the geographical imagination', *Annals of the Association of American Geographers*, 80, 418–434.

Hassler, M. (2003) 'Crisis, coincidences and strategic market behaviour: The internationalization of Indonesian clothing brand-owners', *Area*, 35, 3, 241–250.

Henderson, J., Dicken, P., Hess, M., Coe, N. and Yeung, H. Wai-chung (2002) 'Global production networks and the analysis of economic development', *International Political Economy*, 9, 436–464.

Holt, D.B. (2002) 'Why do brands cause trouble?', *Journal of Consumer Research*, 29, June, 70–90.

Holt, D. (2006) 'Toward a sociology of branding', *Journal of Consumer Culture*, 6, 299–302.

Hughes, A. and Reimer, S. (eds) (2004) *Geographies of Commodity Chains*, London: Routledge.

Humphrey, C. (1995) 'Creating a culture of disillusionment: Consumption in Moscow, a chronicle of changing times', in D. Miller (ed.), *Worlds Apart: Modernity through the Prism of the Local*, London and New York: Routledge, 43–68.

Jackson, P. (2002) 'Commercial cultures: Transcending the cultural and the economic', *Progress in Human Geography*, 26, 1, 3–18.

Klein, N. (2000) *No Logo: Taking Aim at the Brand Bullies*, London: Flamingo.

Kuus, M. (2004) 'Europe's eastern expansion and the reinscription of otherness in East-Central Europe', *Progress in Human Geography*, 28, 4, 472–489.

Lash, S. and Urry, J. (1994) *Economies of Signs and Space*, London: Sage.

Latour, B. (1993) *We Have Never Been Modern*, New York and London: Harvester Wheatsheaf.

Latour, B. (1999) *Pandora's Hope: Essays on the Reality of Science Studies*, Cambridge, MA and London: Harvard University Press.

Lee, R. (2006) 'The ordinary economy: Tangled up in values and geography', *Transactions of the Institute of British Geographers*, NS, 31, 413–432.

Leslie, D. and Reimer, S. (1999) 'Spatializing commodity chains', *Progress in Human Geography*, 23, 3, 401–420.

Lury, C. (2004) *Brands: The Logos of the Global Economy*, London and New York: Routledge.

Marx, K. (1906 [German orig. 1867]) *Capital: A Critique of Political Economy*, vol. I, New York: Modern Library.

Miller, D. (2000) 'Virtualism – the culture of political economy', in I. Cook, D. Crouch, S. Naylor and J.R. Ryan (eds), *Cultural Turns/Geographical Turns: Perspectives on Cultural Geography*, Harlow: Prentice Hall, 196–213.

Moor, L. (2003) 'Branded spaces: The scope of "new marketing"', *Journal of Consumer Culture*, 3, 1, 39–60.

Moor, L. (2007) *The Rise of Brands*, Oxford and New York: Berg.

Patico, J. and Caldwell, M. (2002) 'Consumers exiting socialism: Ethnographic perspectives on daily life in post-communist Europe', *Ethnos*, 67, 3, 285–294.

Pickles, J. (2005) '"New cartographies" and the decolonisation of European geographies', *Area*, 37, 4, 355–364.

Pickles, J., Smith, A., Buček, M., Roukova, P. and Begg, R. (2006) 'Upgrading, changing competitive pressures, and diverse practices in the East and Central European apparel industry', *Environment and Planning A*, 38, 2305–2324.

Pike, A. (2009) 'Geographies of brands and branding', *Progress in Human Geography*, 33, 5, 619–645.

Sennett, R. (2006) *The Culture of the New Capitalism*, New Haven, CT: Yale University Press.

Shankar, A., Whittaker, J. and Fitchett, J.A. (2006) 'Heaven knows I'm miserable now', *Marketing Theory*, 6, 4, 485–505.

Slater, D. (1987) 'On the wings of the sign: Commodity culture and social practice', *Media, Culture and Society*, 9, 457–480.

Slater, D. (2002) 'Capturing markets from the economists', in Paul du Gay and Michael Pryke (eds), *Cultural Economy: Cultural Analysis and Commercial Life*, London: Sage, 59–77.

Stenning, A. (2005) 'Out there and in here: Studying Eastern Europe in the West', *Area*, 37, 4, 378–383.

Stitziel, J. (2005) *Fashioning Socialism: Clothing, Politics, and Consumer Culture in East Germany*, Oxford and New York: Berg.

Thrift, N. (1997) 'The rise of soft capitalism', *Cultural Values*, 1, 29–57.

Thrift, N. (1998) 'Virtual capitalism: The globalisation of reflexive business knowledge', in J.G. Carrier and D. Miller (eds), *Virtualism: A New Political Economy*, Oxford and New York: Berg.

Thrift, N. (2000) 'Pandora's box? Cultural geographies of economies', in G. Clark, M.P. Feldman and M.S. Gertler (eds), *The Oxford Handbook of Economic Geography*, Oxford: Oxford University Press, 689–704.

Thrift, N. (2006) 'Re-inventing invention: New tendencies in capitalist commodification', *Economy and Society*, 35, 2, 279–306.

Timár, J. (2004) 'More than "Anglo-American", it is "Western": Hegemony in geography from a Hungarian perspective', *Geoforum*, 35, 5, 533–538.

Tokatli, N. (2007) 'Asymmetrical power relations and upgrading among suppliers of global clothing brands: Hugo Boss in Turkey', *Journal of Economic Geography*, 7, 1, 67–92.

Tokatli, N. and Kızılgün, Ö. (2009) 'From manufacturing garments for ready-to-wear to designing collections for fast fashion: Evidence from Turkey', *Environment and Planning A*, 41, 146–162.

Veenis, M. (1999) 'Consumption in East Germany: The seduction and betrayal of things', *Journal of Material Culture*, 4, 1, 79–112.

# 8. Sensing brands, branding scents: On perfume creation in the fragrance industry

**Bodo Kubartz**

## INTRODUCTION

> Compare also the physical capitalist commodity with the metaphysical brand. Brands also operate in a sea of inequivalence. A brand's product lines may be tangible, but the brand itself is not. It is abstract. Yet every brand is different from every other. The exchange-value of a commodity is comprised of units of identity. If a brand is not different from another it has no (brand) value. The commodity is divisible into parts consisting of quantities of exchange-value. A brand is not divisible without changing into something else. (Lash 2008: 7)

The development towards a knowledge economy and society has been theorized for the last two decades (Castells 1996; Leadbeater 1999). The end of the industrial economy and the emergence of post-Fordist production and consumption regimes have been examined. Economic geographers have been quite engaged and put their focus on how to conceptualize and understand knowledge (inter alia Amin and Cohendet 2004; Amin and Roberts 2008b; Faulconbridge 2007; Grabher and Ibert 2006; Ibert 2007, 2010; Jones 2008). However, the driving motors of the economy also have to be addressed. To this end, the increasing economic significance of brands has, so far, not been examined in great detail.

Two gaps exist. First, an in-depth discussion of brands and branding as crucial socio-economic activities has only recently begun in economic geography (Pike 2009; Power and Hauge 2008). The gap is substantial, since competitive success is increasingly brand-driven in numerous economic activities (Olins 2003; Pavitt 2000). Second, a gap in economic geography exists in terms of connecting the knowledge debate with the study and examination of brands and branding. This chapter focuses on these gaps.

First, I present the two discourses on knowledge and practices of knowing in economic geography (Amin and Cohendet 2004; Amin and

Roberts 2008a, 2008b; Ibert 2007, 2010) and the general literature on brands and branding (Pike 2009; Power and Hauge 2008). Second, I introduce the example of the fragrance industry, explain the merits of studying this cultural-product industry, and discuss the interactions of major players as well as the major processes. Third, I look at the significance and the attributes of branding to focus on the organizational and geographical challenges for knowing. I spatialize the analysis and point to key geographical and temporal characteristics in the industry. Connections between the two discourses are mentioned. A conclusion follows.

## TWO THEORETICAL DISCOURSES IN CONTEXT

### Knowledge and Knowing

Knowledge plays a key role in the discussion of successful economic activity in current Western knowledge economies. The traditional view conceptualized knowledge as an input, throughput, and output (Vallance 2007). It was argued that tacit knowledge is difficult to communicate other than through direct interaction (Morgan 2004; Storper and Venables 2004; Vallance 2007). It therefore requires spatial proximity for its production and dissemination. In contrast, the recent practice-based approach to knowledge in economic geography has questioned the association between tacit knowledge and the local scale (Amin and Roberts 2008a, 2008b; Ibert 2007; Jones 2008). It seeks a more expansive understanding that recognizes the varied spatialities of knowledge (Ibert 2007, 2010). In order to understand knowledge, research focuses on the specific work processes of 'how knowledge happens'. These processes are conceived as knowing that is understood as a social practice (Amin and Cohendet 2004; Amin and Roberts 2008a, 2008b; Ibert 2007). Theories of practice understand knowing through activities that are distributed between different entities of humans and non-humans. Practice is conceived as 'embodied, materially mediated arrays of human activity centrally organized around shared practical understanding' (Schatzki 2001: 2) including the human body as well as materials as agents. Gherardi (2006: 34) defines a practice 'as a mode, relatively stable in time and socially recognized, of ordering heterogeneous items into a coherent set'. Accordingly, knowing is only recognizable through research on what is done in action and practical accomplishment. The terms 'practice of knowing', 'knowing in action', and 'knowing-in-practice' are equivalents since knowledge can only be studied though the focus on and understanding of doing (Amin and Roberts 2008a; Gherardi 2006). In general, knowing is only partially mental and cognitive but, much more, based on social practice. Knowing in action depends on the industry context.

Accordingly, economic geographers have been keen to study how knowing is practised and how practices of knowing are geographically configured (Amin and Cohendet 2004; Amin and Roberts 2008b; Ibert 2007, 2010). The units of analysis where knowing is practised have shifted in accordance with the above shift: not individuals or clearly defined organizations but 'socially distributed activity systems' (Amin and Cohendet 2004: 30; Amin and Roberts 2008a; Gertler 2008) are the reposi- tories that social scientists increasingly investigate. Knowing practices are characterized in inter-organizational networks emerging out of firms, projects, and careers, for instance (Amin and Roberts 2006; Grabher and Ibert 2006; Jones 2008).

The thrust to better understand practices in knowledge economies has led economic geographers to study diverse industries from manufactur- ing to professional services (Faulconbridge 2007; Hall 2008; Jones 2008). Based on these studies, the understanding is that the sector-specific differ- ences between practices of knowing are created and take place in commu- nities of practice (CoP) which cover the 'social interactive dimensions of situated learning' (Amin and Roberts 2006: 2; Amin and Roberts 2008a; Wenger 1998). Most recently, a sympathetic critique of the CoP literature indicates a range of different forms of communities and knowing prac- tices within them (Amin and Cohendet 2004; Amin and Roberts 2006, 2008a; Grabher and Ibert 2006; Ibert 2010). In contrast to a territorial view, knowledge is seen as practised across space, creating multi-faceted networks where the spatialities of knowledge are multiple and constantly unfolding (Amin and Cohendet 2004). Amin and Roberts (2008b) as well as Gertler (2008) conceive of situated practices of knowing as developing and coming up in 'many spatial forms and intensities, involving entangle- ments of knowledge that cannot be reduced to the local/global choice' (Amin and Roberts 2008b: 29). 'Spaces of knowing' (Amin and Cohendet 2004: 86–111) are based on a combination of interaction of involved par- ticipants in knowing. Thus economic geography reads spatialities that form and change on the basis of social action (Amin and Cohendet 2004; Bathelt and Glückler 2003; Ibert 2007).

**Brands and Branding**

Sociologists conceptualized the shift towards the knowledge economy by focusing on the transition of a capitalism that is grounded in physical entities in the direction of a more metaphysically grounded and substanti- ated capitalism (Lash 2008; Lash and Lury 2007; Lury 2004). Brands are major representatives of this change (Lash and Lury 2007; Lash 2008). They characterize advanced capitalisms that constitute 'econom[ies] of the invisible' (Bolz 2005: 31; also in Leadbeater 1999), where knowledge seemingly plays a focal role. Brands are not new; however, their significance and penetration in the economy have gained global recognition not least through information and communication technologies.

The American Marketing Association (AMA) (in Bengtsson and Ostberg 2006: 84, emphasis added) defines a brand as 'a name, term, design, symbol, or any other feature that *identifies* one seller's good or service as *distinct* from those of other sellers'. Manufactured goods have often been discriminated by their technological and 'hard facts'. However, against the traditional understanding and the above definition, a brand is less about a clear identification than about open-ended and discursive creations of meaning that are based on individual and collective sense-making (Lury 2004). Brands represent a shift from manual or craft-based and mechanical labour towards design-intensive and knowledge-driven functions.

Thus what is branding and who is involved? First, the purpose of branding is to charge a product with intangible qualities and construct a link between the character of an object with a brand image (Lury 2004; Pavitt 2000; Power and Hauge 2008). The emphasis of symbols, the association of a product with a brand, and the representation of the perfectly blended mix of a product with the brand are 'at the heart . . . for many of the goods we buy and sell' (Pavitt 2000: 16; also in Lury 2004). This replaces the previous pragmatic and functional description of an object. However, it is a challenging endeavour to make an often mass-produced good distinctive and ready for a consumer-specific and individualized identification: a product 'seeks to obscure homogeneity' (Sennett 2006: 143), although it is often a physical copy of another item. Often, not only does the understanding of what a good or a service is blur but also what the consumed good or service means to the consumer (i.e. identity) and to the community (i.e. signification). In order to develop its sign value, the implied function of a brand as a symbol for something needs to be organized and recognized (Bengtsson and Ostberg 2006; Lury 2004). 'Being' and 'meaning' are entangled and constructed in the processes of becoming.

Second, the orthodox understanding particularly in the marketing and business literature is that a brand manager is like a 'high priest' and non-creative manager capable of solving problems in branding. However, a more realistic understanding is that of the brand manager as an ambiguity-coping co-author (Kärreman and Rylander 2008). Bengtsson and Ostberg (2006), for instance, discuss that a number of brand authors exist. Other co-creators of a brand are popular culture (TV programmes, magazines, movies, books, etc.), stakeholders (competitors, labour unions, and retailers), and consumers (Bengtsson and Ostberg 2006). A number of these co-creators have been investigated in cultural studies and consumer research. However, since a brand is always negotiated and relational, the orthodox delineation of 'producers' and 'consumers' diminishes particularly in the case of cultural-product industries (Allen 2002; Kubartz 2009; Power and Hauge 2008; Power and Scott 2004; Pratt 2004). Since the consumer co-creates the values of a brand, he is (re-)recognized as a significant construct and player for economic geography (Aoyama 2007; Grabher *et al.* 2008). The productivist logic in economic geography is challenged by the question of how value creation of brands takes place in the creative spheres and spaces between production and consumption (Pike 2009; Pratt 2004). At the same time, the multiplexity of potential authorship of a brand traces back to the question of how brand managers are 'steering the brand ship' and how they are enabled to do what they do.

**Contextualizing the Discourses**

The two literatures on knowledge and the practices of knowing in economic geography and the literature on brands and branding hardly interact (Pavitt 2000). Not only have brands and the processes of branding in cultural-product industries hardly been discussed by economic geographers (Power and Scott 2004), but they have been under-researched at the level of gaining a deeper understanding of how organizational and geographic contexts are configured in the economic activity of branding (Lury 2004). The relation to the knowledge discussion in the discipline and the particular role of brands as engines of growth are research areas worth a further investigation. I intend not to come up with 'best practices' of organizing brands and branding in order to make products successful. Branding is not understood as a normative fashion or managerial tool. Brands and branding imply social (inter-)action and ties. The purpose of branding is to charge a product with intangible qualities and build a link between the 'brand-less character' of an object and specific images so that a particular brand image develops that is communicated through a product (Pavitt 2000; Lury 2004; Power and Hauge 2008). In the short run, the goal is to maximize sales per brand and to guarantee a high and quick return of investments. The ultimate goal in the long run is to increase the credibility and authenticity of a brand in comparison to other brands (i.e. brand positioning) in order to build long-term linkages with the consumer. Branding characterizes a postmodern economy with cultural products where the trade with symbols and experiences is key.

Branding is understood as a diverse set of practices of knowing that are recognizable in their geographical spatialities (see also Amin and Cohendet 2004). In this context, Pike (2009: 360), for example, speaks about the entanglement of brands and branding with space and place: 'space and place are written through branded objects and the social practices of branding', which are, he adds, geographically differentiated and uneven. The chapter underscores this mutual affection and inscription of brands and branding in spatial settings and is sympathetic to the idea of 'entangled geographies of brands and branding' (Pike 2009: 621). Thus branding is a social accomplishment. Branding means social (inter-) action and characterizes social ties in their spatialities. It belongs to the wider field of marketing and is crucial for the manufacturing of cultural products.

However, in this chapter I connect the discourse on brands and branding with the one on knowledge and knowing in economic geography. The investigation of branding as a set of practices of knowing (Amin and Cohendet 2004; Amin and Roberts 2008a; Ibert 2007) should enable: first, a better understanding of how competitive economic success is maintained in praxis; second, which organizational characteristics in branding play crucial roles; and, third, which geographical associations and contexts emerge out of these examinations (Ibert 2007; Pike 2009).

The fragrance industry serves as an example to shed light on these points. It is an intriguing cultural-product industry for investigating brands and branding through the example of perfumes for the following reasons. A perfume walks the material–metaphysical line of being a tangible good that dematerializes and comes into effect in use, of being represented by a smell but with value added by several intangible illuminations. Abstract, expressive, affective, and aesthetic symbolic registers span the material–metaphysical boundary in this particular case (Allen 2002). The creation, performance, and maintenance of a brand are exceptional in comparison to the case in other cultural-product industries, since perfume is evanescent and, unlike many other branded products, demands recognition through all senses but especially the olfactive competencies. The performance of branding in this case is very communication intensive; it demands long-term experience in the sector, and a well-tempered mix of rational and sensible argumentations. 'The brand is the prefix, the qualifier of character', as Pavitt (2000: 16) claims. Is that possible for a perfume? The characteristic of a brand as an identifier is challenging to realize in the case of a perfume, and this has also to do with the specific ways of entering this particular industry. What is a typical smell of a brand? People, such as celebrities or fashion designers, and abstract qualities, like femininity, sensuality, or truth, are signified and articulated in forms, colours, and scents. This signification is hard to grasp as far as the brand values and their connections to scents are concerned: what does classiness smell like and how does it differ between brands that consider themselves classy? The question is how material and immaterial characteristics are affiliated and fused in a perfume through branding.

I focus on the role of the brand manager, look at her participation in the branding process, and examine branding as a knowing practice as part of developing a new perfume. The phrase 'brand manager' is not a corporate term or function but rather a characterization of the responsibilities of this person. Brand managers are typically marketers. This view is connected to an examination of the repositories where knowing takes place. I argue that brands are another social logic and organizing framework for knowing practices besides the previously discussed aspects of firms, projects, and careers (Amin and Roberts 2008a, 2008b; Grabher and Ibert 2006).

This chapter includes empirical material from 66 semi-structured interviews with industry personnel. These were conducted between January 2007 and April 2008 in New York and Paris as the two main centres of the international fragrance industry. The interviews were with multiple functions on the manufacturers' side (brand manager, fragrance developer, for instance), fragrance suppliers (perfumers, marketers, evaluators, sales), and other industry experts. This is a strength, since branding is increasingly performed beyond one single function, and the work of brand management is reflected and affected by other functional roles. Initial interviewees were gathered through the trade and industry press. The industry has been described as small in the sense that 'everybody knows everybody in the industry': although entry into the industry was difficult, participation was secured through a snowballing technique.

## MAJOR CHARACTERISTICS OF THE FRAGRANCE INDUSTRY

The term 'manufacturer' might be antagonistic to a rather artistic understanding of crafting and producing perfumes. However, the reality for the big players is along the lines of manufacturing in post-Fordist times. Manufacturers of perfumes are involved in the creation of a variety of fragranced commodities. Functional fragrances are separated from fine fragrances. Functional fragrances (i.e. they fulfil a certain function) are in various household goods such as detergent, fabric softener, and washing-up liquid; fine fragrances are in products ranging from toiletries (soaps, hair colourant, and body lotion, for example) to perfume. The latter one can be differentiated into a so-called masstige (a neologism developed out of the conceptual understanding of products that provide 'prestige for the masses'), or mass market, premium market or prestige market (including fashion, designer, celebrity, and lifestyle brands), and a niche market. However, it is not precisely clear where to draw boundaries between those idealized segments. Segmentation is possible according to market prices, brand ownership, geographical markets, retail environments, and consumer target groups, for example. Furthermore, the significant international manufacturers are characterized by differing internal management philosophies of the perfume brands. The market share for premium fragrances is even more concentrated, and in 2006 three companies held a share of almost 40 per cent of the whole market (Dodson 2008). However, the industry is fragmented beyond that point. The manufacturers are umbrella corporations that are organized according to brand portfolios. This set-up pursues particular market logics: 'the more brands you put on the shelf the better the chance of being picked' (Olins 2003: 106). The customer is often not aware that several brands are managed and marketed by the same company. Thus, *corporate* branding in the fragrance industry is weak compared to other consumer product segments (Olins 2003). In addition to the increased number of brands, a re-organization of the market has been perfume as a fast-changing consumer product on a launch-intensive market has been taking place over the last 10 to 15 years (Berthoud *et al.* 2007). It is a pro-cyclical market where general economic prosperity is contributing and positively affecting growth (Dodson 2008). The fragrance market had grown to $30.5 billion in sales in 2006 and is forecasted to grow to $35 billion by 2011; Western Europe and North America, with 60 per cent of global sales, are the most significant markets (Dodson 2008). In the first half of 2007 alone, more than 800 new perfumes were launched (Jeffries 2007). The launch intensity has implications for the internal functioning of the 'perfume behemoths', but it also leads to questions about the upstream links to suppliers and the downstream relationships with distributors and retailers. In the subsequent parts of this discussion I will focus only on the interactions of the large perfume manufacturers with the fragrance suppliers.

First, the creative independence per brand is relatively high. The manufacturing firm provides mainly central functions that are accessible for all brands. The function of the umbrella corporation is to play a coordinating role: brand equities are compared, brand plans and product launches coordinated, general market development observed, and potential harm monitored (e.g. brand cannibalization and market exclusion). The manufacturer is often a licence holder of designer or fashion brands and is enabled to produce fragrances for 10 to 15 years until renewal or divestment (Burr 2008). This guarantees long-term financial and planning security and enables the development of brand familiarity and experience.

Initiatives to coordinate between different branded products (clothing, jewellery, accessories, etc.) – building brand unity (Burr 2008) – are typically organized by the licensor.

Second, the manufacturers are 'hollowed out'. Several companies supply a manufacturer. The fragrance suppliers are crucial. They provide scents for all kinds of fragranced products and work in close collaboration with the manufacturers (Berthoud *et al.* 2007; Burr 2008). The number of fragrance suppliers has decreased over the last few years. Five major ones currently exist (Burr 2008). It is an interesting feature that the biggest manufacturers compete with each other on brands, but they work with the same suppliers. Often perfumers work on projects for brands that are competing for the same targeted consumer groups. Fragrance suppliers compete against each other in an increasingly self-regulated and exclusive market environment. The regulatory device is the phenomenon of core lists: fragrance suppliers have exclusive rights to compete in a small pool in order to deliver scents for particular brands. Reasons for this market solution are guaranteed fixity of material prices, quantities, and qualities as well as temporal flexibility. This supply oligopoly supposedly harms creativity; however, in order to remain competitive and creative, the suppliers relocate competition internally and brief numerous perfumers – the creative noses and artistic developers of new scents – in-house throughout the world. Creating a perfume scent is a competitive, interactive, and, in fact, globalizing task (Burr 2008; Turin 2006). The interaction with fragrance suppliers is crucial but difficult in the context of branding, since it crosses firm and sensory boundaries.

The manufacturers actually have a mediating role between the brand owner and suppliers upstream and the distributors and retailers downstream. The brand manager coordinates the production of a new perfume in close connection to the brand owner; the companies have suppliers of tangible materials (bottles, packages, fragrances) and intangible characterizations (design, market, advertising, communication, and even brand). The brand manager coordinates the different production processes in a temporal and creative sense: all delivered tangible and intangible parts have to be in line with the brand. The links in this upstream part are characterized through 'briefs' that initiate and structure the relationship for each product. However, producers are also involved in the downstream part of the business, since circulation through advertising, distribution, and retailing is to different degrees also coordinated and arranged by the manufacturers. Thus the chains of value creation also have to be coordinated in space (Pike 2009).

Brand management is key for the manufacturers of a perfume (Lash and Urry 1994; du Gay and Pryke 2002). General differentiations understand product brands and service brands (for example Olins 2003). Perfumes are both a product and a service brand. While a perfume is a tangible and fragrant product, it serves consumers in that it connects them to the consumption and experience of luxury. The pure materiality is necessarily extended to include non-tangible, symbolic registers (Allen 2002). The challenge for a brand manager is to situate the perfume in a:

> domain, where words, sounds, and images function as an expressive system of signs, which makes possible cultural understanding, regardless of whether such features can be fully articulated by those involved in the appreciation of a particular art form like film or music. (Allen 2002: 47)

A perfume is an expressive and experiential good. Sign values instead of functional or exchange values are important in the communication with and documentation for consumers (Baudrillard 1998). The aspect of value creation in brands is discussed as a significant theme (Arvidsson 2005; Lash 2008; Lury 2004; Pavitt 2000). Sign values emerge not out of the materiality of a branded product by itself but out of the general experience with the brand as a whole (Lash and Lury 2007). The meticulous maintenance, engineering, and manoeuvring of meaning is a key challenge for the manufacturers (Bolz 2005; Kärreman and Rylander 2008). This aspect is connected to spatial circuits of creating meaning: in order to achieve these goals, the tangible and intangible materials have to travel between different involved actors. Circulation, particularly important during the latter downstream stages of distribution and retail, matters also during the manufacturing of a perfume. The mechanics to construct meaning are, however, increasingly challenged: 'The brand is no longer a monolith. It is many different things to many different people' (Michael Edwards, perfume expert, in Jeffries 2007). 'If fragrance doesn't have *noise or word of mouth*, it is just business; that's not designing a brand . . . To excite today's consumer, we have to make her feel that fragrance is too exciting to not use' (Edwards, in Jeffries 2007, emphasis added). This unusual approach towards marketing forces the brand manager to rethink her agenda and to make noisy perfumes and create ways to be heard. It is about the creation of needs and cool (see also Lury 2004). Thus, in the case of a perfume, the question is how 'the distinctive combination of various kinds of symbolic dexterities and knowledges' (Allen 2002: 47) is invented, fabricated, and communicated for the potential consumer. Brand managers in the fragrance industry are symbol analysts and symbol creators (Reich 1993). Symbols are produced in order to signify specific meaning: perfumes are simulacra; they are constructed out of nothing and have no original relation to reality (Baudrillard 1998; Burr 2007). Brand managers qualify products through the management of relations between attributes such as place, packaging, promotion, and product qualities (the orthodox marketing mix; Lury 2004; Pike 2009). The brand manager is not completely free to invent. The brand demands creative continuation and effective communication to consumers. Thus the area of key interest and a challenge of branding as a set of practices of knowing in the fragrance industry are the processes to invent, stamp, and communicate meaning of tangible and intangible product characteristics (Sennett 2006). The specific point in case is that the brand manager is collaboratively working on these tasks. The questions are: what guides the work with other experts, and which spatialities develop out of branding?

## ON BRANDING IN THE FRAGRANCE INDUSTRY

Amin and Roberts (2006, 2008a) differentiate between different forms of knowing in action. The work of a brand manager shows close similarities with epistemic or creative knowing (Amin and Roberts 2006, 2008a.). It is embedded in sectors with high degrees of ambiguity and openness as far as outcomes are concerned and is characterized by (a) individuals with a high degree of individual skills, experience, and reputation, (b) strong loyalty bonds to a shared problem, (c) organized slack (elsewhere characterized as 'consciously cultivated informality'; Thompson in Amin and Roberts 2008a: 362) and (d) other forms of alignment (all in Amin and Roberts 2008a: 361–362). The authors connect each knowing practice with a particular form of community (Wenger 1998). Brand managers practise creative knowing in a community of experts (see Amin and Roberts 2006, 2008a, 2008b; Brown and Duguid 1991). This type of creative community is similar to the crafts- or task-based community of perfumers. Amin and Roberts's first three characterizations provide a checklist for examining the brand manager's performance. The three following subdivisions, about branded managers, b(r)ands of loyalty, and sensing brands as well as branding scents, reflect this checklist. The discussion illustrates that a brand provides a significant socio-economic logic and organizing mechanism for the particular practices of creative knowing in branding.

### Branded Managers

Questions about skills and experiences relate back to the professional development and enculturation of the brand manager. Typically, brand managers have a marketing or business school background. This characterization suggests how they approach and visualize work tasks (see Cochoy 1998; Lury 2004). Branding, just like marketing, is a performative discipline (Lury 2004) or performative science (Cochoy 1998). This means that subject matters are simultaneously described, constructed, and, consequently, altered in the process of doing. '"Performation" of the economy by marketing directly refers to the double aspect of marketing action: conceptualizing and enacting the economy at the same time' (Cochoy 1998: 218). Thus brand managers are both disciplining the market economy through branding and reshaping it through their own activities (Cochoy 1998).

The individual skills, experience, and reputation of a brand manager are intensively coordinated and maintained. This coordination and maintenance demands a mix of labour stability or immobility and labour mobility of marketers within the fragrance industry (see also Grabher and Ibert 2006). This is for two reasons.

First, companies prefer to keep brand employees loyal, because they can be sure that personnel 'know the brand'. This is reflexively integrated into the self-understanding of employees as belonging to a club or elite (Kärreman and Rylander 2008). Labour immobility is an intended goal of the employer to enhance group building capacities; from a creative and managerial point of view, it strengthens the mentality to belong to a particular brand and know the ins and outs of the decision-making processes.

Second, job changes enable individuals to be confronted with new brands and branding environments. Temporality enhances employability and enables both the brand and the brand managers to remain fresh and creative (Arthur 2008; Kärreman and Rylander 2008). Professional temporality helps in understanding the different facets of branding; brand managers often work for time periods between six months and a year in sales, communication, or PR for a manufacturer or supplier. The understanding of fast-changing consumer goods (i.e. breadth) is more crucial than being involved in one or two branding environments only (i.e. depth). In order to remain mobile in a highly competitive labour market it is imperative to understand the different aspects and ways of how branding at different edges in the industry is performed. Overall, labour mobility enhances the individual career and the brand's inventiveness and creativity.

Thus the individual skills, experience, and reputation of a brand manager are based on immobile and mobile phases during a career. Crucial for the decision to become mobile is also the potential to create and re-create a brand. Experiencing different brand environments to stay creative over time is an important knowing practice at this stage.

This trade-off clearly has geographical connotations: a brand manager is experiencing her understanding in geographical terms of how a brand is embedded in major markets. Thus, vice versa, the brand manager is branded through her occupation: by (a) the occupation itself and the function, (b) the brand and the socio-economic brand environment, and (c) the work in specific geographical markets. These characterizations all contribute to her employability and to the construction of a career. The brand is inscribed in a brand manager's career and vice versa. Employability has a significant geographical connotation.

## B(r)ands of Loyalty

The strong loyalties to shared problems and the creative requirements to solve these problems connect the brand managers rather with the suppliers than the umbrella corporation. Below, I will look at two examples of how the umbrella corporation supports each brand with certain functions and how loyalty is shared across firm boundaries. Combining competences for successful creations and sharing loyalties across different interest holders are two sets of knowing practices that characterize the procedures of solving problems during a product development cycle.

First, the firm mainly orchestrates the work of the brand manager. The umbrella firm provides central functions for all brands. Two examples are market research and fragrance development. Market research helps the brand manager to understand the strengths and weaknesses of a scent. It consists of several sets of research procedures such as portfolio analysis where the general market per segment and regional market analyses of similar brands and their products are examined. Market research is a solution to visualize the market in olfactory and conceptual ways and to see prospects for future developments of a brand. Fragrance development is usually involved in writing briefs. Briefs describe an intended perfume in words and characterize the intended product with general characteristics, target group, price margins, and potential ingredients (for a critical view see Burr 2008). Different fragrance suppliers receive the brief. The brief is forwarded internally to several perfumers, who start to compose, change, and adjust fragrant creations in numerous reiterations with the manufacturers until the final scent is determined (Burr 2008; Turin 2006). However, fragrance development at the manufacturer is recurrently testing and evaluating fragrance submissions of suppliers. Furthermore, market research and fragrance development provide market research and olfactory suggestions to the brand manager that enable her to alter or adjust a fragrance or its other components in a perfume when necessary (see also Berthoud *et al.* 2007).

Second, the market set-up, firm sizes, and geographical organization of markets per company allow interactions to recur. Fragrance suppliers work with brands and brand managers on a recurring basis, also between brands. This implies that brand managers develop and are known for some individual characteristics of 'doing business' independently from the current brand environment. Brand managers and perfumers, for instance, develop loyalties towards a particular project and brand. These loyalties emerge out of the actual problem whereby trust and problem-solving competencies develop. Over the last few years, a shift of responsibilities has taken place. Fragrance suppliers take a more proactive role. Two examples are given: the fragrance suppliers duplicate some of the technical efforts of the manufacturers to understand and make sense of the final consumers. The large suppliers invest significant amounts of money into quantitative and qualitative market research (see Catterall and Maclaran 2006). Market research characterizes a long-term value that developed out of the initiative to link fragrances with brands through the vehicle of emotions. Gobe (2007: 49) explains that one of the key suppliers 'chart[s] the emotional profile of the fragrances' based on a global database with emotional responses of people to almost 5000 scent ingredients and fragrances. The goal is to 'create fragrances that will leave an indelible mark on consumers and brands that will have sustainability in the marketplace' (Gobe 2007). Thus a big supplier has integrated 'emotionally driven discovery techniques' which are 'used as a way to develop fragrances for its clients that has now become a source of inspiration for major fragrance brands as well' (Gobe 2007: 45). Thus branding is not only increasingly pre-run by the suppliers but backed up by and intertwined with 'scientific evidence' of emotional research on consumers (see also Falk 2008). In an interview, Falk's (2008: 48) interview partner explained that 'IFF [International Flavors & Fragrances Inc. (www.iff. com), one of the five major fragrance suppliers] is a company that doesn't simply manufacture fragrances, it's a company that *creates* fragrances while understanding the emotional impact that fragrances have on consumers.' Fragrance suppliers become proactive in emotional branding. Thus, they proactively work on the aspects of time and quality. The intentions are to secure short- and long-term collaborative links to the manufacturers and to develop forecasting skills as to which scents work for which brands per market in order to stay competitive and become more flexible and independent from the clients. This case also documents that, in the end, both manufacturers and suppliers have the same denominator: the consumer. Loyalties are relationally shared between the fragrance supplier and the manufacturer. The loyalties are devoted, in essence, to each individual problem and project per brand. However, broadly speaking, they are shared in order to affirm and reassure that the target consumer is attained.

**On Sensing Brands and Branding Scents**

However, the above characteristics do not cover the longevity of the brand as a socio-economic logic and organizing mechanism. Economic geographies of knowledge in cultural-product industries increasingly require an understanding and examination of the role of brands for action, interaction, and creative knowing. So far, firms, projects, and individual careers as three types of socio-economic organization have been researched as systems that are fuelled by motivations to achieve certain economic goals. These organizations have been characterized by different degrees of cohesion and group-think (Grabher 2002; Grabher and Ibert 2006). While Amin and Roberts (2006, 2008a, 2008b) discuss the lack of a source for cohesion and mutuality in expert communities, a brand is a potential enabler of mutuality within and across this community. Brands as socio-economic ideas and guidelines are pervasive and transported beyond firm and project boundaries. They serve as potential organizing mechanisms and platforms for the interaction of different communities involved in the production of branded goods (see also Power and Hauge 2008). The discussion below examines two significant procedures to 'conduct' branding: sensing a brand and branding a scent. The next section contextualizes these procedures in spatial and temporal terms.

**Sensing a brand**

At the beginning of the product development process the invention, development, and presentation of a concept for a new perfume are critical. A crucial capacity here is the understanding of what a brand signals (i.e. deciphering the brand DNA) and how a brand can be reinterpreted, remixed, and integrated into new products (i.e. modelling and projecting facets of the brand DNA). In contrast to the term in biology, 'brand DNA' is a dynamic metaphor for something that exists outside of and contributes to a producer-oriented discourse about a brand (Gobe 2007). This DNA consists of unique core values, a particular history and heritage, and a general ethos, soul, and outlook on the world. The term 'brand DNA' implies the possibility of creating something out of the information in an imaginatively pre-given stock of this cultural, and not biological, DNA. Thus the brand manager has to breathe, live, and represent a brand in a business-to-business context, just as the legal brand owner represents the perfume in front of potential consumers. This conceptual approach of skimming through the brand DNA is exemplified by Burr (2008: 194) through L'Oreal's Armani fragrances licence:

L'Oreal has ensured that the perfumer weaves in the same filaments. Brand unity. You smell the links subtly but distinctively, not as materials but as style, the juice olfactorily finished in that instantly recognizable matte, sleek, silver-gray Armani polish. An aluminum carapace, one part light to two parts dark, and the perfumers manage to convey it in smell.

Thus the brand serves as a trajectory for potential creations. In order to come up with new concepts, brand managers sense a brand. The characterization of 'sensing a brand' has different dimensions.

Sensing a brand is both a single task of the brand manager and a few affiliates and an interactive task: trend agencies and market research, for instance, provide advice up front. Those actors present feedback during the early stages of product development as far as general trends on the fragrance and fashion market are concerned. Trend agencies provide information in generalized terms and through the publication of trend books. One major international creator of trends and publisher of different trend book products explains online that 'our publications are polysensorial to the eye and the touch, combining photos, fabrics, material samples, swatched colour palettes, prints, patterns, silhouettes, sketches and print descriptions' (NellyRodi 2008). These multi-material and -sensorial trends serve as a starting point for creative thinking. Thus a first task is to understand:

> where the market is going to go. We are very linked to fashion also . . . let's say ecological, natural, organic etc.: where are we, where are we not, and where is our competition, and is there a spot there? And if we find that there is a spot there then based upon this we will define our concept. (Vice-President, Global Marketing, June 2007)

Depending on the status of a perfume brand in a geographical market and within a manufacturing firm, the concept authenticity varies between what Power and Hauge (2008: 128) for the case of fashion call 'hierarchical brands' (new technologies and trends that are prototyped, tested, and launched in a smaller high-value or niche market) and those that adapt them to the mass markets. Thus product concepts trickle down within and between companies.

Furthermore, market research (performed internally and bought externally) makes a contribution. A concept is usually tested at different points for a number of times. The common result is that the concept is altered according to the test results and targeted geographical consumer markets. The initial concept is often tested in focus groups (Catterall and Maclaran 2006):

> We went in [into focus group research] and it [i.e. the concept] was all about being outside, all about being free, it was all about being open, and it was all

about sunshine. That is what that [product] brand is about on a very simplistic level. Simultaneously we went in with a number of different names . . . If we are far enough ahead we may also have some very preliminary packaging ideas that we may put on the table to sort of gauge what would be the consumers' point of view and where do we stand? And obviously we are not so black and white, but we try to zone in on some key comments where we can potentially shift in: is there white space in the marketplace that we can ultimately explore and develop a real brand? (Vice-President, Global Marketing, September 2007)

This quote presents the intentional proximity to the aggregated final consumer – a point that continues during the following stages of product development. Market research is only one device reflexively to create and visualize a market (Burr 2008; Cochoy 1998). However, the manager is guided by the brand's past, present, and intended future. A major difference is between those fragrances that drive versus those that merely reflect the brand. The latter are characterized by a strong position of the brand itself, and the fragrance is developed based on that:

We are feeding off what the brand is; the fragrance has to live underneath the brand . . . If you work on designer brands I think what drives that brand forward is much more image and positioning and emotion and then the consumer will follow. (Vice-President, Global Marketing, September 2007)

The time- and cost-intensive process of sensing is backed up by intensive talks with the brand owner and brand team members but also by the understanding of economic performance of a brand amongst particular consumer groups. Furthermore, the brand manager contextualizes this in a geographical sense: does the concept work and fit into a particular market? This brings into question how the development of brand conscience is enabled and maintained over time. 'What I bring to the party is not only a full understanding of the fragrance industry but also just brand imaging and also how to make brands slightly more global versus more regional' (Vice-President, Global Marketing, September 2007). Thus brand performance is still recognized by national markets of economic performance. Usually, international brand managers are located both functionally and bodily in the headquarters offices in either New York or Paris. They elaborated a general understanding of a brand and the potential performance of a concept in different markets. However, in addition (and also during the developmental process) the brand manager receives feedback from brand affiliates for particular countries or regions. Talks with these regional experts focus on the upstream creation and initiation of a new concept and ultimate product but also on the downstream characteristics of implementation of the product (distribution, retail), where questions deal with brand positioning in a market. Parallel to and/or shortly after the confirmation of a concept, the manufacturing firm starts to brief all suppliers.

Within the fragrance supplier, perfumers learn to understand a brand in its symbolic characterization and organizational environment and are encouraged to present scents according to their understanding of a brief and a brand. If a perfume is about a particular celebrity or designer, or abstract qualities like femininity, independence, or love, for instance, the perfumer links verbal descriptions in a brief with adequate materials that represent and symbolize these characterizations. She expresses these qualifications through the estimated and calculated use of particular olfactory notes in a perfume (for a discussion of the role of the perfumer see Burr 2008; Turin 2006). What successful perfumers do is to 'embed into each juice a strand of [in this case] Armani's DNA, this scent signature, as invisible and powerful as a silicon locator chip' (Burr 2008: 195). How does a perfumer become knowledgeable as far as the brand requirements are concerned? The market set-up of the major manufacturers (i.e. the fragrance suppliers) and the development of core lists (Burr 2008) lead to a streamlining of creative competition between the major fragrance suppliers. While on the one hand core lists are formal agreements that mirror strong ties between the manufacturer and supplier, creative work that takes place within the fragrance supplier between competing perfumers characterizes weak ties between the perfumer and the brand (see Grabher and Ibert 2006). Perfumers learn over time what a brand is about. However, depending on a new brief, they are constantly urged to reconsider what they have learned. A brand remains ambiguous (Burr 2008; Grabher and Ibert 2006). However, what perfumers learn to do about a brief is: to smell and decipher where the brand with its other perfumes stands in the market, to work with key personnel on the manufacturer's side, and to know what the intention behind a new perfume launch is. Other functions, such as marketing and evaluation, support the perfumer (Berthoud *et al.* 2007; Falk 2008). The marketer's role is 'to develop tools – marketing tools, which both help [to] understand and analyze trends' (in Falk 2008: 49–50) in advertising, semantics, and packaging. The evaluator critically reflects on whether, and which, scents are ready for competition and submission; evaluators act as a mirror for the perfumer.

### Branding a scent

This description of the tasks at the fragrance supplier indicates that, in turn, a brand ensures that the brand manager has a basic understanding and fluid security in an uncertain environment. The manager senses and evaluates scents in order to brand the scent. Sensing scents includes the understanding of ingredients and the motivation of the perfumer to submit a particular scent. Evaluating scents implies the recognition if a scent fits for a brand. The fragrance that wins the competition is integrated and fitted into the network of other product components (bottle, bottle format and colour, package, name, retail environment, etc.) – thus it is branded. The brand manager has usually only a limited olfactory background, and the interactive knowing with fragrance development in-house and fragrance suppliers reassures her. In subsequent steps, the winning fragrance continues to be slightly altered and tested in order to forecast the likely performance. Thus a brand is an inter-organizational 'symbol of belonging' (Kärreman and Rylander 2008: 117) and a potential enabler of mutual understanding.

## CONTEXTUALIZATION IN SPATIAL AND TEMPORAL TERMS

As mentioned above, territorially defined knowledge spaces are seen as only one example of the geographies in and through which knowing takes place (Ibert 2007, 2010). Practice-based accounts in economic geography work in reverse: they examine practices of knowing first in order to 'spatialize' and characterize emerging spatialities thereafter (in different scales) (Amin and Roberts 2008a; Bathelt and Glückler 2003; Ibert 2007; Pike 2009). It is the 'reading of space that emerges from a heterogeneous interpretation of knowing in action' that is required in order to delineate geographies based on the 'shapes and sizes of knowing in action' (Amin and Roberts 2008a: 365). In this section I will follow 'the argument of place' (Ibert 2007: 111) by examining localized practices but also spatially distributed action. I relate the spatial and temporal characteristics of branding in the fragrance industry to distanciated creative knowing and learning (Amin and Roberts 2008a; Faulconbridge 2007; Ibert 2007; Wenger 1998). I claim that both sensing a brand and branding a scent are procedures that are maintained and enabled through interactions across distances. Branding consists of knowing practices that evolve out of the communal engagement in a particular place as well as through spatially distributed action (Amin and Roberts 2008a, 2008b; Ibert 2007).

First, the brand manager acts and co-develops new concepts in particular places such as her working desk. The particular practices of knowing that characterize this step during the creative process are developing a perfume conceptually and estimating the legitimacy and credibility of this concept. This is typically done at desks and through talk in corporate offices, most often at the headquarters of the brand. It is about building a vision for a brand and getting initial feedback from the closest colleagues working for a brand. Thus 'the conception desk' of the brand manager materializes as a conceptional space where the concept is organized.

However, the initial development of a new fragrance concept and sensing a brand also require that ideas travel. The brand manager manoeuvres between different actors: local brand affiliates, the brand owner, market research, and the fragrance supplier, for instance. Distanciated creative knowing and learning emerge out of the co-alignment of different viewpoints in working on a perfume. The creative practices of knowing that they perform are, at different points during the creative process of inventing a concept, those of shaping and testing the marketability of a concept. Brand affiliates are located within the most important consumer markets and represent the brands of the market. This is a device to represent a brand in a country and, vice versa, to summarize a country for the brand-licensing manufacturer. The local brand affiliate, for instance, looks at perfume concepts according to the question: under which circumstances and with which attributes would the concept for this product brand work in this specific market? This thinking involves not hierarchical decision making but work in exchange with the international brand manager. The initial general conceptualization is checked against the portfolio of fragrances in each target market. The brand affiliates stay familiar within quickly changing brand environments. Situating an affiliate in the local context of consumption allows for a relational understanding of challenges, problems, and opportunities of conceptual implementation within the specific country.

The coordination with the brand owner and market research takes place at a range of geographical distances. Fragrance concepts travel across spaces, and coordination takes place in relational proximity (Amin and Cohendet 2004; Amin and Roberts 2008a; Bathelt and Glückler 2003; Ibert 2010). The uniqueness of a concept in a particular context is maintained even if globalizing forces of brand homogenization speak against that. Uniqueness is a value that contributes to the cachet of a brand. Market research has often been criticized for 'dumbing down' a perfume (Burr 2008). However, product creativity and complexity might only be traded against market success. Thus what is sensed at the conception desk and through concept mobility are two significant aspects: the *ex ante* likelihood of creating and coordinating a branded product that is conceptually credible and graspable for the target audience; and the overall direction, cachet, and operationality of a brand for the creation of a particularly conceptualized fragrance.

Second, at the stage of 'branding a scent' (thus at the end of the development process), the 'conception desk' of the brand manager changes into and becomes a 'coordination desk'. Not all materials and immaterials reach the manufacturer at the same point in time; however, it has to be guaranteed that the highlighted spectrum of the brand DNA is adequately represented and integrated in the overall market appearance of a brand. In the end, the ultimate perfume is intended to tell an interesting story on its own in order to be uniquely positioned on the market. The brand manager keeps the object coherent. She is doing that at the coordination desk. At the end of the developmental process, the product not only is branded by itself through its material and immaterial features, but it brands back: the involved actors are understood and memorized through their particular participation in the creative process of becoming as well as the market success that it receives once it reaches the consumer environment.

Interactions with major collaborators such as the fragrance suppliers take place in a setting of organized slack that promotes spatial proximity. A fragrance is increasingly connected and related to all other material and metaphysical product characteristics towards the end of the creative process. During the fragrance and product development process and towards the end of it, branding a scent is based on shifts in project pace and ruptures (Burr 2008). By 'pace and ruptures' I mean the frequent change of working speed between the manufacturers and suppliers: manufacturers accelerate or delay project work through in-house decision making. Towards the project end, geographical proximity between the fragrance supplier and the client gains importance. Frequent interaction at short notice is preferred by the clients of the fragrance suppliers: while creative processes for consumer products are taking place in New Jersey or the 'Cosmetic Valley' (Berthoud *et al.* 2007), the work on fine fragrances is done in proximity to the headquarters of the manufacturers. The quick and easy access and accessibility are also stressed by the creative materialization and materiality of fragrances that let suppliers co-locate in proximity to their clients. This proximity can be conceptualized under the term and idea of 'the neighbourhood'. Geographic proximity in the neighbourhood is backed by the necessity of interaction to explain as well as discuss fragrant submissions on an ad hoc basis: scents are presented by the supplier and altered based on face-to-face interactions where the brand manager, marketing, sales and evaluation, and the fragrances are co-present. The practice of knowing that is performed in the neighbourhood is ad hoc interacting: flexibility though organized slack is enabled through geographical proximity. Different professionals comment and contribute to alterations of a formulation from their specific viewpoint. However, the potential social solutions that are inherent in geographical proximity are added by frequent exchanges via telephone, email, or short-notice visits. The exchange is continuous but based on temporal ruptures: it is hard to anticipate when the client will come back with further demands and suggestions.

## CONCLUSION

A discussion of the relevance and role of brands is missing from the knowledge debate in economic geography. Knowing in action in the fragrance industry increasingly takes place around brands. This chapter has elaborated on this for the particular case of the brand manager. It is sympathetic to the view that brands are based on processes of negotiation and interaction between multiple economic actors (Power and Hauge 2008: 125). Branding is a set of creative knowing practices that demands an understanding of the relationship between a brand, the brand manager, and the networked relationships in action. A brand complements the concepts of the firm, the individual career, and the project, for instance in its logic to structure, create, and destroy emerging strong or weak networked relationships (Amin and Cohendet 2004; Amin and Roberts 2008a, 2008b; Grabher and Ibert 2006).

The brand is a social logic and an organizing framework that provides guidance for action and an orientation as a path-dependent trajectory. Branding implies multiple practices of knowing that take place over time in order to challenge and re-ensure the boundaries of a brand. The chapter discussed the work and sets of procedures, practices and geographies of collaborative participants during the product development phase. It made an exemplary distinction between the initial process of sensing a brand (i.e. coming up with and testing a concept in the targeted consumer markets) and – after the processes of sensing and evaluating scents – branding a scent (i.e. inter-relating the scent with other material and metaphysical components). Thus the set of applied creative practices necessarily involves distanciated creative knowing and learning at a distance where the mutually understood brand provides meaning. It also involves knowing in geographical proximity (such as particular types of desks and in the neighbourhood) where the materialization, materiality, and demand for the explanation of a scent characterize specific places of innovation. Thus the geographies of knowing and learning are dynamic, and that is, in part, because of the necessity to communicate about the materializing and ambiguous object of perfume (Ibert 2010).

The research has the following implications. First, this chapter focused on the upstream part of the industry, while a focus on the downstream part of branding would be beneficial in providing further insights in terms of other actors and their different relations and co-creative practices on sign-value creation during distribution and retail (e.g. Pratt's call for a retail focus in economic geography, Pratt 2004; also Pike 2009). Second, further research needs to extend the discussion about different and interacting communities of practice within the fragrance sector. Third, research on other brand-intensive industries could further the understanding of branding as a practice of creative knowing and illustrate the idiosyncrasies and similarities between cultural-product industries.

# REFERENCES

Allen, J. (2002) 'Symbolic economies: The "culturization" of economic knowledge', in P. du Gay and M. Pryke (eds), *Cultural Economy: Cultural Analysis and Commercial Life*, London: Sage, 39–58.

Amin, A. and Cohendet, P. (2004) *Architectures of Knowledge: Firms, Capabilities, and Communities*, Oxford and New York: Oxford University Press.

Amin, A. and Roberts, J. (2006) 'Communities of practice? Varieties of situated learning', Paper presentation for EU Network of Excellence: Dynamics of Institutions and Markets in Europe (DIME), October.

Amin, A. and Roberts, J. (2008a) 'Knowing in action: Beyond communities of practice', *Research Policy*, 37, 353–369.

Amin, A. and Roberts, J. (2008b) *Community, Economic Creativity, and Organization*, Oxford and New York: Oxford University Press.

Aoyama, Y. (2007) 'The role of consumption and globalization in a cultural industry: The case of flamenco', *Geoforum*, 38, 103–113.

Arthur, M.B. (2008) 'Examining contemporary careers: A call for interdisciplinary inquiry', *Human Relations*, 61, 2, 163–186.

Arvidsson, A. (2005) 'Brands: A critical perspective', *Journal of Consumer Culture*, 5, 2, 235–258.

Bathelt, H. and Glückler, J. (2003) 'Toward a relational economic geography', *Journal of Economic Geography*, 3, 2, 117–144.

Baudrillard, J. (1998) *The Consumer Society: Myths and Structures*, London: Sage.

Bengtsson, A. and Ostberg, J. (2006) 'Researching the cultures of brands', in R.W. Belk (ed.), *Handbook of Qualitative Research Methods in Marketing*, Cheltenham, UK and Northampton, MA, USA: Edward Elgar Publishing, 83–93.

Berthoud, F., Ghozland, F. and d'Auber, S. (2007) *Stakes and Professions in Perfumery*, Paris: Editions d'Assalit.

Bolz, N. (2005) 'Sinn-Designer: On the management of cultural meaningfulness', in H. Voesgen (ed.), *What makes sense? Cultural Management and the Question of Values in a Shifting Landscape*, Brussels: ENCACT, 27–32.

Brown, J.S. and Duguid, P. (1991) 'Organizational learning and communities-of-practice: Toward a unified view of working, learning, and innovation', *Organization Science*, 2, 1, 40–57.

Burr, C. (2007) 'Ghost flowers', *New York Times*, 25 February.

Burr, C. (2008) *The Perfect Scent: A Year inside the Perfume Industry in New York and Paris*, New York: Henry Holt and Company.

Castells, M. (1996) *The Rise of the Network Society*, Malden, MA: Blackwell.

Catterall, M. and Maclaran, P. (2006) 'Focus groups in marketing research', in R.W. Belk (ed.), *Handbook of Qualitative Research Methods in Marketing*, Cheltenham, UK and Northampton, MA, USA: Edward Elgar Publishing, 255–267.

Cochoy, F. (1998) 'Another discipline for the market economy: Marketing as a performative knowledge and know-how for capitalism', in M. Callon (ed.), *The Laws of the Market*, Oxford and Malden, MA: Blackwell, 194–221.

Dodson, D. (2008) 'Global fragrance market booms', *Global Cosmetic Industry*, February, 44–46.

Du Gay, P. and Pryke, M. (2002) *Cultural Economy: Cultural Analysis and Commercial Life*, London: Sage.

Falk, J. (2008) 'Collaboration and the golden rule', *Global Cosmetic Industry*, February, 48–51.

Faulconbridge, J. (2007) 'Relational networks of knowledge production in transnational law firms', *Geoforum*, 38, 925–940.

Gertler, M. (2008) 'Buzz without being there? Communities of practice in context', in A. Amin and J. Roberts (eds), *Community, Economic Creativity, and Organization*, Oxford and New York: Oxford University Press, 203–226.

Gherardi, S. (2006) *Organizational Knowledge: The Texture of Workplace Learning*, Oxford: Blackwell.

Gobe, M. (2007) *Brandjam: Humanizing Brands through Emotional Design*, New York: Allworth.

Grabher, G. (2002) 'The project ecology of advertising: Task, talents and teams', *Regional Studies*, 36, 245–263.

Grabher, G. and Ibert, O. (2006) 'Bad company? The ambiguity of personal knowledge networks', *Journal of Economic Geography*, 6, 3, 251–271.

Grabher, G., Ibert, O. and Flohr, S. (2008) 'The neglected king: The customer in the new knowledge ecology of innovation', *Economic Geography*, 84, 3, 253–280.

Hall, S. (2008) 'Geographies of business education: MBA programmes, reflexive business schools and the cultural circuit of capital', *Transactions of the Institute of British Geographers*, 33, 1, 27–41.

Ibert, O. (2007) 'Towards a geography of knowledge creation', *Regional Studies*, 41, 1, 103–114.

Ibert, O. (2010) 'Dynamische Geographien der Wissensproduktion: Die Bedeutung physischer wie relationaler Distanzen in interaktiven Lernprozessen', IRS Working Paper 41, Leibniz-Institut für Regionalentwicklung und Strukturplanung, Erkner.

Jeffries, N. (2007) 'Selling the experience: New York focuses on fragrance and marketing, and re-experiencing the segment', *Global Cosmetic Industry*, September, 32–35.

Jones, A. (2008) 'Beyond embeddedness: Economic practices and the invisible dimensions of transnational business activity', *Progress in Human Geography*, 32, 1, 71–88.

Kärreman, D. and Rylander, A. (2008) 'Managing meaning through branding: The case of a consulting firm', *Organization Studies*, 29, 1, 103–125.

Kubartz, B. (2009) 'Scent and the city: Perfume, consumption, and the urban economy', *Urban Geography*, 30, 4, 340–359.

Lash, S. (2008) 'Capitalism and metaphysics', *Theory, Culture and Society*, 24, 5, 1–26.

Lash, S. and Lury, C. (2007) *Global Culture Industry: The Mediation of Things*, London: Polity Press.

Lash, S. and Urry, J. (1994) *Economies of Signs and Space*, Thousand Oaks, CA: Sage.

Leadbeater, C. (1999) *Living on Thin Air: The New Economy*, London: Penguin.

Lury, C. (2004) *Brands: The Logos of the Global Economy*, New York: Routledge.

Morgan, K. (2004) 'The exaggerated death of geography: Learning, proximity and territorial innovation systems', *Journal of Economic Geography*, 4, 1, 3–21.

NellyRodi (2008) NellyRodi Trend Publications, http://www.nellyrodi.com, accessed 1 April 2008.

Olins, W. (2003) *On Brands*, New York: Thames and Hudson.

Pavitt, J. (2000) *Brand.New*, London: V&A Publications.

Pike, A. (2009) 'Geographies of brands and branding', *Progress in Human Geography*, 33, 5, 619–645.

Power, D. and Hauge, A. (2008) 'No man's brand – brands, institutions, and fashion', *Growth and Change*, 39, 1, 123–143.

Power, D. and Scott, A.J. (2004) *Cultural Industries and the Production of Culture*, London and New York: Routledge.

Pratt, A. (2004) 'The cultural economy: A call for spatialized "production of culture" perspectives', *International Journal of Cultural Studies*, 7, 117–128.

Reich, R. (1993) *The Work of Nations*, London and New York: Simon & Schuster.

Schatzki, T.R. (2001) 'Introduction: Practice theory', in T.R. Schatzki, K. Knorr Cetina and E. von Savigny (eds), *The Practice Turn in Contemporary Theory*, London and New York: Routledge, 1–14.

Sennett, R. (2006) *The Culture of the New Capitalism*, New Haven, CT: Yale University Press.

Storper, M. and Venables, A.J. (2004) 'Buzz: Face-to-face contact and the urban economy', *Journal of Economic Geography*, 4, 4, 351–370.

Turin, L. (2006) *The Secret of Scent: Adventures in Perfume and the Science of Smell*, New York: Ecco.

Vallance, P. (2007) 'Rethinking economic geographies of knowledge', *Geography Compass*, 1, 4, 797–813.

Wenger, E. (1998) *Communities of Practice: Learning, Meaning, and Identity*. Cambridge: Cambridge University Press.

# 9. Constructing brands from the outside? Brand channels, cyclical clusters and global circuits

**Dominic Power and Johan Jansson**

## INTRODUCTION

Traditionally, both the business and research worlds have posited direct links between products and place: Sheffield steel, Hollywood films, Paris fashion, Belgian chocolates, Swiss watches and Scandinavian design. It has been thought that regional and industrial success can be at least partly explained by mutually reinforcing effects: a locally embedded industry adds to the brand and vice versa. This view, we suggest, is too one-dimensional to explain the 'origins' of products or to explain how origins embed a place. In this chapter we explore the notion that the 'origins' of products can be considered to be 'collective brands' with considerable power. As such they are built up in a dialectical relationship between the product industries and their places. In particular, we suggest that it is important to understand that what happens outside the place can be as important to 'place-based brands' as what happens at home. The suggestion we put forward is that understandings of connections between products and place could benefit from thinking about the role and geographies of the 'brand channels' (Jansson and Power 2010) in which brands are constantly worked on. These brand channels are the spaces and conduits for the messages and various iterations that brands rest upon. However, just because the brand is about one place does not mean that the channels are constructed and transmitted locally. Rather we argue that it is important to think that brand channels are rooted in global circuits that are constantly reworked and renewed. This leads us to emphasize the role of 'cyclical events' and 'cyclical clusters' (Power and Jansson 2008) in both brand narratives and channels. In short we suggest that a whole series of processes on the outside, happening somewhere else, can be important to the place-based brands that many regions trade upon.

Before we move on, it is worth asking why thinking about where the communication lines and locus of power in place-based brands are might be important. In recent decades there has been considerable interest in the idea that certain places and regions act as particularly nurturing environments for product innovation and the creation of globally successful products. This idea is backed by an enormous body of research and policy that has shown that investing in regional industrial networks and systems can help boost places' economy and sustainability. Whilst this field of research has carefully directed attention at many aspects of product innovation and production it has tended to ignore the ways in which brands are built around products. Rather, it is often assumed that the brands will be best formed in a similar way to other aspects of product development: in the milieu the product is developed within. An implicit emphasis then is put on the primacy of the geography of the artefact's development and origination: where stuff, rather than brands, comes from. This chapter takes a rather different starting point. It suggests that value in the economy and industry is in many cases highly related to brands that have a significant attachment to and reliance on particular places and spatial processes. But these place-based brands often rely on narratives which are constructed and communicated through processes 'located' outside the place of origin.

Later in the chapter we use the example of Scandinavian design, which in its 50-year history has become an important identifier and brand used by design, architecture and fashion consumers and industries around the world to imbue cultural products and firms with various intangible values. This example is used to show that:

1.  industrial narratives can be crucial to producing imagined geographies of cultural production; and
2.  narratives of place have complex geographies that should be understood less in terms of their roots in that place than in terms of their roots in discursive fields played out through brand channels rooted in cyclical clusters in global circuits.

The chapter starts off with a discussion of brands and images as central to product and value chains in design- and fashion-based industries. The idea of using design-based industries and products as a focus is because these are industries where branding is often a crucial element in how firms create value and in how consumers understand product offerings. It is suggested that there are particular economic geographies and spaces for images and brands, and we attempt to illustrate this with the story of Scandinavian design as a constructed narrative formed by actors and processes outside Scandinavia's borders. The chapter concludes by suggesting that we must go beyond thinking about products' 'origins' in terms of place-based constructs and instead think about how spatial narratives are constructed in global brand circuits.

## PLACE-BASED BRANDS AND GLOBAL BRAND CIRCUITS

In recent years it has become clear that brands have a vital role in the economy and that brands have a widespread informational importance in modern society. It is no longer certain that firms engaged in selling even the most functional items are solely defined by their technical and manufacturing capacity. This is especially so for firms operating in design- and fashion-intensive sectors, such as the furniture and interiors sectors that much of this chapter uses as a case. In this example something as simple as a chair becomes a commodity defined as much by the quality of its construction and ergonomic functionality as by the fashion- and design-based brands that its creators use to package, market and sell it (McRobbie 1998). At a basic level, brands are nothing more than well-labelled information packages created in the hope of offering individual consumers (rather biased) help in negotiating the many chairs available to them. Brands are thus a proprietary set of product-specific characteristics, narratives and images that firms propagate. However, since brands are based on intangible product characteristics – look, feel, meaning and associations – it is obvious that they may connect with registers of meaning and association other than those intended by the brand proprietor. This raises an important question: if specific brands are judged on more than just the meanings and associations their owners ascribe to them then where else could these meanings and associations come from?

One answer to the above is that brand 'origins' matter. As Pike (2009) notes, place relates to brands through material and/or constructed connotations, associations, attachments, narratives, ties and so on: brands become entangled in 'inescapable spatial associations'. Many, if not most of, the brands that surround us are entangled with and inextricably linked to specific places; and this link is an element in the commercial fortunes of the brands. Many brands are thus, at least partly, place-based brands, since they trade upon their origins or where they come from.

However, the origins of something as intangible as a brand are hard to pin down, and understanding of brands' associations to place need to recognize that brand origins may be actual, constructed or perceived. They may be actual in the sense that it is possible to trace where they originally come from, for example Colombian coffee that is grown on farms in Colombia. Equally they may be constructed in the sense that different commercial actors process them and include them in their own firm's brand narratives, for example the Colombian coffee gets French roasted or becomes part of Brand X's instant coffee. Ultimately origins are always subject to consumers' perceptions, interpretations and misinterpretations, for example 'I don't care if it is Colombian or roasted by a French person as long as Brand X treats the farmers in a fair way.'

Thus place-based brands, like all brands, are only partially controlled by stakeholders or proprietors, since the value of the brand is as much a result of how a brand is received by relevant audiences or markets and/or consumers. By this we mean that the value of a brand is less an outcome of its simple positive or negative links to a place than a result of how it works in 'brand channels' that tap into global brand circuits (a topic we pick up further in the section on brand channels). In addition, individual product and firm brands are seldom isolated from the general context of where they come from. In a sense some sort of 'collective brand' or neighbourhood reputational effect arises around where a group of similar producers can be found (e.g. IT and Silicon Valley), or around where a particularly successful product was first developed (e.g. Guinness and Dublin). As soon as individual brands become entangled with place they have a share in the associations and brands developed by others in a place and in how consumers perceive that place.

The collective brand is thus a label that is commonly applied to and shared by a wider range of different activities. As such it can work as a unifying force, though it can also work as a restraining straitjacket, especially if the brand is forced upon a place through top-down processes (Jensen 2007): no matter what you do it can be hard not to be pigeonholed or be affected by the actions of others in your place of origin.

Economic geographers have long drawn attention to the importance of embedding within specific specialized industrial locations or milieus. Since later in this chapter we will be dealing with a place-based collective brand (Scandinavian design) it is important to note that there is a considerable body of work focused on agglomeration tendencies within fashion- and design-oriented industries. This work demonstrates how global competitiveness in fashion and design is intertwined with the existence of localized industrial systems for creative inspiration (McRobbie 1998; Breward *et al.* 2004), product innovation (Rantisi 2002b; Breward and Gilbert 2006; Weller 2007), knowledge and learning (Zukin 1991; Rantisi 2002a), inter-firm or inter-actor linkages (Hirsch 1972; Scott 1996; Barrera 2002; Hauge 2007; Weller 2007), labour availability and mobility (Zukin 1991; Neff *et al.* 2005; Vinodrai 2006), technological updating (Segre Reinach 2006), specialized services and institutions, and links to global commodity

chains (Leslie and Reimer 2003; Weller 2007). These accounts are primarily focused on production-related internalities and externalities: on the
idea that inter-firm and firm-based knowledge production, innovation or
learning are linked to regional specialization and excellence (Malmberg
and Power 2005). What these accounts generally lack is a more detailed
treatment of the role of these places as powerful markers of quality, specialization and agglomeration: that being associated with such places can
have a defining role in those firm- and product-specific branding processes.

For market segments where products' competitive and commercial
value ultimately rests in immaterial qualities and in differentiation from
competitors (Levitt 1975 [1960], 1981; Power and Scott 2004) – in the
products, positionality, acclaim, recognition and reputation – 'origins'
are central but also complex and potentially fluid. In particular, for these
sorts of products the crucial moments of value creation might not happen
behind the factory gates but in other places where products are received,
reviewed, consumed and recycled. Products here are commodities that are
framed by aesthetic, cultural and symbolic values that are constituted in
knowledge communities that are highly time and space sensitive (Storper
2000; Power and Scott 2004; Weller 2007). Such knowledge processes are
increasingly encapsulated in brands: negotiated and constructed fields that
act as markers and carriers for a range of aesthetic, symbolic and cultural
values and knowledge (Power and Hauge 2008). Brands are a reflection of
firms' consciousness of their need to differentiate themselves from competitors, as well as a reflection of consumers' needs both for cognitive ciphers
or navigation aids that help make choices easier and for identity kits that
allow them to position themselves in socio-cultural worlds. Branding is
an attempt strategically to 'personify' products, to give them a history,
personality and geography: to 'place' them.

The construction of origins does not, necessarily, mean that the origins
assigned to a product will be authentic or genuine. Indeed for many of the
products that surround us today it is hard to say exactly where and who
the producers are. For example, for the Danish furniture manufacturer
Eilersen is it most important that the firm has its history, design functions
and headquarters in Denmark even though much of its production occurs
in China? Or where do we place the origin of an iPhone when on the back it
states the phone is 'Designed by Apple in California. Assembled in China',
but is full of software and content from all over the world? Such examples
underline the complexity of origins in a globalized world and point to
the illusionary and interchangeable nature of origins. Firms often simultaneously try to highlight certain place associations whilst attempting to
mask or gloss over other elements of products' origins. Indeed many firms
try to obscure geographical associations and create somehow placeless,

mobile brands. One could add that it is not just the construction of origin that might matter here: destinations also matter to brands. If a product becomes fashionable in certain status markets can help add value in other markets: 'Success in New York' can thus be a sales argument alongside 'Origin: Stockholm'. Globalized value chains seem to make it difficult to say exactly where something comes from (or is going to). Nevertheless many actors seem to think it is important to attempt to place products.

Despite difficulties in assigning origins, the place of origin remains important to consumers: for example, Copenhagen and Milan have more positive design credentials than Limerick or Vladivostok. Places and sites can be of great importance as firms try to contribute to brands, protect them, use them, and manipulate them to appeal to key audiences. Place-based associations can have a significant effect on situating the knowledges and values brands aspire to utilize. Molotch (2003) suggests that place-based associations are often indivisible from products and that consumers attach place-informed evaluations to products of all sorts. The value of these place-based brands lies partly in their ability to persuade consumers of products' excellence, quality and innovation. Also the brand infuses products (and firms) with the 'feel' of the city or the region: for example, cool clothes come from cool places. Labels of origin such as 'Made in Italy', 'Scandinavian Design', or 'Rive Gauche' are far from neutral in their affect and are commonly used as strategic tools in the fashion industry (Hauge *et al.* 2009). Inherent in these differentiation processes is that they may produce and/or reproduce economic and social inequalities as well as amplifying unequal divisions of labour (Pike 2009). Positive connections between product images and place may create a kind of monopoly rent and can therein create entry barriers for products from competing places, and give firms an incentive for being in the 'right' place.

If brands and branding processes are important to global value chains then we must remember that economic geography has long drawn attention to the idea that connections through networks (be these networks of actors commodities, or production chains) are necessary for how we explain and understand the spaces that make up economic activity. Dicken *et al.* (2001: 95) argues:

> It becomes meaningless to talk of local versus global processes as in much of the global–local literature; instead we should think in terms of networks of agents (such as individuals, institutions or objects) acting across various distances and through diverse intermediaries.

Thus we must direct our efforts to understanding the complexities inherent in image-producing practices: practices which are seldom clearly local, global or extra-local, but set in global brand circuits. In a relational approach the spatial processes and anchoring of brands involve not just local actors but also ones that may never visit a place. Brands that have a global reach are entirely relational in their construction and should not be seen as 'bounded' indigenous creations but as constantly contested, changing and negotiated collections of fragmented artefacts that are subject to intertwined as well as isolated processes that can be local, global or, more often, multi-scalar.

## CHANNELLING THE BRAND: BRAND CHANNELS, CYCLICAL EVENTS AND GLOBAL CIRCUITS

Branding theory and practice tell us that effective brand vehicles or channels are needed to both maintain and disseminate brands. We thus need to look at how actors and products connect into global circuits: at the circuits and channels in which brands are constructed and communicated.

By the term 'brand channel' we mean a set of related or similar (and identifiable) spaces and activities through which many brands and messages can be simultaneously communicated and negotiated. The term implies that certain types of communicative space or media exist together as a connected channel (or as a collection of connected communities and channels) or as a network of activities, spaces and media in which various authors and consumers can publish their opinions about a type of meta-brand or narrative. Examples of such brand channels are: interlinked promotional events such as fashion and design weeks or seasons which are all about simultaneously promoting many firms and actors involved in the sale of seasonal collections and the wider branding of luxury goods conglomerates; specialized trade press and blogospheres that focus on specific types of product and activity; boosterist urban narratives aimed at using various techniques for the promotion of a positive reading of one place; or specialized retail districts where all the elements of the environment and product offer are geared towards the construction of desire enabling certain types of consumption (Jansson and Power 2010). Brand channels thus can be a series of organized events, a set of specific spaces, a dedicated communications or media sphere, or a coordinated branding campaign.

Rather like a TV channel, a brand channel acts as a communicative platform in which various messages and programmes can be delivered and consumed. As with TV channels they have their own particular identity and form, but unlike TV channels they do not have a general controller and it is hard to exclude actors from using or programming the channel.

This means that brand channels are shaped by various actors, stakeholders, stockholders and audiences. Each thus works according to a mess of countervailing organizational, individual and collective motivations. Despite being messy and unmanaged, these processes collectively and cumulatively constitute systems of communication. Thus brand channels may be formed by actors interested in individual acts of commercial branding (e.g. a designer) as well as broader coalitions acting towards collective branding (e.g. an aesthetic movement, a city authority's efforts). Through these various actors' use of, and investment in, similar types of spatially rooted branding vehicles (e.g. temporary promotional events, entrepreneurial narratives) they cumulatively give shape to effective communication channels. These channels are the result of local-level actions, initiatives and forces that most often do not have the promotion of particular places as their primary goal but rather the promotion and commercialization of fashion and design knowledge.

An example of such a brand channel would be a design and furniture trade fair, such as the one held annually in Milan (Power and Jansson 2008). This fair attracts a great deal of attention from around the world to the city of Milan and undoubtedly helps promote the city as a design capital. The effectiveness of the Milan design week though is not down to one actor alone but to the thousands of exhibitors and journalists that create content and invest in the design week's global promotion. The success of the design week is also down to the hundreds of thousands of trade visitors who visit the spaces created around the exhibits and the numerous professionals, critics and ordinary consumers who dissect the images and messages emitted by the design week into a myriad of websites, TV reportages and magazine columns around the world. A channel like this is used to broadcast messages about the meaning of design for, and in relation to, a variety of different actors (as we shall see, be they Scandinavian or Italian). Such channels are characterized by contested participation, recognition and ownership; and it is perhaps this contestation that is essential to explaining their dynamism.

In order for a brand channel to gain any longevity, a semblance of permanence must be achieved: if a brand channel is not regularly revisited and reused it will eventually fade from sight. It is thus important to note that, though many brand channels seem to be populated by temporary and pop-up events or phenomena, an underlying cyclicality or constancy to participation is necessary. In this sense they are 'cyclical clusters' of actors, actions and events: they are complexes of overlapping spaces that are timed and arranged in such a way that messages, markets and innovations can be reproduced and continuously renewed over time. The types of phenomena and action that characterize brand channels should not be viewed as freak extra-local happenings or as fragile globally stretched strings of periodic communication that are sideline outliers to the real business of embedded and enacted localized brands. Rather they should be seen as interlinked micro-phenomena arranged in global circuits which aggregate to form vital planks in global value constructions. Thus the effects of these channels reach beyond the single events that they may be concerned with and have long-lasting effects on brands and industries.

This theoretical framework suggests a strong relation between products, place and the idea of place-based brands. The relation between products, place and place-based brands is a complex weave of processes embedded in global circuits where temporary clusters or events contribute to the brand building of place-based products. Important elements in these processes are brand channels that throw out the brands' messages, although it is never entirely possible to manage these, since the message is constantly negotiated and re-negotiated in the microcosms of temporary clusters or events.

## CONSTRUCTING PRODUCT MEANING AND ORIGINS – SCANDINAVIAN DESIGN

In the chapter so far we have frequently referred to design and furniture as market segments where various types of brand are important: product-specific brands such as 'It's a Billy bookcase' (the IKEA bookcase that has sold more than 40 million units since 1979), corporate brands such as 'It's from IKEA', and more diffuse regional brands such as 'It's an example of Scandinavian design'. In this section we will look a little more closely at the latter: the regional brand Scandinavian design.

Scandinavia has been closely associated with interiors and furniture design for many decades. As design critics have noted, it is however hard to pin down a term with multiple meanings. Most commonly, the term 'Scandinavian design' indicates products that share a certain type of modernist artistic and design philosophy. In cultural circles it invokes certain stylistic and ideological approaches to design, handicrafts and architecture (Fiell and Fiell 2002; Halén and Wickman 2003): a philosophy that emphasizes democratic design principles, simplicity and functionality or, as Gregor Paulsson put it in 1919, 'Better things for everyday life' (Creagh *et al.* 2008). Paradoxically much of the everyday design produced in Scandinavia has been (or become regarded as) high-end and high-value design, and 'Scandinavian design' is a term often used to denote expensive modernist minimalist design pieces. Yet another meaning for the concept is that it is used as a catch-all term for twentieth-century big-name designers and architects who happen to come from Northern Europe, for example Arne Jacobsen, Alvar Aalto, Verner Panton and Jørn Utzon. At a completely different end of the furniture market, 'Scandinavian design' has been used by various firms to describe and aggressively mass-market mass-produced furniture. The most prominent of these firms is Dutch-registered IKEA, which has built much of its brand around its 'Scandinavian' heritage (it was founded in Sweden) and elements of Scandinavian culture (such as using the colours of the Swedish flag on its storefronts and the use of Nordic languages in its product naming).

'Scandinavian design' then is a slippery term, since it covers a range of things from a philosophical or stylistic marker to a term associated with high-cachet marketable design products as well as low-cost mass-produced furniture. Many place-based brands are similarly slippery, since they stand for, or are used for, a wide range of different things. It may be surmised that it is this very diversity of use and exposure that marks out particularly successful and sustainable place-based brands.

Apart from the difficulty in defining exactly what Scandinavian design denotes, there is a difficulty defining the geographical area itself. There is indeed a far longer history of ideology, power, confusion and discourse involved in the term 'Scandinavia' than there is in the term 'Scandinavian design'. In a very general sense Scandinavia denotes the geographical and cultural proximity of Denmark, Norway and Sweden, and in some interpretations includes Finland. The term however masks a diversity of cultural, linguistic, governmental and historical backgrounds and experiences. For these reasons the term 'the Nordic countries' is more commonly used in the area of Northern Europe that 'Scandinavia' is thought to denote: Norway, Sweden, Denmark, Finland and Iceland, including their associated territories (Greenland, the Faroe Islands, and Åland).

If the term has many different connotations then it has also had many different proponents. What is interesting in looking at these voices in defining the brand narrative is that many of the loudest and earliest voices were not local actors attempting to create for themselves a positive brand. The term 'Scandinavian design' first appeared in 1951 in conjunction with two parallel exhibitions of home decoration and furniture run in London: 'Scandinavia at Table' organized by the British Council of Industrial Design and 'Scandinavian Design for Living' at Heal's store in London (Davies 2003). The exhibition was the first of a series of showcases for Nordic design, decoration and furniture. In 1954–57 'Design in Scandinavia' toured Canada and the United States to great success, and similar collaborative exhibitions in Milan during the 1950s and Paris in 1958 ('Formes Scandinaves') helped to form a globally recognized label that has been used to brand a wide variety of products (though most

particularly furniture). Its first outings then were largely marketing and
co-branding attempts to promote the furniture trade.

The term first started entering more esoteric design discourses and
circles when it was used in critical debates within Italy on the direction of
Italian design. In fact Milan-based design events have had a significant
role in the history and formation of Scandinavian design: the formative individual and group exhibits of various combinations of products
from Nordic nations at the *Triennale di Milano* during the late 1940s
and throughout the 1950s; and as the key site for a debate within Italian
design circles that used the term as a focus for discussion on Italy's design
direction. The term then has been used as a signifier in wider cultural and
political projects as well as a signifier used in the marketing of commercial
commodities:

> Clearly Britain and the United States were not the countries where
> Scandinavian design came from but they were two of the world's major
> markets for such things and formed significant venues in and for which ideas
> about this peculiarly transnational commodity were given shape. Because of
> this market basis . . . Scandinavian design can be understood as something of
> a marketing ploy, and the ideas generated about it as, in effect, a sales pitch.
> (Davies 2003: 102)

In the region itself this 'sales pitch' has met with sometimes mixed
responses. For many it was welcomed, since it was a very positive recognition that Scandinavia's reputation for competitive design commodities is not entirely unfounded. This has meant that in recent years trade
organizations and public actors in the region have been happy to help
promote the brand abroad. As recently as 2007 a travelling showcase
for Scandinavian design was promoting the idea in museums around the
world: the exhibition 'Scandinavian Design beyond Myth', sponsored
by the Nordic Council of Ministers, was shown in Berlin, Milan, Ghent,
Prague, Budapest, Riga, Glasgow, Copenhagen, Gothenburg, Oslo, Vigo,
La Coruña, Sofia, Belgrade and Zagreb. However, if the history of the
brand has been one written largely outside the Nordic region at 'home',
it is one that has drawn frequent attack from 'Scandinavian' designers
who have rejected it as overly general, dangerously homogenizing, irrel-
evant and inaccurate. In Oslo in 1980 a group of designers even staged a
mock burial for the term. Though the creation of regional images is often
fraught with questions of authenticity and validity there is a deeply rooted
tradition of design in these countries: both as an input into industrial production and as an everyday presence (Fiell and Fiell 2002; Power 2009).
In Sweden design has long had a prominent place in society and been supported by design-conscious consumers and a set of supporting institutions:

the Swedish Society of Crafts and Design (Svensk Form), founded in 1845, is the world's oldest design association. In addition, many of the countries' more successful companies have consciously used design in order to establish their competitive edges. The brand or set of myths that is Scandinavian design is then not merely an overly general external imposition, though nor is it purely a self-construction for marketing purposes. As Davies suggests:

> Whilst there is a good case to suggest that these meanings may have been 'a fiction to suit the South', that is for the consumption of the non-Nordic world, they were also fictions, often flattering, that suited the North – especially Nordic manufacturers – and, in reality must have largely originated there. (Davies 2003: 109)

'Scandinavian design' then is a slippery term that has been used to denote a diversity of products, designs and characteristics. Equally it has been used by both 'insiders' and 'outsiders' to denote regional, supra-national and trans-national spaces, though in the context of the relational flows, networks, brand channels, cyclical clusters and global circuits we describe such scalar distinctions are hard to maintain. The strength of the brand may indeed lie less in its local roots or origins than in the diversity and complexity of the discursive fields it is played out through.

## CONCLUSION

The example of Scandinavian design may be interesting in several ways to readers of this book. Firstly, it is an example of a long-running product-oriented narrative that has a powerful role in defining and marketing design and furniture. This means that it mirrors most of the characteristics of a brand. However, it is different to the majority of commercially successful brands that surround us. It is a collective brand in the sense that many actors are involved and affected and there is no single controlling or owning structure behind its development. Secondly, it is a brand with very strong regional and geographical associations and implications. In this sense it is an important unifying and defining narrative that connects all sorts of different regions, products and sectors: from Danish furniture production to Finnish and Norwegian architecture. Equally it may also represent an oppressive identity with long roots that could potentially stifle and filter out alternative emerging imageries. Thirdly, it is an example of an imagined geography and community that has largely been constructed by actors and in channels from outside the places the brand explicated links to.

In this chapter we have used several concepts we hope can help in understanding brands in general and place-specific brands in particular. We have used the term 'brand channels' to underline our view that it is crucial to understand brands not only in terms of what they signify and symbolize (their emotional impact, etc.) but also in terms of the infrastructure around the narrative circuits they are based on. These brand channels are not the same as local production milieus or image factories. However, they do share some of the characteristics that typify successful localized clusters. For example, these brand channels rest upon cyclical and reproducible interactive processes, and these interactive processes or relations are in many ways spatially embedded, bounded, policed and made up of actors linked together around a core product: a collective brand.

Thinking about branded commodities in terms of brand channels helps one appreciate the complex geographies that underpin an economy of signs and symbols. These geographies go far beyond easy dualisms such as global versus local. We are talking about a space economy, but it is one where hybrid globalized connections and circuits abound: a space economy where the brand capacities and opportunities that firms from one region may rely upon are reflexively related to multi-scalar and cyclical collective processes. Indeed, as the Scandinavian design story attests, even explicitly regional brands may be subject to a set of construction spaces that need not be the same as, or intersect with, those involved in material construction or distribution. For firms and regions linked to such brands, what happens at home is of course important, but so too is how they connect into global brand channels and circuits: the medium and the message can have a very separate life to the product.

## REFERENCES

Barrera, T.O. (2002) 'Enterprise clusters and industrial districts in Colombia's fashion sector', *European Planning Studies*, 10, 5, 541–563.

Breward, C. and Gilbert, D. (eds) (2006) *Fashion's World Cities*, New York: Berg.

Breward, C., Ehrman, E. and Ewans, C. (2004) *The London Look: Fashion from Street to Catwalk*, London: Museum of London.

Creagh, L., Kåberg, H. and Lane, B. (eds) (2008) *Modern Swedish Design: Three Founding Texts*, New York: Museum of Modern Art.

Davies, K. (2003) 'Marketing ploy or democratic ideal? On the mythology of Scandinavian design', in W. Halén and K. Wickman (eds), *Scandinavian Design beyond the Myth: Fifty Years of Design from the Nordic Countries*, Stockholm: Arvinius Förlag/Form Förlag, 101–110.

Dicken, P., Kelly, P.F., Olds, K. and Yeung, H.W.-C. (2001) 'Chains and networks, territories and scales: Towards a relational framework for analyzing the global economy', *Global Networks: A Journal of Transnational Affairs*, 1, 2, 89–112.

Fiell, C. and Fiell, P. (2002) *Scandinavian Design*, Köln: Taschen.

Halén, W. and Wickman, K. (eds) (2003) *Scandinavian Design beyond the Myth: Fifty Years of Design from the Nordic Countries*, Stockholm: Arvinius Förlag/ Form Förlag.

Hauge, A. (2007) *Dedicated Followers of Fashion: An Economic Geographic Analaysis of the Swedish Fashion Industry*, Uppsala: Uppsala University.

Hauge, A., Malmberg, A. and Power, D. (2009) 'The spaces and places of Swedish fashion', *European Planning Studies*, 17, 4, 529–547.

Hirsch, P. (1972) 'Processing fads and fashions: An organization-set analysis of cultural industry system', *American Journal of Sociology*, 77, 639–659.

Jansson, J. and Power, D. (2010) 'Fashioning a global city: Global city brand channels in the fashion and design industries', *Regional Studies*, 44, 889–904.

Jensen, O. (2007) 'Culture stories: Understanding cultural urban branding', *Planning Theory*, 6, 3, 211–236.

Leslie, D. and Reimer, S. (2003) 'Fashioning furniture: Restructuring the furniture commodity chain', *Area*, 35, 4, 427–437.

Levitt, T. (1975 [1960]) 'Marketing myopia', *Harvard Business Review*, 53, 5, 26–42.

Levitt, T. (1981) 'Marketing intangible products and product intangibles', *Harvard Business Review*, 59, 3, 94–103.

Malmberg, A. and Power, D. (2005) '(How) do (firms in) clusters create knowledge?', *Industry and Innovation*, 12, 4, 409–431.

McRobbie, A. (1998) *British Fashion Design: Rag Trade or Image Industry?*, London: Routledge.

Molotch, H. (2003) *Where Stuff Comes From: How Toasters, Toilets, Cars, Computers and Many Other Things Come to Be as They Are*, London: Routledge.

Neff, G., Wissinger, E. and Zukin, S. (2005) 'Entrepreneurial labor among cultural producers: "Cool" jobs in "Hot" industries', *Social Semiotics*, 15, 3, 307–334.

Pike, A. (2009) 'Geographies of brands and branding', *Progress in Human Geography*, 33, 619–645.

Power, D. (2009) 'Creativity and innovation in the Scandinavian design industry', in P. Jeffcutt and A. Pratt (eds), *Creativity and Innovation in the Cultural Economy*, London: Routledge, 200–216.

Power, D. and Hauge, A. (2008) 'No man's brand – brands, institutions, fashion and the economy', *Growth and Change*, 39, 1, 123–143.

Power, D. and Jansson, J. (2008) 'Cyclical clusters in global circuits: Overlapping spaces and furniture industry trade fairs', *Economic Geography*, 84, 4, 423–448.

Power, D. and Scott, A. (2004) 'A prelude to cultural industries and the production of culture', in D. Power and A. Scott (eds), *Cultural Industries and the Production of Culture*, London: Routledge, 3–15.

Rantisi, N. (2002a) 'The competitive foundations of localized learning and innovation: The case of women's garment production in New York City', *Economic Geography*, 78, 4, 441–462.

Rantisi, N. (2002b) 'The local innovation system as a source of variety: Openness and adaptability in New York City's garment district', *Regional Studies*, 36, 6, 587–602.

Scott, A. (1996) 'The craft, fashion, and cultural-products industries of Los Angeles: Competitive dynamics and policy dilemmas in a multisectoral image-producing complex', *Annals of the Association of American Geographers*, 86, 2, 306–323.

Segre Reinach, S. (2006) 'Milan: The city of prêt-à-porter in a world of fast fashion', in C. Breward and D. Gilbert (eds), *Fashion's World Cities*, Oxford: Berg.

Storper, M. (2000) 'Globalisation and knowledge flows: An industrial geographer's perspective', in J. Dunning (ed.), *Regions, Globalisation and the Knowledge-Based Economy*, Oxford: Oxford University Press, 42–62.

Vinodrai, T. (2006) 'Reproducing Toronto's design ecology: Career paths, intermediaries, and local labor markets', *Economic Geography*, 82, 3, 237–263.

Weller, S. (2007) 'Fashion as viscous knowledge: Fashion's role in shaping trans-national garment production', *Journal of Economic Geography*, 7, 1, 39–66.

Zukin, S. (1991) *Landscapes of Power: From Detroit to Disney World*, Berkeley: University of California Press.

# 10. The making and recontextualizing of 'competitiveness' as a knowledge brand across different sites and scales

**Ngai-Ling Sum**

## INTRODUCTION

Research on brands and branding is emerging as an important new area in interdisciplinary studies. Studies range from commercial brands to cities (and nations) as brands and objects of branding. With the growing demand for fast strategy and policy in a globalized world marked by space-time compression and acceleration, knowledge is increasingly subject to commodification – justified in many cases in the name of the knowledge-based economy, knowledge-intensive business services, and intellectual property rights. In this context some forms of knowledge are branded and marketed for profit through consultancy in the fields of business strategy and public policy. Such brands are not confined to the scientific or intellectual 'mainstream', however defined; knowledge and ideas are also branded and marketed for profit at the margins of the mainstream and beyond – with more successful cases sometimes being 'mainstreamed' in due course. In this regard, if we accept that the primary purpose of knowledge brands is to maximize profit or revenues from the sale of knowledge-intensive services, it would be misleading to apply this notion to the activities of public intellectuals (e.g. Noam Chomsky, Umberto Eco) in seeking intellectual influence or to the mobilization of 'knowledge from below' (e.g. Paulo Freire, Italian automomists) to challenge political authority, professional expertise, or commodified knowledge. It is interesting to note here the self-reflection by Naomi Klein in the introduction to the tenth anniversary edition of *No Logo* (2010) on whether her critique of branding has become a brand in its own right – an idea she claims to have explicitly disavowed and avoided for 10 years.

This distinction allows this chapter to focus on some leading examples of (mainstreamed) knowledge brands. The latter include Porter's 'competitive advantage' in cluster development, Florida's 'creative class' in urban regeneration, Lundvall's 'national/regional innovation system' in science, technology and capability building, and Lall's 'technological capabilities' in developing countries. These brands, which are promoted by academic gurus, research centres, business schools, think tanks, consultancy firms, international and regional organizations, service-oriented NGOs and so on, may be selectively hybridized and recombined in the (inter-)national academic-consultancy policy circuits in order to secure a particular geographical-historical fit. It is beyond the scope of this chapter to examine a wide range of knowledge brands in the policy circuits and their hybridizations in different scales and sites. Instead I will take the Harvard-Porterian brand of 'competitive advantage' to illustrate some of the practices and processes involved in the making of a knowledge brand without claiming that it represents a typical or ideal average example.

The chapter has three sections. The first argues that the knowledge of competitiveness was translated into a brand through three overlapping stages: theoretical paradigm, policy paradigm and knowledge brand. The second section examines the geography of the redefinition and recontextualization of this brand at various scales (from global to local) and for different kinds of site at each scale with a view to demonstrating the spatio-temporal and substantive specificities of knowledge brands. The final section concludes with reflections on brand negotiation (e.g. 'responsible competitiveness') in times of financial crisis and the material issues related to this process.

## THE DEVELOPMENT OF 'COMPETITIVENESS' AS A KNOWLEDGE BRAND

Discourses on 'competitiveness' date back centuries and have been linked to very diverse economic imaginaries in different times and contexts (see Reinert 2008). This section tracks the development of 'competitiveness' as a knowledge brand from the 1960s through three overlapping stages (see Table 10.1). Stage one saw the development of the theoretical paradigm that underpins the neoliberal competitiveness imaginary. This paradigm draws in part on a Schumpeterian body of knowledge that emphasizes the creatively destructive nature of innovation and the virtues of entrepreneurial competition and in part on the neoliberal concern with the role of market forces as the key driver in competition (Schumpeter 1934). With the end of the post-war boom and the emergence of major new technologies (especially information and communication technologies), his theory

*Table 10.1*    *Three overlapping stages in the development of 'competitiveness' as hegemonic policy discourses since the 1960s*

| Overlapping stages in the development of the 'cultures of competitiveness' | Articulation of major discourses and practices | Major authors/ institutions |
|---|---|---|
| **Stage 1** Theoretical paradigm | Technology, innovation and national competitiveness research monographs and papers | Schumpeter, Posner, Vernon, Freeman, etc. |
| **Stage 2** Policy paradigm | Competitiveness policy, competitiveness commissions, white papers and technology policy | Commission of Industrial Competitiveness, Council on Competitiveness, OECD, EU, etc. |
| **Stage 3** Management/consultancy knowledge and knowledge brand | Diamond model, clusters, cluster charts, indices, pilot projects, workshops and training courses | Porter, Harvard Business School, Monitor Group, World Economic Forum, etc. (see also Table 10.2) |

*Source:*    Author's own compilation.

was used to highlight technological change and innovation as central to long-run economic dynamics. In this stage competitiveness was largely framed in terms of academic accounts of technological and organizational innovation, R&D in enterprises, the role of patents, competitiveness and trade policy (e.g. Posner 1961; Vernon 1966; Freeman 1982).

These theoretical accounts were translated into policy discourses around questions of national geo-economic competitiveness at this second stage. Policies were narrated in terms of innovation- and technology-driven growth corresponding to a competitiveness framework (for two overviews of this development, see Dosi and Soete 1988; Fagerberg 1996). This occurred in a conjuncture when the USA and UK were experiencing low growth, rising unemployment, high inflation and techno-economic decline vis-à-vis Japan and East Asia in the 1980s (D'Andrea Tyson 1988; Krugman 1995). These changes were narrated in terms of a 'loss of competitiveness' compared to faster-growing economies in Europe and the East. The Reagan Administration responded in 1983 by establishing the Commission on Industrial Competitiveness, followed in 1988 by the Council on Competitiveness. Both bodies comprised industrial, labour and academic leaders and placed national competitiveness at the centre of national policy discourses and public consciousness. A parallel trend, influenced by Lundvall's 'national system of innovation', occurred in the Organisation for Economic Co-operation and Development (OECD), which is a service-oriented think tank for its member states, in its emphasis on science and technology. This theme was raised as early as 1962 (OECD 1962a), but the OECD's engagement intensified in the 1980s and 1990s, producing detailed policy data and analyses on technology, productivity and economic growth (e.g. OECD 1962b). Narrated more in the languages of 'technology policy' and 'national system of innovation' (see Miettinen 2002), this gradual move from theoretical to policy paradigm was reinforced by the reorientation of the EU on similar lines with the publication of the European Commission's White Paper on Growth Competitiveness and Employment (1993), Green Paper on Innovation (1995), Lisbon Strategy for Competitiveness (2000) and so on.

This rise of Schumpeterian-inspired accounts of competitiveness as a major policy paradigm was reinforced and supported by parallel developments in management theories and business studies. This introduced stage three, when the new policy paradigm was translated into management or consultancy knowledge about 'getting the competitiveness right'. The latter was articulated by experts such as business school professors (e.g. Michael E. Porter from Harvard Business School), consultancy firms and think tanks. These had become an important part of the transnational knowledge-policy circuit and constructed 'marketable' meaning-making models or apparatuses bundled with claims to problem-solving competencies.

Porter, as a Harvard Business School professor and consultant, was renowned for his analyses of the competitiveness of firms and industries (1980, 1985). His work won early attention in the policy field (e.g. he served on Reagan's first Presidential Commission on Competitiveness), and he later applied his firm-level approach to national and regional case studies. His best-selling 1990 book, The *Competitive Advantage of Nations*, studied the industries of 10 nations to explain both why a nation succeeds in some industries but not all and why some industries were more competitive in some nations than others. On this basis, he constructed the interactive 'diamond model' (see Figure 10.1) based on four factors conducive to the development of competitiveness: demand conditions; factor conditions; firm strategy, structure and rivalry; and related and supporting industries. These were reinforced by 'chance' and the 'government' as additional, but not decisive, factors. For Porter, the co-evolution

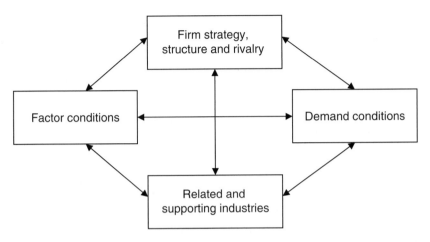

*Source:*    Adapted from Porter (1990: 127).

*Figure 10.1    Porter's diamond model of national advantage*

of these factors creates the 'microeconomic foundations of prosperity' that enable national firms to gain and sustain competitive advantages. He added that these micro-foundations would be strongest when they formed a 'cluster', a concept that depicts 'a geographic concentration of competing and cooperating companies, suppliers, service providers, and associated institutions' (Porter 1990). Such concentration enhances interaction among the four factors in Porter's diamond to boost productivity, growth, employment and, hence, competitiveness.

Porter's model has provoked debates, criticisms and support. Some business and management scholars (e.g. Gray 1991; Stopford and Strange 1991) criticized it for lack of formal modelling, while others (e.g. Thurow 1990; Rugman 1991; Dunning 1992) challenged its originality. Porter's 'cluster' concept has also been criticized in regional studies as chaotic, loose and imprecise, making it hard to deploy for concrete public intervention (Martin and Sunley 2003). Nonetheless the cluster approach is often discussed as a key strand in the 'spatial agglomeration' and 'industrial district' literature and has often been repeated within the policy circuit as one of the leading ideas that frame regional development and proposals for local development. For example, the UK government's Improvement and Development Agency for local government (IDeA) has a special website page on Porter's ideas, noting that, 'despite (the) plethora of competing but similar ideas, Porter's theory became, for some time, the established "industry standard"'.

This status as an 'industry standard' underpins its role as a knowledge brand. It acquires its brand status partly owing to: (1) the cliché and quality guarantee that comes with Harvard University and the Harvard Business School; (2) the generality, simplicity and flexibility of 'competitiveness', which allow diverse interpretations, frequent renewal, and building of possible alliances among actors involved in economic strategies; (3) the promotion and circulation of this body of knowledge by diverse institutions across the global, regional, national and local scales (see Table 10.2); (4) the accumulation of credibility as it echoes within and across idea-policy networks – especially when backed by celebrity guru academics (e.g. Porter) and high-profile conferences, business media and journals; (5) the offer of ready-made policy advice (e.g. cluster-based strategies) as national or regional re-engineering solutions in the face of growing pressures for fast policy and the fear of economic restructuring in a global information age; (6) the high-paid careers possible in consultancy policy work; and (7) the popularization of the 'cluster approach' by Harvard-related institutions (on the consultancy guru industry, see Huczynski 1996; Collins 2000; Jackson 2001; Clark and Fincham 2002).

The growing popularization (and commercialization) of this approach was stimulated by worries about US competitiveness from the late 1980s onwards, leading to various initiatives in different contexts. One important example among many was the establishment in 2001 of the Harvard Business School Institute for Strategy and Competitiveness. The institute is headed by Porter and focuses its research on the strategic implications of competitive forces for firms as well as nations, regions and cities. Its website declares that this international research institute 'is dedicated to extending the research pioneered by Professor Porter and disseminating it to scholars and practitioners on a global basis'. This concern with extending and disseminating Porter's model is reflected in, and facilitated by, the setting up of institutions associated with Harvard Business School (e.g. the Institute for Competitiveness in Barcelona and the Asia Competitiveness Institute in Singapore) and of associated strategy firms (e.g. Monitor Group and ontheFRONTIER Group). Through their joint claims to expertise and efforts, Porter's cluster-based strategy is flexibly applied to quite different countries (e.g. Canada, Denmark, New Zealand, Portugal, Sweden and Switzerland) and regions or cities (e.g. Atlanta, Rhône-Alpes, the Baltic Sea, Singapore, and Hong Kong/Pearl River Delta). Strategy firms like ontheFRONTIER Group have also adapted it to so-called 'emerging markets' (e.g. Mexico, Peru, Bolivia and Rwanda).

Apart from the Harvard-associated organizations, this knowledge brand – albeit not always purely Porterian in content – has been

*Table 10.2    Examples of institutions and discourses related to competitiveness at different scales*

| Scales | Examples of institutions involved | Examples of competitiveness discourses or instruments |
|---|---|---|
| Global/ international | World Economic Forum | ● Global Competitiveness Report and Global Competitiveness Index |
| | Institute for Management Development | ● World Competitiveness Yearbook and World Competitiveness Scoreboard |
| | The Competitiveness Institute | ● The Cluster Initiative Database<br>● The Cluster Initiative Greenbook 2003 |
| | United Nations Industrial Development Organization (UNIDO) | ● Clusters and Networks Development Programme 2005 |
| Regional | Asian Development Bank | ● Asian Development Outlook 2003: III Competitiveness in Developing Countries |
| | African Union | ● Pan African Competitiveness Forum 2008 |
| | Inter-American Development Bank | ● Competitiveness of Small Enterprises: Cluster and Local Development 2007 |
| National | United States Agency for International Development (USAID) | ● African Global Competitiveness Initiative 2006 |
| | Japan International Cooperation Agency (JICA) | ● Strategic Investment Action Plan (Competitiveness/ SME) 2005 |
| Local/city | Numerous (inter-)city competitiveness projects and plans | ● The Hong Kong Advantage 1997<br>● OECD's International Conference on City Competitiveness 2005<br>● Remaking Singapore 2008 |

*Source:*    Author's own compilation based on website information of these institutions, accessed 29 July 2009.

*Table 10.3　Two knowledge apparatuses and knowledging technologies in the construction of 'competitiveness'*

| Knowledge apparatuses/ instruments | Knowledging technologies in meaning-making | Major institutional sites/ actors |
| --- | --- | --- |
| *Benchmarking reports and indices constructed in:* | | |
| Global Competitiveness Report | Technologies of performance and judgement | World Economic Forum |
| Growth and Business Competitiveness Indices and Global Competitiveness Index | | |
| *Cluster-and-chain metaphors constructed in:* | | |
| Asian Development Outlook 2003: III Competitiveness in Developing Countries | Technologies of agency (see Table 10.6) | Asian Development Bank |
| Other reports (see Table 10.5) | | Other institutions (see Table 10.5) |

*Source:*　Author's own compilation.

adopted or adapted on different scales by international authorities (e.g. World Economic Forum and United Nations Industrial Development Organization), regional banks (e.g. Asian Development Bank), national agencies (e.g. United States Agency for International Development and Asia Competitiveness Institute) and city governments and development agencies (for example, see Table 10.2). Complementary sites in these knowledge networks include other business schools, consultancy firms, chambers of commerce, think tanks, research institutes, business and mass media, town hall meetings, luncheon gatherings and public performances (e.g. conferences and speeches). The presence of celebrity consultant gurus magnifies the impact of such media and events (Huczynski 1996; Jackson 2001). In turn this body of management knowledge circulates widely and resonates strongly in policy networks in developed and developing countries, gaining credibility from its promotion by strategists and consultants, opinion-forming journalists, leading policy makers and executives who recontextualize, package and market related discourses. Key apparatuses here include outlooks, reports, indices, scoreboards, databases, cluster plans, best practices, training courses and so on (see Tables 10.2 and 10.3).

These institutions, agencies and actors have quite heterogeneous motives and may produce contrary or contradictory substantive effects. Any coherence they may have in contributing to the circulation of competitiveness as a set of neoliberal discourses and practices is the product of contingent convergence, structural coupling and skilful recontextualization rather than attributable to a single, top-down, global neoliberal project, let alone to a neoliberal 'conspiracy'. For this very reason its reproduction and effects are fragile and require continuing suturing or 'repair work' at many sites and scales (see also below).

Given their 'coherence' and pervasiveness across different scales and sites, Porter-inspired ideas about competitiveness gradually acquired brand status in policy-consultancy circuits. Like consumer brands (Lury 2004), knowledge brands address the rational and irrational aspects of human nature. Cognitively, a brand like Porter's competitiveness 'diamond' or 'cluster' model is rationalized and legitimated by its association with Harvard Business School, circulation among policy elites, distinctive policy advice, re-engineering solutions and individual career benefits. Emotionally, it addresses pride, anxieties, threats and social tensions linked to growth or decline, development, and the intense pressures of economic restructuring in a globalized information age. These rational and irrational effects shape struggles to make a brand hegemonic. In the present context (bearing in mind the purposes for which these brands are being promoted), a knowledge brand can be defined as a resonant hegemonic meaning-making device advanced in various ways by 'world-class' guru academic consultants who claim unique knowledge of the economic and development world and commercially translate this into transnational policy symbols, recipes and tool kits that address social tensions, contradictions and dilemmas and also appeal to pride, threats and anxieties about socio-economic restructuring and changes.

## THE GEOGRAPHY OF THE KNOWLEDGE BRAND: MAKING AND RECONTEXTUALIZING 'COMPETITIVENESS' ACROSS DIFFERENT SITES AND SCALES

In circulating transnationally, this Harvard-related brand offers a stable but flexible template that not only travels but is recontextualized to changing global, regional, national and local contexts. Bernstein's concept of 'recontextualization' denotes that agents selectively appropriate, relocate, refocus and recombine pedagogic discourses in applying them to other discursive fields in ways that both fit and reaffirm existing social relations

*Table 10.4     World Economic Forum and its global competitiveness rankings of the USA and selected Asian countries, 2004–08*

|                | Index 2008–09 | Rank 2008–09 | Rank 2004–05 |
|----------------|:-------------:|:------------:|:------------:|
| United States  | 5.74          | 1            | 2            |
| Singapore      | 5.53          | 5            | 7            |
| Japan          | 5.38          | 9            | 9            |
| Hong Kong      | 5.33          | 11           | 29           |
| South Korea    | 5.28          | 13           | 21           |
| Taiwan, China  | 5.22          | 17           | 4            |
| Malaysia       | 5.04          | 21           | 31           |
| China          | 4.47          | 30           | 46           |
| India          | 4.33          | 50           | 55           |
| Indonesia      | 4.25          | 55           | 69           |

*Source:*   World Economic Forum, Global Competitiveness Reports 2007–09.

(1996: 47). In terms of the geography of knowledge brands, this section examines the recontextualization of 'competitiveness' discourses in two sites and scales, namely (1) the construction of benchmarking reports and indices by the World Economic Forum (WEF) for global application, and (2) the use of metaphors such as 'clusters' and 'chains' in economic outlooks or commissioned reports in the Asian region (see Table 10.3).

**On a Global Scale: Construction of Benchmarking Reports and Indices**

In line with and as part of the rise of global managerialism (Murphy 2008), 'competitiveness' discourses are linked to the development of knowledging apparatuses such as benchmarking reports and indices. The 2004–05 version of the World Economic Forum report was presented by its publisher (Macmillan) as a 'unique benchmarking tool in identifying obstacles to economic growth and assist [*sic*] in the design of better economic policies'. It achieves this partly through its use of 'indices' that are instruments dominated by the language of competition and principle of performance. The composition of the WEF indices has been updated four times between 2000 and 2009 (Sum 2009b: 200). Despite the increasing sophistication in index construction, this knowledge instrument still relies on assigning numbers to countries. It ranks and scores countries in terms of evaluative rules, scoring the presence or absence of certain factors of competitiveness (see Table 10.4). Notwithstanding their relatively short history, these indices are becoming part of a global statistical instrumentarium produced by international private authority. This does not mean that they are not questioned (Krugman 1994; Lall 2001; Kaplan 2003), but their continuous circulation and recognition in the policy-consultancy world reinforce their hegemonic potential within and across many economic and political spaces. As a largely managerial body of economic discourse, it is dominated by the language of competition and performance in and through which indices serve to visibilize countries' competitive strengths and weaknesses. Countries are located in a number order which then operates as a disciplinary tool (or paper panopticon) with surveillance capacities over them. Its draws (more and more) countries into its number order, and countries are compared in terms of economic performance to each other and/or over time (see Table 10.4). It deploys numbers and tables to rank them. Annual revisions create a cyclical disciplinary art of country surveillance that institutionalizes a continuous external gaze through numbers that depicts countries' performance via changing rank and score orders. Its power operates through the hierarchization of countries and their division into high/rising and low/falling economies in the competitive race.

Such performance and judgement technologies provide each government with tools for self-assessment in relation to international benchmarks. Countries are thus subjected to the treadmill of competitiveness and under pressure to change economic and social policies in line with specific recommendations and 'best practices' (e.g. cluster building). Countries with a low or slipping position in the rank order are visibilized and targeted to become more competitive. Such ranking discourses are frequently used by government officials, think tanks and journalists to communicate pride, needs, desires and even panics over economic restructuring. For example, actors may narrate a fall within this index order as threatening and/or a sign of 'hollowing out'. This generates pressures on governments, firms, communities and, indeed, some individuals to refashion themselves to become competitive subjects and economic categories (e.g. entrepreneurs and catch-up economies) in the race to ascend to a world-class ranking or, at least, do better than their immediate comparators. In this regard, there is more to this discursive regime than its disciplinary power. Its benchmarking nature increases the competitive spirit of some actors and encourages them to act upon their own conditions of competitiveness in the hope of enhancing them and acquiring greater capacities. In neo-Foucauldian terms, the WEF's benchmarking devices combine disciplinary and governmental power in that countries are externally regulated by indices and also steered at a distance into becoming more competitive by building clusters, enhancing FDI and promoting SMEs, education, sustainable development and so on in ways conducive to prosperity (see Tables 10.5 and 10.6).

*Table 10.5*    *Institutions and practices in building capacities and organizing themed clusters in Asia*

| Institutions | Spatial focus | Practices | Examples of workshop, report and themed clusters |
|---|---|---|---|
| Asia Development Bank Institute (and Institute for Industrial Policy and Strategy in Vietnam) | Transitional economies in Asia (e.g. Vietnam) | Policy seminars, workshops, courses, pilot projects, technical assistance, etc. | Cluster-Based Industrial Development Workshop (2006)<br>• Vietnam: software/ ICT, fruit, ceramics and agricultural products (rice, coffee, pepper, rubber, etc.) |
| Asia Competitiveness Institute (Singapore) | ASEAN countries | Reports, information repository, training courses (for post-graduates and executives), etc. | Country report on *Remaking Singapore* (2008)<br>• Petrochemical, transport and logistics, finance, information technology and biopharmaceuticals |
| Enright, Scott & Associates Ltd. (Hong Kong) | Hong Kong and Pearl River Delta | Consultancy reports, conferences, seminars, new briefings, luncheon meetings, etc. | City report on *The Hong Kong Advantage* (1997)<br>• Business and financial services, transport and logistics, light manufacturing and trading, property and construction, and tourism<br>Report on *Hong Kong and the PRD: the Economic Interaction* (2003)<br>• Pearl River Delta: electrical/electronic goods, software, toys, furniture, telecommunication products, plastics, clothing, port services, ceramics, etc. |

*Source:*   Author's own compilation based on various websites, http://www.abdi.org/ conf-seminar-papers/2007/04/04/2226.vietnam.cluster.dev/, accessed 8 December 2008; http://www.spp.nus.edu.sg/ACI/home.aspx; and http://www.2022foundation.com/index. asp?party=project1, accessed 26 January 2009.

*Table 10.6    Technology of agency that organizes regional spaces, policies and populations*

| Sites of organising agency | Ways of controlling or mapping agency |
| --- | --- |
| Regional space | ● Market and foreign direct investment promotion<br>● Export-oriented clusters link with MNCs through subcontracting<br>● Themed clusters tied to global value chains |
| Policies | ● Governments playing catalytic or supply-side roles<br>● Promotion of technology, innovation, education and training |
| Population | ● Competitive and entrepreneurial spirits<br>● Self-responsibilized individuals for 'catch-up competitiveness' |

*Source:*    Author's own compilation.

### On Regional-Local Scales: Framed by Catch-up, Cluster and Chain Metaphors

On the regional scale, there have been increasing efforts to combine 'competitiveness' and 'development' discourses since the early 2000s. Notable examples include the USAID's African Global Competitiveness Initiative, Inter-American Development Bank (IADB)'s Multilateral Investment Fund for SME competitiveness, and Asian Development Bank on Asian Development Outlook 2003. This section discusses briefly two ways in which the competitiveness discourses have been recontextualized in Asia by regional actors like the Asian Development Bank (ADB), the Asian Institute for Competitiveness (ACI) in Singapore and strategy firms (see Tables 10.3 and 10.5). The first is the idea of 'catch-up competitiveness', and the second draws on 'clusters and chains' metaphors and related practices.

The ADB, which is a regional counterpart of the World Bank, recontextualized 'competitiveness' in 'developmental' terms. Section 3 of its Asian Development Outlook 2003 narrates Porter-inspired ideas in terms of successive stages of neo-Schumpeterian technological and innovation development. Accordingly, Asian newly industrializing economies (NIEs) are seen as initially engaging in original equipment manufacturing (OEM) which produces standard and simple goods for export to developed countries. It is recommended to imitate and then 'catch up' with the developed countries via the development of own design manufacturing (ODM) and own brand manufacturing (OBM). With the electronics sector as its shining example, the term 'catch-up competitiveness' was coined and narrated thus:

> The nature of catch-up competitiveness in the NIEs contrasts sharply with the traditional definition of technological innovation, namely the production of new (or improved) products, based on R&D . . .
>
> Furthermore, the stages model captures the fact that innovation occurs, not just in technological terms but also, and very importantly, in institutional terms. The technological change which took place in East Asia in electronics probably could not have occurred with such rapidity without the OEM and, later, ODM systems. (*Source*: http://www.adb.org/documents/books/ADO/2003/part3_3-7. asp, accessed 2 August 2009)

'Catch-up competitiveness' deploys 'path and journey' metaphors to frame goals and visions for the future. The 'path' metaphor structures movements of the East Asian NIEs and normalizes them as 'laggards' (with their own internal hierarchy) moving forward. Accordingly, their future trajectory is seen in terms of development through the promotion of technological innovation and market-friendly institutions. Taking Singapore as a paradigmatic case of the export-oriented, MNC-led and FDI-driven growth model propelled by industrial clusters, the building of Porterian clusters is normalized for other parts of Asia (e.g. the 'computer disk-drive' cluster in Thailand) as follows:

> The exploitation of MNC investment began in Singapore (Goh 1996) and was imitated by other countries wishing to export to OECD countries. Although FDI occurred prior to 1960s, the electronics industry brought with it a huge expansion of FDI in Southeast Asia, leading to the development of several industrial clusters. For example, the computer disk-drive cluster in Thailand is the largest of its kind in the world. Similarly, in Penang, Malaysia, the semiconductor assembly and testing cluster is the largest exporter of semiconductors worldwide. (*Source*: http://www.adb.org/documents/books/ADO/2003/ part3_3-7.asp, accessed 2 August 2009)

These themed clusters are then connected in the same section of the Outlook to the global market through the metaphor of 'global value chains' (GVCs). This is another common term (if not another brand) in work on global production (Gereffi and Korzeniewicz 1994). No mention is made here of the issue of whether all these Asian economies can move up the chains and the technology ladder or, indeed, of the uneven power relations between subcontractors or suppliers and global buyers (Sum 2009a). Nonetheless, the 'GVC' term is invoked to indicate how the resulting market opportunities create the following advantages for Asian firms and 'clusters':

> GVCs can enable firms to enter global production networks more easily, allow-ing them to benefit from globalization, climb the technology ladder, and gain wider access to international markets. GVCs provide firms with a wide spec-trum of options to operate in global markets with a view to staying competitive . . . Entry into GVCs is easiest when an agglomeration of local buyers and manufacturers already exists, so that newcomers can learn from the established players. (*Source*: http://www.adb.org/documents/books/ADO/2003/part3_3-5. asp, accessed 26 January 2009)

Framed as 'beneficial' and offering 'opportunities', participation in 'GVCs' is said to offer 'clusters' and firms access to global markets and chances to 'climb the technology ladder'. This way of re-imagining how Asia might compete within the world market deploys a 'nodes and links' metaphor in framing the relationship between 'clusters' and the 'global chains'. More specifically, 'clusters' are presented as 'nodes' (i.e. points of intensive interaction) that can become drivers of development when 'linked' into 'GVCs'.

This combination of the 'path–journey' and 'node–link' metaphors in the 2003 Outlook constructs a regional identity and trajectory based on 'catch-up competitiveness'. This has implications not only for national policy but also for everyday life. Implicit in the 'path' metaphor is movement towards a goal (goal attainment), and this in turn implies the use of 'intervention tools' to guide cluster development. In line with the World Bank's self-description as a 'knowledge bank', the ADB, especially through its management arm operating as the ADB Institute (ADBI), organizes the building of capacity in the region. 'Capacity building' can be seen as a governmental tool that involves a body of training-assistance knowledge that targets specific objects and locations (see Eade 1997; Cornwall 2007). The ADBI, in conjunction with other policy institutes, local governments, strategy firms and service-oriented NGOs, co-constructs this body of knowledge that targets cluster build-ing via discursive practices such as cluster programmes, strategic plans, pilot projects, technical assistance schemes, policy workshops and training courses. More specifically, Table 10.5 illustrates some of these institutions and related discourses, practices and spatial foci on cluster building. For example, the ADBI focuses on the 'transition economies' (e.g. China, Vietnam and Cambodia), Asia Competitiveness Institute targets ASEAN countries, and strategy firms such as Enright, Scott & Associates Ltd. concentrates on Hong Kong/Pearl River Delta (Sum 2010). In the case of Vietnam, the ADBI entered into partnership with local development agencies (e.g. Institute for Industrial Development and Strategy in Vietnam) and, with financial support from international organizations (e.g. UNIDO), promoted cluster building assistance (e.g. the 2006 Cluster-Based Industrial Development Workshop). The latter provided seminars and training courses for senior officials to learn to evaluate the potentials of industrial clusters and make strategic action plans for the maximization of their potentials in specific locations (see Table 10.5).

It is beyond the scope of this chapter to examine the details of cluster-based programmes and related best practices; but the discursive practices of cluster training recall what neo-Foucauldians term the technology of agency (Cruikshank 1999), which combines participation and capacity building in the processes of governing as well as controlling the exercise of agency. This array of discourses and practices on regional development produces 'participatory' actors equipped to perform their constructed but eventually self-guided role in promoting catch-up competitiveness. Despite their capacitating aspects, they also control the organization of regional space and the policy for exercising agency and types of agency (see Tables 10.3 and 10.6).

This knowledging technology encourages actors to treat regional spaces as (potential) clusters in which firms, suppliers, service providers and associated institutions interact to form export-led production- and/or service-oriented nodes (e.g. fruit, transport and logistics, finance, electrical/electronic products, etc.) that are opened to foreign direct investment and multinational-dominated global value chains. It also self-responsibilizes public and private agencies to become competitive, entrepreneurial and world-market-oriented in their journey towards 'catch-up competitiveness'. Depending on their locations and interests, individual subjects may reorganize themselves through training and affective-pragmatic identification with the competitiveness project, whilst others are ambivalent and even resist in the institutional and everyday life of catch-up developmentalism.

## CONCLUDING REMARKS

The preceding sections have outlined a new field for the geographical as well as sociological study of brands. They highlight the emergence of knowledge brands in transnational fast policy contexts marked by time-space compression and acceleration. Deploying the Harvard-Porterian brand as an example, the chapter examines the circulation and recontextualizations of this brand across different sites and scales. Though it is influential, regional and local actors act as sites of translation and centres of policy persuasion in diverse global–regional–local construction relays. The resultant circulation and suturing of heterogeneous knowledging technologies and apparatuses (e.g. the technologies of performance or judgement to apparatuses such as benchmarking reports, indices, numbers, clusters and chains) across different scales and sites contribute to the competitiveness regime of truth. Actors perform, repeat and mimic these neoliberal subjectivities that help to crystallize, condition and reproduce institutions, strategies and social relations that are founded upon clusters, global value chains and regional development. Successful cases (e.g. Dongguan's electronics cluster in southern China as part of the global factory) occur, but even here sub-standard labour conditions and environmental degradation challenge the reproduction of the relevant cluster-chain complex (e.g. Sum and Pun 2005; Sum 2009a). The resulting struggles allow for continuous negotiations and shifting compromises when these MNCs, firms, local governments and so on face challenges from labour unions and social movements related to minimum wage legislation, corporate social responsibility and environmental stewardship.

The onset of the 2008 financial crisis affected export-oriented clusters in East Asia through export sluggishness, production downturns, factory closures, unemployment, a credit crunch and even social unrest. This heightened fears about worldwide depression and 'loss of competitiveness'. Accordingly there was a clamour to refix the global economy and the 'international financial architecture' (e.g. the Stiglitz Commission). Competitiveness discourses remain flexibly stable and are currently undergoing a new round of brand negotiation, recontextualization and reinvention. New economic imaginaries, which range from 'responsible competitiveness' (Zadek 2005, 2009) to 'sustainable competitiveness', are circulating in the transnational policy arenas. They contribute towards the broadening and thickening of this knowledge brand and facilitate the building of discourses and practices related to enhanced neoliberalism.

## ACKNOWLEDGEMENT

This chapter derives in part from an ESRC seminar series on 'Changing cultures of competitiveness' 2007–09 (No. RES-451-26-0439) and from research conducted with a British Academy Research Development Award 2008–10 (No. BARDA-48854).

# REFERENCES

Bernstein, B. (1996) *Pedagogy, Symbolic Control and Identity*, London: Taylor & Francis.

Clark, T. and Fincham, R. (eds) (2002) *Critical Consulting: New Perspectives on the Management Advice Industry*, Oxford: Blackwell.

Collins, D. (2000) *Management Fads and Buzzwords: Critical-Practical Perspectives*, London: Routledge.

Cornwall, A. (2007) 'Buzzwords and fuzzwords: Deconstructing development discourse', *Development in Practice*, 17, 4–5, 471–484.

Cruikshank, B. (1999) *The Will to Empower*, Ithaca, NY: Cornell University Press.

D'Andrea Tyson, L. (1988) 'Competitiveness: An analysis of the problem and a perspective of future policy', in M. Starr (ed.), *Global Competitiveness: Getting the U.S. Back on Track*, New York: W.W. Norton, 95–120.

Dosi, G. and Soete, L. (1988) 'Technical change and international trade', in G. Dosi (ed.), *Technical Change and Economic Theory*, London: Pinter, 401–431.

Dunning, J. (1992) 'The competitiveness of countries and the activities of transnational corporations', *Transnational Corporations*, 1, 1, 135–168.

Eade, D. (1997) *Capacity Building: An Approach to People-Centred Development*, Oxford: Oxfam.

Fagerberg, J. (1996) 'Technology and competitiveness', *Oxford Review of Economic Policy*, 12, 3, 39.

Freeman, C. (1982) *Economics of Industrial Innovation*, London: Pinter.

Gereffi, G. and Korzeniewicz, K. (1994) *Commodity Chains and Global Capitalism*, Westport, CT: Praeger.

Global Competitiveness Reports (2004–09) http://www.weforum.org/en/initiatives/gcp/Global%20Competitiveness%20Report/index.htm, accessed 6 August 2009.

Gray, H.P. (1991) 'International competitiveness: A review article', *International Trade Journal*, V, 503–517.

Huczynski, A. (1996) *Management Gurus: Who Makes Them and How to Become One*, London: Routledge.

Jackson, B. (2001) *Management Gurus and Management Fashions*, New York: Routledge.

Kaplan, D. (2003) 'Measuring our competitiveness – critical examination of the IDM and WEF competitiveness indicators for South Africa', *Development South Africa*, 20, 1, 75–88.

Klein, N. (2010) *No Logo*, 10th anniversary edition, London: Fourth Estate.

Krugman, P. (1994) 'Competitiveness: A dangerous obsession', *Foreign Policy*, 73, March, 342–365.

Krugman, P. (1995) *Trade with Japan: Has the Door Opened Wider?*, Chicago: Chicago University Press.

Lall, S. (2001) 'Competitiveness indices and developing countries: An economic evaluation of the Global Competitiveness Report', *World Development*, 29, 9, 1501–1525.

Lury, C. (2004) *Brands: The Logos of the Global Economy*, London: Routledge.

Martin, R. and Sunley, P. (2003) 'Deconstructing clusters: Chaotic concept or policy panacea?', *Journal of Economic Geography*, 3, 5–35.

Miettinen, R. (2002) *National Innovation System: Scientific Concept or Political Rhetoric*, Helsinki: Edita.

Murphy, J. (2008) *World Bank and Global Managerialism*, London: Routledge.

OECD (1962a) *Minutes of the 4th Session, Committee for Scientific Research*, SR/M (62), Paris: OECD, 2.

OECD (1962b) *Proposed Standard Practice for Surveys of Research and Development*, Paris: OECD.

Porter, M. (1980) *Competitive Strategy: Techniques for Analyzing Industries and Competitors*, New York: Free Press.

Porter, M. (1985) *Competitive Advantage: Creating and Sustaining Superior Performance*, New York: Free Press.

Porter, M. (1990) *The Competitive Advantage of Nations*, Basingstoke: Macmillan.

Porter, M. (1991) 'America's green strategy', *Scientific American*, 264, 168.

Posner, M. (1961) 'International trade and technical change', *Oxford Economic Papers*, 13, 1, 323–341.

Reinert, E. (2008) *How Rich Countries Got Rich . . . and Why Poor Countries Stay Poor*, London: Constable.

Rugman, A.M. (1991), 'Diamond in the rough', *Business Quarterly*, 55, 61–64.

Schumpeter, J. (1934) *The Theory of Economic Development*, Cambridge, MA: Harvard University Press.

Stopford, J. and Strange, S. (1991) *Rival States, Rival Firms: Competition for World Market Shares*, Cambridge: Cambridge University Press.

Sum, N.-L. (2009a) 'Wal-Martization and CSR-ization in Developing Countries', in P. Utting and C. Marques (eds), *Corporate Social Responsibility and Regulatory Governance: Towards Inclusive Development?*, 1, Geneva: UNRISD and London: Palgrave, 50–76.

Sum, N.-L. (2009b) 'The production of hegemonic policy discourses: "Competitiveness" as a knowledge brand and its (re-)contextualizations', *Critical Policy Studies*, 3, 2, 184–203.

Sum, N.-L. (2010) 'A cultural political economy of transnational knowledge brands: Porterian "competitiveness" discourse and its recontextualization in Hong Kong/Pearl River Delta', *Journal of Language and Politics*, 9, 4, 546–573.

Sum, N.-L. and Pun, N. (2005) 'Globalization and ethical production chains: Corporate social responsibility in a Chinese workplace', *Competition and Change*, 9, 2, 181–200.

Thurow, L. (1990) 'Competing nations: Survival of the fittest', *Sloan Management Review*, 32, 1, 95–97.

Vernon, R. (1966) 'International trade and international investment in the product cycle', *Quarterly Journal of Economics*, 80, 2, 190–207.

Zadek, S. (2005) *Responsible Competitiveness: Reshaping Markets through Responsible Corporate Practices*, London: AccountAbility.

Zadek, S. (2009) 'Chatham House: Corporate responsibility 2009', http://www.accountability21.net/events, accessed 6 July 2009.

# PART III

# Brands and branding geographies – spaces and places

# 11. Branding Hoxton: Cultural landscapes of post-industrial London

**Andrew Harris**

## INTRODUCTION

London is one of the foremost centres in the world for creating new brands. Its advertising and public relations industries, including companies such as the communications services group WPP and the brand consultancy Wolff Olins, spawn branding and place marketing strategies that circulate globally. Various localities such as Notting Hill, Chelsea and Brick Lane, as well as London itself, enjoy an international profile equivalent to leading branded products and services. Moreover, the award of the 2012 Olympics to London rather than Paris was arguably facilitated by a more sophisticated marketing and branding of the city. Yet it is often unclear how these brands are created, developed and promoted, and what their relationship is to the spaces and places from which they emerge. This chapter investigates some of the complex and geographically specific social and cultural worlds in which London's recent 'brandscapes' have been forged. It will detail how a distinct new urban brand was established during the 1990s around Hoxton, a formerly down-at-heel inner-city district, by a group of creative entrepreneurs and artists. The chapter will argue, however, that the successful brand they fashioned failed to acknowledge and challenge the incipient gentrification of the area, and proved highly conducive to property developers. The Hoxton case-study is an example of how urban branding often not only promotes new forms of economic activity but also involves new forms of spatial capture and control in the post-industrial city.

## CITIES AND BRANDING

The use of branding to communicate essential features of a commercial product, such as quality, reliability and utility, while marking the product in some way to distinguish it from other similar items, has historically been an inherent part of capitalist economies (Lury 2001). With the increasingly ubiquitous 'culturisation' of consumer goods over the past 20 years, however, branding and accompanying practices of marketing and advertising, rather than the products themselves, have come to dominate efforts at generating 'surplus value' (Lash and Urry 1994). Furthermore, with the growing importance of consumption to everyday life, branding has pervaded not simply economic activity but the fabric of popular culture and social affiliations. As the cultural theorist Hal Foster (2002: 20) comments, 'whether the design object is Young British Art or a Presidential candidate, "brand equity" – the branding of a product name on an attention-deficit public – is fundamental to many spheres of society'.

This widespread deployment of branding practices has extended to the form and function of cities. From buildings and districts to whole metropolitan regions, attempts have been made to re-image perceptions of urban space, and transform the way it is consumed. Although such 'brandscapes', as Walter Benjamin's work on Parisian arcades demonstrates, have always characterised urban economic growth, the last three decades have witnessed an intensification in these processes (Greenberg 2008). From the advertising of certain products and services, to efforts to express particular ideals or lifestyles, and attempts to increase the appeal of urban areas to potential residents, tourists and investors, 'brandscapes' have become a prominent feature of post-industrial urbanism (Klingmann 2007).

It is possible to identify three main groups responsible for this increasing prevalence of urban branding, often in concert and coalition with one another. Firstly, urban space has been branded by large multinational companies such as Nike, Prada and Sega as a method of marketing and corporate identification (Sherry 1998). These companies have, for example, integrated their products into urban built form more fully than ever before by turning many of their retail outlets into themed entertainment destinations such as Niketown and Segaworld – what Susan Davis (1999: 449) describes as 'walk-through public relations'. They have also increasingly branded public space in cities, infiltrating, sponsoring and creating various urban events and festivals (Klein 2000). The oil multinational Shell, for instance, filled a prominent stretch of riverside on London's South Bank with multi-media displays dubbed the 'Shell Electric Storm' in November 2003 as part of its attempts to signal its environmental commitments. In turn, many cultural institutions, such as art museums, have emulated these corporate urban branding techniques, using public space for outdoor events and displays, and opening new retail and entertainment facilities (Wu 1998).

Secondly, urban space, particularly in the centre of cities, has also increasingly been branded by property and commercial elites, recognising and attempting to enhance demand from the new middle classes for distinctive urban landscapes based on cultural consumption, entertainment and leisure (Hannigan 1998). This creation of what Ed Soja (2000: 151) describes as 'simulated and aestheticized cityscapes' is exemplified by the 1990s redevelopment of Times Square in New York. Encouraged by state tax abatements and the impact of public art projects, private investors led by the Disney Corporation have actively re-imaged this area as a hub of upmarket consumption and commercial and entertainment activity, drawing on its early-twentieth-century history as a 'publicity gimmick' for the *New York Times* newspaper, and its reputation for Broadway theatre (Sagalyn 2001).

These commercially orientated attempts to brand urban space have often appropriated and reinvented marginalised and multi-ethnic inner-city areas and the symbolic representations of their communities and cultural life. The bohemian, cosmopolitan and criminal history of London's Soho, for instance, has been reworked since the early 1990s in the establishment of Old Compton Street as a thriving commercial centre for the consumption and performance of gay identities (Andersson 2008). Similarly, the Lower East Side's history as a prominent site for protest, resistance and cultural experimentation in New York has been adopted and adapted by entrepreneurial real estate developers in their creation of a lucrative new 'East Village' brand (Mele 2000).

As well as appropriating, packaging and manipulating forms of cultural diversity and artistic life found in certain inner-city areas, commercial and property elites have also deployed discourses of heritage in their recent attempts at branding urban space. They have increasingly looked to the renovation and adaptive reuse of the built environment in their efforts to cater to the socio-cultural consumption demands of certain residents, businesses and visitors. Through the creation of 'festival marketplaces', such as London's Covent Garden and Boston's Faneuil Hall, the preservation and accompanying branding of historic urban features and architectural ensembles have offered both new commercial opportunities and a way of responding to a greater collective desire and nostalgia in contemporary cities for more stability in urban life (Boyer 1992).

Thirdly, many local and national governments have been instrumental in providing support and finance for these attempts to combine the conservation of historic built fabric with new consumption-orientated branding practices. They have recognised not only the potential enhanced tax revenues and positive civic image generated by these schemes to brand cities' heritage but their contribution to bolstering urban competitiveness.

In Shanghai, for example, state authorities have looked to preserve and restore the city's rich architectural and cultural heritage in a bid to help the city compete for foreign investment and international tourism, despite the political ambiguities and contradictions involved (Abbas 2000).

Political elites have also attempted to brand urban space at both a city-wide and a district level as a means of addressing and managing long-term economic decline. Acknowledging how cities' subjective 'feel', aesthetic qualities and social values have become increasingly crucial in attracting investment, urban managers have not only deployed cultural strategies of economic development but looked to redefine and refashion perceptions of urban space (Kearns and Philo 1993). This has frequently involved the creation of specific place-based 'myths' designed to erase the negative iconography of dereliction and labour militancy associated with the industrial city. Deindustrialised districts of Sydney in Australia, for instance, were extensively re-imaged during the 1980s, in a process that the urban sociologist Sophie Watson (1991) termed 'gilding the smokestacks'. Advertising and place marketing techniques have also been used over the past 20 years to attract new commercial and tourist investment in 'rust-belt' cities such as Pittsburgh and Cleveland in the US, and in cities in the UK such as Birmingham, Glasgow and Stoke-on-Trent hit by industrial retrenchment.

In these attempts at 'imagineering' urban space, urban politicians and planners have often tried to capitalise on distinctive local subcultures, emulating and reinforcing commercially orientated strategies of place-branding, and responding to the seductive policy templates offered by Richard Florida (2004). The US city of Seattle, for example, has manoeuvred its location as the home of Kurt Cobain and 'grunge' music into a viable tourist brand (Hannigan 2004). Manchester City Council in the UK has similarly looked to exploit Manchester's reputation for popular music, hiring the former creative director of Factory Records, Peter Saville, and several other 'renegade' figures in 2003 as part of a 'Creative Panel' charged with forming a brand strategy for the city and instigating marketing strategies emphasising what Guy Julier (2005: 880–882) describes as the 'louche avant-gardism' of 'Manchesterness'.

Urban branding therefore demonstrates the mutation of the brand beyond a two-dimensional role as a largely abstract and deterritorialised logo. Branding strategies by a range of corporate, commercial and political elites have become highly sophisticated in re-imaging and commodifying urban space, and responding to and reinforcing a greater role for cultural activities and identities in the contemporary city. Yet there has been a tendency by scholars to ignore the geographically and historically specific social and cultural worlds in which these new urban brands have been forged, popularised and disseminated. The emphasis has been more on the imposition of new 'landscapes of power' (Zukin 1991) or the Disney-esque 'theme-parking' of cities (Sorkin 1992). The assumption has often been that urban brands are the preserve of public–private coalitions (Greenberg 2008) and have been 'severed from particular and concrete modes of attachment or activity' (Malpas 2009: 195). There is rarely any systematic empirical investigation of the complex social practices of cultural production and consumption involved, and their relation to specific actors and neighbourhoods. For this reason, drawing on archival and interview research undertaken between 2001 and 2004, this chapter will explore how a distinct new urban brand was initiated and developed around a particular area in London – Hoxton.

## JOSHUA COMPSTON AND A NEW HOXTON BRAND

Hoxton is located in the south-west of the London Borough of Hackney just to the north of the City of London (Figure 11.1). Traditionally its boundaries have been defined by Kingsland Road in the east, Regent's Canal in the north, Old Street and City Road in the south, and Shepherdess Walk in the west. But since the mid-1990s the area has also come to encompass the triangle to the south created by Great Eastern Street, Shoreditch High Street and Old Street. Prior to the early 1990s, Hoxton was little known beyond its immediate environs, aside from maybe an association with the far-right political party the National Front, and as the birthplace for the notorious London gangsters the Kray Twins. It was a run-down stretch of inner London containing largely derelict light manufacturing premises in the south and a swathe of social housing to the north. During the 1990s, however, Hoxton acquired a dynamic new cultural image before undergoing considerable property redevelopment. By the turn of the century, it had become recognised throughout London, and indeed further afield, exemplified by the opening of the Hoxton Bar in a post-industrial district of Athens, Greece.

An important figure in instigating this dramatic branding of Hoxton as 'the hippest, most happening neighbourhood in this hip, happening world capital' (Karastamatis 2001: 12) was the eccentric and charismatic cultural impresario Joshua Compston. Compston was not a corporate strategist, property developer or urban planner, but he played an influential if unheralded role in the creation and popularisation of new inner-city branding strategies in London. He first arrived in Hoxton after graduating from the Courtauld Institute of Art in central London, where he had become enamoured by the dynamism and excitement of the city's

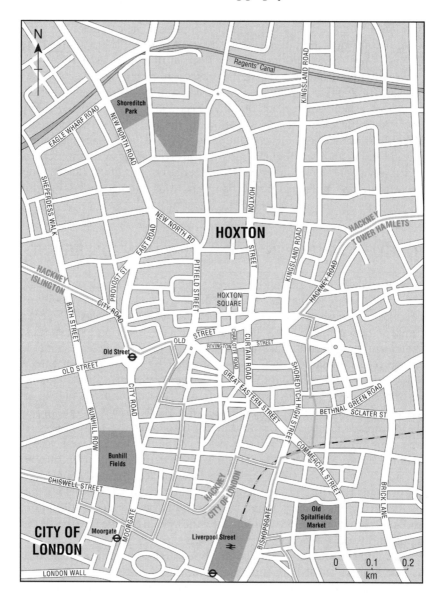

*Source:*   Cartography by Miles Irving, UCL Department of Geography.

*Figure 11.1    Location map of Hoxton*

contemporary art scene during the early 1990s (Cooper 2000). He moved into a former timber yard and French-polisher's on Charlotte Road, where he opened the area's first permanent gallery, Factual Nonsense, in 1992. Compston was drawn to Hoxton not only on account of its cheap rents and central location but also because of its rich collection of nineteenth-century built fabric and a small, close-knit community of artists and other creative individuals living semi-legally in spaces once earmarked for commercial redevelopment prior to the recession of the early 1990s (Harris 2006).

Compston envisaged Hoxton as a 'no-man's land ripe for artistic takeover' (Cooper 2000: 78). He stated in August 1994:

> This is a very charming, very intriguing and essentially very colourful area. Without sounding arrogant, I think it needs companies like Factual Nonsense around it to help it realize its potential . . . [I]t's had a lot of stuffing and guts punched out of it and I'd like to be able to help it realize itself and pick it up. (Factual Nonsense Archives)

He harboured grand ambitions for Factual Nonsense (FN) operating not simply as an art gallery but as a new type of brand-led entertainment conglomerate, declaring in his business plan from 1994 that: 'I'll be defining sites for FN activity in terms of magazines, television, large-scale billboard format advertising and if it really works . . . within all the streets, identifying and thence "branding" certain towns and geographical areas' (Factual Nonsense Archives).

In order to promote this FN brand in Hoxton, Compston staged a conceptual arts festival in July 1993 on the crossroads of Charlotte Road and Rivington Street, which he dubbed the 'Fete Worse than Death'. Compston took advantage of the area's deserted streets by renting stalls for a nominal sum to artists, many of whom lived locally. Highlights of the fete, attended by approximately a hundred people, included John Bishard and Adam McEwan offering advice about absolutely anything for 20p, Gavin Turk using a piece of industrial tubing and a sock to run a 'Bash a Rat' game and Damien Hirst, dressed as a clown, making his first trademark spin paintings before exposing his painted genitals for 50p. Following the success of this first event, Compston held another much larger Fete Worse than Death (FWTD) in Hoxton Square, attended by 4000 people, the following summer, and a further extravaganza he called the 'Hanging Picnic' in 1995. Highlights of the second FWTD, expanded to include music, theatre and circus performances, included Tracey Emin's 'Rodent Roulette' and Leigh Bowery's 'birth' to a naked gold-painted woman live on stage. Compston attempted, in these three outdoor events, to harness the dynamism of the new local creative community to the 'blank canvas' offered by Hoxton's disused spaces in order to advertise what he termed 'perfect FN reality' (quoted in *Smiths Magazine* 1994).

Importantly, in these efforts to stamp the FN brand on to Hoxton, Compston recognised and manipulated the local area's reputation and history. In particular, he mined a perceived working-class tradition for street parties and revelry in the East End of London. As Compston himself stated in 1995 on being asked about his art events, 'what I want to achieve is more in tune with the life of working-class communities a hundred years ago' (quoted in Barklem 1995). This legacy of forms and practices of British working-class popular culture offered Joshua Compston and the artists' community a rich resource and environment from which to promote a new Hoxton brand (Harris 2006). Benefiting from the growing profile and reputation of many of the participating artists, Compston increasingly reaped national media attention for his outdoor events and the local area that was intrinsic to their success. By 1995, he had persuaded London Weekend Television to make a half-hour documentary on the event and the *Guardian* newspaper to devote seven pages to Factual Nonsense and the area's artistic community in its *Weekend Magazine* (Gott 1995).

Prior to Compston's galvanising and promoting the activities and imaginaries of the area's dynamic creative community, Hoxton had been largely synonymous with inner-city deprivation and notoriety. As the philosopher Bryan Magee (2003: 81) notes in his biography of his childhood in Hoxton during the 1930s, Hoxton's name was 'used in speech and writing to represent the ultimate in social degradation, the poorest, most criminal, most uncivilised corner of Britain'. Yet, by the late 1990s, the idea of Hoxton had been refashioned as an exciting hub of cutting-edge contemporary British art. Compston had therefore achieved his ambitions, as he stated in a 1994 press release, to 'buff up and make explicit the profile of . . . Hoxton'; his outdoor events had worked, in his words, as a way of 'shaping and mythologizing the area' and promoting it as 'a funky, upbeat up-and-coming cultural zone' (LWT 1995). The symbolic representation of Hoxton had been comprehensively transformed and rebranded.

## PROPERTY DEVELOPMENT AND HOXTON'S BRANDING

This branding of Hoxton as a cutting-edge artistic hub, however, cannot be reduced simply to the activities and ambitions of Joshua Compston and associated artists. Crucially, property interests also played a role, at first informally collaborating with Compston in the ownership of a new Hoxton brand before claiming it for themselves by the late 1990s. In particular one company called Glasshouse Investments bought several buildings in Hoxton Square during the property recession of the 1990s, and provided sponsorship and amenities for Compston's second event in 1994. Glasshouse's founder, a former sculptor, recounts:

> At the time it was a bit of a nightmare because of the way Joshua [Compston] did things. However, it became clear much later that he had succeeded in raising the profile of the area, which is what we set out to do. (Interview, 2001)

Compston also approached the estate agents Stirling Ackroyd, based in the area, early in 1995, explaining in a letter why he thought they should sponsor his proposed Hanging Picnic:

> I have successfully, through the nature and style of my events over the last two years, manipulated both the media and the general public to perceive Hoxton as a certain sort of desirable area. This has obviously had significant benefits . . . to the property business. (Factual Nonsense Archives)

Stirling Ackroyd became one of the main backers of the Hanging Picnic, with the event proving, as the company's founder recollects, 'very important as a catalyst for the area' (interview, 2003).

These local property businesses supported Compston's energetic efforts to brand Hoxton as a distinct hub of young British art, not only because they were eager to contribute to the life of the area of which they were a part, but because of the possible impact his events might have on Hoxton's down-at-heel image. During the property recession of the early 1990s, aside from the creative community, it was generally difficult to attract tenants, despite the area's close proximity to the City. As one Stirling Ackroyd estate agent recalled, 'nobody wanted to be there; there were drugs, it had a real bad reputation, shootings, and a few crimes happening on a regular basis' (interview, 2001). Compston's urban branding strategy was seen by Glasshouse and Stirling Ackroyd as an important means of changing these negative perceptions.

Hoxton's new art-related brand also offered a distinct cultural cachet that appealed to young professional groups and fractions of the new middle classes. This may explain why despite the departure of nearly all of the area's visual artists since the mid-1990s, and the death of Joshua Compston in March 2006 – aged 25 – from a suspected halothane overdose, Hoxton's art-related brand has continued to prove a useful marketing tool in new property developments. In the 2001 promotional material for a new-build development at 14–15 Hoxton Square, the developers St.

*Source:*  Photographs taken by author 2006–08.

*Figure 11.2    Collage of Hoxton signs and logos*

George depicted Hoxton as the 'chosen home of many of London's "Brit art" celebrities'. City Lofts' 2002 development on the site of a former timber yard similarly declared that Hoxton has 'the largest proportion of working artists of anywhere in Europe'. These clearly demonstrate how property companies fully co-opted and commoditised Hoxton's artistic reputation and brand. The appeal of Hoxton's brand can also be seen in numerous commercial signs and logos that use the name of the local area (Figure 11.2). And it has been bolstered by the arrival of numerous advertising, architecture, new media and indeed brand management companies in the area since the late 1990s (*Economist* 2000; O'Sullivan 2002). Hoxton can now be understood as one of the main clusters and staging-grounds for London's cultural economy.

Owing to the widely recognised and celebrated rebranding of the area, Hoxton has increasingly acted as a model and exemplar for other parts of London. New contemporary art scenes in places such as Deptford or Dalston have often led to these areas being tagged by urban boosters and journalists as the 'new Hoxton' (Hackworth 2001; Flynn 2009). Most notably, the conversion of an old power station in the borough of Southwark into a national art gallery, Tate Modern, betrays a Hoxton legacy. The Tate has repeated and institutionalised a similar branding strategy to the one adopted by Joshua Compston. By associating itself with a traditionally working-class and formerly industrial area not previously connected with contemporary art, the Tate has also successfully deployed inner-city urban space to forge a distinct new identity (Harris 2006).

## CONCLUSIONS

New urban branding in London is obviously part of a much larger story than the role of Joshua Compston, artists and assorted property interests. This includes restructuring processes that led to the deindustrialisation of areas such as Hoxton and the dominance of the City of London within London's economy, regeneration initiatives and investment programmes during the 1990s, and new cultural trends associated with the promotion of what was deemed 'cool Britannia' in this period. But this chapter has shown how urban branding needs to be considered as more than a corporate and political strategy imposed from above. New urban brands are created through the practices, performances and urban visions of particular cultural intermediaries acting in specific locations, and often have resonance and impact across a city. Indeed invariably it is the most sustainable and dynamic branding strategies that recognise this. Hoxton's artistic brand, initially forged through Joshua Compston's dreams of diversifying Factual Nonsense as an entertainment conglomerate, has catered for many of the lifestyle tastes and investment priorities within post-industrial inner London. It has involved complex entanglements of culture and economy, of motivations and geographical influences, that disrupt simplistic notions of 'soft' versus 'hard' urban branding.

Nevertheless, Compston's promotion of a new art-related brand for Hoxton was easily co-opted by urban commercial and corporate capital. Arguably, if the new cultural landscape which was developed by Compston and friends had actively tried to critique and challenge widespread structural inequalities in the area, rather than prioritising casual spectacle and the mass media, it would not have received the same support from property interests (Harris 2006). The media hoopla over Hoxton's new brand can be seen as acting as a *fait accompli* for the gentrification of the area and wider political failures to address ongoing inequalities in housing, employment and education provision in inner London. Like the burning of a mark to indicate ownership of animals, urban branding can also convey capture and control over space and place.

Yet urban branding need not act as an example of 'inauthentic' urbanism, invariably bound up with the mechanisms and logics of the 'neoliberal' and 'revanchist' city. Cities are always contested cultural terrains offering a range of branding possibilities and opportunities for detournement that cater less to corporate and governmental attempts at reshaping cities for post-industrial consumption and emphasise the more ordinary, diverse and conflictual qualities to contemporary urban life. An example of this can be found in Hoxton itself. In 2005, the Red Room theatre group collected, performed and disseminated testimonies from residents of local council estates detailing their dreams and disappointments in relation to the transformation of the area. The potential therefore remains for London to be one of the foremost centres in the world not only for creating brands, but also for counter-branding events, efforts, narratives and tactics.

## REFERENCES

Abbas, A. (2000) 'Cosmopolitan de-scriptions: Shanghai and Hong Kong', in C. Breckenridge, S. Pollock, H.K. Bhabha and D. Chakrabarty (eds) *Cosmopolitanism*, Durham, NC: Duke University Press, 209–228.

Andersson, J. (2008) 'Consuming visibility: London's new spaces of gay nightlife', Unpublished Ph.D. thesis, Bartlett School of Planning, University College London.

Barklem, N. (1995) 'Life on the edge of the Square', *Detour Magazine*, December.

Boyer, C. (1992) 'Cities for sale: Merchandising history at South Street Seaport', in M. Sorkin (ed.), *Variations on a Theme Park: The New American City and the End of Public Space*, New York: Noonday, 181–203.

Cooper, J. (2000) *No Fun without U: The Art of Factual Nonsense*, London: Ellipsis.

Davis, S. (1999) 'Media conglomerates build the entertainment city', *European Journal of Communication*, 14, 4, 435–459.

*Economist* (2000) 'Clustering in Hackney', 4 March.

Florida, R. (2004) *The Rise of the Creative Class: And How It's Transforming Work, Leisure, Community and Everyday Life*, New York: Basic Books.

Flynn, P. (2009) 'Welcome to Dalston, now the coolest place in Britain', *Guardian*, 27 April.

Foster, H. (2002) *Design and Crime*, London: Verso.

Gott, R. (1995) 'Where the art is', *Guardian*, 7 October.

Greenberg, M. (2008) *Branding New York: How a City in Crisis Was Sold to the World*, New York: Routledge.

Hackworth, N. (2001) 'Why Saatchi shops in Deptford', *Evening Standard*, 5 April.

Hannigan, J. (1998) *Fantasy City: Pleasure and Profit in the Postmodern Metropolis*, London: Routledge.

Hannigan, J. (2004) 'Boom towns and cool cities: The perils and prospects of developing a distinctive urban brand in a global economy', Unpublished paper from Leverhulme International Symposium: The Resurgent City, LSE, 19–21 April.

Harris, A. (2006) 'Branding urban space: The creation of art districts in London and Mumbai', Unpublished thesis, University College London.

Julier, G. (2005) 'Urban designscapes and the production of aesthetic content', *Urban Studies*, 42, (5/6), 869–887.

Karastamatis, J. (2001) 'A real London revival', *Toronto Star*, 15 December, 12.

Kearns, G. and Philo, C. (1993) *Selling Places: The City as Cultural Capital, Past and Present*, Oxford: Pergamon Press.

Klein, N. (2000) *No logo: No Space. No Choice. No Jobs*, London: Flamingo.

Klingmann, A. (2007) *Brandscapes: Architecture in the Experience Economy*, Cambridge, MA: MIT Press.

Lash, S. and Urry, J. (1994) *Economies of Signs and Spaces: After Organised Capitalism*, London: Sage.

Lury, G. (2001) *Brandwatching: Lifting the Lid on Branding*, Dublin: Blackhall.

LWT (1995) Transcript to 'Opening shot' directed by Liz Friend, broadcast October.

Magee, B. (2003) *Clouds of Glory: A Childhood in Hoxton*, London: Jonathan Cape.

Malpas, J. (2009) 'Cosmopolitanism, branding and the public realm', in S. Donald, E. Kofman and C. Kevin (eds), *Branding Cities: Cosmopolitanism, Parochialism and Social Change*, Oxford: Routledge, 189–198.

Mele, C. (2000) *Selling the Lower East Side: Culture, Real Estate, and Resistance in New York City*, Minneapolis: University of Minnesota Press.

O'Sullivan, F. (2002) *Dot Com Clusters and Local Economic Development: A Case Study of New Media Development in London's City Fringe*, London: Middlesex University Business School, Centre for Enterprise and Economic Development Research.

Sagalyn, L. (2001) *Times Square Roulette: Remaking the City Icon*, Cambridge, MA: MIT Press.

Sherry, J. (ed.) (1998) *Servicescapes: The Concept of Place in Contemporary Markets*, Lincolnwood, IL: NTC Business Books.

*Smiths Magazine* (1994) 'Situating alternatives', Round-table discussion, Autumn.

Soja, E. (2000) *Postmetropolis: Critical Studies of Cities and Regions*, Oxford: Blackwell.

Sorkin, M. (ed.) (1992) *Variations on a Theme Park: The New American City and the End of Public Space*, New York: Noonday.

Watson, S. (1991) 'Gilding the smokestacks: The new symbolic representations of deindustrialised regions', *Environment and Planning D*, 9, 59–70.

Wu, C.-T. (1998) 'Embracing the enterprise culture: Art institutions since the 1980s', *New Left Review*, 230, July–August, 28–57.

Zukin, S. (1991) *Landscapes of Power: From Detroit to Disneyworld*, Berkeley: University of California Press.

# 12. Branding provincial cities: The politics of inclusion, strategy and commitment

## Anette Therkelsen and Henrik Halkier

## INTRODUCTION

In recent years urban development strategies increasingly try to appeal to what Richard Florida dubbed the creative class (Florida 2002), and, in order to attract attention in the competition for 'the right kind of citizens' whose presence is believed to improve prospects of economic development, the image and brand of the city are clearly important (Jensen 2007; Turok 2009). Understanding why some brands have greater longevity and penetration than others, however, requires investigation not just of the communicative outcomes and reception in targeted markets but also of the processes through which the brands have been created, or what Ooi (2004) has termed 'the politics of place branding', because several dilemmas present themselves in the context of place branding processes. Firstly, what aspects of the city are to be highlighted and possibly developed constitutes a potential dilemma. Is holding on to an established identity that has characterized the place through a longer period of time the preferred strategy, what could be termed a strategy of continuity, or do preferences exist for a change of course towards presenting a different place identity, e.g. in line with trendy 'creative class' ideals through what could be called a strategy of change? What is to be branded will have consequences for who is to be included and, as an implicit consequence of this, who is to be excluded from the branding process, which constitutes a second dilemma of place branding. Though comprehensive umbrella place brands are meant to cover the interests of the place across a wide range of stakeholders and social activities (Therkelsen and Halkier 2008), the branding initiator, typically public authorities, will frame the branding initiative in a particular context (e.g. the need for changing the existing place identity and image or the need for reinforcing place identity and image), something which will have consequences for who is included and excluded and may result in a division between primary decision-making stakeholders and secondary stakeholders less intensely consulted. Thirdly, targeting the brand towards particular audiences also constitutes a dilemma, because whether to sell the place to external consumer groups and/or build community among internal public and private actors is a fundamental strategic choice, and in the process public and private actors may pursue their own interests rather than the 'public good' of a common place brand. Fourthly, the type of place-making preferred, i.e. place branding via communication and/or through product development, would also be central to understanding the dynamics of the place branding process. It has been argued that poorly managed place branding efforts in which synergy effects are not obvious to the participating stakeholders will tend to focus on a common communication platform rather than a more holistic approach to place branding which also involves reshaping the city itself (Hankinson 2007), something which suggests a link between process and outcome. The fifth, and final, dilemma concerns commitment versus non-commitment of stakeholders, and would seem to be a consequence of the extent to which stakeholders have been included in the place branding process and the degree to which their strategic preferences have been heard. It has, however, been demonstrated elsewhere that stakeholders may pay lip service to the place branding effort despite early and prominent inclusion (Therkelsen *et al.* 2010). All in all the politics of place branding is clearly highly complex, and it is therefore perhaps surprising that relatively limited research appears to have been undertaken in relation to this central aspect of place branding.

The purpose of the present chapter is to contribute with insight into the politics of place branding, combining theoretical reflection with an empirical study of city branding processes as they unfold in the case of the two Danish provincial cities of Aarhus and Aalborg, where three types of local stakeholders are interviewed: the municipalities, the tourism organizations and the city retail organizations, which are central actors in place branding efforts in general and in these two cases in particular. Hence the focus is on the role of stakeholders related to different sectors of socio-economic activity, how these stakeholders influence the process and the practice of place branding, and, eventually, the long-term viability of the resulting place brands. Through discussions of three salient elements of place branding processes – inclusion, preferred strategies and commitment – the chapter seeks to contribute to the existing knowledge on place branding by means of conceptual developments that combine the above-mentioned elements and by empirical discussions underscore the necessity of shared strategic priorities among the stakeholders included to generate commitment to the brand. Contrary to what is widely held in the existing literature, inclusion per se does not ensure long-term stakeholder commitment.

## CONCEPTUAL FRAMEWORK

As both scholarly and more applied consultancy research has approached the field of place branding from a marketing angle, limited attention has been given to internal stakeholder relations and the processes behind place branding initiatives. Thus there is still a scarcity of literature which accounts for the success of branding campaigns in terms not just of appropriate marketing choices but also of understanding these choices in the light of the way the branding process itself has unfolded, i.e. the politics of place branding.

In order to identify and understand the often contrasting interests, influences and different degrees of ownership towards the brand that characterize many place branding initiatives, it is expedient to combine an approach inspired by studies of corporate branding processes (Pedersen 2004; Kavaratzis and Ashworth 2005; Hankinson 2007) with an approach to public policy inspired by institutionalism and network theory (Thorelli 1986; Rhodes and Marsh 1992; Halkier 2006, ch. 3). This involves focusing on the interaction of actors within the branding process around three key elements, namely when and how different actors are included in the process, actor preferences in relation to the branding strategies implemented, and the commitment of key actors to participating in the process. Taken together, these elements should illuminate the inter-organizational processes around branding initiatives while also accounting for the latent tensions between different perceptions of what the city currently is and how it is envisioned, physically and representationally, in order to be able to position itself as attractive to current and potential place consumers. The remainder of this section will elaborate on each of these three dimensions in dialogue with existing contributions to the literature.

In line with mainstream policy analysis literature (Hogwood and Gunn 1986; Parsons 1995), place branding involves a potentially contested process where questions of inclusion (and exclusion) of particular actors may be of crucial importance (Hankinson 2007). This is because internal stakeholders are also part of the internal target group that may have preferences that concur to a greater or lesser extent with external target groups with regard to wanting change or continuity in the city brand. However, although broad inclusion would seem to ensure a broad social and political foundation for a place brand viable in the long term, the fact that the ideal-type process is clearly a complex, difficult and time-consuming one also makes it more likely that deviations will occur, such as limited involvement of local stakeholders in order to maximize appeal to external target groups or, conversely, using the brand primarily to sanction particular brand-compliant local activities with limited relevance to the outside world. The question of the roles of different actors in the various phases of the place branding process, from initiation via design to implementation, is, in other words, a crucial feature to uncover. A special role is played by the branding initiator, most often a public organization, which formulates a need for a branding strategy in view of the envisaged challenges facing the place. How the place branding effort is framed in terms of challenges to be overcome is likely to influence who is included in the process and will have a bearing on what public and private stakeholders assume the role of brand champions vis-à-vis partners with more peripheral roles during the process. Whereas this way of acting assumes a certain level of problem analysis and definition on the part of the branding initiator, a less well-reflected approach may be applied. Perhaps especially in situations where the branding initiative is a kind of copy-cat activity driven by unease about similar activities in cities perceived as competitors, stakeholder selection may reflect path dependency where the 'old boys' network' is summoned, i.e. the actors of the major public and private organizations in the city, who have shown their worth in other contexts. Hence they are invited to join the process not owing to their specific relevance in a branding context but because of their general political standing.

With regard to strategies, place branders are faced with balancing their activities along three different lines. Is the branding process aimed at strengthening the existing image of the city or creating a new and different one? Are external and/or internal place consumers being targeted? And to what extent are symbolic representations and physical place-making involved? The choice between reinforcing existing or furthering new perceptions among place users or consumers is clearly important for the branding process for several reasons: stakeholders may disagree or not about the direction in which to move, and it may be perceived as easier (but also less urgent) to strengthen the existing brand rather than comprehensively reposition the city. Moreover, recent contributions (see Kavaratzis and Ashworth 2005; Hankinson 2007) have started to draw attention to both the internal and the external challenges of place branding and highlight the importance of taking into consideration the diverse interests of various groups of locals, thereby facilitating their identification with the place and contributing to community building. In theory external and internal audiences may be mutually supportive target groups, because local pride can be furthered by external demand for one's place, and satisfied local citizens are likely to function as ambassadors of the place towards external target groups. However, in practice a salient question is still how to combine the highly diverse interests of different groups of local citizens and simultaneously maintain a clear external message. The third strategic balance to be struck, between symbolic representation and physical place-making, has traditionally been skewed in the direction of a communication-oriented approach, resulting in numerous city brands consisting of a vision, four to six values and a communication toolbox. Recently, contributions from both urban planning and marketing research have, however, emphasized the importance of the quality of the place as an important prerequisite for long-term durable branding, because no place branding strategy can be made without a spatial referent, and therefore understanding the relationship between the narrative and its place-bound context is of great importance (Morgan and Pritchard 2001; Eckstein and Throgmorton 2003; Jensen 2007; Turok 2009; Therkelsen *et al.* 2010). Clearly, strategic choices in relation to brand positioning, market focus and concrete branding activities are closely intertwined and will be influenced by the role of stakeholders in the place branding policy process.

A certain level of inclusion and influence on branding strategies would seem to be core prerequisites for brand commitment of stakeholders and hence the long-term viability of the brand. In her account of consumer brand relationships, Fournier understands commitment as continual dedication to the brand despite foreseen and unforeseen circumstances as well as a public statement of one's loyalty to the brand (in Keller 2003: 474), and also research on corporate branding has demonstrated that brand commitment in organizations takes on emotional forms (Thomson *et al.* 1999; Ind 2003). This internationalization of the corporate brand may, in fact, constitute a serious challenge to place branding initiatives, because commitment to cross-sectoral umbrella brands will be secondary to network partners unless clear synergy effects are obvious between the brand of one's own organization and that of the place (Hankinson 2007: 248). In other words, a utilitarian approach among stakeholders is likely to characterize the start of a place branding initiative – 'what is in it for our organization' – and, for stakeholders to become more whole-heartedly committed, Hankinson argues that early inclusion in the specification of the brand values is necessary. Indeed, a central task in a well-managed branding process is to establish compatible partnerships (Hankinson 2007: 250), as simply stemming from the same place is unlikely to be enough to forge brand commitment and eventually loyal actions among stakeholders. In other words, added value for the individual stakeholder has to be evident.

All in all, the study of place branding initiatives clearly requires an approach that is capable of accounting for the ongoing interaction between individual actors and the overall branding process. While the discussion above has demonstrated that the three key dimensions and the associated analytical categories (summarized in Table 12.1) must be illuminated in empirical analyses, it is also clear that the three dimensions of the place branding process are likely to be linked. Although branding

*Table 12.1    Place branding processes: Analytical dimensions*

| Dimensions | Variables |
| --- | --- |
| Inclusion | • Initiator / central partner / peripheral partner / exclusion |
| Strategy | • Positioning: continuity / change |
|  | • Target: external / internal |
|  | • Means: symbolic representation / physical place-making |
| Commitment | • Instrumental / emotional |

*Source:*   Authors' own elaboration.

strategies are the product of discussion and possibly consensus among key stakeholders, the commitment of individual actors will reflect not only the importance attached to branding at the outset of the process but also their evaluation of the activities initiated and, indeed, the ongoing process and their own role in its different phases. In short, the object of study is a complex, moving target, and therefore the need for a systematic approach to the study of place branding processes is all the more pressing.

## EMPIRICAL DATA AND CASE DESCRIPTIONS

The primary data for this study was generated through qualitative research interviews. Although the number of relevant stakeholders is considerable in place branding efforts, it has been deemed expedient in the context of this qualitative study to narrow down the number of stakeholders to three in the cities of Aalborg and Aarhus respectively:

- the municipalities which have initiated the branding processes and which, despite being formally unitary actors, also represent potentially diverging interests with regard to internal and external target groups in terms of securing attractiveness for current and future citizens, students, investors and visitors;
- the local tourism organizations which are actively involved in the branding initiative and have a strong interest in domestic and international visitors;
- the city retail organizations which have their main focus on short-term domestic or regional visitors.

The interviews were conducted according to the principles of semi-structured qualitative interviews (Kvale 1996), and priority was given to letting the respondents speak freely on themes pre-defined by the research-ers, just as room was made for unforeseen topics that might appear.

Use has also been made of strategy papers and marketing material relating to the branding efforts in the two case cities. The stakeholder-directed websites of the two cities, www.brandingaalborg.dk and www.aarhuskommune.dk, have functioned as a supplement to the interviews in terms of descriptions of the brand values, design, merchandise and events, though the detail of information varies significantly, with the Aalborg website being far more informative than the Aarhus website (Figure 12.1).

*Source:*    Wikimedia Commons.

*Figure 12.1    Map of Denmark*

The branding efforts of Aalborg and Aarhus are characterized by a number of similarities and differences. In terms of similarities, both cities initiated branding efforts around the turn of the millennium, and thus the general socio-cultural context is similar, because both initiatives were formulated with recent notions of the 'creative class' as the backdrop. Moreover, judging from media coverage and debates, neither of the two branding campaigns appears to have gained a strong foothold with the general public, something which could perhaps reflect inadequate assess-ments of the external or internal markets or inefficient cooperation among stakeholders. At the same time the two branding processes have clearly taken place in very different social locales: Aalborg is an old industrial city which has only recently moved decisively towards a knowledge- and service-oriented economy, while Aarhus is historically a cultural city strongly influenced by its university, one of the oldest in Denmark, and by its lively performing arts environment, and thus different configurations of social actors are likely to influence the two processes of brand development. Moreover, a recent Danish survey (Epinion 2006) has demonstrated that the image of Aarhus is considerably stronger than that of Aalborg among the general public and that Aarhus possesses the 'right' associations of a creative and cultured place, as opposed to Aalborg, which is still associated with being an old industrial place. Hence from an external market perspective the city of Aalborg faces more severe challenges in establishing itself as an attractive contemporary city compared to Aarhus. While the Aarhus process was initiated to reinforce existing strengths (Århus Kommune 2004), the need to emphasize that Aalborg has changed and will continue to change is prominent in the strategy documents produced here (www.brandingaalborg.dk/). It is, furthermore, worth noting that the efforts to re-brand Aalborg must be seen in a wider context of urban change centring on the remaking of an extensive semi-derelict waterfront close to the city centre (Jensen 2007). These differences with regard to internal and external relations constitute the core of a very real and practical branding challenge for the two cities, and the subsequent description of their respective brands will illustrate whether the two places have interpreted their past and future differently and, indeed, whether it is an advantage or a disadvantage in terms of stakeholder involvement that the branding process involves a further development of an existing place identity, as in the case of Aarhus, or an attempt fundamentally to change the existing place identity, as in the case of Aalborg.

## ANALYSIS AND FINDINGS

The starting point of the analysis is stakeholder inclusion and how it compares across the two cases. In the case of Aalborg the municipality-led branding secretariat is the main actor in all phases of the branding process – from agenda setting, through design, to implementation. It is important to note that the branding secretariat is centrally placed as part of the mayor's office, and it does not appear to include other municipal actors like the business development department or the city's planning department as central partners in the process (Therkelsen *et al.* 2010). Other non-municipal actors have been included in the branding process in the design and implementation phases, among these VisitAalborg, the local tourism organization, which has been a member of the brand board since it was established. Despite early inclusion, the tourism organization only half-heartedly supports the city branding initiative, which among other things is seen by the tourism organization's limited usage of the communication platform developed for the brand. The city retail organization has throughout the process been on the sideline, only joining in as an active partner in connection with specific events where it sees an added value in joining forces with the municipality and other local actors. The Aarhus case bears some resemblance to the Aalborg case in that the initiative has been led by the municipality in the agenda-setting and design phases, but unlike the Aalborg case it has been more solidly anchored in the municipality across departments. Broad stakeholder inclusion of non-municipal actors through discussion groups has characterized the process, and these have from the start included both the tourism organization and the city retail organization. In the implementation phase, responsibility has, however, been handed over to the tourism organization, which may jeopardize the umbrella status of the brand, as it may be 'degraded' to a sector-specific brand in the eyes of both stakeholders and markets. Furthermore, this action may be interpreted as a sign of loss of commitment on the part of the municipality, something we will return to below.

*Source:*   ©www.brandingaalborg.dk; ©www.aarhuskommune.dk.

*Figure 12.2   Logos of city brands in Aalborg and Aarhus*

In terms of strategic choices, the aim of the two place branding cases falls into the category of either repositioning (change) or confirming a position (continuity), as illustrated by the two symbolic representations chosen (Figure 12.2). By making use of the slogan 'Aalborg – seize the world', as well as a logo with an exploding globe (the 'o' in the city name), the Aalborg brand clearly emphasizes a global identity – reaching out and welcoming the world – which in many ways stands in contrast to what this old industrial place has traditionally been associated with. This is also supported by the value platform of the brand ('wide prospects', 'diversity'), although elements of continuity are also present ('teamwork', 'drive') which draw on a local self-perception of being strong and peripheral with a culture of collaboration and entrepreneurship that has its roots in the industrial past (www.brandingaalborg.dk). The logo of the Aarhus brand consists of the city name shaped as a smile, which refers to the slogan 'The smiling city' that has been associated with the place since 1938 when the local tourism association invented it, thereby reinforcing an existing image as well as widespread self-perception. The value platform of the brand also communicates continuity (Århus Kommune 2004): 'roots' refers back to the historical heritage of Vikings and other relics of the past; 'pulse' refers to the cultural offerings of the place, not least the diversified music scene, which caters especially for young people; and 'knowledge' links up with the long-standing university status of the city. Like other former industrial cities in Western Europe such as Glasgow and Bilbao, and the German Ruhr area (Gomez 1999; Belina and Helms 2003), Aalborg follows a strategy of change by which it tries to reposition itself as a cosmopolitan place, but with roots in its industrial background, which gives warmth and closeness to the brand. Aarhus, on the other hand, pursues a strategy of continuity, seeking to reinforce its present image and identity as a cultural place with a heritage of university traditions and a diversified arts and music scene, and with little explicit interest in and hospitality extended to the outside world.

In terms of market orientation, selling the place to external target groups is in focus for all stakeholders in both cases, as attracting new residents, companies, tourists and shoppers contributes to the economic foundation of the stakeholders. Interesting to note, however, is the fact that even the municipality actors in the two cases give limited attention to internal target groups, as installing pride and engagement in the cities among their citizens is not seen as an integral part of the branding effort, although it was in both cases presented as an initial ambition.

With regard to the means by which branding is being pursued, both municipalities have a clear focus on symbolic representation, and hence place branding has not been seen as integrated with wider plans for urban development in the two cities. Interestingly, only two private actors, the Aarhus tourism and retail organizations, display a fairly holistic understanding in that they see symbolic representation and physical place-making as two sides of the same coin which have to be closely integrated for the place branding effort to make sense. Conversely, among the private Aalborg actors it is only the concrete place-making initiatives that are seen as attractive – particularly events that are appealing to their specific target groups of tourists and shoppers and which they prefer to market by means of their own communication concepts and tools and thus with limited use of the Branding Aalborg communication platform.

Finally, the level and kind of commitment displayed among the three types of actors across the two cases vary significantly. The municipality actor in the Aalborg case considers the branding campaign as imperative in that it sees itself fighting the outdated industrial image which appears to linger on in Danish public opinion (Epinion 2006) and which is out of touch with the present socio-economic reality of the city. In this process of repositioning, the Aalborg branding campaign is seen as an important tool. Quite contrary to this, the municipality actor in the Aarhus case sees its own branding campaign as less important, as it perceives itself as having a strong and positive image, which is supported by an existing image analysis (Epinion 2006). Its reason for embarking upon a branding campaign hence seems rather obscure, and this limited commitment by the branding initiator may be one reason why responsibility for the campaign was handed over to the tourism organization in the implementation phase. Interestingly, the level of commitment among the private actors is the reverse of that of the public actors in the two cases. In the case of Aalborg the tourism and retail organizations perceive the place branding effort as being of importance only as a means of product development (i.e. event-making) for their tourist and retail target groups, and the common communication platform appears to have little value to them. Hence a utilitarian 'What's in it for me?' approach characterizes these two organizations. In the case of Aarhus, on the other hand, both the tourism and the retail organizations see the common branding initiative as an important cross-sector effort that will help position the city as attractive in the experience economy. Hence the commitment of the tourism and retail organizations goes beyond their own organizational gains, and they even appear to be more dedicated to the city branding project than the municipal initiator.

## CONCLUSION

This chapter has analysed place branding efforts in two Danish provincial cities on the basis of a theoretical framework based on three concepts – inclusion, strategy and commitment – in order to explain how stakeholder interaction influences place branding processes. In the existing literature it has been argued that significant overlaps of stakeholders in the agenda setting, design and implementation phases of the branding process are necessary to develop place branding viably in the long term. However, the empirical case study has demonstrated that this does not guarantee stakeholder commitment, as agreement on visions and goals does not spring from inclusion alone but just as importantly from sharing strategic priorities. By comparing the two case studies we have found that despite the different positioning strategies involved – while Aarhus attempts to reinforce an existing image, Aalborg aims to project a new (post-industrial) one – in practice the two branding strategies are quite similar. Both of them focus on selling place to external would-be users or consumers rather than building community internally, and both of them give priority to communication efforts without integrating these with tangible place-making to any great extent, and thus in practice the two branding processes would seem to resemble traditional place promotion rather than comprehensive place branding. In the light of this it is particularly interesting to note that in both cases the commitment to the branding process would appear to be uneven, with a proactive municipal branding office facing somewhat reluctant external partners in Aalborg, and an apparently more half-heartedly committed municipal actor in Aarhus that transfers the responsibility to the tourism agency, which together with the retail organization seems strongly engaged in the branding initiative. This clearly suggests that early inclusion, not even acting as initiator, is not enough to ensure commitment to place branding, and that both public and private actors may be influenced by other reasons for engaging more or less extensively in a branding process. In order to ensure commitment, inclusion has to be coupled with development and acceptance of a common strategy, identifying not only overall aims but also target markets, communication efforts and, not least, concrete place-making activities. If an *ex ante* assessment has not been made of the need for a branding strategy, including the problems it is supposed to address, and if stakeholders have not been included on a strategically informed basis, then the stakeholders involved may end up being the well-established 'old boys' network' (i.e. prominent organizations of the city), and this may result in highly different levels of commitment among stakeholders that will constitute significant challenges to inter-organizational cooperation as well as to producing a coherent and durable brand as the outcome. From a theoretical perspective, this conclusion suggests that study of the politics of place branding can be furthered through the adoption of a multi-dimensional conceptual framework like the one employed in the current text, and it would therefore be interesting to widen the geographical focus of research through a systematic comparison of place branding processes in medium-sized cities across Europe.

## REFERENCES

Århus Kommune (2004) *Branding af Århus*, Århus: Århus Kommune.

Belina, B. and Helms, G. (2003) 'Zero tolerance for the industrial past and other threats: Policing and urban entrepreneurialism in Britain and Germany', *Urban Studies*, 40, 9, 1845–1867.

Eckstein, B. and Throgmorton, J.A. (eds), (2003) *Story and Sustainability: Planning, Practice and Possibility for American Cities*, Cambridge, MA: MIT Press.

Epinion (2006) *Måling af Horsens som dynamisk by*, København: Epinion.

Florida, R. (2002) *The Rise of the Creative Class: And How It Is Transforming Work, Leisure, Community and Everyday Life*, New York: Basic Books.

Gomez, M.V. (1999) 'Reflective images: The case of urban regeneration in Glasgow and Bilbao', *International Journal of Urban and Regional Research*, 22, 1, 106–121.

Halkier, H. (2006) *Institutions, Discourse and Regional Development: The Scottish Development Agency and the Politics of Regional Policy*, Brussels: PIE Peter Lang.

Hankinson, G. (2007) 'The management of destination brands: Five guiding principles based on recent developments in corporate branding theory', *Brand Management*, 14, 3, 240–254.

Hogwood, B.W. and Gunn, L.A. (1986) *Policy Analysis for the Real World*, Oxford: Oxford University Press.

Ind, N. (2003) 'Inside out: How employees build value', *Journal of Brand Management*, 10, 6, 393–402.

Jensen, O.B. (2007) 'Culture stories: Understanding cultural urban branding', *Planning Theory*, 6, 3, 211–236.

Kavaratzis, M. and Ashworth, G.J. (2005) 'City branding: An effective assertion of identity or a transitory marketing trick?', *Tijdschrift voor Economische en Sociale Geografie*, 96, 5, 506–514.

Keller, K.L. (2003) *Building, Measuring, and Managing Brand Equity*, 2nd edition, Upper Saddle River, NJ: Prentice Hall, Pearson Education International.

Kvale, S. (1996) *InterViews: An Introduction to Qualitative Research Interviewing*, London: Sage.

Morgan, N. and Pritchard, A. (eds) (2001) *Advertising in Tourism and Leisure*, Oxford: Butterworth-Heinemann.

Ooi, C.-S. (2004) 'Poetics and politics of destinational branding: Denmark', *Scandinavian Journal of Hospitality and Tourism*, 4, 2, 107–128.

Parsons, W. (1995) *Public Policy: An Introduction to the Theory and Practice of Policy Analysis*, Aldershot, UK and Brookfield, VT, USA: Edward Elgar Publishing.

Pedersen, S.B. (2004) 'Place branding: Giving the region of Øresund a competitive edge', *Journal of Urban Technology*, 11, 1, 77–95.

Rhodes, R.A.W. and Marsh, D. (1992) 'New directions in the study of policy networks', *European Journal of Political Research*, 21, 1–2, 181–195.

Therkelsen, A. and Halkier, H. (2008) 'Contemplating place branding umbrellas: The case of coordinated national tourism and business promotion', *Scandinavian Journal of Hospitality and Tourism*, 8, 2, 159–175.

Therkelsen, A., Halkier, H. and Jensen, O.B. (2010) 'Branding Aalborg: Building community or selling place?', in G. Ashworth and M. Kavaratzis (eds), *Towards Effective Place Brand Management: Branding European Cities and Regions*, Cheltenham, UK and Northampton, MA, USA: Edward Elgar Publishing.

Thomson, K., de Chernatony, L., Arganbright, L. and Khan, S. (1999) 'The buy-in benchmark: How staff understanding and commitment impact brand and business performance', *Journal of Marketing Management*, 15, 8, 819–835.

Thorelli, H.B. (1986) 'Networks: Between markets and hierarchies', *Strategic Management Journal*, 7, 1, 37–51.

Turok, I. (2009) 'The distinctive city: Pitfalls in the pursuit of differential advantage', *Environment and Planning A*, 41, 1, 13–30.

# 13. Design activism meets place-branding: Reconfiguring urban representation and everyday practice

**Guy Julier**

## INTRODUCTION

A brand tells a story. A story employs a text set across a structure. Place-branding involves the deployment of a coordinated and homogenised campaign of aesthetic features and attitudinal markers across a location. But the resulting weave is also open to unpicking, frottage or re-use. Any story is helped along with an attention-grabbing opener, so, on 26 September 2005, the Leeds City Council's place-marketing arm, Marketing Leeds, unveiled its city brand at the city's famous Victoria Quarter. This arcade includes such key up-market retail brands as Harvey Nichols, Ted Baker and Louis Vuitton, which underline Leeds's national reputation as a shopping destination. The event featured support messages from Leeds-connected celebrities such as Chris Moyles, the BBC Radio 1 DJ, and local bands Embrace and the Kaiser Chiefs. The brand carried the slogan 'Leeds. Live It. Love It'. In developing this identity, the local branding and communications group entitled An Agency Called England undertook a survey of Leeds residents to discern, if the city was a person, what kind of person that would be. As if to underline the consumeristic bias of its launch, the 'research' that came back was that Leeds would be 'a young male, friendly, your best friend, a really nice person to know, an ambitious person, living in a trendy apartment, driving a Volkswagen Golf GTi' (Scott 2005).

Outside the 'official' identity for Leeds sit a number of cues that provide alternative narratives for the city. That Leeds is home to the largest Jewish population and the most extensive Afro-Carribean carnival in the UK outside London was absent at the launch party. So too were other causes for celebration, such as the city's long history that melded creative practices and political activism, evidenced through bands such as the Mekons and Chumbawamba. Additionally, it is home to the Leeds Animation Workshop, founded in 1976 as a group of women friends who came together to make a film about the need for pre-school childcare. Since then they have produced numerous titles on social issues. Leeds is also the home of Leeds Postcards. Founded in 1979, this group set the standard for activist stationery in the 1980s. Leeds is also where, via a slow process of community participation, steps were taken in the 1990s towards the establishment of Britain's first Home Zone, turning residential streets into mixed-use civic spaces. By 2008, a group of what I will call 'design activists' had instigated a counter-brand with the slogan 'Leeds. Love It. Share It', connecting into a number of other initiatives (Figure 13.1).

The subversion of brands, by their decollage or rewriting, has become a common trope within activism. Examples of 'subvertising' are abundant. Witness, for example, www.subvertise.org or the journal *Adbusters*, where visual or literary puns on company names, ads or slogans are made in order to reveal how they conspire in systems of exploitation. Hence, 'Ford' becomes 'Fraud', and so on. Such incursions are nonetheless reactive. They provide critiques of dominant actors and processes within neoliberal capitalism, but they do not necessarily propose alternative actions. Subvertisements, I hold, might be effective in jogging political consciousness, but by existing wholly in the same cultural field – print and digital media – they do not offer any specific indicators as 'the next step'.

By contrast, a counter-brand may extend from critique into the instigation of alternative attitudinal markers for action. The slogan 'Leeds. Love It. Share It' is, at a basic level, a subversion of the official line of 'Leeds. Live It. Love It'. This takes some inspiration from the historical tradition of culture-jamming activities, some of which were, indeed, energised through the aforementioned Leeds Postcards, but it also offers the suggestion that local enthusiasms can be mustered toward a more equal and inclusive practice of urban life. The Leeds of the official brand slogan is almost an abstract concept. Loving it is loving an idea of Leeds. However, sharing it raises the questions 'Share what? Amongst whom? In what proportions?' and so on. Thus focus is diverted toward the specifics of its physical and economic resources and its people. A more concrete notion of Leeds is considered to be acted upon.

With reference to the case of Leeds, this chapter reviews the ways that design activism contests and disrupts the assumed spatiality that is inherent in place-branding. In particular, folded into the dominant spatial ideology is the notion, within their governance, of postindustrial urban agglomerations as, primarily, sites of consumption in the context of neoliberal global networks. The economic and spatial logic on which this

*Source:* ©Marketing Leeds; ©Leeds Love It Share It CIC.

*Figure 13.1* *'Leeds. Live It. Love It' and 'Leeds. Love It. Share It' city brand logos*

ideology is founded becomes challenged by the dual exigencies of financial meltdown and climate change. This opens up a space within which its own protaganists begin to question their own assumptions. However, as 'political intermediaries', activists – including those working in the design sphere – have already anticipated the need for changes in tempo and focus in local governance.

## PLACE-BRANDING AND GLOBALISM

The *a priori* casting of urban identities in a globalist way is common among many academic accounts. For example, Anna Klingmann takes a critical view of international architectural traditions that foreground landmark buildings as a tactic for making a place recognisable. She sees the tactics of branding – in her case, thinking about the orchestration of the users' experience of spatial phenomena – as an antidote to this. Nonetheless she begins her book by positing that 'It is a fact that people and places must differentiate themselves in a global economy' (2007: 27). The emphasis here is on the outward orientation of locations and the users of them. The latter's everyday dispositions therefore become automatically imbricated into their role as actors on a world stage rather than in their own right or oriented toward more localised outlooks. Being cosmopolitan is part of being urban; being urban is part of participating in the global order of things and their economy.

The need for differentiation through place-branding exists within assumptions with regard to inter-territorial competition for investment, jobs, residents and visitors (Storper 1997; Buck *et al.* 2005). This is derived in part from a logic formed with management studies, in particular Porter's notion of 'competitive advantage' (Porter 1990). Here, differentation is concerned with providing a niche within the marketplace rather than head-on competition with other companies or, in this case, places. Thus the features of a place are refined and articulated in order to attract certain forms of capital investment, entrepreneurial expertise and labour resources according to that script (Jensen 2007).

This is a defensive strategy in that it responds to perceived demands of the global marketplace rather than proposes an alternative approach to the healthy economic, social and environmental maintenance of a place. Recent much quoted examples suggest that alternative frameworks of existence for urban agglomerations may be pursued. Regeneration specialists in Rotterdam are investigating the notion of reframing the city as a 'skill city'. By focusing on the existing and latent faculties of its population, it is expected that alliances, dispositions and relationships may be forged that provide new social models for conviviality (Oosterling 2007). Detroit is emerging from terminal deindustrialisation and depopulation as an energetic model for urban agriculture (Boggs 2003).

Critiques have emerged that problematise the easy alliance of urban identity, globalism and a homogenising view of cities. Fraser and Weninger (2008: 1436) argue that the narratives of globalisation and neoliberal governance are 'increasingly deployed as the lens through which the transformation of urban space is written'. Smith (2001: 43) maintains that early accounts to understand globalisation in terms of finance and flexible accumulation (in particular, for example, Harvey 1985) leave out politics as a social and cultural force. They omit an analysis of power in all its criss-crossing forms as opposed to the power of capital. Robinson (2006) adds that the dominant account of globalisation privileges a Western notion of modernity within whose discourse cities are subsequently ranked.

These assumptions about the operation of urban agglomerations automatically lead to some quite basic problems. Within days of the Leeds brand launch it was revealed that Hong Kong had already carried the 'Live It. Love It' marketing slogan for three years. This confirms one of the perennial problems of place-branding: that, in fixing the image of a location in a readable and understandable way for a global audience, the message is reduced to broad rhetorical devices. Equally, a brief survey of cities shows that Singapore, Brisbane and Birmingham have described themselves as 'dynamic' and 'cosmopolitan' or 'diverse'. Johannesburg and Manchester were both 'vibrant'; Birmingham, Glasgow and Johannesburg were 'cultural'; Santo Domingo and Brisbane, they claimed, were 'sophisticated' (Julier 2005). Theirs is a quest to ally themselves with notions of being modern and cosmospolitan while at the same time differentiating themselves from each other. However, they show that the limited scope allowed in the former leads to failure in the latter (Turok 2009).

Nevertheless, slogans and tags are merely one part of the codification of urban identities and their formation through promotional graphics, urban design, architecture and marketing strategies. Place-brands are subject to guidelines that rigorously set out such details as allowable applications of colour palettes, typefaces or textual copy. These provide legally enforceable standards, transposing research into local characteristics and/or their global reputation into intellectual property. In so doing they also establish a marque of authority over specific spatial contexts.

## AUTHORITARIANISM BEYOND PLACE-BRANDS

This authoritarianism extends into the built environment through planning processes whose aesthetic features are also informed by localised design guides. Urban design is redolent with compendia and 'best practice' guidelines that involve the codification of its practice and outcomes. These are invariably arrived at by careful appraisal of the architectural and planning features of the city, but at the same time they are tightly bound into assumptions with regard to notions of 'character' and 'modernity' and how these are communicated (Julier 2009).

In the UK, this process has been folded into urban regeneration strategies. The UK government's Urban Task Force, founded soon after New Labour's election to power in 1997, published its highly influential policy statement *Towards an Urban Renaissance* (Urban Task Force 1999). This and the subsequent Urban White Paper (2000) came amongst a plethora of government policy that attempted to address urban living in the postindustrial era. For the first time, design was placed as a key component in the revitalisation of urban areas. Nonetheless, its translation into government policy and thence into application at local level has tended to focus largely on a narrow interpretation of design as engaging its purely formal rather than processual features. Implicit in this is a behaviouristic model of urban design that is deeply embedded in its theoretical backgrounds (see Cuthbert 2006). In brief, this approach is firmly rooted in a view of space as the assemblage of typologies that are based entirely on their material facets rather than on practices of everyday life. Thus, for example, we hear of 'settlement pattern', 'urban form', 'urban space' and 'built form' (e.g. Department for Communities and Local Government 2006: 65) rather than the human infrastructure of, say, 'kinship', 'mobility', 'social networks' or 'labour'.

Whether it be the guides on 'best practice' in developing design codes or the design codes themselves, the emphasis is on design that produces attitudes and behaviours in and toward places. Put the other way around, despite the recurrent reminders that public consultation is generally a good thing in the development of design guidelines, the end result is a particular, specifically cast narrative of what urban living should be. This narrative is, in turn, served up as something to be consumed, adhered to and adopted as a disposition or, as Bourdieu (1984) would have had it, an urban habitus. Citizens are to complete the scenography, in other words.

This is perhaps more implicit in design codes and guidelines for urban design and planning. In place-branding the message is perhaps clearer or, even, more brutal in that it requests a particular form of performativity in response to the brand values that are laid down. Branding orthodoxy involves the fixing of core themes that describe the essential features of the object. These are, in turn, translated into aesthetic gestures that begin with a fixing slogan. These are further rolled out into a logo, websites, print material and beyond, sometimes into aspects of urban design, planning and architecture (Julier 2005). Brand guidelines provide rigorous rules on the use of such details as colour, typography and 'voice'. Design implementations of the brand may be controlled by the restriction of any subcontracted work to an approved roster of design studios, which make legal agreements to adhere to the guidelines. In this way, the message is tightly controlled.

## THE POLITICAL ECONOMY OF PLACE-BRANDING

Mommaas (2002: 34) usefully provides a summary of the conundrums that are felt through place-branding and its connection to an authoritarian view of development and globalisation. He argues that not addressing the particularities of local culture produces the following tensions:

1.  the tendency to gear city brands to the dynamic of an external cash-rich market rather than to that of internal cultural practices and feelings;
2.  the tendency to objectify and generalise specific cultural meanings by the means of 'brands' and then to link these meanings materially to spectacular places and projects;
3.  the possible danger that 'brands' preclude renewal rather than stimulate it, the long-term effect being that urban practices are dragged along on their necessary inflation. (Mommaas 2002: 34)

In Leeds, the intense instrumentalisation of design in the fixing of an image and practice of urban living goes hand in hand with a set of priorities with regard to its political economy. Over the past 20 years, Leeds and its city-centre in particular have undergone significant change. Key features include:

- re-imagining of the city as a 24-hour city, with 'European' allusions to being the 'Barcelona of the North', 24-hour café society and city-centre living from the early 1990s (Haughton and Williams 1996);
- growth of its city-centre population from a few hundred to a projected 20 000 by 2015 (Knight Frank 2005) – note, however, that this will account for only 2 per cent of the city's population (Fox and Unsworth 2003);
- £1.4 billion worth of office and apartment schemes under construction at the end of 2006 and a further £5.8 billion proposed – a total of £10.4 billion since 1997 (Leeds City Council, cited in Chatterton and Hodkinson 2007);

- reduction of social housing stock by 40 000 over the past 25 years, with a further reduction of 10 000 by 2016 (Leeds City Council, cited in Hodkinson and Chatterton 2007);
- adherence to the largest public–private partnership or private funding initiative programmes in schools, health and other welfare provision (£880 million) in the UK and a consequent tying in of their operation and governance with a range of private services in accountancy and law and other forms of private sector service delivery (Fauset 2009).

In short, then, the visual and material transformation of Leeds – intensely focused on its city-centre – has stood to confirm and, even, celebrate its participation in neoliberal policies on the financialisation of its operations at a regional or national level while, at the same time, to implicate it even more deeply into global flows of capital. The place-brand, architectural and urban design inputs to the city must be read in the context of capitalisation and financialisation processes (Molotch 1976; Minton 2009). Challenges to the city's prevailing dominant design strategies must also be read as challenges to its dominant ideological discourse with regard to its economic and, thus, spatial structure.

This drive itself came about in response to the perceived poor performance of Leeds against an ascendant verve for ranking global cities (see CWHB 2002; Sperling and Sander 2005). At a city envisioning event in 2002 ('The Big Meeting') it was noted that Leeds did not figure amongst the top 20 European cities to do business in. For a city of only 700 000 inhabitants competing against the likes of Frankfurt, Amsterdam and Barcelona, this should hardly be a thwarted ambition. However, the exterior perception of Leeds certainly riled. In 2003, the local advertising agency Brahm was commissioned by the city council to carry out research on external perceptions of Leeds. Out of this, but also out of a more general sense of insecurity shared amongst the city officials and leadership, came the notion of 'going up a league'. This was coined as the first aim of the umbrella group of city council, agencies and leaders, the Leeds Initiative. According to a Leeds Initiative member who followed this development closely, this was made in response to a comment by Hans Anders, Senior Planner of Gothenburg. Reflecting on 'The Big Meeting', he argued that, 'If you don't work on going up a league, you will end up going down one' (Unsworth 2010). The Leeds Initiative went on to state that this involved 'making Leeds an internationally competitive city, the best place in the country to live, work and learn, with a high quality of life for everyone' (Leeds Initiative 2004). The 'Leeds. Live It. Love It' brand was therefore constituted in this boosteristic context.

## CHALLENGES TO PLACE-BRANDS

Place-brands may not always go in one direction, either on the part of their originators or on that of interlopers. Dismantling or understating a place-brand may be a deliberate process on the part of its originators. Medway and Warnaby (2008) raise the notion of strategic 'demarketing' of places. They draw attention to the occasional need to manage visitor numbers in order to avoid supply outstripping demand or to discourage the 'wrong kind' (e.g. disruptive stag parties). They also argue that 'perverse place marketing' may be effective, for example, by drawing attention to the quirkiness of a location (e.g. Whitby as a 'goth town' to attract a niche visitorship) or its underside (e.g. the London Borough of Hackney advertising itself as 'Britain's Poorest Borough' in the 1980s in order to influence policy makers).

Subculturally orientated entrepreneurialism may also trigger unofficial place identifiers. The 'Birmingham: It's Not Shit' website (see www.birminghamitsnotshit.co.uk) was established in 2002. It acts as a mildly sarcastic celebration of the city, delivering paeans to such features as its 1960s Bullring shopping centre or the city's No. 11 bus route. For its author, the humourist Jon Bounds, this site also provides a shop-window for his writing and an opportunity to sell related merchandise. However, it also provides an important opportunity for listings of gigs and other events and has an enthusiastic blog following. The website gently mocks notions of city pride whilst providing an alternative lens through which the city may be seen.

Similarly, even before the 'Leeds. Live It. Love It' brand was released, local radio station Aire FM had promoted an alternative identity for the city. In 2004, it ran a billboard advert adjacent to the annual temporary ice-rink in the city-centre that read, 'No La-De-Da Skating, No Lycra Outfits, No Cheesy Smiles, Remember This Is Leeds'. Bell (2009) argues that city-centre ice-skating provides a regulated ludic space – the engineering of affect (Thrift 2004) – while at the same time underscoring notions of individual and collective risk as well as entrepreneurialism. It provides a materialisation of 'official' city aspirations and an opportunity for participants to adopt these as dispositions. But Aire FM had other thoughts. There was another narrative of Leeds, and Yorkshire, as unfussy, solid and down to earth (Sandle 2004) to be got over, and heady city ambitions were not going to detract from this other story.

The image of 'going up a league', of Leeds as the international, 24-hour city to do business in, of retail-fuelled loving-it-while-you-live-it, got severely dented by the economic recession of 2008–10. Employment had peaked at 455 000 in 2007 and was expected to decrease by 18 800 over the following three years (Leeds City Council 2009). Of a total of 5653 city-centre apartments, 15.51 per cent were empty at the beginning of 2009, 7 per cent of which had been so for more than 12 months (BBC 2009). As the city's River Aire burst its banks – the second major flooding of the city-centre inside a year – this gave visible evidence of the need to build a more sustainable approach to urban planning and design. In the background, the development boom had passed its zenith. The credit crunch of early 2008 and loss in demand led to many schemes being put on hold, including the £160 million Spiracle tower, a building for which the city's only city-centre public swimming pool was closed to make way.

Set against this recessionary backcloth was the rise of a number of new activist initiatives in the city which were centred on issues of sustainability, urban form and governance. These included Stop Climate Chaos Leeds, a Transition Towns group, the Leeds Eco-Village project, the Leeds: Are We Going in the Right Direction? initiative and Climate for Change. Amidst these, and drawing on the city's 'alternative' historical roots, a revindication of design activism was sought amongst several of its creative practitioners. While, needless to say, some impetus for such activist initiatives may be read in the context of global concerns with regard to climate change, peak oil and economic crises, their focus was highly localised in that they rested on questions of the ways that Leeds is and could be. The official brand was a useful point of reference for contestation for design activists.

## DESIGN ACTIVISM IN THEORY

Fuad-Luke (2009: 27) puts forward a definition of design activism as 'design thinking, imagination and practice applied knowingly or unknowingly to create a counter narrative aimed at generating and balancing positive social, institutional, environmental and/or economic change'. It could be claimed that design activism has as long a pedigree as the profession itself. The emergent, modern conception of design in the latter half of the nineteenth century located it in terms of an 'added value' that was to temper a Kantian notion of endless production that filled out the later industrial revolution. Design was an ethical challenge that harnessed taste and control as against the rampant commercialism of modern production and consumer culture (Dutta 2009). Thus, as propagated by John Ruskin, William Morris, Christopher Dresser and their progenies, design was to be a moral filtering system. Since the early 1970s, design for social need and ecological concerns have been recurrent themes, as witnessed by the enduring success of Victor Papanek's seminal text *Design for the Real*

*World* (1972), which became an international cult book for designers and non-designers alike.

The activist impulse amongst many designers has been given further impetus since 2000. Needless to say, this may be allied with general concerns for environmental amelioration and social justice, as echoed in such books as *Massive Change: A Manifesto for the Future Global Design Culture* (Mau 2004) and *Design Like You Give a Damn: Architectural Reponses to Humanitarian Crises* (Architecture for Humanity 2006). In such accounts, following in the footsteps of Papanek, the designer's work keys into globalist ambitions wherein expertise is lent to specific local challenges (such as fresh water or mobility) as part of a world view on responsibility. Here, creative solutions are largely technical before they are social.

There is another design activist approach that foregrounds social practices. This focuses on innovations that individuals or communities create for themselves, seeing that 'unofficial customisation' of resources may be of significance. The designer's job is to recognise these and facilitate their development and possible up-scaling. Thus, for example, turning informal arrangements for lift-sharing into a neighbourhood scheme supported by internet booking may be a social innovation that the designer develops upon (Manzini and Jégou 2004). In this approach the emphasis is on the small-scale and local and on the analysis of the everyday ways by which people live and their capabilities. While this verve for localism may be a starting point, it is accepted that cultures are not territorialised but exist in extended relational networks and flows. Thus, to borrow from Fraser and Weninger (2008: 1438), the design activist enters into these networks and becomes 'part of the dynamic that produces futures'.

## DESIGN ACTIVISM IN PRACTICE

The 'Leeds. Love It. Share It' counter-brand was established in 2008 by a seven-strong group of creative practitioners and members of the academic community who were concerned about the direction of Leeds. The 'Leeds. Live It. Love It' slogan was seen to typify the globalist ideology, powered by neoliberal financialisation, as already discussed above. However, to recap, 'Leeds. Love It. Share It' was more than a cheeky rebuff or a challenge to the authoritarianism of the official brand and what it stood for. Its implication in 'sharing it' was to shift attention from the city-centre as a site of tourism, shopping and night-time economies, to a participative city, encompassing all its spatial and demographic features.

The activism that was intended in producing an alternative logotype was in a moral position held by the group that the city's population deserved 'something better', both visually and in its message. It was also driven by an awareness of the need imaginatively to re-think the ways that everyday urban life is practised and identified in the face of climate change, peak oil and global economic recession.

The management of the counter-brand would have to be distinct from the official Leeds brand. The official 'Leeds. Live It. Love It' logotype could be liberally applied to merchandise and communications that existed in the dominant neoliberal domain of the city's urban culture. The 'Leeds. Love It. Share It' counter-brand had to honour the autonomy of other activist groups in Leeds (thus not being seen to appropriate their own energies). Any alternative space that it inhabited would, effectively, have to be created by itself. Distribution of the counter-brand was therefore low-key and, thus, it was largely ignored by Marketing Leeds, which managed the official city brand. In any case, since it was of entirely original design, the counter-brand was not in any breach of any legal guidelines governing trade marks.

In seeking another space for the counter-brand to become embedded and meaningful, 'Leeds. Love It. Share It' worked to model design activist practice. Whilst the counter-brand deliberately set out to challenge dominant conceptions of the city, it was also necessary to instigate activities that demonstrated the possibilities of alternative approaches to the city's economic, social and environmental make-up.

'Leeds. Love It. Share It' could therefore not work entirely independently of the systems of local governance. It would look to building relationships with interested departments of the Regional Development Agency, Yorkshire Forward and other agencies that were engaged in the development and delivery of regeneration and neighbourhood management services. In so doing, it exploited the very system of what Whitfield (2006) calls 'agentification' that neoliberal governance had itself established. Here, delivery of public sector services may be developed and managed through the alliance of local authority social services, semi-public agencies and the voluntary sector. These in turn may be financed through a mixture of recurrent local authority expenditure, specific national or European government grants or charitable donation. 'Leeds. Love It. Share It' could therefore insert itself into this complex web of interests, benefiting from partnerships, while not so stridently challenging the status quo as to alienate itself from potential funders or allies. The balancing act of activism and collaboration was most probably achieved through careful targeting of interested parties (e.g. speaking to sympathetic people in the Regional Development Agency), coupled with demonstrating that the aims and expertise of 'Leeds. Love It. Share It' could be of longer-term benefit to the city at large. Finally, for legal-financial reasons it thus had to constitute itself as a community interest company in order to manage externally funded projects.

Through a one-year project entitled 'Margins within the City', funded by Yorkshire Forward and the Local Enterprise Generation Unit, 'Leeds. Love It. Share It' undertook a mapping of social networks, skills and space use in the Leeds inner suburb of Richmond Hill (population 17 000) during 2009. This revealed the hidden potentials that exist in a maligned and little-understood neighbourhood that carried a reputation for long-term unemployment, social fragmentation and a poor environment. However, the chief concern of this project was to design and prototype mapping tools that could be rolled out to other neighbourhoods. In so doing, the emphasis was on discovering and drawing attention to their productive capacities. These may reside in an expanded field of economic practices and social skills – ones that do not appear in business listings – such as mending cars or informal caring arrangements. The mapping process itself thus becomes a way that a neighbourhood knows itself. Focusing on its productive capacities (both extant and in potentia and in their broadest conception) provides a means to forge new place-identities that are flexible, dynamic and specific to the everyday lives of citizens.

Why should this be seen as design activism rather than, more generally, as activist work? At a banal level, the generation of a counter-brand involves design decisions as to its form and content. But it is the more extended activities of 'Leeds. Love It. Share It' that lend themselves to 'design thinking'. More specifically, its approach resonates with the emergent specialism of 'service design' (Kimbell 2009). This is very much concerned with investigating the relations and exchanges that go on between citizens and environments. Its method involves deep user research in order to understand the variety of requirements and experiences that they engage. In addition, notice may be taken of small-scale innovations that users and producers of services create themselves, seeing that their 'unofficial customisation' may be of significance and applicability that can be up-scaled. In the case of 'Margins within the City', mapping such things as the distribution of social centres or corner shops, what they provide and how community members access them pays attention to the micro-levels of everyday life and how, in turn, these relate to a larger sense of neighbourhood.

Such data can then be returned to community stakeholders so that they can engage in the design and development of services that are most appropriate to their needs. The project has revealed the 'hollowing out' of the neighbourhood through the progressive removal of power, place-identity, finance, economic opportunity and services in preference to the capital and infrastructural intensity of the city-centre and elsewhere (Leeds. Love

It. Share It 2010). But, in the small-scale innovations, the adaptations and the exploitation of low costs that may be found in economically marginal neighbourhoods or the forging of informal economies, alternative forms of resilience and adaptability that challenge the dominant scales through which a neighbourhood is conceptualised (see Pike *et al.* 2010) may be developed. For Richmond Hill it may not be so much a case of 'going up a league' as inventing a new game.

The overall process outlined above involves a shift from place-brand as representation to counter-brand as a design approach to regeneration. Rather than imposing a top-down conception of city living (one that privileges a mythical lifestyle of an affluent minority, reflecting a city-centre bias) the 'Leeds. Love It. Share It' counter-brand favours the flourishing of multiple identities in a multi-centred urban agglomeration. In moving swiftly from political rhetoric to an on-the-ground project, the 'Leeds. Love It. Share It' group was keen to demonstrate that it could be part of that 'dynamic' of urban life that 'produces futures'. It could be argued that the project conspires with the downloading of responsibility for macro-economic failure to communities and individuals (Perks 2008; Julier 2009). The citizens of Richmond Hill are asked to find in their own meagre resources the social and productive capital to deal with problems caused through a national decline in manufacturing and the emptying out of welfare support. How much 'ethical surplus' (see Arvidsson 2006) is available in the neighbourhood to lend to the creation of a new sense of its own identity might be questionable. Alternatively, by presenting a different 'story' of a locality, this project may help citizens realise their own potential for political, social and economic agency.

## CONCLUSION

Place-branding, as with branding in general, is founded in perceived perception. It is outwardly oriented to the globalist gaze. How an urban agglomeration is framed is dependent on how its dominant authority believes it should be seen. This is driven by a spatial model that sees the city as a node in global flows of finance and people. Thus, in order to make it attractive to the right finance and the right people, it has to invent itself with a language that appeals to this presumed global audience. Meanwhile, its citizens are required to play bit parts within this carefully designed scenario of global (or Western) modernity.

An alternative is to reverse this process, giving prominence to the actors that make up the city, allowing its many practices and identities to provide a multi-layered urban conception. This acknowledges the agency of human action. Design activism may involve re-working the urban habitus or, at least, finding new ways of representing what's there but overlooked.

By shifting from slogan and logotype to action, by only establishing a counter-brand as a starting point for a more extensive, activist approach, the 'Leeds. Love It. Share It' initiative might avoid the pitfalls of mimicry. An official place-brand involves the reduction of a complex spatial and social organism to an oversimplified and easily contestable utterance. A counter-brand can easily do the same. However, if the latter is presented as just the starting point for a debate with regard to the kinds of places we want to live, learn and work in, then it may open out on to other practices.

Reflecting on attempts to re-brand Britain as 'Cool Britannia' during the 1990s, Robert Hewison argued that:

> it is up to the creators of symbolic goods – the designers, artists and architect[s] . . . to scribble all over the marque, to break in from the margins of an ersatz, marketised identity and reveal just what our collective sense of ourselves could be. (Hewison 1997: 31)

However, design activism can do more than just scribble. It can produce alternative narratives or, at least, provide some of the tools to write new stories.

## REFERENCES

Architecture for Humanity (2006) *Design Like You Give a Damn: Architectural Reponses to Humanitarian Crises*, London: Thames and Hudson.

Arvidsson, A. (2006) *Brands: Meaning and Value in Media Culture*, London: Routledge.

BBC (2009) 'Inside Out: Leeds city centre', press release available at http://www.bbc.co.uk/pressoffice/pressreleases/stories/2009/01_january/28/leeds.shtml, accessed 20 November 2009.

Bell, D. (2009) 'Winter wonderlands: Public outdoor ice rinks, entrepreneurial display and festive socialities in UK cities', *Leisure Studies*, 28, 1,: 3–18.

Boggs, G.L. (2003) 'Living for change: Urban agriculture in Detroit', *Michigan Citizen*, XXV, 42, B8.

Bourdieu, P. (1984) *Distinction: A Social Critique of the Judgement of Taste*, trans. Richard Nice, Cambridge, MA: Harvard University Press.

Buck, N., Gordon, I., Harding, A. and Turok, I. (eds) (2005) *Changing Cities: Rethinking Urban Competitiveness, Cohesion and Governance*, London: Palgrave.

Chatterton, P. and Hodkinson, S. (2007) 'Leeds: Skyscraper city', *Yorkshire and Humberside Regional Review*, Spring, 24–26.

Cuthbert, A.R. (2006) *The Form of Cities: Political Economy and Urban Design*, Oxford: Blackwell.

CWHB (2002) 'European cities monitor' Report.

Department for Communities and Local Government (DCLG) (2006) *Preparing Design Codes: A Practice Manual*, London: RIBA Publications.

Dutta, A. (2009) 'Design: On the global (r)uses of a word', *Design and Culture*, 1, 2, 163–186.

Fauset, C. (2009) 'Leeds: Live it, lease it', *Corporate Watch*, 30, http://www.corporatewatch.org.uk/?lid=2573, accessed 20 November 2009.

Fox, P. and Unsworth, R. (2003) 'City living in Leeds – 2003' Report.

Fraser, J. and Weninger, C. (2008) 'Modes of engagement for urban research: Enacting a politics of possibility', *Environment and Planning A*, 40, 6, 1435–1453.

Fuad-Luke, A. (2009) *Design Activism: Beautiful Strangeness for a Sustainable World*, London: Earthscan.

Harvey, D. (1985) *The Urbanization of Capital: Studies in the History and Theory of Capitalist Urbanization*, Baltimore, MD: Johns Hopkins University Press.

Haughton, G. and Williams, C. (eds) (1996) *Corporate City? Partnership, Participation and Partition in Urban Development in Leeds*, Aldershot: Avebury.

Hewison, R. (1997) 'Fool Britannia', *Blueprint*, 144, 30–31.

Hodkinson, S. and Chatterton, P. (2007) 'Leeds: An affordable, viable, sustainable, democratic city?', *Yorkshire and Humberside Regional Review*, Summer, 24–26.

Jensen, O.B. (2007) 'Culture stories: Understanding cultural urban branding', *Planning Theory*, 6, 3, 211–236.

Julier, G. (2005) 'Urban designscapes and the production of aesthetic consent', *Urban Studies*, 42, 5–6, 689–888.

Julier, G. (2009) 'Designing the city', in G. Julier and L. Moor (eds), *Design and Creativity: Policy, Management and Practice*, Oxford: Berg, 40–56.

Kimbell, L. (2009) 'The turn to service design' in G. Julier and L. Moor (eds), *Design and Creativity: Policy, Management and Practice*, Oxford: Berg, 157–173.

Klingmann, A. (2007) *Brandscapes: Architecture in the Experience Economy*, Cambridge, MA: MIT Press.

Knight, F. (2005) 'Future city' Report.

Leeds City Council (2009) 'Leeds economy briefing note', Report, 40.

Leeds Initiative (2004) *A Vision for Leeds*, Leeds: Leeds City Council.

Leeds. Love It. Share It (2010) 'Margins within the City: Social networks, undervalued enterprise and underutilised spaces', Report.

Manzini, E. and Jégou, F. (2004) *Sustainable Everyday: Scenarios of Everyday Life*, Milan: Edizioni Ambiente.

Mau, B. (2004) *Massive Change: A Manifesto for the Future Global Design Culture*, London: Phaidon.

Medway, D. and Warnaby, G. (2008) 'Alternative perspectives on place marketing and the place brand', *European Journal of Marketing*, 42, 5/6, 641–653.

Minton, A. (2009) *Ground Control: Fear and Happiness in the Twenty-First Century City*, London: Penguin Books.

Molotch, H. (1976), 'The city as a growth machine: Toward a political economy of place', *American Journal of Sociology*, 82, 2, 309–332.

Mommaas, H. (2002) 'City branding: The necessity of socio-cultural goals', in V. Patteeuw (ed.), *City Branding: Image Building and Building Images*, Rotterdam: NAI Publishers.

Oosterling, H. (2007) 'Rotterdam skill city' Report.

Papanek, V. (1972) *Design for the Real World*, London: Thames and Hudson.

Perks, M. (2008) 'A radical re-think of what "change" means', *Spiked*, 28 August, http://www.spiked-online.com/index.php/site/reviewofbooks_article/5669, accessed 1 April 2010.

Pike, A., Dawley, S. and Tomaney, J. (2010) 'Resilience, adaptation and adaptability', *Cambridge Journal of Regions, Economy and Society*, 2010, 1–12.

Porter, M. (1990) *The Competitive Advantage of Nations*, New York: Free Press.

Robinson, J. (2006) *Ordinary Cities: Between Modernity and Development*, London: Routledge.

Sandle, D. (2004) 'The Brick Man versus the Angel of the North – public art as contested space', in E. Kennedy and A. Thornton (eds), *Leisure, Media and Visual Culture: Representations and Contestations*, Eastbourne: Leisure Studies Association.

Scott, N. (2005) 'Brand loyalty', *Yorkshire Evening Post: Marketing Leeds Special Supplement*, 27 September.

Smith, M. (2001) *Transnational Urbanism: Locating Globalization*, Oxford: Blackwell.

Sperling, B. and Sander, P. (2005) *Cities Ranked and Rated*, Hoboken, NJ: Wiley Publishing.

Storper, M. (1997) *The Regional World: Territorial Development in a Global Economy*, New York: Guilford Press.

Thrift, N. (2004) 'Intensities of feeling: Towards a spatial politics of affect', *Geografiska Annaler*, 86B, 1, 57–78.

Turok, I. (2009) 'The distinctive city: pitfalls in the pursuit of differential advantage', *Environment and Planning A*, 41, 1, 13–30.

Unsworth, R. (2010) Personal correspondence with the author, 28 March.

Urban Task Force (UTF) (1999) *Towards an Urban Renaissance*, London: ODPM.

Whitfield, D. (2006) *New Labour's Attack on Public Services*, Nottingham: Spokesman.

# 14. Place branding and cooperation: Can a network of places be a brand?

**Cecilia Pasquinelli**

## INTRODUCTION

In light of distinct trends of discussion, place branding can be considered as an approach 'to integrat[ing], guid[ing] and focus[ing] place management', while the change of place perception and the 'creation of place identity' are only 'the simplest level' (Kavaratzis 2005: 334). Beyond any definition, it is worth considering the scale at which place branding is analysed. The existing literature focuses on cities, regions and nations, whereas a significant gap concerning brands for networks of places remains to be filled in. These consist in systems of places cooperating for development, through the pooling of resources and the pursuit of economies of scale.

While cities may be strong brands thanks to their richness in assets and diversity, the areas lacking leading urban centres and characterized by minor economic patterns struggle to be 'on the map'. Indeed, to attract and retain investors, visitors and talents, small and peripheral communities need sources of diversity to trigger economic revitalization. Concerning the rural US, Cai (2002) underlines the need to achieve a critical mass across multiple communities, thus suggesting a cooperative approach to destination branding. Accordingly, Lee *et al.* argue that not only 'by encouraging a single and unified sense of identity in a rural area, the territory can be marketed as a tourist destination and for consumption of niche products', but also 'the region can be marketed to itself as a way of creating social capital since a stronger sense of shared identity will foster trust and cooperation' (2005: 273).

The point is that the network brand can help break path dependency by providing a new visibility to both political and economic viewpoints. That is, by encompassing multiple towns, the network brand can be a framework where coordination is pursued and diversity spills out. In addition, networks of places may trigger image change by recasting a new space fuelling imagery. This is a fundamental issue for old industrial regions where the decline of the socio-economic and cultural system compels the reconsideration of place identity. For instance, to cope with the decline of the coal and iron industry, the Ruhr city-region chose cooperation involving 45 local governments coordinated by the inter-communal agency marketing the network (Kunzmann 2004). According to the 'flexible functional boundaries' theorized by Kunzmann (2004), the Ruhr brand involves increasing the towns willing to cooperate under the label Ruhr Metropolis, capitalizing on regional culture and the related economic potential.

To deal with the legacy of deindustrialization, many cities have focused on branding in order to shift from a negative industrial image to a post-industrial one. Glasgow, Bilbao, Turin, Newcastle upon Tyne and Pittsburgh are only a few examples. All these cases demonstrate the fundamental role of the city centre and the urban dimension alongside the attempt to present 'their freshest faces' (Gómez 1998: 110). Indeed, regeneration and iconic projects, cultural or sport events, and crucial urban resources like universities able to mobilize talents for new tracks of development are all viable 'tools' for change within the urban contexts. How can a peripheral non-urban area cope with deindustrialization challenges? Networking existent material and immaterial resources including imagery is here suggested as a viable way to carry out post-industrial branding in marginal areas.

Accordingly, this chapter will investigate a network of places cooperating under an umbrella brand. Usually intended as cross-sector brands spanning several functional contexts (Therkelsen and Halkier 2008), 'umbrellas' are here considered in a spatial perspective. This means the analysis of brands crossing institutional borders and, consequently, spanning cooperating municipalities in the need to re-launch development. A relational reading of umbrella brands leads to a network representation, giving the chance to analyse and evaluate interconnections among the involved communities.

The case study of Val di Cornia will test the capacity of the network brand to produce re-branding effects, by changing the image of a rural area hosting a declining old industry. Originally an important industrial area in Italy, Val di Cornia is composed of five municipalities, led by Piombino town, where steel factories historically provided jobs and economic security to locals. Since the 1980s, a crisis has arisen, and this chapter will investigate the capacity of the network brand to re-launch place image through the shaping of a new space nurturing local identity. Accordingly, the emergence of the Val di Cornia brand will be tested, and its 'creators' will be analysed in light of the industrial crisis meta-narrative (Somers 1994).

# PLACE BRAND: STATIC VERSUS DYNAMIC READING

Generally, product and corporate branding concepts are critically adapted to places by stressing the intrinsic differences between the two branded objects, i.e. product or corporate brand and place. It is said that 'place branding differs significantly from conventional products and product branding' because of the place identity (Therkelsen and Halkier 2008: 161). However, it seems that the rationale is offering the place as the best 'package' possible to the relevant targets, being residents, tourists, investors or rather all of them. Certainly, place identity plays a vital role, and often branding efforts consist in entangling the place in its positive or, even better, unique characteristics. However, by treating places as 'packed' objects, brands end up being mere static entities confined to a set of attractive features and selected symbols.

Alongside the 'packaging' process, place identity is supposed to guide branding, since the lack of rootedness in reality will produce unsustainable brands, even provoking negative reactions across local communities (Greenberg 2008). For this reason, local authenticity and the genius loci are at the core of the discussion. However, in the pursuit of distinctiveness, the selection of authentic brand components may 'freeze' the place into becoming a closed set of symbols and characteristics, i.e. a static brand. Paradoxically, in the effort to 'package' distinctiveness, cities end up promoting the same features. Turok (2009) argues that the result is sameness, which, emerging from serious lack of imagination and risk aversion, is very ineffective.

# THE RELATIONAL PARADIGM: DYNAMIC BRANDS

To deal with the dynamic dimension of brands, the relational paradigm helps in considering the immaterial, ever changing and invisible world around brands. Indeed, it draws attention to the relationships established between all stakeholders and the brand (Figure 14.1). In fact, the rationale is that the focus should no longer be on the object in itself, i.e. the place, but, rather, on the set of relationships built with and around it.

The relational paradigm has already been considered in the place branding debate. Hankinson (2004) claims brands are relationship-builders and conceptualizes a brand model based on the 'relation exchange paradigm'. Lury defines brands as 'new media objects' capable of activating multi-directional communication flows (2004) and suggests that place brands

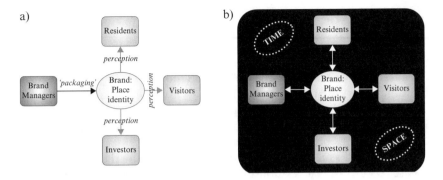

*Source:* Author's own elaboration.

*Figure 14.1    a) Static interpretation of brands; b) Dynamic interpretation of brands*

may be interpreted as 'meeting points' for the actors interacting with them (n.d.). Govers and Go (2009) argue that place marketers have to deal with 'the space of flows', since the network society makes participatory relations and global interactions crucial to place brands. Although the arguments demonstrate the need to fill this theoretical gap, little attention has been paid to the relational content of place brands.

Thus, assuming branding mechanisms of internal and external visibility, the relational paradigm suggests that brand relational capacity should be at the core of brands, as a strong source of distinctiveness. Indeed, this provides a durable competitive advantage, because the relationships established locally and with the outside world constitute those attributes that, as Turok (2009) says, other places cannot easily reproduce. Such a relational perspective on brands is particularly in line with the relational nature of place identity. In fact, Allen *et al.* (1998) argue that the discontinuity in the pattern of relationships within space is the condition for different regional identities to exist.

In this regard, relationship marketing calls for attention. It is defined as 'a marketing perspective on the network organization and the network society', and its purpose is 'to identify and establish, maintain and enhance, and when necessary terminate relationships' (Gummesson 2002: 257) with the relevant actors. The rationale is that all actors' goals are to be met through a continuous 'mutual exchange and fulfilment of promises' (Gronroos, 2000, cited in Gummesson 2002: 293). Accordingly, the concepts of exchange and relationship are at the core of the dynamic interpretation of place brands, as the next section shows.

## THE RELATIONAL PARADIGM: A TOOLKIT FOR ANALYSIS

The theoretical platform for the investigation of relational brands borrows an alternative lens for observation from relationship marketing, i.e. 'relationship eye-glasses' (Gummesson 2002). Through this lens, traditional branding variables, i.e. brand image, identity and reality, are interpreted. First, conventionally defined as 'the perception of the brand that exists in the mind of the consumers or audience' (Anholt 2007: 5), brand image is here conceived as a bundle of relationships boosted by the brand. This is the set of 'parasocial relationships' (Gummesson 2002) that, relying on objects, symbols and other non-tangible phenomena, links targeted people to the brand. Such relationships define the 'whole of the invisible world of perceptions' (Linn, in Gummesson 2002: 112) around the brand so that they are intended as a proxy of brand relational content.

Second, arguments support a relational interpretation of brand reality, i.e. place tangible and intangible assets including institutions like norms, rules and habits (Hankinson 2004). In light of the relational paradigm, brand reality requires the analysis of both the intensity and the nature of the relationships local players develop under a common label. In this regard, Hankinson proposes 'the relational network brand' (2004: 114), while Lee *et al.* (2005) argue the strong connection between a shared place identity and relationships, spilling over into social capital. This means that, behind a brand, there may be dynamics of membership that are potentially capable of building communities through collective dialogue, exchange and, in some cases, even conflict among the actors.

Similarly, relationship marketing focuses on 'nano-relationships' inside an organization. This is represented as a network composed of 'many-headed' actors, i.e. bearing a set of diverse interests, each establishing formal and informal relationships with all the others. Furthermore, the 'relationscape', i.e. the set of relationships consciously included in the network, is a useful concept for brand analysis, since it helps deal with the fact that relationships are 'active and visible or passive and invisible but still influential' (Gummesson 2002). In the same vein, it is said relationships have to be steered with and within a place, by involving a multiplicity of actors. Accordingly, beyond the traditional outside-looking place marketing, mainly aimed at attracting foreign direct investment and visitors, internal place branding is increasingly taken into account in light of the need to establish relationships with internal audiences.

In contrast to what happens with product and corporate brands, place managers cannot select the relationships enriching the brand by cutting off the useless or even harmful ones. On the one hand, it is claimed the list of branding participants can never be fully inclusive (Kavaratzis and Ashworth 2005); on the other hand, inclusiveness seems to be the only possible approach to managing place brands. In fact, who is entitled to add meanings to the brand and who is not? The question of 'what kind of brands and branding and for whom?' (Pike, 2011) is to be answered.

Finally, brand identity is usually defined as the mix of tangible and intangible attributes representing the way in which managers want the place to be perceived (Kavaratzis and Ashworth 2005). In relationship marketing, brand identity is represented as a process of exchange of promises to be delivered in order to maintain trust. In this regard, inclusiveness is relevant alongside its formation. In addition, Christopher *et al.* (2002) reflect on the importance of a collective determination of brand identity, but admit this may not be viable owing to conflicts emerging, especially in the case of radical change within organizations.

Similarly, in place branding, Trueman and Cornelius emphasize tensions among public and private actors fighting about what the city 'has to symbolize and should be symbolized by' because of the 'multiple layers of place identity' (2006: 4). According to much evidence, the problematic determination of collective brands can hardly be solved with a collective selection of brand values, since even the most sophisticated mix of symbols cannot fully represent the complexity of identity. Furthermore, Govers and Go (2009) underline how place identity is constructed through political processes, especially at the local level, thus echoing local power struggles.

However, may collective behaviours emerge through the steering of multiple relationships with brands? In *Relationship Marketing*, Christopher *et al.* (2002) suggest a 'vanguard group' should pioneer the new brand values until all the others are persuaded, by creating ferment and momentum. This means brand aggregating power has to be triggered over time so that an increasing degree of complexity can be represented. Put simply, instead of focusing attention on the packaging of brand identity, more effort should be expended on developing brand relational content. For this reason, from the analytical perspective, monitoring brand identity components is useful in identifying the brand governance, i.e. the set of formal participants, and in understanding the extent to which the relational process succeeds in being collective or, rather, led by an elite holding the brand.

## A NETWORK OF PLACES: THE CASE OF VAL DI CORNIA

Val di Cornia is in Southern Tuscany (Italy) and is deemed part of Maremma (Pazzagli 2003), whose image of 'otherness' in relation to the

| Val di Cornia, Tuscany (Italy), 2008 | | |
|---|---|---:|
| Population | *Circondario* | 58 689 |
| | *Piombino* | 34 825 |
| | *Campiglia* | 13 197 |
| | *Sanvincenzo* | 6 973 |
| | *Suvereto* | 3 104 |
| | *Sassetta* | 590 |
| Population natural increase | | −289 |
| Net migration | | 757 |
| Total surface (km²) | | 366 |
| | *Hills* | 63% |
| | *Plain* | 37% |
| | *Coast (km)* | 64 |

*Source:*   Author's own elaboration.

*Figure 14.2   Val di Cornia map and description*

rest of the region is claimed (see Bellini *et al.* 2010). Five communities compose the network, among which Piombino, the industrial town, leads the surrounding municipalities (Figure 14.2). Feeling 'far from the urban contexts', the 'awareness of homogeneity and the subsequent need for integration' compelled the rise of a network in order to counterbalance the absence of a strong leading city (Pazzagli 2003). This case is an example of the cooperative approach to (re-)branding in the effort to foster change and overcome lock-ins due to a local economic and identity crisis.

A multi-method strategy was adopted for empirical research, including both primary and secondary data sources. After the analysis of documents, reports, websites and local newspapers, primary data were gathered through a survey questionnaire (100 respondents, 20 for each municipality) and 10 in-depth semi-structured interviews to key informants. The empirical research was carried out from March to July 2009. Interviewees were selected on the basis of their role in the network, i.e. mayors and representatives of organizations relevant to local development. They were identified as formal participants in the institutional setting, while their cooperation was investigated through face-to-face interviews.

The name Val di Cornia (VdC) means the valley of the River Cornia, but this geographical definition was replaced by a political one when, in 1998, Circondario was established. Recently abolished by a national law

*Table 14.1　Employment 1981–2001 and employment per sector in Val di
Cornia: Trends*

| | Total Employment: Units | | |
| --- | --- | --- | --- |
| | 1981 | 1991 | 2001 |
| *VdC* | 25 149 | 21 252 | 20 132 |
| | – | −16% | −5% |
| *Tuscany* | 1 259 398 | 1 212 312 | 1 367 876 |
| | – | −2% | +4% |
| *Italy* | 16 883 286 | 17 430 784 | 19 410 556 |
| | – | +3% | +11% |

| *VdC* | Employment per sector in VdC | | | | |
| --- | --- | --- | --- | --- | --- |
| | *Manu-facturing (steel)* | *Trade* | *Health system* | *Professionals and entrepreneurs* | *Hotels and restaurants* |
| *Composition % (2001)* | *19.40* | *19* | *7.50* | *9.40* | *6* |
| *Trend% 1991–2001* | *−34.60* | *−7.80* | *+21.50* | *+77* | *+4* |

*Source:*　IRPET (2005); Luzzati and Sbrilli (2009).

(L.42, 2010), Circondario was the inter-municipal institution in charge of rural and urban planning in the space of the network. Network boundaries are an 'ongoing, debated issue' (Mayor, Suvereto municipality, author's interview, 8 July 2009). This is confirmed by survey results, showing that 80 per cent of respondents cannot identify the institutional borders. Actually, 76 per cent of respondents know of Circondario and its functions, but evidently this is not enough to frame the area.

Historically, VdC has been characterized by a closed economic system. Since the 1950s, it has seen flows of workers into the steel factories, on the one hand making Piombino town the socio-economic epicentre and on the other hand reducing the rest of the area to a steel-workers' dormitory. Accordingly, Piombino has been defined as 'the little Manchester' of Tuscany, and similarly '[it] is hardly trying to be also something else' (Pazzagli 2009). Indeed, since the 1990s, a new equilibrium between steel and other sectors, Piombino and the rest of VdC (Casini and Zucconi 2003), has been sought. In fact, while 'in the past young generations dreamt of the steel factory, now they escape and everybody looks at it as a giant condemned to death' (Caracciolo 2009: 49). Table 14.1 and

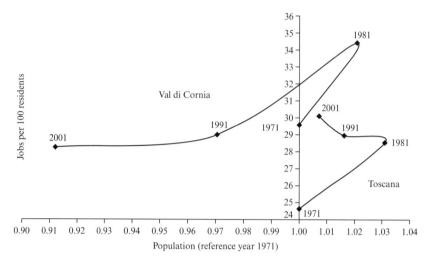

*Source:*   IRPET (2005); Luzzati and Sbrilli (2009).

*Figure 14.3    Trajectory of development in Val di Cornia*

Figure 14.3 report the dramatic loss of jobs that compelled the 'irreversible change' (Casini and Zucconi 2003) and the claim of 'the end of the Iron Age' (Unknown 1997).

## BRAND IDENTITY: FRAGMENTS OF THE EMERGING CHANGE

The VdC brand emerged along with the rising interest for cooperation, deemed crucial to facing the economic crisis. In the 1980s to 1990s the local political elite had to be nurtured from scratch, since until then the local arena was composed of national government owning the steel companies and trade unions as symbols of blue-collar culture. On the basis of coordinated planning since 1970s (IRPET 2005) and strong political cohesion, Circondario Val di Cornia provided important competences locally. In addition, regional and national authorities fostered network governance. For example, in 1999 the *patto territoriale Piombino-Val di Cornia*, i.e. a public funding programme, triggered cooperation for a new deal in the area and, since then, the label 'Val di Cornia' has become synonymous with regeneration.

A proper branding activity was never carried out, yet a series of brand identity components emerged. The narrative of change became crucial.

This was fuelled by the idea of economic diversification and, consequently, tourism started being a priority in the pursuit of a post-industrial economy (IRPET 2002). In fact, Val di Cornia arose as a post-industrial brand that was sought by a community experiencing a dramatic identity crisis and seeing the only local economic engine sink without leaving anything to build on for its future. The old industry was even said to have stolen human capital from alternative development, while local actors became familiar with the idea of deindustrialization. Only recently, official documents have spoken of 'reindustrialization', thus explicitly retaking into account the old industry (Comune di Piombino 2008).

In 1993, Parchi Val di Cornia SpA was founded. Deemed 'the clue of Val di Cornia' (Caracciolo 2009), the company is owned by the five municipalities and is in charge of managing the biggest natural and archaeological parks system in Tuscany (IRPET 2005). This has been a source of innovation and has provided material and non-material advantages not only to tourists but also to inhabitants (Luzzati and Sbrilli 2009). Politicians have claimed 'a project aimed at modifying place identity and image' (Luzzati and Sbrilli 2009: 22), while local newspapers have contributed to widespread awareness of change, by steering the 'VdC debate' and making an overarching narrative emerge.

Accordingly, a 'green' vision for the area emerged on the basis of the 'enlightened politicians' brave decisions' (Casini and Zucconi 2003) that, in the 1980s, introduced strict planning rules for natural resources protection. The strong reference to environmental sustainability (Circondario 2004) is distinctive and in clear opposition to the uncontrolled pollution characterizing the steel industry. This contrast contributes to the local interpretation of tourism as the green economy, as the clean alternative to steel beyond the likely impact on natural resources of ever increasing visitors.

## BRAND IMAGE: HOW DO RESIDENTS RELATE TO THE BRAND?

To analyse brand relational content, a residents' target was chosen. The related parasocial relationships are investigated and measured through both the degree of brand awareness and the associated meanings. Although the survey is merely explorative, the five communities seem to be fairly familiar with the Val di Cornia concept. In relation to its institutions, i.e. Circondario and Parchi SpA, 76 per cent and 78 per cent respectively of respondents clearly know their mission. In addition, the sample shows close attachment to the area, since 74 per cent would not like to move elsewhere, having been born in the place (73 per cent) or having arrived more

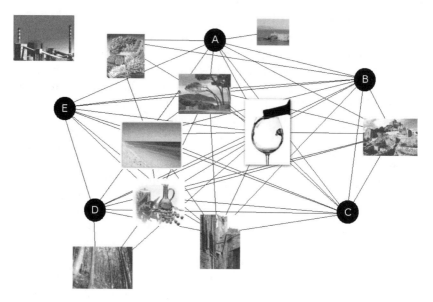

*Source:* Author's own elaboration.

*Figure 14.4 Respondents' associations: A graphical representation*

than 10 years ago (18 per cent). The claimed sense of belonging goes with the high quality of life perceived, since 88 per cent of respondents declare they live well or very well in VdC.

Generally, respondents show a clear but not completely realistic idea of VdC. They identify tourism (94 per cent) and agriculture (89 per cent) as successful economic engines, while 80 per cent deny the relevance of traditional industry, which actually employs about 20 per cent of local workers (IRPET 2005). The lack of trust in the industrial heritage goes with an emerging vision focused on tourism and relying on 'nature' as the value-guiding economic and political choices. It is significant that Piombino, the industrial town, is no longer clearly identified as leader, while small rural municipalities are, in relation to their strong tourist vocation.

By answering 'When you think of Val di Cornia, what comes to mind?' (James 2005; Keller 1998), respondents elicited the elements composing the brand associations' map, shedding light on the qualitative dimension of parasocial relationships. Accordingly, wine seems to be a core association (40 respondents), followed by countryside villages (35), sea landscape (27), Baratti Archaeological Park (26) and olive oil (22). That is, natural landscapes, agricultural products and historical heritage are crucial to residents' sense of place. In addition, brand associations analysis across the five sub-samples shows a fairly cohesive perception of the brand (Figure 14.4). In particular, the five communities seem to converge on both the recognition that wine and natural landscapes are local icons, and the denial of industrial imagery. In fact, there is no reference to steel symbols, though they are still rooted and evident on-site.

## BRAND REALITY: THE RELATIONSCAPE

Intended as the set of relationships that multiple players develop under the brand, brand reality offers a further perspective on the relational content. To operationalize this variable, first the brand governance, i.e. the set of formal participants, is analysed in light of the relationships attaching meanings to the brand. Second, the contributions of those actors not directly participating in brand formation yet somehow enriching it are stressed.

Thus participants are those players working for local development in the space of the network. According to the interviews, only Circondario and Parchi SpA seem to play a clear role in the definition of the VdC brand. Both attach new values by defining a discontinuity with political and economic backwardness (Figure 14.5). That is, 'Circondario has helped face the mental distance from provincial and regional authorities which traditionally have been treating the area as peripheral on all points of view' (Mayor, Piombino municipality, author's interview, 26 June 2009). Further, 'the tourism agency of the province in charge of local promotion does almost nothing for the area', while, as widely confirmed, 'Parchi SpA is the only one to promote VdC, facing a quite challenging context' (CEO, Parchi SpA, author's interview, 24 June 2009).

Despite the central role that the local network ascribes to Parchi SpA, the company cannot provide appropriate support to all local assets as a consequence of its specific mission and limited resources. For example, there is a gap in the VdC network concerning the wine sector, which, despite being core to residents' perceptions, is featured by almost non-existent individual or collective actions under the VdC label. Neither national initiatives, i.e. Strade del Vino and Città del Vino, nor the DOC Val di Cornia consortium, i.e. the local organization in charge of assuring the wine quality of the Val di Cornia DOC label, is actively fostering the place brand in relation to wine production (President, Città del Vino, author's interview, 8 July 2009). They have missed the opportunity to foster a relational thickness around the brand so that they are not likely to have attached any meanings to it.

Nevertheless, local vineyards are reaching international visibility not

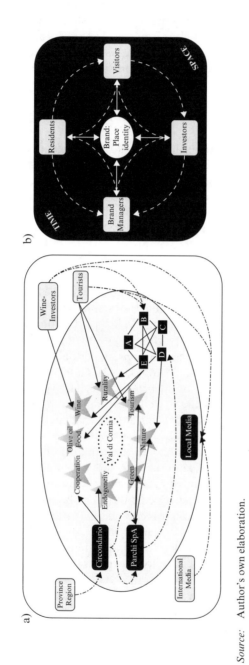

*Source:* Author's own elaboration.

*Figure 14.5* a) Val di Cornia network brand; b) Dynamic concept of brand

only for the high quality of their wine but also for attracting relevant wine entrepreneurs from outside. Much visibility is also given by the media in celebrating local wine-cellars, designed by popular Italian architects and hosting world-class cultural events, which are local icons. However, while locals refer to wine as representing their place, wine producers often prefer to position their vineyards in Maremma, thus avoiding any reference to Val di Cornia (http://www.petrawine.it/territorio.html). It seems that wine entrepreneurs do contribute to the brand even though they are not participants in VdC brand governance.

## DISCUSSION

The investigation of brand relational content proves the rise of a new local narrative growing in the space of the network. This is the framework within which the narrative of change was nurtured in favour of regeneration. In the absence of a proper branding strategy, major facts, for example the foundation of Circondario and Parchi SpA, and stories, for example the death of the steel industry and 'tiger' tourism, have worked as a re-branding strategy. Networking material and immaterial resources have effectively provided diversity and richness in the local offer so that a new vision became possible. This implied a radical change whose claimed pillars were cooperation, economic diversification and protection of natural resources.

The emergence of a new network brand is confirmed by the analysis of residents' perceptions. It seems that the network narrative holds local communities and drives respondents to develop new relationships with the place, where rurality, history, nature and wine are crucial. The residents' sample is persuaded by tourism and its potential, while the steel industry is forgotten or no longer considered as a way to explain the place. Such a perspective is strongly shared across the five communities, evidently rushing to overcome the sense of frustration induced by the decline of the industrial town. Not only the sense of place, but also the politics of brands seems to play a role in explaining the evident re-branding effect. Indeed the forgetting of the old industry goes with the emergence of a new economic and political elite that earned legitimacy along the path of change.

Nevertheless, the VdC brand is losing its source of differentiation, i.e. the history of steel and metals, characterizing this place since the ninth century BC. Consequently, VdC is becoming 'the umpteenth stereotyped postcard from Tuscany' (Pazzagli 2009), a beautiful and natural place where wine is produced. Such an image carries risks for VdC, whose small size and recent entry into tourism and the wine sector make it a weak brand in the highly competitive regional arena. Instead of Val di Cornia using the distinctiveness of its pattern of relationships, including steel, the analysis of the brand relational content suggests it risks disappearing from the map, since its identity is fading.

In the overall effort to understand whether the network brand can re-launch place image according to the definition of a new space for local identity, three propositions arise. First, the network space for brands may result in a successful re-branding strategy, making even local residents, who are said to be the most difficult to persuade, think of their place in a new fashion and (re)discover local values and symbols. Second, the network brand may be created through facts, the media and political communication provided that a new set of stories at network level introduces discontinuities with the past and single communities. Third, in the absence of a branding strategy, the rush for change may result in the forgetting of reality and history, which could provide the basis for developing unique relationships with the brand.

Furthermore, the analysis of brand governance makes the gap between brand identity and brand image emerge. Circondario and Parchi SpA are the only actors actively fuelling the brand. The former has attached the value of cooperation and the idea of endogenous development, making VdC the geography of resurgence. The latter has pushed forward a green vision and the concept of sustainability, translated into the management of natural and cultural resources for tourism (Figure 14.5a). However, beyond the meanings formally attached by brand participants, residents' perceptions reveal further elements, for example rurality and wine.

Thus, in addition to residents' experience of the place, other stakeholders may be fuelling the brand by influencing locals' perceptions. If the relationscape indicates that the actors in charge of promoting VdC wine and tourism are completely or partially inactive, why are these elements rooted in the inhabitants' mind? The concern is that other players have enriched the VdC brand. Regarding wine, both international reward and the attraction of wine entrepreneurs from outside may have persuaded residents of their land's excellence, while product coolness may have convinced them of this local vocation. Second, national and international tourists visiting the countryside and being in close touch with locals may have persuaded them theirs is a beautiful and natural place worthy of being visited and lived in, rather than a declining and polluted area.

Put simply, residents' attention seems to be captured by those assets attracting other targets, especially external ones, i.e. investors and visitors, while among different targets there seem to be flows of tacit communication and influence, i.e. relationships developing the brand (Figure 14.5b).

This is a relevant issue for place branding, especially in light of the need to deal with multiple audiences through investing scarce resources. Whereas mechanisms of residents' influence on outsiders are usually claimed in place branding, there is room for recognizing and exploiting the influence outsiders exert on insiders.

Moreover, it is confirmed that brands are bundles of relationships that 'visible or invisible, passive or active [are] still influential' since a huge set of communities, internal or external and of diverse nature, for example residents, entrepreneurs and visitors, contributes to the brand. The communities defining the brand's tracks of evolution necessarily go beyond the ones composing brand governance, i.e. participants explicitly building the brand.

Thus, in place branding, is it worth referring to brand governance for understanding a brand? If brand governance implies a static reading of brands where participants are intended as a repository of place identity or authenticity, it can be heavily misleading, since only a small part of the whole bundle of relationships around the brand will emerge, especially in the case of complex network brands along the path of change.

On a relational perspective, brand governance is a relevant concept because it allows the evaluation of the risk of losing control of brands. The larger the gap between brand identity and brand image, the weaker the capacity of the brand governance to give direction to the relationships established with the brand. On the other hand, brand governance provides a reference to assess the extent to which the gap is bridged over time by building relationships with those actors that, though not being formal participants, attach meanings to the brand so that higher degrees of inclusiveness may be achieved.

## CONCLUSION

The chapter analysed a network brand labelling cooperation for development and, according to the 'relationship eye-glasses', its relational content has emerged. A framework composed by concepts coming from relationship marketing, critically adapted to places, drove the analysis. The overall contribution of the chapter was to prove the usefulness of the relational approach, looking at place brands as complex bundles of relationships. Furthermore, a set of propositions arose concerning both the feasibility of the network brand as a re-branding strategy and the multiplicity of communities that attach meanings to the brand. Mutual influence among brand communities emerged from empirical evidence that inductively improved the theoretical model.

However, the relational approach implies structural limitations on both theoretical and empirical points of view. Theoretically, the resulting insight into brands is constrained by the adopted perspective on reality, i.e. the relational one. This means that the achievable understanding is necessarily partial and shaped by the lens used. Empirically, all the existing relationships adding meanings to brands are hardly taken into account. Indeed, the case study analysed only the most evident relationships, for example residents, politicians, local institutions, tourists and wine entrepreneurs, but this is certainly not exhaustive. For this reason, further research is needed to identify analytical categories of relationships rendering the complexity of place brands.

## REFERENCES

Allen, J., Massey, D. and A. Cochrane (1998) *Rethinking the Region*, Routledge: London.
Anholt, A. (2007) *Competitive Identity: The New Brand Management for Nations, Cities and Regions*, Basingstoke: Palgrave.
Bellini, N., Loffredo, A. and Pasquinelli, C. (2010) 'Managing otherness: The political economy of place images in the case of Tuscany', in G. Ashworth and M. Kavaratzis (eds), *Towards Effective Place Brand Management: Branding European Cities and Regions*, Cheltenham, UK and Northampton, MA, USA: Edward Elgar Publishing, 89–116.
Cai, L.A. (2002) 'Cooperative branding for rural destinations', *Annals of Tourism Research*, 29, 3, 720–742.
Caracciolo, E. (2009) 'Paesaggi da film', *Itinerari e Luoghi*, 18, 189, 48–59.
Casini, A. and Zucconi, M. (eds) (2003) *Un'impresa per sei Parchi: Come gestire in modo imprenditoriale e innovativo il patrimonio culturale e ambientale pubblico*, Milano: il Sole24Ore.
Christopher, M., Payne, A. and Ballantyne, S. (2002) *Relationship Marketing: Creating Stakeholder Value*, Oxford: Elsevier.
Circondario Val di Cornia (2004) *Progetto VASVAS: Valutazione Ambientale Strategica per la Val di Cornia Sostenibile*, Piombino: Circondario.
Comune di Piombino (2008) 'PIUSS – Piombino 2015: Progetto Città Futura. Documento di orientamento strategico, Comune di Piombino', http://www.comune.piombino.li.it/cittafutura2015/normativa_documenti/Del_GC_27062008_doc_orientamento_strategico.pdf.
Gómez, M.V. (1998) 'Reflective images: The case of urban regeneration in Glasgow and Bilbao', *International Journal of Urban and Regional Research*, 22, 1, 106–121.
Govers, R. and Go, F. (2009) *Place Branding: Glocal, Virtual and Physical Identities, Constructed, Imagined and Experienced*, Basingstoke: Palgrave.
Greenberg, M. (2008) *Branding New York: How a City in Crisis Was Sold to the World*, London: Routledge.
Gummesson, E. (2002) *Total Relationship Marketing: Rethinking Marketing Management: From 4Ps to 30Rs*, Oxford: Elsevier.

Hankinson, G. (2004) 'Relational network brands: Towards a conceptual model of place brands', *Journal of Vacation Marketing*, 10, 2, 109–121.

IRPET (2002) *Piano Locale di Sviluppo della Val di Cornia*, Firenze: Regione Toscana.

IRPET (2005) *Il mosaico dello sviluppo territoriale in Toscana*, Firenze: Regione Toscana.

James, D. (2005) 'Guilty through association: Brand association transfer to brand alliances', *Journal of Consumer Marketing*, 22, 1, 14–24.

Kavaratzis, M. (2005) 'Place branding: A review of trends and conceptual models', *Marketing Review*, 5, 329–342.

Kavaratzis, M. and Ashworth, G.J. (2005) 'City branding: An effective assertion of identity or a transitory marketing trick?', *Tijdschrift voor Economische en Sociale Geografie*, 96, 5, 506–514.

Keller, K.L. (1998) *Strategic Brand Management: Building, Measuring, and Managing Brand Equity*, New York: Prentice Hall.

Kunzmann, K.L. (2004), 'An agenda for creative governance in city regions', DISP 158/5, http://e-collection.ethbib.ethz.ch/eserv/eth:22383/eth-22383-34.pdf.

Lee, J., Arnason, A., Nightingale, A. and Shucksmith, M. (2005) 'Networking: Social capital and identities in European rural development', *Sociologia Ruralis*, 45, 4, 269–283.

Lury, C. (n.d.) 'The doing and the living of the business of Barcelona: Brandspace, brandvalue and brandpower', Unpublished paper, Goldsmiths, University of London.

Lury, C. (2004) *Brands: The Logos of the Global Economy*, London: Routledge.

Luzzati, T. and Sbrilli, L. (eds) (2009) *Tra cultura e ambiente: Verso un bilancio sociale per la Parchi Val di Cornia*, Milano: Gruppo24Ore.

Pazzagli, R. (2003) 'Ambiente, territorio e istituzioni in un sistema locale della Toscana: La Val di Cornia', in A. Casini and M. Zucconi (eds), *Un'impresa per i sei Parchi: Come gestire in modo imprenditoriale e innovativo il patrimonio culturale e ambientale pubblico*, Milano: il Sole24Ore.

Pazzagli, R. (2009) 'Fra storia e turismo: Beni culturali, parchi e politiche del territorio', in M. Paperini (ed.), *Leggere il Territorio: Montioni: storia e beni culturali nell'alta Maremma*, Pisa: Felici Editore.

Pike, A. (2011) 'Placing brands and branding: A socio-spatial biography of "Newcastle Brown Ale"', *Transactions of the Institute of British Geographers*, 36, 2, 206–222.

Somers, M.R. (1994) 'The narrative constitution of identity: A relational and network approach', *Theory and Society*, 23, 5, 605–649.

Therkelsen, A. and Halkier, H. (2008) 'Contemplating place branding umbrellas: The case of coordinated national tourism and business promotion in Denmark', *Scandinavian Journal of Hospitality and Tourism*, 8, 2, 159–179.

Trueman, M. and Cornelius, N. (2006) 'Hanging baskets or basket cases? Managing the complexity of city brands and regeneration', Working Paper 06/13, Bradford University School of Management.

Turok, I. (2009) 'The distinctive city: Pitfalls in the pursuit of differential advantage', *Environment and Planning A*, 41, 13–30.

Unknown (1997) 'Amministratori, tecnici e studiosi a convegno concordano: Lavoriamo a un sistema integrato Parchi', *il Tirreno*.

# 15. Branding a Roman frontier in the twenty-first century

## Gary Warnaby, David Bennison and Dominic Medway

## CONTEXT: PLACES, PRODUCTS AND BRANDS

Traditional marketing theory conceptualises a product as 'anything that can be offered to a market for attention, acquisition, use or consumption' (Kotler *et al.* 2008: 994), which is 'capable of satisfying customer needs' (Jobber 2007: 1002). A brand is a name given to a particular product or service or range of products or services (Kotler *et al.* 2009), and has been defined as 'a distinctive product offering created by the use of a name, symbol, design, packaging or some combination of these' (Jobber and Fahy 2009: 343). Indeed, the interconnectedness of the concepts of 'product' and 'brand' is a constant refrain in the marketing literature (see, for example, Jobber 2007; Kotler *et al.* 2008, 2009). A key purpose of branding is to identify a product offering as being that of a particular organisation, and to differentiate that offering from the offerings of competitors (de Chernatony and McDonald 2003) – a factor reiterated in a place context by Kavaratzis and Ashworth (2005: 510), who state that the fundamental aim of city branding is to endow an urban place with 'a specific and more distinctive identity'.

However, in the context of places, traditional marketing theory needs to be modified if it is to be relevant (Ashworth 1993; Ashworth and Voogd 1990a; Corsico 1993; Kavaratzis 2007; Kavaratzis and Ashworth 2005; van den Berg and Braun 1999), and the inherent difficulty of defining places as products which can then be commodified and marketed has been identified as an important factor distinguishing place marketing from more stereotypical marketing contexts (Warnaby 2009). Ashworth and Voogd (1990a, 1990b) emphasise the complex, multi-layered nature of the (urban) place product, consisting of a 'holistic' product, incorporating numerous 'contributory elements' (that is, individual attributes or attractions), which can be considered in isolation, or in terms of related clusters (van den Berg and Braun 1999).

This has consequences for the application of related branding concepts – the subject of much recent place marketing research, manifested in the existence of dedicated journals (for example, *Place Branding and Public Diplomacy*) and books (Anholt 2006; Dinnie 2008; Govers and Go 2009; Moilanen and Rainisto 2009; Morgan *et al.* 2004), and many articles in more general management or marketing and geography journals. However, branding theory, likewise, requires modification if it is to be applied effectively in a place context. Moilanen and Rainisto (2009: 19–22) identify various factors whereby 'building a place brand differs significantly from branding consumer goods', and they regard place branding as somewhat analogous to building service brands – indeed, Govers and Go's (2009) '3-gap place branding model' draws from the services marketing literature. However, Moilanen and Rainisto (2009) acknowledge differences between services and place marketing contexts, although Warnaby (2009) suggests that the emerging service-dominant logic of marketing has the potential to achieve some convergence here.

In their seminal exposition of city marketing, Ashworth and Voogd (1990a) identify various 'subdisciplines' of marketing, including marketing in non-profit organisations, social marketing and 'image' marketing, as having some utility in understanding the specific nature of place marketing. This use of different aspects of marketing theory to inform and deepen understanding of the specific place context is also evident in more recent work, relating specifically to branding. In his discussion of 'relational network brands' for places, Hankinson (2004) draws not only on classical branding theory, but also from relationship marketing, services marketing, tourism marketing and urban planning. Kavaratzis and Ashworth (2005) draw from the corporate communications literature to argue that, if the full potential of the branding concept is to be realised in a place context, then the city's brand should operate as some form of 'umbrella' that can cover a multitude of stakeholders and audiences (see also Iverson and Hem 2008). However, they acknowledge the implications of product complexity, and another key factor distinguishing this specific context – the complexity of organisational mechanisms for place marketing (Warnaby 2009). These factors may lead to difficulties in ensuring consistency of approach in articulating a place's brand values. Indeed, clarity and consistency in communicating the attributes or benefits of the brand – or its 'core values' (de Chernatony and McDonald 1992) – are recognised as vital in its market positioning (see Jobber 2007).

The majority of the place marketing literature has focused on the urban (Barke 1999), and more recent branding-oriented literature has continued in this vein (see Hankinson 2001, 2004; Kavaratzis 2004, 2005, 2007; Kavaratzis and Ashworth 2005, 2007; Trueman *et al.* 2004), although there is greater emphasis on nation branding (see Anholt 1998, 2004, 2006; Dinnie 2002, 2008; Iverson and Hem 2008; Kotler and Gertner 2002; Kotler *et al.* 1997; O'Shaughnessy and O'Shaughnessy 2000). Notwithstanding the inherent difficulties in product definition mentioned above, spatial entities such as towns or cities and nations have clear spatial definition, relating to administrative or jurisdictional boundaries. The definition of other types of places as products to be marketed or branded may be more amorphous and 'fuzzy' (Medway *et al.* 2008). Such 'fuzzy' places could include regions, which can be shaped as much by symbols, institutions and social practice and consciousness (Hospers 2006; Paasi 2002) as by territorial criteria. Such places may also be 'imagined' in that they relate to literary personalities or creations (see Ashworth 2007) or link to the heritage of an area.

The main focus of this chapter is Hadrian's Wall in the North of England, inscribed as a World Heritage Site (WHS) in 1987, which can be considered an archetypal 'fuzzy' place. Maddern (2004: 311) emphasises that heritage landscapes – especially popular World Heritage Sites – can be 'particularly contested' in that 'a wide range of stakeholders from a variety of institutional contexts have a legitimate interest in the sorts of knowledge and identities there inscribed', with obvious implications for marketing and branding. This fuzziness is also evident spatially. At one level, Hadrian's Wall is relatively easily defined in terms of the materiality of Roman remains, with the spatial parameters of WHS inscription indicated in the Hadrian's Wall WHS Management Plan closely aligned to the surviving archaeology (Austen and Young 2002). It is, however, also part of the 'realm of meaning' (Cresswell and Hoskins 2008) that constitutes 'Hadrian's Wall Country' – a concept actively marketed by various Wall stakeholders.

## HADRIAN'S WALL: BRIEF HISTORY AND MANAGEMENT STRUCTURES

Hadrian's Wall is the most spectacular and best-known Roman *limes* or frontier system (Dudley 1970 – see Breeze and Dobson 2000 for a detailed account of the building of, and life on, the Wall). The Wall has a long history of antiquarian interest (see Hingley and Nesbitt 2008) and also, in relation to historical monuments in the UK, has one of the longest traditions of conservation efforts (see Mason *et al.* 2003; Young 2006 for more detail).

Dating from AD 122, the Wall stretches across the narrowest part of England, from the River Tyne in the east to the Solway Firth in the west, and is described as a 'linear monument' (Nesbitt and Tolia-Kelly 2009).

This linearity creates its own problems, as ownership of the Wall has been (and remains) fragmented. Indeed, Young (2006: 207) states that, before the 1970s, 'there was little attempt to visualise the Wall as an entity, and to manage it as such'. In recent years this has changed, in part catalysed by its WHS inscription, and the subsequent requirement for a management plan has led to various initiatives to coordinate management of the Wall. The initiation of the Management Plan process (led by English Heritage) began in 1993, and 'these initiatives created institutions and partnerships to manage the Wall and setting resources in ways that were coherent geographically and across sectors' (Mason *et al.* 2003: 18).

When the second iteration of the WHS Management Plan covering the period 2002–07 was published (see Austen and Young 2002), its content was influenced by the 2001 outbreak of foot and mouth disease, which had a major impact on the area's rural economy. This in turn catalysed the publication in 2004 of the *Hadrian's Wall Major Study Report*, commissioned by the two regional development agencies (RDAs) in the North of England, the aim of which was 'to assess the potential of Hadrian's Wall to support the regeneration of the North of England through the growth of tourism revenues and to deliver a new Vision for Hadrian's Wall' (Northwest Development Agency and One North East 2004: 1). This document articulated the vision: to move Hadrian's Wall from a Northern 'ought to see' to a global 'must see, stay and return for more'. This was to be achieved by positioning the Wall as 'the Greatest Roman Frontier'. Indeed, highlighting the interconnection between the concepts of product and brand mentioned previously, this appellation is described in the document in terms of both a 'core product development objective' and a 'brand'. This 'Greatest Roman Frontier' concept was regarded in terms of an 'umbrella' (see Kavaratzis and Ashworth 2005; Iverson and Hem 2008), under which various stakeholders (and their activities) could coalesce, thereby serving to facilitate cohesion and coordination, and also serving to create a specific place identity (Kavaratzis and Ashworth 2005).

Following this, specific recommendations regarding organisational structures were produced in 2005, proposing that the organisation responsible for the Wall should be a non-charitable, not-for-profit company limited by guarantee. In May 2006, Hadrian's Wall Heritage Limited (HWHL) was created, with the aim:

> To realise the economic, social and cultural regeneration potential of the Hadrian's Wall World Heritage Site and the communities and environment through which it passes by sustainable tourism development, management and conservation activities which benefit local communities and the wider region. And all that done in a way that reflects the values embodied in the World Heritage Site Management Plan. (HWHL 2007a: 1)

HWHL remains the main coordinating stakeholder of the subsequent branding activities of the Wall.

## A FRAMEWORK FOR BRANDING 'FUZZY' PLACES

This chapter argues that with regard to the marketing of 'fuzzy' places such as Hadrian's Wall and the associated concept of 'Hadrian's Wall Country' – which are more amorphous in terms of their spatial definition – there may be an enhanced role for branding in the articulation of the specific place 'offer'. Indeed, as noted above, there are analogies between the marketing of more amorphous 'fuzzy' places and that of intangible services, where reduced (or minimal) tangibility creates an additional communication imperative in terms of differentiating an offer where the differences with competitors may not be overtly demonstrable (Grönroos 2007).

Such issues are thrown into even sharper relief arising from the multiplicity of stakeholders with potential responsibility for the marketing of a place (and especially a 'fuzzy' place). In a services marketing context, Brodie *et al.* (2006) argue that a service brand can perform an important integrating role for the complex sets of interactions which co-create value in this context. Kavaratzis (2007: 704) recognises this integrating role in the context of places, regarding branding as encompassing both the 'functional–rational' aspects of the place and the 'mental, psychological and emotional ties' associated with it. This has resonance with Cresswell and Hoskins's (2008) interlinked aspects of the materiality of places and their evocation of a less concrete realm of meaning. Hankinson highlights the importance of the integrative role of branding in a place context, stating its success as being ultimately reliant on 'the effective extension of the core brand through effective relationships with stakeholders, each of which extends and reinforces the reality of the core brand through consistent communication and delivery of services' (2004: 116).

Brodie *et al.* (2006) link brands, value creation and relationships in the concept of the service brand-relationship-value (SBRV) triangle. The original SBRV triangle has been modified in the context of places by Warnaby (2009), and this is applied to the specific situation of Hadrian's Wall, as shown in Figure 15.1.

Thus there will be interaction between the coordinating agency responsible for the marketing of Hadrian's Wall as a holistic entity and those organisations that manage and market individual place product elements along the Wall. These could be core, supplementary or complementary elements, reflecting their level of association with Roman materiality (as discussed in the next section). Such interaction helps to develop a coherent

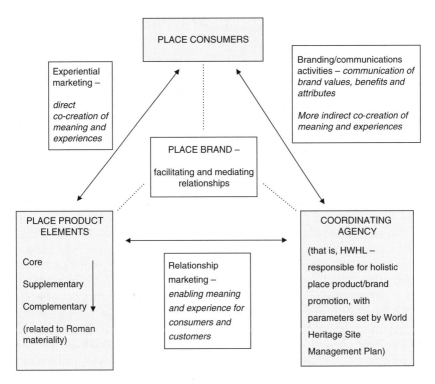

PLACE CONSUMERS

Experiential marketing –

*direct co-creation of meaning and experiences*

Branding/communications activities – *communication of brand values, benefits and attributes*

*More indirect co-creation of meaning and experiences*

PLACE BRAND –

facilitating and mediating relationships

PLACE PRODUCT ELEMENTS

Core

Supplementary

Complementary

(related to Roman materiality)

Relationship marketing – *enabling meaning and experience for consumers and customers*

COORDINATING AGENCY

(that is, HWHL – responsible for holistic place product/brand promotion, with parameters set by World Heritage Site Management Plan)

*Source:* Adapted from Brodie *et al.* (2006); Warnaby (2009).

*Figure 15.1 SBRV triangle applied to Hadrian's Wall*

and consistent brand image for Hadrian's Wall as a whole. In this manner, the coordinating role of HWHL has been acknowledged by various place product organisations as an essential driver of recent marketing activity (and success) for the Wall.

In turn, place consumers of Hadrian's Wall interact with the coordinating agency responsible for its marketing as a holistic place product, and with those organisations responsible for Hadrian's Wall place product elements (either in isolation or in combination). In addition, place consumers may help to co-create meanings and experiences of Hadrian's Wall as a place through such interactions. The linkages between coordinating agency, organisations responsible for the various place product elements and place consumers are mediated by branding or communications, experiential marketing and relationship marketing, each of which is considered in more detail below, after a brief discussion of the nature of the specific place 'product' in this context.

## THE HADRIAN'S WALL 'PLACE PRODUCT'

Mainstream marketing theory conceptualises a product offering as consisting of different levels, incorporating core, supplementary and complementary features (although specific terminology varies – see Baines *et al.* 2008; Brassington and Pettitt 2006; Kotler *et al.* 2008). Cresswell and Hoskins (2008: 409) emphasise the importance of 'material persistence' in the perception of historic significance, and the degree of materiality of the Roman remains is an indicator of the levels of product that can be applied to Hadrian's Wall.

Thus the core Hadrian's Wall place product could be thought of as those spaces where this materiality is most evident: in other words, the primary Roman attractions – the Wall itself and associated forts and milecastles, and perhaps also where 'meaningful association' (Cresswell and Hoskins 2008: 393) is at its greatest. The supplementary product elements could include Roman-related aspects constituting the broader Roman frontier area delineated by the World Heritage Site, including museums and exhibitions with a strong Roman component (for example, Tullie House Museum in Carlisle).

The complementary part of the Hadrian's Wall place product could incorporate the multitude of non-Roman attractions and businesses several miles either side of the Wall, which together are often collectively referred to as 'Hadrian's Wall Country' by those responsible for its marketing and branding. At this level, there is less emphasis on Roman materiality, and the area becomes more of a heterogeneous tourist space (Edensor 2007), where visits to the area are motivated by reasons other than its Roman heritage. Moreover, for some residents in this area, its historical materiality may be mundane and routine (Edensor 2007), and tangential to their everyday lives. Edensor (2007) identifies various elements which could constitute this complementary aspect, including hotels, bed and breakfast accommodation, cafés, tea shops, information centres, souvenir shops, craft shops, cycle hire businesses, farm life centres and so on. Indeed, recent advertising by HWHL emphasises the amount and variety of contributory place product elements (from the three product 'levels' above) in 'Hadrian's Wall Country', which include '25 Roman forts and museums . . . 89 historic houses & museums, 38 art galleries, 469 places to stay, 273 cafes, 802 restaurants and 1004 pubs', all of which make up 'one epic adventure'.

## BRANDING HADRIAN'S WALL

As noted above, according to mainstream marketing theory (which emphasises the interconnectedness of the concepts), branding can be the means by which a product offering is made distinctive, and, as noted above with regard to Hadrian's Wall, the publication of the *Major Study Report* in 2004 emphasised the importance of branding and positioning the Wall as 'the Greatest Roman Frontier' in contributing to the wider regeneration objectives for the area. Indeed, branding and communication have been an important aspect of the activities of Hadrian's Wall Heritage Limited during the first years of its operation – both explicitly articulated as important aspects of raising awareness of HWHL and its activities (see HWHL 2007b, 2008). Moreover, it could be argued that a number of key activities developed over this period have resulted in a more holistic approach to product definition and subsequent marketing activities. These are: (1) branding and communications; (2) experiential marketing; and (3) relationship marketing. These issues are discussed in more detail below, illustrated with quotations from key Hadrian's Wall management stakeholders, interviewed by the authors between January and September 2008.

**Branding and Communications**

A key activity for HWHL has been the branding of the Wall to create a distinct and coherent identity, and more effectively communicate the product benefits to relevant audiences. Attempts to build the brand have occurred through the development of a distinctive logo. An important part of the communications activity has been geared towards moving perceptions of the Wall from being simply a wall to a Roman frontier:

> A major area of work is improving the interpretation of what we're beginning to call the Roman frontier, because the story of the Roman frontier is much more interesting than the story of just the Wall. (Respondent 1)

In its first 18 months of operation HWHL undertook numerous marketing initiatives 'to build brand awareness, encourage more and prolonged visits, and grow the longer term visitor economy' (HWHL 2007b: 24). Crucial in this was the development of a website, www.hadrians-wall. org, regarded as an important element in the perceptual repositioning of the Wall. Linked to this, in 2007, the summer marketing campaign was built around the theme 'Plan Your Invasion'. The main focus of this was a stand-alone web-based journey planner, with an interface that actively promoted the various destinations, facilities and attractions of 'Hadrian's Wall Country'. In addition, there were full-colour press adverts which ran in July and August. These adverts emphasised the range of activities, facilities and attractions located in the area – not only those explicitly linked to the Roman heritage, but also those with a more tangential relationship (for example, art galleries, cafés, restaurants, etc.), but which nevertheless contribute to the overall visitor experience. This has been supported by promotional literature designed to be used by visitors before and during their visit, and also HWHL has been actively engaged in public relations activities designed to stimulate and maintain media interest at local, regional and national level through national and local print and broadcast media as well as relevant websites, with a view to aligning coverage to marketing campaigns and key messages (see HWHL 2007b, 2008).

In doing this, HWHL acted as a conduit for other stakeholders. For example, other management stakeholders in the Wall send information to the PR agency acting on behalf of HWHL, so that this can be incorporated into PR effort relating to the Wall place product as a whole. Such cooperation helps to maintain a consistency of approach:

> We work with Hadrian's Wall Heritage and we send them our events programme so that when they're putting together press releases about events at Hadrian's Wall they can promote them . . . We have quite a lot of dealings with their PR company as well . . . a lot of contact comes through them in terms of arranging and PR activity. (Respondent 3)

Lack of funding is a perennial problem in place marketing (Warnaby *et al.* 2002), and public relations is traditionally recognised as a way of getting significant media exposure for a small amount of money (Fill 2009; Warnaby and Medway 2004 in a specific place context). This fact is not lost on stakeholder organisations directly involved with the Wall, all of which operate under the funding constraints typical of charitable trusts and publicly funded bodies. As one key informant explained:

> We're in contact with the local press and when we find an interesting or an astounding find we will try and get publicity on the back of that, because, as I said, we can't compete on marketing budgets, but we know the sites along the Wall can't compete with what we find, so we sort of work that way. (Respondent 4)

## Experiential Marketing

In line with some recent developments in marketing practice to focus on the experiential (see Tynan and McKechnie 2009 for a useful review of this area), HWHL has also been keen to develop a move from marketing the Hadrian's Wall product simply as a physical place or a collection of linked places to one of an opportunity for experience and adventure. This also fits with the notion of moving the Hadrian's Wall place product from merely being a Wall to being a frontier. The experiential marketing stance has been enthusiastically bought into by various key stakeholders. For example, the Vindolanda Trust has been keen to invite voluntary battle re-enactment societies in full Roman dress to undertake special events at its sites and to enhance its visitors' experience. HWHL has also worked hard to develop the notion of a frontier experience by funding a bus service (called the AD122 bus – a reference to the date of the Wall's construction) which travels along the length of the Wall and back so that people can start to appreciate the scale and scope of the Wall as a whole, rather than simply experiencing it as merely a pile of stones in one location.

This experiential marketing concept is also supported by, and in line with the marketing activities of, the large regional-level stakeholders in the Hadrian's Wall place product, one of whom notes that:

> What we are moving towards is more experience-driven campaigns. So let's think about what experience your visitor wants to have and let's develop what we have around that and bring the products into the experience that we have to offer. (Respondent 2)

Cresswell and Hoskins (2008: 394) conceptualise places in terms of their materiality (in that they have a tangible form), but also in terms of a 'less concrete realm of meaning', and these aspects have been discussed above in relation to Hadrian's Wall. However, Cresswell and Hoskins also suggest a third aspect of place, which involves different levels of practice and performance, relating explicitly to experiential dimensions, stating that '[p]lace is a lived concept' (2008: 394), and this aspect is rec-ognised as crucial in developing an attractive place product offer. Here, the importance of the interpretation of the materiality of the Wall is acknowledged:

> Interpretation, lifelong learning, events and displays need to engage with individuals and families from many different backgrounds and interests and to enrich their experience and understanding of the Roman frontier and its landscape. Much of HWHL's work with the multiplicity of sites and museums along the Wall concerns improving interpretation and access – giving visitors the tools to absorb as much as they wish of 2,000 years of history. (HWHL 2007b: 16)

In branding terms, consistency of approach and message is crucial (Fill 2009), and coordinating the activities of a disparate collection of stake-holders is important in ensuring appropriate positioning, which leads to the next aspect of activity.

## Relationship Marketing

The multiplicity of stakeholders and complexity of their interaction are a characteristic of the marketing of places which distinguishes it from more traditional marketing activity (Warnaby 2009), and the investigation of actor interaction and relationships has been a key theme in the place marketing literature. This is analogous to the concept of relationship marketing, defined by Gummesson (2004: 16) as 'interactions in networks of relationships'. In a place marketing context, the critical importance of networks – defined in a marketing context by Iacobucci (1996) as a collection of actors and their structural interactions – in the successful planning and implementation of activities has been emphasised (van den Berg and Braun 1999). The complex networks typical of place marketing organisational mechanisms, such as that of Hadrian's Wall, are arguably the embodiment of Gummesson's concept of many-to-many marketing, 'which utilises the network properties of marketing', thereby allowing for 'complexity, context and dynamism' (2006: 349). In this specific context, the coordinating role of HWHL is regarded as crucial in bringing the various stakeholders together and coordinating action. One respondent mentioned that in the period before the creation of HWHL (after the folding of the previous tourism partnership) there was a period when 'there was no worldwide marketing happening; it just ceased and stopped', and that since HWHL's creation things were 'definitely on the right track' (Respondent 4). A consensual approach to management and marketing – which hopefully ensures coordinated action – is therefore critical in this context if the contestation symptomatic of marketing in a place context is to be minimised. As one respondent stated, 'there's an awful lot of consultation with many different groups of people in order to achieve specific objectives' (Respondent 1).

However, such relationship marketing should not only occur within the strategic network of place marketing actors, but also with visitors to, and residents within, the area in order to develop what mainstream marketing theory would term 'brand loyalty', through the co-creation of meaning and experiences. What one respondent termed a 'sense of place' agenda was seen as a means of 'building a sense of connection in the places that people live using culture or an actual heritage of the place, and it can also mean building stronger community links and more opportunities to connect with other people in your community' (Respondent 1). The experiential elements described above could be regarded as a means by which relationships with visitors could be developed further.

# CONCLUSION

Figure 15.1 suggests that a fully formed sense of the place brand emerges from a triad of interactivity (encompassing branding/communications, experiential marketing and relationship marketing) between place consumers, place product elements and the coordinating agency. Hence the place brand could be viewed as the outcome of dialogue between three key stakeholder blocs about what the place entity 'Hadrian's Wall' actually means. This emphasises the fact that place brands such as Hadrian's Wall are negotiated concepts which can change over time. In a similar way, dialogue and contestation between these three stakeholder blocs can also alter the delineation of territory which a place brand represents. Thus the concept of 'Hadrian's Wall Country', an idea intimately tied to the Hadrian's Wall place brand, would appear to be in flux, not only over time, but also depending on which stakeholder bloc defines it.

In his discussion of the importance of distinctiveness in the competition between places, with particular reference to cities, Turok (2009: 14) describes them as 'complex adaptive systems comprising multitudes of actors, firms, and other organisations forming diverse relationships and evolving together'. Linking back to the services marketing literature, such a perspective has resonance with the principles of the emerging area of 'service science' (see IfM and IBM 2008; Maglio and Spohrer 2008), which is defined as the study of service systems, which in turn are defined as 'dynamic configurations of people, technologies, organizations, and shared information that create and deliver value' (IfM and IBM 2008: 1). Maglio and Spohrer (2008) explicitly identify the spatial entities (i.e. cities and nations) which have been the subject of much of the place marketing literature to date as service systems. However, the same concepts could apply to an equal (if not greater) extent to 'fuzzy' places (especially those with historic or heritage attributes), given their amorphous nature, in terms of spatiality, the potentially contested 'realm of meaning' (see Cresswell and Hoskins 2008; Maddern 2004), and the organisational mechanisms for their marketing (such places having an even more extensive stakeholder network than more readily definable place entities, precisely because of their pliability). It could be thus argued that, as research into places and their branding often falls in the interstices between disciplines, this tendency may be even more apposite in relation to 'fuzzy' places, with consequently greater potential for the development of understanding.

# REFERENCES

Anholt, S. (1998) 'Nation brands of the twenty-first century', *Journal of Brand Management*, 5, 6, 395–406.

Anholt, S. (2004) 'Nation brands and the value of provenance', in N. Morgan, A. Pritchard and R. Pride (eds), *Destination Branding: Creating the Unique Destination Proposition*, Oxford: Elsevier Butterworth-Heinemann, 26–39.

Anholt, S. (2006) *Competitive Identity: The New Brand Management for Nations, Cities and Regions*, London: Palgrave Macmillan.

Ashworth, G. (1993) 'Marketing of places: what are we doing?', in G. Ave and F. Corsico (eds), *Urban Marketing in Europe*, Turin: Torino Incontra, 643–649.

Ashworth, G. (2007) 'Personality association as an instrument of place branding: Possibilities and pitfalls', Paper presented at EUGEO Conference, Amsterdam.

Ashworth, G. and Voogd, H. (1990a) *Selling the City*, London: Belhaven.

Ashworth, G. and Voogd, H. (1990b) 'Can places be sold for tourism?', in G. Ashworth and B. Goodall (eds), *Marketing Tourism Places*, London: Routledge, 1–16.

Austen, P. and Young, C. (2002) *Hadrian's Wall World Heritage Site Management Plan 2002–2007*, Hexham: English Heritage/Hadrian's Wall World Heritage Site Management Plan Committee.

Baines, P., Fill, C. and Page, K. (2008) *Marketing*, Oxford: Oxford University Press.

Barke, M. (1999) 'City marketing as a planning tool', in M. Pacione (ed.), *Applied Geography: Principles and Practice*, London: Routledge, 486–496.

Brassington, F. and Pettitt, S. (2006) *Principles of Marketing*, 4th edition, Harlow: Financial Times Prentice Hall.

Breeze, D.J. and Dobson, B. (2000) *Hadrian's Wall*, 4th edition, London: Penguin Books.

Brodie, R.J., Glynn, M.S. and Little, V. (2006) 'The service brand and the service-dominant logic: Missing fundamental premise or the need for stronger theory?', *Marketing Theory*, 6, 3, 363–379.

Corsico, F. (1993) 'Urban marketing, a tool for cities and business enterprises, a condition for property development, a challenge for urban planning', in G. Ave and F. Corsico (eds), *Urban Marketing in Europe*, Turin: Torino Incontra, 75–88.

Cresswell, T. and Hoskins, G. (2008) 'Place, persistence, and practice: Evaluating historical significance at Angel Island, San Francisco, and Maxwell Street, Chicago', *Annals of the Association of American Geographers*, 98, 2, 392–413.

de Chernatony, L. and McDonald, M.H.B. (1992) *Creating Powerful Brands: The Strategic Route to Success in Consumer, Industrial and Service Markets*, Oxford: Butterworth-Heinemann.

de Chernatony, L. and McDonald, M. (2003) *Creating Powerful Brands in Consumer Service and Industrial Markets*, 3rd edition, Oxford: Butterworth-Heinemann.

Dinnie, K. (2002) 'Implications of national identity for marketing strategy', *Marketing Review*, 2, 3, 285–300.

Dinnie, K. (2008) *Nation Branding: Concepts, Issues, Practice*, Oxford: Butterworth-Heinemann.

Dudley, D. (1970) *Roman Society*, Harmondsworth: Penguin Books.

Edensor, T. (2007) 'Mundane mobilities, performances and spaces of tourism', *Social and Cultural Geography*, 8, 2, 199–215.

Fill, C. (2009) *Marketing Communications: Interactivity, Communities and Content*, 5th edition, Harlow: Financial Times Prentice Hall.

Govers, R. and Go, F. (2009) *Place Branding: Glocal, Virtual, and Physical Identities, Constructed, Imagined and Experienced*, Houndmills: Palgrave Macmillan.

Grönroos, C. (2007) *Service Management and Marketing: Customer Management in Service Competition*, Chichester: John Wiley & Sons.

Gummesson, E. (2004) 'From one-to-one to many-to-many marketing', Paper presented at QUIS 9 Symposium, Karlstad, Sweden.

Gummesson, E. (2006) 'Many-to-many marketing as grand theory: A Nordic school contribution', in R.F. Lusch and S.L. Vargo (eds), *The Service-Dominant Logic of Marketing: Dialog, Debate, and Directions*, Armonk, NY and London: M.E. Sharpe, 339–353.

Hadrian's Wall Heritage Ltd (HWHL) (2007a) 'Hadrian's Wall Heritage Limited strategic plan March 2007', http://www.hadrians-wall.org/ResourceManager/ Documents/HWHL_Strategic_Plan_March_2007.pdf, accessed 13 November 2008.

Hadrian's Wall Heritage Ltd (2007b) *Annual Review 2006–07: Bringing History and Landscape to Life*, Hexham: HWHL.

Hadrian's Wall Heritage Ltd (2008) *Annual Review: Bringing History and Landscape to Life 2007–2008*, Hexham: HWHL.

Hankinson, G. (2001) 'Location branding: A study of the branding practices of 12 English cities', *Journal of Brand Management*, 9, 2, 127–142.

Hankinson, G. (2004) 'Relational network brands: Towards a conceptual model of place brands', *Journal of Vacation Marketing*, 10, 2, 109–121.

Hingley, R. and Nesbitt, C. (2008) 'Hadrian's Wall: A wall for all times', *British Archaeology*, 102, September/October, http://www.britarch.ac.uk/ba/ba102/ feat2.shtml, accessed 3 November 2008.

Hospers, G.-J. (2006) 'Borders, bridges and branding: The transformation of the Øresund region into an imagined space', *European Planning Studies*, 14, 8, 1015–1033.

Iacobucci, D. (ed.) (1996) *Networks in Marketing*, Thousand Oaks, CA: Sage Publications.

Institute for Manufacturing (IfM) and IBM (2008) *Succeeding through Service Innovation: A Service Perspective for Education, Research Business and Government*, Cambridge: University of Cambridge Institute for Manfacturing.

Iverson, N.M. and Hem, L.E. (2008) 'Provenance associations as core values of place umbrella brands: A framework of characteristics', *European Journal of Marketing*, 42, 5/6, 603–626.

Jobber, D. (2007) *Principles and Practice of Marketing*, 5th edition, Maidenhead: McGraw-Hill.

Jobber, D. and Fahy, J. (2009) *Foundations of Marketing*, 3rd edition, London: McGraw-Hill.

Kavaratzis, M. (2004) 'From city marketing to city branding: Towards a theoretical framework for developing city brands', *Place Branding*, 1, 1, 58–73.

Kavaratzis, M. (2005) 'Place branding: A review of trends and conceptual models', Paper presented at Academy of Marketing Conference, Dublin.

Kavaratzis, M. (2007) 'City marketing: The past, the present and some unresolved issues', *Geography Compass*, 1, 3, 695–712.

Kavaratzis, M. and Ashworth, G. (2005) 'City branding: An effective assertion of identity or a transitory marketing trick?', *Tijdschrift voor Economische en Sociale Geografie*, 96, 5, 506–514.

Kavaratzis, M. and Ashworth, G. (2007) 'Partners in coffeeshops, canals and commerce: Marketing the city of Amsterdam', *Cities*, 24, 1, 16–25.

Kotler, P. and Gertner, D. (2002) 'Country as brand, product and beyond: A place marketing and brand management perspective', *Journal of Brand Management*, 9, 4–5, 249–261.

Kotler, P., Jatusripitak, S. and Maesinsee, S. (1997) *The Marketing of Nations: A Strategic Approach to Building National Wealth*, New York: Simon & Schuster.

Kotler, P., Armstrong, G., Wong, V. and Saunders, J. (2008) *Principles of Marketing*, 5th European edition, Harlow: Financial Times Prentice Hall.

Kotler, P., Keller, K.L., Brady, M., Goodman, M. and Hansen, T. (2009) *Marketing Management*, Harlow: Pearson Education.

Maddern, J. (2004) 'Huddled masses yearning to buy postcards: The politics of producing heritage at the Statue of Liberty–Ellis Island National Monument', *Current Issues in Tourism*, 7, 4&5, 303–314.

Maglio, P.P. and Spohrer, J. (2008) 'Fundamentals of service science', *Journal of the Academy of Marketing Science*, 36, 18–20.

Mason, R., MacLean, M.G.H. and de la Torre, M. (2003) *Hadrian's Wall World Heritage Site, English Heritage: A Case Study*, Los Angeles: Getty Conservation Institute.

Medway, D., Bennison, D. and Warnaby, G. (2008) 'Branding a Roman frontier in the 21st century', Paper presented at Association of American Geographers Annual Conference, Boston.

Moilanen, T. and Rainisto, S. (2009) *How to Brand Nations, Cities and Destinations: A Planning Book for Place Branding*, Houndmills: Palgrave Macmillan.

Morgan, N., Pritchard, A. and Pride, R. (2004) *Destination Branding: Creating the Unique Destination Proposition*, 2nd edition, Oxford: Elsevier Butterworth-Heinemann.

Nesbitt, C. and Tolia-Kelly, D. (2009) 'Hadrian's Wall – embodied archaeologies of the linear monument', *Journal of Social Archaeology*, 9, 3, 368–390.

Northwest Development Agency and One North East (2004) *Hadrian's Wall Major Study Report Summary September 2004*, Manchester and Newcastle upon Tyne: NWDA and One North East.

O'Shaughnessy, J. and O'Shaughnessy, N.J. (2000) 'Treating the nation as a brand: Some neglected issues', *Journal of Macromarketing*, 20, 1, 56–64.

Paasi, A. (2002) 'Bounded spaces in the mobile world: Deconstructing regional identity', *Tijdschrift voor Economische en Sociale Geografie*, 93, 2, 137–148.

Trueman, M.M., Klemm, M., Giroud, A. and Lindley, T. (2004) 'Can a city communicate? Bradford as a corporate brand', *Corporate Communications: An International Journal*, 9, 4, 217–224.

Turok, I. (2009) 'The distinctive city: Pitfalls in the pursuit of differential advantage', *Environment and Planning A*, 41, 13–30.

Tynan, C. and McKechnie, S. (2009) 'Experience marketing: A review and reassessment', *Journal of Marketing Management*, 25, 5–6, 501–517.

van den Berg, L. and Braun, E. (1999) 'Urban competitiveness, marketing and the need for organising capacity', *Urban Studies*, 36, 5–6, 987–999.

Warnaby, G. (2009) 'Towards a service-dominant place marketing logic', *Marketing Theory*, 9, 4, 403–423.

Warnaby, G. and Medway, D. (2004) 'The role of place marketing as a competitive response by town centres to out-of-town retail developments', *International Review of Retail, Distribution and Consumer Research*, 14, 4, 457–477.

Warnaby, G., Bennison, D., Davies, B.J. and Hughes, H. (2002) 'Marketing UK towns and cities as shopping destinations', *Journal of Marketing Management*, 18, 9–10, 877–904.

Young, C.J. (2006) 'Hadrian's Wall: Conservation and archaeology through two centuries', in R.J.A. Wilson (ed.), *Romanitas: Essays on Roman Archaeology in Honour of Sheppard Frere on the Occasion of his Ninetieth Birthday*, Oxford: Oxbow Books, 203–210.

# 16. Packaging political projects in geographical imaginaries: The rise of nation branding

**Nick Lewis**

## INTRODUCTION

In October 2007, New Zealand prime minister Helen Clark opened a giant inflatable rugby ball in the shadows of the Eiffel Tower in Paris. The ball, which acted as a theatre for an innovative audio-visual showcase of New Zealand's tourism products, a stage for Maori performing arts, and a temporary venue for trade and diplomatic cocktail parties, formed a three-dimensional billboard for New Zealand as a national product. It was erected at the time of the 2007 Rugby World Cup and aimed to promote New Zealand's hosting of the 2011 Cup. Three years later, it was erected in Tokyo and opened by a different prime minister (Figure 16.1). It was again staged to coincide with a game of rugby and to advertise the 2011 World Cup, but was also expected to reinvigorate a declining market for New Zealand tourism in Japan and to add lustre to government–government trade talks and a meeting of the New Zealand–Japan Business Association. The example demonstrates both the creative application of nation branding and prominent nation brander Simon Anholt's (2007b) conception of it as a mix of destination branding, place of origin marketing, and public diplomacy.

There is nothing fundamentally new about the use of spatial imaginaries to sell products or attract inward investment. Place of origin marketing and destination branding have long histories in trade shows, lobbying, and tourism advertising. Brands are often tightly interwoven with geographical and even national imaginaries, as in the case of kiwi fruit, Vegemite or Foster's (Sinclair 2008). However, nation branding as a 'named' phenomenon is something different. It calibrates geographical imaginaries in national terms and mobilises them in terms of sophisticated 'integrated marketing' and globalising political projects. In so doing, nation branding extends branding expertise into the field of national economic development and the production of national identity.

*Source:* Author's images.

*Figure 16.1*    *Images of the New Zealand giant rugby ball performing in Tokyo, November 2009: (i) ball at foot of the Tokyo Tower; (ii) prime minister John Key opens the ball in front of a temporary Shinto shrine erected within it; and (iii) Japanese schoolchildren pose for photos with members of Te Arawa Kapa Haka group*

In this chapter I ask how Brand NZ has taken form, been mobilised and made coherent, what subjects and spaces it has fostered, and for what ends and to what effects. To answer these questions, I use the language of cultural economy (du Gay 2002; Lury 2004; Lash and Lury 2007) rather than that of the nation branders themselves (see Anholt 1998, 2003a, 2009; Olins 1999, 2003; Dinnie 2008). In this language, nation branding is a set of strategically developed practices that mobilise imaginaries of nation, the values of place in consumption, and the reputational effects of identities on investment and purchase decisions. I use the idea of 'political project' to focus attention on how nation branding is assembled into an active, expansive and co-constitutive project of globalisation and has itself become a key globalising space (Lewis *et al.* 2008).

The chapter draws on a review of policy documents and media reports, and field research that has included attending a Simon Anholt nation branding masterclass in London, participant observation of the giant rugby ball in action in Tokyo, and interviews with industry leaders and trade policy officials in New Zealand. It begins by extending the cultural economy literature on branding into a focus on geographies of branding, and interprets nation branding in these terms. The next sections examine Brand NZ by tracing the emergence, form and application of two formal nation brands – 100% Pure New Zealand (100% Pure) and New Zealand New Thinking (NZNT). I use this discussion to highlight the implication of Brand NZ in the constitution of a globalisation that fosters and depends upon economic nationalism.

## BRANDING

Branding is portrayed in the marketing literature as a strategic exercise to attach reputational and symbolic values to products. Much is made of the brand as a site of value generation and for the application of expertise to affect the production–consumption nexus, by communicating messages, attaching values and so on. Attention is given to calculating consumer responses to brands, measuring the value generated by brands, and intervening to enhance consumer responses and the value of the brand. The nation branding literature begins from this point.

However, whilst brands are increasingly seen in the branding literature as establishing or enhancing relationships along the value chain between product and consumer (de Chernatony 2009), they are not seen as fully relational. Their sociologies and genealogies are unexplored, while consumers are generally treated as unproblematic subjects (pre-formed bundles of attributes who are open somehow then to manipulation). For Lury (2004), the rise of brands is related to post-modern sensitivities and post-industrial economies, in which the cultural and symbolic values of objects are elevated relative to their use values, and consumers take a more active role in relations between producer and consumer. Brands are crucial in the interplay of symbolic, cultural and economic value in the cultural economy and in mediating relations between production and consumption. They frame connectivities, ease tensions, mediate exchanges of symbolic and material values, and co-constitute supply and demand.

For Lury (2004) and Klein (2000), as for Anholt (2007a), Stern (2006) and the standard marketing text, brands are far more than simply the logo and are worthy of closer study. In mainstream marketing thought, the proliferation of branding is part of the inexorable logic of globalisation and inscribed into a globalising moral economy of creativity, choice and self-expression (Saren *et al.* 2007; Maclaran *et al.* 2010). Whilst there are alternative and critical streams of marketing theory (see, for example, Araujo and Kjellberg 2010), a sociology or geography of branding takes a different starting point – that brands come from somewhere, are performative, and have consequences. They make the worlds that they seek to facilitate by acting on and through the consumers whose subjectivities they shape and by qualifying and enacting globalisation. For Klein, brands are constitutive of globalisation and branding a performative practice of commodity fetishism. Brands reinscribe capitalist power relations, and reproduce the social and environmental injustices of globalisation. For Lury they make globalising capitalism possible. They are signs for negotiating globalising economies and identifying, calculating and constituting a new status order and the selves of a globalising elite. They can be understood in Miller's terms (2002) as a metrology – a regime of calculative practices, calculating technologies, representations and institutional forms. Brands are power laden, culturally, socially and politically transformative, and tightly connected to the constitution of post-modernity.

I take four points from this discussion. First, brands are the products of the work of marketing agents and others. They must be studied in terms of their strategic intent and the context of the complex of practices and agents that mediate them. Second, brands have genealogies, geographies and architectures. Third, brands are performative rather than acting on pre-constituted worlds. And, fourth, they are as a result constitutive – they have effects and affects, and co-constitute moral economies or at least zones of qualification with moral forms.

## A GEOGRAPHY OF BRANDING

Geographers have developed some recent interest in brands (Pike 2009; Pawson 1997; Power and Hauge 2008; Jackson 2004), although less than one might imagine given the role of geographical imaginaries and provenance in the construction of value and of brands in the globalisation of value chains (Banks *et al.* 2007; Lewis 2008; Morgan *et al.* 2006; Jackson *et al.* 2007). Streams of geographical scholarship examine how products and consumption values are invested with place-based meanings, cultural and environmental associations, traditions, and reputations for quality (Pike 2009). At its bluntest, place can come to substitute for more technical, experiential or otherwise material understandings of product qualities, especially where these are difficult to measure or otherwise qualify, as in the case of wine or international education. More subtly, all cultural economies have geographies and are constituted geographically. As Pike (2009) observes, brands are inherently geographical and enmeshed in geographical referents – to product provenance, in spatial circuits of meaning, and in the spatiality of production–consumption relations.

As performative imaginaries with more or less materialised and co-constitutive conjunctions of meanings, practices and networks of association among people, objects, places and cultural economy trajectories, brands are constitutive of economic spaces. Such economic spaces are far less stable than conventionally imagined (Allen 2008; Jessop 2008; Larner and Le Heron 2002). They may be connected to place-making projects such as the creative city, innovation region, competitive nation or even transnational nation (Lewis *et al.* 2008; Gibson and Klocker 2004; Larner 2007). These new relational spaces escape the hierarchical scalar or institutional grids of predefined structures such as the nation state. Rather, they are emergent spaces or spaces 'in the framing'. They reconfigure territory, governance and identities into new geographical imaginaries for political work (Allen 2008; Larner and Le Heron 2002).

A view of economic space as relational, emergent and co-constituted embraces the constitutive dimensions of discourse, calculation and geographical imaginaries. It spatialises three key post-structural insights into 'the economy'. First, the characteristics of a good are not prior and waiting to be described; 'their objectification implies specific metrological work' (Callon *et al.* 2002: 198–199). Second, the economy is co-constituted with politics and culture or, in Mitchell's (2008) terms, 'a series of competing projects . . . to establish metrological regimes based on new technologies of organisation, measurement, calculation and representation'. This chapter directs attention to representation in such regimes. Third, political actors are at work mobilising the potentialities of these regimes by fostering political projects (Larner *et al.* 2007).

For Lewis and colleagues (2008) political projects are 'strategically mobilized narratives' that marshal governmental and spatial imaginaries, diverse interests, institutions, and cultural and economic trajectories into a calculated and calculative project. Writing from the New Zealand context, they identify a set of co-constitutive political projects related to a particular political moment in the early 2000s. They argue that, whilst born of their times, these projects reconnect with enduring struggles to build a nation and secure international competitiveness for a small, isolated, trading economy. Prominent among the projects was a 'globalisation' project that sought to inscribe the global deeply into the daily economy, social practice and identities. More expansive than earlier understandings of globalisation as increasing exports and encouraging foreign investment, this framing of economic and social policy was about enhancing global connectedness and cultivating global subjects and spaces to facilitate global competitiveness. Policy interventions included the Growth and Innovation Framework (GIF), an economic development strategy that identified four sectors for programmes of industry building, investment facilitation, and market development support. In this chapter I demonstrate how Brand NZ became a co-constitutive dimension of this project.

## NATION BRANDING

'Nation branding' refers to the application of sophisticated marketing expertise and branding techniques to cultivate understandings of the nation. Its aim is: to market the nation as a destination for tourism and inward investment; to add value to its final products; to stimulate interest, attach values and regulate practices along value chains; to build reputations; and to reconstitute economic and political subjectivities domestically. Nation branding connects the traditions and aspirations of place marketing (destination branding and events marketing) and place of origin branding of products to national politico-legal aspirations (public diplomacy) and reputations (democracy dividend), trading reputations (value chain marketing) and national economic development programmes (Anholt 2007a). Nation branding is most apparent in trade shows and in the now ubiquitous advertisements for nations as tourism destinations, sites for major cultural events, high-technology production sites, and investment opportunities on international news networks and in glossy global business magazines. Nation branding has taken hold in different groups of aspirational nations (Table 16.1). At the risk of creating a category for all nation states and reproducing the rhetoric of the branders, these include: advanced or rapidly advancing smaller nations seeking to take (or retain) seats in the second tier of nations; those with uninspiring or unexciting national images; the awakening economic powers of the Gulf states, Brazil and India and other pretenders such as Turkey and South Africa; those looking to nation brands to overcome histories of cultural or economic marginalisation or particular moments of political infamy; and those seeking desperately to find economic salvation (the nations of Brand New Justice – Anholt 2003a).

Despite its antecedent practices, nation branding was only 'named' in the mid- to late 1990s by British advertisers Simon Anholt and Wally Olins. Nation branders define nation branding as the coordination if not

*Table 16.1    Author's classification of attendees at Simon Anholt's nation branding masterclass, London, November 2007*

| Nation state type | Delegates |
| --- | --- |
| Scandinavian | 9 |
| Baltic | 6 |
| Other small, wealthy suspects | 5 |
| Dull North | 16 |
| Aspiring South – Ecuador, Botswana, Swaziland | 5 |
| Consultants | 10 |
| Gulf states | 7 |
| Others: Caymans, Cyprus, Mauritius, Malta | 15 |
| Plus: Sponsors and speakers* | 18 |

*Note:*   * Many representing or seeking to represent other nations.

*Source:*   Author's research.

orchestration of the overt and passive acts of communication performed by national agents (including businesses and citizens) in economic, cultural and political relation. These acts include: formal promotional activities in trade, tourism and investment; the production of associated logos and brand collateral; the public management of nation state policy; representations of environmental iconography and cultural heritage; and the reputations earned by the qualities of exports and citizen behaviour (Anholt 2007a). Nation branding mobilises extant and generates new geographical imaginaries (cultural, environmental and economic, such as reputations for reliability, quality, consistency, prompt payment and trustworthiness). It scales and coordinates them to the nation, and translates them into texts and supporting practices. The objective is to create and attach distinctiveness, place of origin values, and meanings to cross-border economic and political relations.

Formal nation brands are developed, framed, legitimated, documented and evaluated in formal policy documents. They coordinate and/or work alongside nation branding developed and deployed by non-state actors at other sites. They give both logic and content to the work of economic development agencies as intermediaries along value chains and in establishing trade networks, lobbying and fostering national identities. They also give form to the work of state agents and industry peak bodies in seeking economies of scale in marketing, advertising and PR.

Simon Anholt insists that in a globalised world every country, region and city has to compete with every other for customers, visitors, business, talent, investment, attention and respect (Anholt 2007a). In a passage on his website publicising his 2007 book *Competitive Identity*, he argued that to compete effectively 'every place needs to be *known* for something'. He went on to argue that brand strategy recognises special qualities as assets and thinks through how to use and combine them into 'a unique, truthful, distinctive and attractive proposition'. Crucially, he insisted, 'none of this happens by accident'. Behind the logos, advertisements, promotions and other collateral lies an extensive architecture of aspiration, strategy and practice. A place brand strategy, he argues, must be linked to a vision and a set of supportive practices. The vision must be realistic, competitive and compelling, and be reinforced and enriched by every act of investment and communication with the rest of the world and backed by 'the right policies, the right economic, social, cultural and educational climate' (Anholt 2007b). The national imaginary must be authentic, sincere and credible, and be mobilised consistently and effectively. This will require, Anholt insists, design and management from corporate branding experts and leadership at the highest level of government.

## BRAND NEW ZEALAND

Brand New Zealand (Brand NZ) is a loosely defined signifier for the set of national imaginaries and representations of them that link New Zealand and New Zealanders to New Zealand products. Various authors have recognised their significance in social and economic change (Dürr 2007b; Bell 2006; Skilling 2005; Cloke and Perkins 2002). For nation branders, Brand NZ is an important example of effective nation branding, and is cited repeatedly as a case study (Dinnie 2008; Anholt 2003b). For New Zealand economic development agencies it is a pivotal, tangible and manageable object for management. For advertising agencies it is a plum account. For New Zealand tourism researchers it is the source of considerable economic value creation – in effect the tourism product at the core of New Zealand's leading export industry.

## THE NEW ZEALAND WAY

Brand New Zealand was first named and mobilised in the New Zealand Way (NZW), a marketing campaign launched in 1991 and formalised as a company co-owned by Trade New Zealand and Tourism New Zealand a year later. The NZW was seen as a designer marque that would secure a market edge and/or premium based on the 'unique New Zealand personality' (New Zealand Way 1993). Established against the background of neoliberal policy rhetoric of market-driven economic development, it fell short of nation branding in the Anholt sense. While a more permanent institutional form than one-off advertising campaigns, it was product centred rather than expected to fulfil the whole range of functions and aspirations of a nation brand. As collective economic action, it was compromised by its constitution as a licensed marque for accredited firms or 'brand partners'.

This nascent nation brand was developed at a time when government was committed to user-pays rationalities rather than collective national economic development. The agencies that developed it did not hold a coordinated national development vision behind which it could have been crafted into a more fully fledged nation brand. Nonetheless, NZW introduced the language of Brand NZ and built networks of relationships among individuals working at the interface of advertising, tourism marketing and trade development that became its soft infrastructure (Warren 2002). These networks incorporate the expertise and institutional memory of the brand, as well as having made instrumental contributions to its development. In Anholt's terms they form part of the brand equity.

The content of NZW was held to be a clean green environmental imaginary, based on a reputation for trusted trading and good international citizenship. The latter was largely unproblematised, but clearly relied on a domestically understood national identity, historical relations with Commonwealth nations and their consuming publics, English language and Westminster political traditions, and relations of trust established by New Zealand's earlier national marketing boards. These foundations were assumed and treated as prior. The substance or identity of Brand NZ was not itself seen as requiring construction.

This changed with the reinvention of active economic development planning at the end of the 1990s. In 1998 the destination brand 100% Pure was launched as the earlier market-led NZW crumbled amidst the contradictions of private funding of a collective asset and the complexities of practices established to deal with them. The programme of nation branding that we have come to understand as Brand NZ was named. By the end of the Clark government in 2008, Brand NZ had become increasingly understood within government and more widely as a co-constitutive family of brands (corporate, national industry, 100% Pure, New Zealand New Thinking) and complex of branding practices by multiple actors (Figure 16.2).

*Source*: Author's own elaboration.

*Figure 16.2   Family of brands New Zealand: A selected sample*

## 100% PURE NEW ZEALAND

Developed by M&C Saatchi, the 100% Pure New Zealand (100% Pure) campaign was launched in 1999. At core a destination brand, it is tourism centred, and administered by tourism authorities, although its potential to brand the nation more widely and do political work was inscribed into its early strategy (Morgan *et al.* 2002). The 100% Pure campaign replaced fragmented market-by-market advertising centred on print media and characterised by montage presentations of over-coloured images of tourism activities and pastoral landscapes. A major investment in market development, it pooled funding into a single campaign. At a time of dramatic increases in tourism worldwide, Tourism New Zealand (TNZ) (2009) credits 100% Pure for increasing visitor numbers by 50 per cent from 1999 to 2005, significantly above Australia (23 per cent), the UK (18 per cent) and Canada (4 per cent). In 2009 100% Pure was rated as the leading global destination brand by the European Travel Commission and the United Nations World Tourism Organization (UNWTO and ETC 2009).

The search was for a consistent brand that would capture the national 'essence' (Tourism New Zealand (TNZ) 2009). The campaign drew on research that suggested overseas visitors look first for natural landscapes and then for adventure and culture. It is based on images of dramatic landscapes into which people are minimally inserted, generally engaged in adventure – be it exhilarating or romantic. It built on the double meaning of 'pure' behind the arresting, language-neutral claim of '100%' to capture earlier 'green' message lines and extend them into the realms of excitement and the dramatic. At a time when wealthy post-industrial urban classes around the globe turned simultaneously to the Discovery Channel, extreme sports, and tourism generally, 100% Pure changed the perception of New Zealand from a place at the end of the earth to a 'hip' place. The dramatic landscapes appealed directly to adventure tourists as well as those who preferred to be voyeurs in such landscapes.

Images from 100% Pure were reinforced and extended by New Zealand's emerging reputation for landscape-centred wine and film, especially the *Lord of the Rings* (*LoTR*) phenomenon, which itself created a niche tourism market (Le Heron 2004, 2008; Jones and Smith 2005; Tzanelli 2004) and expansionary cultural and political economy (Lawn 2005, 2006). TNZ (2009) recognises that destination branding is about marshalling and crafting such diverse reputational effects as much as it is about creating new collateral. The '100% Pure' tagline is designed to open up space for diverse images of nation, which can reinforce or take form around the campaign, or be layered on to existing messages. In the same way, it provides a platform for New Zealand-specific iconography (Maori performing arts and wider Maori society, sheep, geothermal activity, pastoral landscapes, food and sport) to be grafted to globalised aesthetics of mountains, fjords, winescapes, adventure and seclusion.

This assemblage of the local and global is given substance by its resonance with New Zealanders and its appeal to a sense of nation and national pride. It crafts and adds production values to a set of identities to which many New Zealanders aspire, especially the well-travelled young who were in the vanguard of the emerging global class of adventure landscape tourists and have dominated the production of popular imaginaries of nation in other settings. Its edgy elementalism complemented well-established understandings of New Zealand as open, rugged and pioneering. Adding narratives of success in the global and a defiant new world urbanity in the wild, and setting scenes to globally recognisable popular music made by New Zealanders have helped 100% Pure to foster a national identity in its image. Market research suggests that consumers believe it to have successfully distilled New Zealand (TNZ 2009) – that is, that it both attracts and is an authentic representation.

At the heart of this successful intervention in the production of national identity and appeal to tourists lie the high production values in film and photography in which the 100% Pure imagery is captured and presented. The landscapes are dramatic and the human presence minimalist, and the film and photography are highly sophisticated (Pan *et al*. 2010). Much of the photography, for example, is shot downwards, accentuating the drama of the landscapes and the exhilaration of the human presence (Lawn 2010). The production values, links to New Zealand film and wine reputations, and careful insertion of human presence allow image makers to localise global aesthetics and carefully craft a local distinctiveness in tune with global post-industrial aesthetics.

This craft extends beyond the image making itself to an orchestrated 'leveraging' of the brand. TNZ invested in documentary-making to ensure that New Zealand landscapes appeared on the Discovery Channel through deals with Pacific Broadcasting and National Geographic. Its media placement group has brought television programmes such as Billy Connolly's *World Tour of New Zealand*, Jack Osbourne's *Adrenaline Junkie*, and *The Bachelor* to film in New Zealand, as well as attracting image makers. TNZ made a deal with the distributors of *LoTR* to facilitate advertising of New Zealand landscapes, while the success of *LoTR* at the Oscars was built into a special set of advertisements claiming New Zealand to be 'Best Supporting Country in a Motion Picture' and run in key US cities. TNZ commissioned a gold-medal-winning garden at the Chelsea Flower Show in 2004 and another that earned silver in 2007. TNZ placed 100% Pure imagery around the America's Cup in 2002–03, and developed the giant rugby ball.

## NEW ZEALAND NEW THINKING

Market research among businesses in key export markets commissioned by New Zealand Trade and Enterprise (NZTE) in the mid-2000s confirmed that New Zealand was known as a great place for a holiday, high-quality agricultural products, and honesty, safety, and legal and political transparency, but was not seen as a place to do business. As in tourism markets, these images are strongest in places where cultural contacts are greatest. New Zealand New Thinking (NZNT) was established 'to accelerate the change in global awareness of New Zealand as being innovative and technologically advanced, creative and successful'. It seeks to brand New Zealand as an innovative knowledge economy. Developed by NZTE, NZNT is about business–business relations, buyer and investor networks and value chain relations rather than popular national identity. It is understood as a relational branding exercise – making, fostering and sustaining connections and adding value along the chain from gaining access to investment capital to securing paths through distribution agencies to market. It is the brand of the GIF.

NZNT was developed as a complementary brand to 100% Pure, to which it is linked by imaginaries of New Zealand floating elsewhere. These imaginaries broker connections, foster conversations and gain access to the target audience of potential investors and key decision makers along value chains of interest (those signalled by the GIF). The brand is not communicated by high-production-value mass images, but by trade magazine articles and documentary narratives of successful high-technology-driven business ventures, urban sophistication and science successes. Branding includes targeted editorial and beach-head programmes targeting investment or trade networks off-shore, as well as brand collateral to attract attention at trade fairs. Thus *LoTR* is again an opening, and the fame attained by its landscapes an attraction, but it is celebrated as evidence of high-technology image and film-making and computer graphics. The objectives (and often also the metric of success) are column inches achieved in business or high-brow sections of key newspapers and other influential publications in target markets (the *New York Times*, for example), and invitations to business meetings. Both are often facilitated by 100% Pure imaginaries.

## WIDER FAMILY OF BRANDS NEW ZEALAND

These formal brands are complemented by other initiatives located at the edges or beyond the state. Individual firms can become brand partners, which permits licensed users (exporters meeting certain requirements) to place the Fern Mark (a registered marque) on their products (see Florek and Insch 2008). This links these companies into the wider family of 'brands NZ'. Air New Zealand is one prominent example among the multiple firms deploying Brand NZ, and an obvious benefactor of the success of 100% Pure in bringing more tourists to New Zealand, and has been a significant player in its development. It is the national carrier and since 2001 has been 76.5 per cent owned by the government. It exerts a significant voice in tourism policy, and in 2005, when domestic communications agency Assignment Group took over the brand from M&C Saatchi, its CEO was outspoken in his support for continuing 100% Pure (TNZ 2009). Air New Zealand co-sponsors events such as the giant rugby ball that celebrate 100% Pure, runs complementary advertising campaigns, and carries 100% Pure message lines and collateral in its in-flight magazines and advertising. This type of alliance adds micro-detail to Brand NZ. The company's reputation as a high-class carrier adds lustre.

## Industry Brands NZ

National industry associations are significant mobilisers of Brand NZ – particularly those that rely on selling products through geographical imaginary or place of origin marketing. Wine and international education are two such industries. Both are highly significant in the New Zealand context, have grown spectacularly in the last 15 years, and have developed their own nation brands. Both have drawn at different times on the same brand gurus active in Brand NZ. Both have also in the last three years reworked national imaginaries through brand audits that have grafted the dynamics, dramatics and production values of 100% Pure and elements of NZNT on to imaginaries of clean green and little England forged in the 1990s (Lewis 2007, 2008).

The rapid export growth of New Zealand wine has drawn on the spatial imaginaries celebrated in 100% Pure, while its success has added new layers of possibility to 100% Pure and NZNT. Wine culture draws heavily on the discourse of *terroir*, which draws direct associations between place and wine quality. Much of the value of mid- to high-priced wines derives from narratives and images that develop this association, especially in wine media commentaries. In the higher price brackets these need to be compelling and sophisticated (Vaudour 2002). Brand NZ is important to New Zealand wines, which sell at higher than average prices. Wine tourism is also important – to tourism and its marketing, as well as the sale and marketing of wine. Wine landscapes appear in 100% Pure advertising and feature as tourism activities and narratives of place in glossy and in-flight magazines and below-the-line tourism advertising, while New Zealand wines provide social context, talking points, and demonstration of craft and innovation in the relationship building of NZNT.

Generic national marketing and branding of New Zealand wine have been in place for two decades. Run by peak organisation WINZ (later NZ Winegrowers), the early campaign was based around clean green imagery and relied heavily on extant images of New Zealand's greenness and familiar or sleepy exoticness. It communicated New Zealand's arrival on global markets as a wine producer. The rebranding of New Zealand wine in 2007 from the 'Riches of a Clean Green Land' to 'New Zealand Wine: Pure Discovery' reflects dimensions of defensive strategy around claims of greenness, but also new appreciation of the value of both high production values in marketing and the targeting of more sophisticated post-industrial aesthetics than the first-round rural idyll (Lewis 2008). The rebranding shifted much of the material into black and white and cleaner, more minimalist lines and directed new attention to value chain relations (the colours, aesthetics and objectives of NZNT), while the high production values and more dramatic landscapes reflected 100% Pure. The new tagline incorporates elements of both. It shifts New Zealand wine into a more sophisticated market space, which reflects its higher-priced aspirations.

The branding of New Zealand international education has experienced a similar journey to that of wine, although effective national industry branding was initiated later (Lewis 2007). In the early 2000s NZTE and TNZ in conjunction with the association Education New Zealand established a marketing network (NZIEMN) and website to facilitate market development. Geographical provenance (New Zealand) was recognised as the product: its educational history, qualities and reputation; its physical, cultural and political environments; its colonial history; its cities and their cultural infrastructure; and its families and their homes. NZIEMN developed a nation brand that sought to assure parents and agents of New Zealand's educational capacities and accentuate its advantages of safety, friendliness, English language and environment. With the tagline 'New World Class: Educated in New Zealand', it targeted the 'the aspirational group that international students seek to join' ('New World Class') and placed New Zealand within that aspiration. The logo was supported by 'seven perfect growing conditions' that celebrated New Zealand's 'difference': world-leading courses, association with fresh thinkers, world-class institutions, a British-based education system, high-quality living conditions, warm and welcoming environments, and recreation in paradise. These represented four place-specific claims interwoven with three assertions about New Zealand's ability to deliver desirable generic qualities.

Brand NZ Education was used to design extensive brand collateral, underpin a national message at trade fairs, support the website, and provide a banner behind which to attract and do business with agents. It was reviewed in 2007 in response to falling demand, diversification objectives, the increasing sophistication of the global market, and the knowledge economy aspirations expressed in NZNT (Lewis 2007). Higher production values, a new tagline 'New Zealand Educated' and techno-urban imagery cultivate more professionalised, globalised and technologised images of educational quality and New Zealand's capacity to deliver it. Clean green is replaced by 100% Pure and NZNT. New Zealand is portrayed as a place to prepare young people to perform as part of a networked and mobile global elite. Instead of the seven growing conditions, the brand is centred on seven benefits of a New Zealand education beneath the strapline 'First Light Thinking': connected, lively, inventive, adventurous, personal, trusted and welcoming.

### NZEdge.com

Established and supported by advertising professionals, including New Zealander Kevin Roberts, who is CEO Worldwide of Saatchi & Saatchi in New York, NZEdge.com is a website that claims to be 'a new way of thinking about New Zealand identity . . . and place in the world'. It aims to:

> strengthen national identity and foster the global community of New Zealanders – to introduce metaphors for NZers to articulate who they are; articulate and leverage New Zealand's difference; increase its prosperity in spirit and in pocket; build an emotional connection with the global community of New Zealanders; and build the de-facto global brand for New Zealand.

This rhetoric of success and champions places into circulation multiple identity-building narratives. New Zealand can point to high-profile, successful daughters and sons who have succeeded on global stages: from splitting the atom to climbing Mount Everest, inventing bungy jumping, making *LoTR* or jet engines, or succeeding in sporting arenas. They are celebrated on NZEdge.com in a roll of honour labelled 'heroes'.

NZEdge brands New Zealand for New Zealanders domestically and overseas. It uses the term 'compatriation' to create the country outside the country. Its aim is to make visible 'overseas New Zealanders' (estimated to number one in four of all New Zealanders), connect them (in part through the site), and internationalise New Zealanders' view of themselves. NZEdge resources 100% Pure and NZNT by cataloguing champions, cultivating a national identity of achievement, and making possible new global connections. In this expression of globalisation the spatiality of nation is being explicitly reimagined and the diaspora enrolled into the national project (Larner 2007). NZEdge facilitates the efforts of NZNT and various other brands NZ to mobilise the diaspora as pre-existing business networks and *in situ* 'brand ambassadors' (a strategy recognised as a practice of nation branding – Kuznetsov 2006), whilst producing for the diaspora an identity that is explicitly New Zealand yet also a platform for New Zealanders to take on the global subjectivities necessary to participate in the global from the edge or connected through the edge.

## BRAND NEW ZEALAND ARCHITECTURE

Brand NZ is then assembled from a mix of geographical imaginaries (cultural and environmental), agencies, practices, artefacts, events and virtual presences. Its practices involve creating images and text and putting them into circulation – formally through film, posters, brochures, pamphlets, ticketing material, and relationship-building moments and events, and less formally through conversations, spontaneous relationships, and viral release through social networking sites, blogs and YouTube (an important strategy in promotion of the work of the giant rugby ball beyond the site itself). They also involve close attention to placement and shaping the channels of circulation (domestically and in key global cities): marketing, public relations and communications strategies; staging events; and establishing and building connectivity, networks and alliances through beach-head programmes, receptions and conferences.

Events are an important part of these strategies – purpose-specific, such as the rugby ball, or the imaging of more general activities and cultural spectacles such as New Zealand Fashion Week (Lewis *et al.* 2008). Other events include the privately inspired initiative that saw 1000 New Zealanders and a couple of big diggers build a giant silver fern on Santa Monica beach in February 2007. Inspired by a communications agency the event was designed to launch 'Made from New Zealand' online, a social and business marketing network of New Zealand businesses and entrepreneurs. Funded by the sale of T-shirts specially designed by celebrity designers and supported by Air New Zealand, the fern was built by Inside Out, the same firm that built and managed the giant rugby ball event. These events provide moments for displaying and generating textual and visual brand collateral.

The stuff that relates these elements and practices, makes Brand NZ cohesive and gives it shape and meaning is its shared imaginaries – the images themselves, their meanings, and the commitments that make them shared. In the case of Brand NZ, nation is linked to alluring post-industrial lifestyles and aesthetics by a rich base of environmental and cultural iconography and narratives of achievement. Its material forms include the brand collateral crafted to capture this base, as well as advertorial, travel and food media, beach-head programmes for targeted investors off-shore, national trade fairs and one-off events in key global places, industry trade fairs, sports and cultural festivals, industry and exporter awards rounds, and the virtual platforms of TNZ, NZTE, 100% Pure, NZEdge and industry associations. Holding them together has been 100% Pure, a relatively stable circle of brand architects, the absence of significant challenges to the authenticity of the imaginaries (internally and externally), and a careful cultivation of economic nationalism.

Economic nationalism, which reduces national identity building to a calculus of economic success in the global from the edge, is deeply embedded. It is cultivated by popular media, industry actors, education curricula, science funding and even much domestic art, as well as national development agencies, and is exemplified in NZEdge.com. New Zealand identifies with national branding – so closely that Brand NZ is roundly parodied in, for example, the highly successful *Flight of the Conchords* television comedy aired on HBO in the United States and around the world (success in the global – and used as a marker!). The character Murray, the manager of the band and a middle manager in the New Zealand trade consulate, is routinely filmed at his desk in front of cheaply veneered wall panelling decorated with a 100% Pure poster tacked to the wall slightly askew. The point, that New Zealanders have a deeply entrenched drive to sell their country (in the best sense of that metaphor), is lost on neither New Zealanders themselves nor others viewing the show.

Stewarded by NZTE and TNZ respectively, which own their taglines and co-own the iconic silver fern used in promotional material, and the NZ.com web address, NZNT and 100% Pure and the partnership between TNZ and NZTE provide a pivotal part of the architecture of Brand NZ. They direct the brand strategically in terms of government policy, allocate resources and monitor effects. TNZ produces extensive brand collateral, including the film and print images of 100% Pure, while NZTE published the bi-monthly glossy magazine *Bright* which celebrated business and technology achievement, and maintained databases of key business contacts and business networks in different export markets. The wider family of brands NZ extends the number and range of agents involved in nation branding, the sites of branding, and the range and volume of brand collateral (artefacts, individual capacities, relations, and reputation building). Daily newspapers, editorials, coffee-table magazines, airline cabins, staff rooms, dentists' waiting rooms, art galleries and many more spaces, sites, publics and artefacts are drawn into making Brand NZ. And, in each of the moments, the 100% Pure images have a domestic and internal register that celebrates a certain New Zealandness via its landscapes – connecting them to globalising aesthetics and aspirations as well as local cultural histories.

As long as the principal messages, spatial imaginaries and aspirations remain understood, accepted and coherent, Brand NZ achieves what it is intended to achieve – to help New Zealand 'punch above its weight' and transcend its small size and isolation into global presence and globalisation. The brands are heavily enrolled behind what has become known as NZInc (the economic relations and overarching purpose and project that will 'enable New Zealand to win' in the global – the challenge that the Clark government explicitly set itself in 2001). The brand gurus and their related spin-doctors are invited into the engine rooms of NZInc (Prince 2010; Lawn 2006). Celebrating nation makes sense to producers and consumers of geographical imaginaries in (and of) a small nation at the far edge of the world. There is a certain inoffensiveness, appropriateness or perhaps even nobility about high-class nation branding in this context. Small nations can shout about themselves if they have something to say in interesting ways. The enrolment into NZInc of award-winning expertise in branding and image production embedded in the local offices of global advertising agencies has secured this 'right', and high production values remain central to the architecture of Brand NZ.

## CONCLUSION

This chapter has used the case of Brand NZ to highlight the phenomenon of nation branding and the work performed by nation brands. It reveals the architecture, genealogy and practices of a coordinated initiative to define and promote New Zealand as a tourism destination, add value to goods and services produced in New Zealand, mobilise a globalising national identity, and nurture globalising business relationships. The New Zealand context confirms just how ambitious nation branding has become. The project of the nation is to be an all-embracing struggle to globalise successfully from the edge.

Brand NZ is thus, like other brands, far more than a logo. It is a calculated and calculating entanglement of territory, imaginary, measurement technology, practice and identity building (Pike 2009). At its narrowest, it is market making and value adding, but also a relational equity that does different work in different parts of the value chain from imagining new products and investment through to consumption and the reproduction of social relationships. More broadly, it is performative, helping to make in virtual and real terms the landscapes and globalising relations that it describes, and fostering the national identities of economic nationalism and success in the global that it represents. In fashioning relations, practices and identity it has constituted a global space of cultural economy – a nation extending beyond New Zealand's territorial borders that is most clearly exemplified by the compatriated New Zealand. This is a space in which geographical imaginaries and cultural and economic objects and practices are generated and circulated, and the international economic, social and political relations that sustain this circulation are built and fostered.

The chapter has interpreted the strategic assemblage of Brand NZ as a political project to drive an expansionary globalisation more deeply into economic practice and social identity. Brand NZ seeks to enrol all New Zealanders in a project of global competitiveness, together with anyone who has ever visited the country (physically or virtually). It fosters the economic nationalism, pride in landscapes, and images of success that it uses to sell products overseas, including tourism. The spatialities of nation are being reimagined strategically and played out in everyday lives, especially those of the diaspora and those agents living the brand in their daily work (often off-shore). Brand NZ reassembles in a particular global form the now fractured alignments of nation, state and society of an earlier more inwardly framed development agenda.

Nation branding provides one example of the sorts of globalising strategies, rhetorics and practices run by nation states, the ways in which these are aligned across policy spheres, and the ways in which cultural practices, identities and geographical imaginaries are mobilised for what is a new game of competitive national development. However, like other brands, Brand NZ is far from politically, culturally, socially or economically innocent. There is more at stake even than an extension of Klein's (2000) critique of the work of brands in contemporary capitalism to the anxieties of nation states facing a neoliberal globalising race to the bottom. This includes what is represented in the brand and whose interests are served by it – the question of what and whose nation.

Whilst this chapter has not pursued this line of critique, it does allow me to conclude by posing three connected questions. First, will nation branding stimulate enlightened policy formation so as to sustain a positive national image, as Anholt (2007a) claims? We should have a healthy scepticism (Mayes 2008). While a cultural economy entity, the nation is more than a brand. At the very least, in its coupling with the state, it confers rights, bounds activities, regulates, exercises legitimate force and allocates resources. Nonetheless, whilst the development ambitions of Lagos (Anholt's example) are conditioned in far more complex ways than a negative 'continent branding effect', and suggestions that Africa's problems reduce to branding deserve derision, nation branding is political and has political effects. A government is vulnerable to overt contradictions in the geographical imaginaries that it promotes, as well as the wider politics of identity and the narrower political economy of brand resourcing. This vulnerability may open up opportunities to contest the claims made, or provide platforms for critical political projects.

In New Zealand's case environmentalists and critics routinely mobilise contradictions in claims about 'clean and green' and pristine landscapes in political rhetoric and efforts to secure resources for environmental projects – within the state and in direct negotiations with corporates (Westgate 2010; Bell 2006; Coyle and Fairweather 2005). Similarly, Maori may contest their portrayal in Brand NZ, which is dominated by performing arts and at odds (at least for foreign audiences) with their ownership of significant chunks of NZ tourism and their increasingly corporate presence in New Zealand's many globalising relationships. While those involved perform Brand NZ very much as their own and on their own terms, the 100% Pure representation has the potential to become embroiled in wider contests over representations and benefits (Dürr 2007b).

Second, how localised is Brand NZ – how much of New Zealand is inscribed into Brand NZ and how much is it about competing to best exemplify global aesthetics? Certainly the architecture and practices of assemblage are distinctive – the economic nationalism and the wealth of nation at geographical margins. So too are some of the images: the prominence of Maori; the bungy cords; the youth of the nation; the symbology of the colour black, the silver fern and the kiwi; the playful use of 'NZ'; and the juxtaposition of mountains, bush and geothermal activity. To date the play of local and global has been skilfully negotiated to produce a globally valued distinctiveness. The crucial feature of high-end production values (locally specialised global technology) is a case in point. Monitoring this play will remain important for the nation branders – particularly the ways in which it plays out in different markets.

The deeper political question is just how localised or inclusive of diversity the geographical imaginaries can become. Brand NZ knows and performs New Zealand in a particular and largely singular way – a particular assemblage of cultural and environmental iconography and successful competitive participation in the global. Many New Zealanders may not see themselves or their visions for the future in these images – even if they find the images alluring (Dürr 2007b). Social groups struggling with poverty and health issues and increasing inequalities in income, education and health are masked, as is a complex politics of multiculturalism and less-than-green environmental practices.

Third, in what ways does nation branding reframe neoliberalising globalisation's race to the bottom, and to what effects? Whilst a far from novel insight, nation branding reveals how nations remain significant imaginaries and states important actors in globalisation. It highlights the implication of geographical imaginaries and their production in globalisation, interventionist practices in these terms, and the renewed attention to social institutions and identities. Unlike the destructive neoliberalism of 'roll-back' (Peck and Tickell 2002), nation branding is a proactive project in which geography is reinscribed as important and the potential to launch social projects is expanded. Against this, it is still about cross-border investment and trade flows and a deeper, more expansionist globalisation. The technologies are global, as are many of the underpinning geographical imaginaries, and global branders are available for hire and thus to eliminate advantages and flatten the field. Brand NZ is about succeeding in the global, not about local aspiration or any challenge to the global that it is performing. More positively, such aspiration is not precluded from the brand or its inherent cultural project or governmental technologies. By asking what is included and excluded in the imaginaries mobilised, whose identities are being framed and for whom, and whether this might be done differently to imagine a more local future, it offers some political potential that does not necessarily reduce to another move in the race to the bottom.

## ACKNOWLEDGEMENT

This research is funded by the Marsden Fund administered by The Royal Society of New Zealand. I wish also to thank those officials of New Zealand Trade and Enterprise and industry organizations to whom I talked in the course of this research. Special thanks to Tourism New Zealand's Major Events Coordinator David Burt, who made possible my observation of the Giant Rugby Ball in Tokyo, and to all those involved in inflating and promoting the ball.

## REFERENCES

Allen, J. (2008) 'Powerful geographies: Spatial shifts in the architecture of globalization', in S. Clegg and M. Haugaard (eds), *The Handbook of Power*, Los Angeles, CA: Sage, pp. 157–173.
Anholt, S. (1998) 'Nation brands of the twenty-first century', *Journal of Brand Management*, 5, 6, 395–406.
Anholt, S. (2003a) *Brand New Justice: The Upside of Global Branding*, Oxford: Butterworth-Heinemann.
Anholt, S. (2003b) 'Branding New Zealand', Interview with Linda Clark, National Radio, New Zealand, 13 June.
Anholt, S. (2007a) *Competitive Identity: The New Brand Management for Nations, Cities and Regions*, Houndmills: Palgrave Macmillan.
Anholt, S. (2007b) *http://www.simonanholt.com/*, accessed 15 November 2007.
Anholt, S. (2009) *Places: Identity, Image and Reputation*, Houndmills: Palgrave Macmillan.
Araujo, L. and Kjellberg, H. (2010) 'Shaping exchanges, performing markets: The study of marketing practices', in P. Maclaran, M. Saren, B. Stern and M. Tadajewski (eds), *The Sage Handbook of Marketing Theory*, London: Sage, 196–218.
Banks, G., Kelly, S., Lewis, N. and Sharpe, S. (2007) 'Place "from one glance": The use of place in the marketing of New Zealand and Australian wines', *Australian Geographer*, 1, 15–35.
Bell, C. (2006) 'Branding New Zealand: The national greenwash', *British Review of New Zealand Studies (BRONZS)*, 15, 13–28.
Callon, M., Méadel, C. and Rabeharisoa, V. (2002) 'The economy of qualities', *Economy and Society*, 31, 2, 194–217.
Cloke, P. and Perkins, H. (2002) 'Commodification and adventure tourism in New Zealand', *Current Issues in Tourism*, 5, 6, 521–549.
Coyle, F. and Fairweather, J. (2005) 'Challenging a place myth: New Zealand's clean green image meets the biotechnology revolution', *Area*, 37, 2, 148–158.
de Chernatony, L. (2009) 'Towards the holy grail of defining "brand"', *Marketing Theory*, 9, 1, 101–105.

Dinnie, K. (ed.) (2008) *Nation Branding: Concepts, Issues, Practice*, Oxford: Elsevier.

du Gay, P. (2002) 'Cultural economy: An introduction', in P. du Gay and M. Pryke (eds), *Cultural Economy*, London: Sage.

Dürr, E. (2007a) 'Arcadia in the Antipodes: Tourists' reflections on New Zealand as nature experience', *Sites: A Journal of Social Anthropology and Cultural Studies*, 4, 2.

Dürr, E. (2007b) 'Representing purity: National branding, nature, and identity in New Zealand', Paper given at Transformations '07: Composing the Nation: Ideas, Peoples, Histories, Languages, Cultures, Economies, Congress of Te Whāinga Aronui, Council for the Humanities, Wellington, 27–28 August, http://www.humanitiesresearch.net/news/representing_purity_national_branding_nature_and_identity_in_new_zealand_1, accessed 6 June 2010.

Florek, M. and Insch, A. (2008) 'The trademark protection of country brands: Insights from New Zealand', *Journal of Place Management and Development*, 1, 3, 292–306.

Gibson, C. and Klocker, N. (2004) 'Academic publishing as a "creative" industry: Some critical reflections', *Area*, 36, 423–434.

Jackson, P. (2004) 'Local consumption cultures in a globalising world', *Transactions of the Institute of British Geographers*, 29, 165–178.

Jackson, P., Russell, P. and Ward, N. (2007) 'The appropriation of "alternative" discourses by "mainstream" food retailers', in D. Maye, L. Holloway and M. Kneafsey (eds), *Alternative Food Geographies: Representation and Practice*, Amsterdam: Elsevier, 309–330.

Jackson, P., Ward, N. and Russell, P. (2009) 'Moral economies of food and geographies of responsibility', *Transactions of the Institute of British Geographers*, 34, 1, 12–24.

Jessop, B. (2008) 'The knowledge-based economy', *Naked Punch*, 10, http://www.nakedpunch.com.

Jones, D. and Smith, K. (2005) 'Middle-Earth meets New Zealand: authenticity and location in the making of *The Lord of the Rings*', *Journal of Management Studies*, 42, 5, 923–945.

Klein, N. (2000) *No Logo*, London: Flamingo.

Kuznetsov, Y. (2006) 'Leveraging diasporas of talent: Toward a new policy agenda', in Y. Kuznetsov (ed.), *Diaspora Networks and the International Migration of Skills: How Countries Can Draw on Their Talent Abroad*, Washington, DC: World Bank.

Larner, W. (2007) 'Expatriate experts and globalising governmentalities: The New Zealand diaspora strategy', *Transactions of the Institute of British Geographers*, 32, 331–345.

Larner, W. and Le Heron, R. (2002) 'The spaces and subjects of a globalising economy: A situated exploration of method', *Environment and Planning D: Society and Space*, 20, 6, 753–774.

Larner, W., Le Heron, R. and Lewis, N. (2007) 'Co-constituting neoliberalism: Globalising governmentalities and political projects in Aotearoa New Zealand', in K. England, and K. Ward (eds), *Neoliberalization: States, Networks, People*, 223–247.

Lash, S. and Lury, C. (2007) *Global Cultural Industry*, Cambridge: Polity Press.

Lawn, J. with Beatty, B. (2005) 'Getting to Wellywood: National branding and the globalisation of the New Zealand film industry', *Post Script*, 24, 2–3, 125–143.

Lawn, J. (2006) 'Creativity Inc.: Globalising the cultural imaginary in New Zealand', in Janet Wilson and Clara A.B. Joseph (eds), *Global Fissures: Postcolonial Fusions*, Amsterdam: Rodopi, 225–245.

Lawn, J. (2010) 'Branding the landscape: Ian Wedde's literary critique of the 100% Pure NZ campaign', School of Social and Cultural Studies seminar, Massey University, Albany, 11 August, 2010.

Le Heron, E. (2004) 'Placing geographical imagination in film: New Zealand film-makers' use of landscape', *New Zealand Geographer*, 60, 1, 60–66.

Le Heron, E. (2008) 'Making film-landscapes and exploring the geographical reso-nances of *The Lord of the Rings* and *Whale Rider*', Doctoral thesis, Department of Geography, University of Sheffield.

Lewis, N. (2007) '"New Zealand Educated": Rebranding New Zealand to attract foreign students', GlobalHigherEd Weblog (editors: K. Olds and S. Robertson), 11 December, http://globalhighered.wordpress.com/2007/12/11/new-zealand-educated-rebranding-new-zealand-to-attract-foreign-students/.

Lewis, N. (2008) 'Brand New Zealand wine: Where are we at, and what more should we be doing?', in C. Moore and K. Moore (eds), *Building Wine Brands: Proceeding of the Inaugural New Zealand Wine Business Symposium*, EIT, Napier, 17–18 June.

Lewis, N., Larner, W. and Le Heron, R. (2008) 'The New Zealand designer fashion industry: Making industries and co-constituting political projects', *Transactions of the Institute of British Geographers*, 33, 42–59.

Lury, C. (2004) *Brands: The Logos of the Global Economy*, Oxford: Routledge.

Maclaran, P., Saren, M., Stern, B. and Tadajewski, M. (eds) (2010) *The Sage Handbook of Marketing Theory*, London: Sage.

Mayes, R. (2008) 'A place in the sun: The politics of place, identity and branding', *Place Branding and Public Diplomacy*, 4, 2, 124–135.

Miller, D. (2002) 'Turning Callon the right way up', *Economy and Society*, 31, 2, 218–233.

Mitchell, T. (2008) 'Rethinking economy', *Geoforum*, 39, 1116–1121.

Morgan, K., Marsden, T. and Murdoch, J. (2006) *Worlds of Food: Place, Power, and Provenance in the Food Chain*, Oxford: Oxford University Press.

Morgan, N., Pritchard, A. and Piggott, R. (2002) 'New Zealand, 100% pure: The creation of a powerful niche destination brand', *Journal of Brand Management*, 9, 4/5, 335–354.

New Zealand Way (1993) *Brand New Zealand*, Auckland: New Zealand Way.

Olins, W. (1999) *Trading Identities: Why Countries and Companies Are Taking Each Other's Roles*, London: Foreign Policy Centre.

Olins, W. (2003) *On Brand*, London: Thames and Hudson.

Pan, S., Tsai, H. and Lee, J. (2010) 'Framing New Zealand: Understanding tourism TV commercials', *Tourism Management*, 32, 33, 596–603.

Pawson, E. (1997) 'Branding strategies and languages of consumption', *New Zealand Geographer*, 53, 2, 16–21.

Peck, J. and Tickell, A. (2002) 'Neoliberalising space', *Antipode*, 34, 3, 380–404.

Pike, A. (2009) 'Geographies of brands and branding', *Progress in Human Geography*, 33, 619–645.

Power, D. and Hauge, A. (2008) 'No man's brand – brands, institutions, fashion and the economy', *Growth and Change*, 39, 1, 123–143.

Prince, R. (2010) 'Policy transfer as policy assemblage: making policy for the crea-tive industries in New Zealand', *Environment and Planning A*, 42, 169–186.

Saren, M., Maclaren, P. and Goulding, C. (2007) 'Blurring the boundary: Towards a conceptual reconstruction of the relationship between production and consumption', *Revista Romana de Marketing*, 2, 1, 21–36.

Sinclair, J. (2008) 'Branding and belonging: Globalised goods and national identity', *Journal of Cultural Economy*, 1, 217–231.

Skilling, P. (2005) 'Trajectories of arts and culture policy in New Zealand', *Australian Journal of Public Administration*, 64, 4, 20–31.

Stern, B. (2006) 'What does brand mean? Historical-analysis method and construct definition', *Journal of the Academy of Marketing Science*, 34, 216–223.

Tourism New Zealand (TNZ) (2009) 'Pure as: Celebrating 10 years of 100% Pure New Zealand', available at: http://www.tourismnewzealand.com/media/106877/10%20year%20anniversary%20of%20100%20%20pure%20new%20zealand%20campaign%20-%20pure%20as%20magazine.pdf.

Tzanelli, R. (2004) 'Constructing the "cinematic tourist": the "sign industry" of *The Lord of the Rings*', *Tourist Studies*, 4, 1, 21–42.

United Nations World Tourism Organization (UNWTO) and European Travel Commission (ETC) (2009) *Handbook on Tourism Destination Branding*, Brussels: ETC and UNWTO.

Vaudour, E. (2002) 'The quality of grapes and wine in relation to geography: Notions of *terroir* at various scales', *Journal of Wine Research*, 13, 2, 117–141.

Warren, S. (2002) 'Branding New Zealand: Competing in the global attention economy', *Locum Destination Review*, Winter, 54–56, http://www.locumconsulting.com/pdf/LDR10BrandingNZ.pdf, accessed 7 June 2010.

Westgate, J. (2010) 'Brand value: the work of ecolabelling and place-branding in New Zealand tourism', unpublished Masters thesis, The University of Auckland, Auckland, Summary available at: http://www.tourismresearch.govt.nz/Documents/Scholarships/JustinWestgate_BrandValue_ecolabellingNZ-Tourism.pdf.

# 17. Beyond the nation brand: The role of image and identity in international relations

**Simon Anholt**

## INTRODUCTION

I first began to write about an idea I called 'nation brand' in 1996. My original observation was a simple one: that the reputations of countries (and, by extension, of cities and regions too) behave rather like the brand images of companies and products, and that they are equally critical to the progress, prosperity and good management of those places. Unfortunately, the phrase 'nation brand' soon become distorted, mainly by naive governments in willing collusion with ambitious consulting firms, into 'nation branding' a dangerously misleading phrase which seems to contain a promise that the images of countries can be directly manipulated using the techniques of commercial marketing communications. Yet, despite repeatedly calling for it over the last 15 years, I have never seen a shred of evidence to suggest that this is possible: no case studies, no research, and not even any very persuasive arguments. I conclude that countries are judged by what they do, not by what they say, as they have always been, yet the notion that a country can simply advertise its way into a better reputation has proved to be a pernicious and surprisingly resilient one.

I also have to admit that, despite studying the topic for many years, I'm not at all sure I even know what 'branding' is. 'Brand' can mean at least three different things in the world of commerce: first, it can refer to the designed identity of a product (the look of the product itself, its packaging, its logo, its livery, its communications and so forth); second, it is sometimes used more ambitiously to refer to the culture of the organisation behind the product; and, third, it can refer to the product's or corporation's reputation in the minds of its target audience (this is the sense in which I used the word in my first essay on the subject in 1998, 'Nation brands of the twenty-first century', although the term 'brand image' is a more precise one in this context). Hence, one might suppose, brand*ing* must be related to one or another of these meanings: it is the business of designing the livery of products (which is indeed what branding agencies do); or else it has something to do with building or creating an enhanced sense of corporate culture or 'mission' within the organisation (in fact the word is not often used in this context); or it is the means by which the product acquires its reputation, and this is where the trouble starts. Used in its first sense, branding actually does have some relevance to countries and the ways they present themselves to the rest of the world, but it is a humdrum business which doesn't begin to justify the excitement about 'nation branding'. Countries, through their many state agencies, have numerous dealings with various professional audiences around the world, and one can certainly argue that it gives a better impression of the country if all those agencies use consistent, well-designed materials when they carry out their transactions. A single logo, and a professional 'look and feel' on their stationery, business cards, corporate videos, information leaflets, communiqués, press releases, websites and so forth undoubtedly reinforce the impression of a well-organised, modern, self-respecting state with effective and efficient structures, processes and mechanisms. If this is 'nation branding' then I withdraw all my objections: it's an eminently sensible, perfectly achievable standard to aspire to; all countries should try to do it well; and it's certainly as important as, for example, making sure that diplomats offer the right kinds of canapés when entertaining foreign heads of state; but it's hard to understand why anybody in their right mind would want to spend time theorising about it, still less write books about it.

The point is that 'branding' in this sense of the term is essentially a passive operation: it can't win any new customers, change anybody's mind, increase market share or affect the country's prospects in any significant way. It is simply good practice, a useful exercise of reassurance, a piece of housekeeping. Certainly, for low-cost, fast-moving consumer products in a busy retail environment, the branding (in this sense of graphic design or corporate identity) can be almost as important as the product itself, because design is one of the few things that distinguish a product from its competitors; the attractiveness of the product and its wrapper may even be a more significant driver of consumer choice than advertising. This is why branding agencies, accustomed to the emphasis placed on brand identity in their native field of commerce, talk so impressively about such matters, and public officials are often swayed by their talk. But countries aren't for sale, aren't easily mistaken one for another, aren't fast-moving consumer goods, and certainly don't come in wrappers, so the principles simply don't transfer.

The real confusion starts when people want 'branding' to mean a technique, or set of techniques, by means of which brand image is directly built or enhanced: 'Nike's fantastic brand image is the result of fantastic branding.' It is not. Nike's fantastic brand image is the result of fantastic products sold in fantastically large numbers. Brand *building* is primarily achieved through product development and marketing, and has relatively little to do with branding (except, as I mentioned before, if branding means logo and packaging design, in which case it certainly helps the marketing process along). If people buy a product and find it good, this will begin to create a powerful brand image for the product; the product will earn a good reputation. This reputation gradually spreads to non-users; even people who haven't bought the product will 'know' that it's a good product. The reputation spreads, drives up sales and increases the value of the corporation. It's one of the most significant factors of business success.

But the use of the term 'branding' to imply a method for building brand equity is both incorrect and unjustifiable – there is simply no such method. Good products and services produced by a good corporation acquire a positive brand image, which eventually reflects on the corporation and becomes its principal asset. Similarly, good products, services, culture, tourism, investments, technology, education, businesses, people, policies, initiatives and events produced by a good country also acquire a positive brand image, which eventually reflects on the country, and perhaps also becomes its principal asset.

The message is clear: if a country is serious about enhancing its international image, it should concentrate on 'product development' and 'marketing' rather than chase after the chimera of 'branding'. There are no short cuts. Only a consistent, coordinated and unbroken stream of useful, noticeable, world-class and above all *relevant* ideas, products and policies can, gradually, enhance the reputation of the country that produces them.

I have often summarised this process as consisting of three main components: strategy, substance and symbolic actions.

*Strategy*, in its simplest terms, is knowing *who* a nation is and *where* it stands today (both in reality and according to internal and external perceptions), knowing where it wants to get to, and knowing how it is going to get there. The two main difficulties associated with strategy development are (a) reconciling the needs and desires of a wide range of different national actors into a more or less single direction, and (b) finding a strategic goal that is both inspiring and feasible, since these two requirements are frequently contradictory.

*Substance* is the effective execution of that strategy in the form of new economic, legal, political, social, cultural and educational activity: the real innovations, businesses, legislation, reforms, investments, institutions and policies which will bring about the desired progress.

Symbolic actions are a particular species of substance that happen to have an intrinsic communicative power: they might be innovations, structures, legislation, reforms, investments, institutions or policies which are especially suggestive, remarkable, memorable, picturesque, newsworthy, topical, poetic, touching, surprising or dramatic. Most importantly, they are emblematic of the strategy: they are at the same time a component of the national story and the means of telling it.

Some good examples of symbolic actions are the Slovenian government donating financial aid to their Balkan neighbours in order to prove that Slovenia wasn't part of the Balkans; Spain legalising single-sex marriages in order to demonstrate that its values had modernised to a point diametrically opposed to those of the Franco period; the decision of the Irish government to exempt artists, writers and poets from income tax in order to prove the state's respect for creative talent; Estonia declaring internet access to be a human right; or Bhutan charging a hefty fine to visitors in order to demonstrate its great respect for its own cultural identity and for the fragility of its environment.

A single symbolic action will seldom achieve any lasting effect: multiple actions should emanate from as many different sectors as possible in order to build a rounded and believable image for the place; they must also continue in unbroken succession for many years. Symbolic actions should never be empty – they must be communicative substance rather than just communication. I argue that governments should never do things purely for brand-related reasons; no action should ever be conceived of or dedicated to image management or image change alone. Every initiative and action should first and foremost be done for a real purpose in the real world or else it runs the risk of being insincere, ineffective, and perceived as propaganda (not to mention a use of taxpayers' money that is often extremely hard to justify).

It is clear that places require new and dedicated structures to coordinate, conceive, develop, maintain and promote such an unbroken chain of proof. None of the traditional apparatus of trade or government is fit for such a purpose.

## WHY PLACE REPUTATION IS IMPORTANT

In order to sidestep the terminal confusion surrounding the notion of brands, I coined the deliberately unsexy term *Competitive Identity* as the title of a book on this subject in 2007. It probably compromised sales of the book, but it made the point that national image has more to do with national identity and the politics and economics of competitiveness than with branding as it is usually understood in the commercial sector (or as it is usually meant by people who know nothing about it).

Today, every place on earth appears to want to enhance, reverse, adapt or otherwise manage its international reputation. Yet we are still far from a widespread understanding of what this means in practice, and just how far commercial approaches can be effectively and responsibly applied to government, society and economic development. Many governments, most consultants and even some scholars persist in a tiresome and superficial interpretation of 'place branding' that is nothing more than standard product promotion, public relations and corporate identity, where the product just happens to be a country, a city or a region rather than a tin of beans or a box of soap powder.

The need for proper understanding in this area is crucial. Today, the world is one market; the rapid advance of globalisation means that whatever countries try to pull in (investors, aid, tourists, business visitors, students, major events, researchers, travel writers and talented entrepreneurs), and whatever countries try to push out (products, services, policies, culture and ideas), is done with a discount if the country's image is weak or negative, and at a premium if it's strong and positive.

In this crowded global marketplace, most people and organisations don't have time to learn much about other places. We all navigate through the complexity of the modern world armed with a few simple clichés, and they form the background of our opinions, even if we aren't fully aware of this and don't always admit it to ourselves: Paris is about style, Japan about technology, Switzerland about wealth and precision, Rio de Janeiro about carnival and football, Tuscany about the good life, and most African nations about poverty, corruption, war, famine and disease. Most of us are much too busy worrying about ourselves and our own countries to spend too long trying to form complete, balanced and informed views about 6 billion other people and nearly 200 other countries. We make do with summaries for the vast majority of people and places – the ones we will probably never know or visit – and only start to expand and refine these impressions when for some reason we acquire a particular interest in them. When you haven't got time to read a book, you judge it by its cover.

These clichés and stereotypes – positive or negative, true or untrue – fundamentally affect our behaviour towards other places and their people and products. It may seem unfair, but there's nothing anybody can do to change this. It's very hard for a country to persuade people in other parts of the world to go beyond these simple images and start to understand the rich complexity that lies behind them. Some quite progressive places don't get nearly as much attention, visitors, business or investment as they need because their reputation is weak or negative, while others are still trading on a good image which they acquired decades or even centuries ago, and today do relatively little to deserve.

So all responsible governments, on behalf of their people, their institutions and their companies, need to measure and monitor the world's perception of their nation, and to develop a strategy for managing it. It is a key part of their job to try to earn a reputation that is fair, true, powerful, attractive and genuinely useful to their economic, political and social aims, and honestly reflects the spirit, the genius and the will of the people. This huge task has become one of the primary skills of administrations in the twenty-first century.

When it comes into office, a government inherits a sacred responsibility for its electorate's most valuable asset: the good name of its country. Its task is to hand that good name down to its successors in at least as good condition as it received it.

## THE CASE OF KOREA

President Lee Myung-bak of the Republic of Korea is one leader who appears to have taken this responsibility seriously, and has identified the task of improving South Korea's rather weak performance in my survey, the Anholt-GfK Roper Nation Brands Index (NBI), as a particularly important challenge for the country's future success and prosperity. South Korea is an interesting case: this is a country which, by any account, has made remarkable progress during the last three decades, achieving great advances in prosperity, stability, transparency, productivity, education and many other important areas. The 'Korean Wave' of high-quality film, music and television has made Korea into something of a media star in East and South-East Asia, yet its image remains decidedly weak, if not actually negative, outside the region: research suggests that people in many countries aren't even quite sure which of the two Koreas is the good one and which the bad one – or whether perhaps they are both bad.

The reason why Korea has a weak international image is not, of course, because it has spent too little money on promoting itself: it's because most people in most other countries simply aren't interested in Korea, any more than they are interested in Peru, Jordan, Estonia or Namibia. And there is, currently, no compelling reason why they should be.

Most people in most countries aren't even very interested in their *own* country, let alone the 200 or so other countries around the world. They are interested in their own lives, their own families, their own neighbourhood. Perhaps they sometimes think about America or China or Afghanistan or some other country that's regularly in the news. Perhaps they occasionally give a thought to their neighbouring countries, another country where friends or relatives live, or another country they would like to visit one day as tourists or migrant workers or students. But the idea that large numbers of people in Europe, the Americas, South Asia or anywhere else would spend time thinking about South Korea is, at least at the moment, merely fantasy. Korea could spend a hundred billion or a trillion won on promoting its image, and it still wouldn't make itself relevant to the daily lives of foreigners. The cutest logo in the world can't make people admire a country that has no relevance to them: governments might as well burn the money.

Tourism promotion – it should be stressed – is a different matter. This is primarily about selling a product to a consumer, rather than trying to change people's minds about a country, and advertising is a legitimate and proven method to achieve this. In one sense, despite all the mystique and complexity surrounding the concept of nation 'branding', the basic principle is actually a very simple one, and it comes from marketing: the consumer wants to know 'What's in it for me?' At this basic level, it is clear that a country's achievements for its *own* population, its successes and its prosperity, will never automatically result in any kind of enhanced reputation, simply because they don't benefit the (foreign) 'consumer'.

I was consequently all the more delighted to hear Chang See-jeong, Director of the Korea International Cooperation Agency, announce at the Jeju Peace Forum in 2009 that it was Korea's intention to increase its overseas development assistance to 0.25 per cent of GNI by 2015. This means that Korea is still a long way from joining the tiny club of nations that have met the UN's recommendation of 0.7 per cent of GNI, but it is certainly better than either the United States or Japan has achieved in recent years. Clearly a country can't simply buy itself a better reputation by spending more money on poverty reduction, but the voluntary increase is a powerful symbolic gesture that Korea is ready and prepared to start making a serious contribution to the issues that matter to humanity – and not just to Koreans.

## CORPORATE SOCIAL RESPONSIBILITY FOR COUNTRIES?

So, if a country wants to be admired, it must be relevant, and in order to become relevant it must participate usefully, productively and imaginatively in the global 'conversations' on the topics that matter to people elsewhere and everywhere. The list of those topics is a long one: climate change, poverty, famine, narcotics, migration, economic stability, human rights, women's rights, indigenous people's rights, children's rights, religious and cultural tolerance, nuclear proliferation, water, education, corruption, terrorism, crime, war and arms control are just a few of the most obvious ones. It's hard to imagine any country that couldn't pick at least one item on this list with a special relevance to its own needs or resources, and find a way to make a prominent, thoughtful, meaningful and memorable contribution to the debate and to the global effort. There is a strong precedent for this kind of behaviour in the commercial world. For the past 20 years or so, it has become more and more evident that corporations which fail to demonstrate and maintain high ethical standards, transparency and social responsibility will soon lose the trust and respect of their consumers.

The critics of 'corporate social responsibility' claim that the approach has become devalued because, in many cases, it is no more than window-dressing. But, in the face of such attempts at free-riding, the media and consumers naturally tend to increase scrutiny and demand higher standards, reducing the opportunities for corporations to get away with 'green-wash' or empty propaganda. Corporations are at last being forced to treat their social responsibilities as a matter for the board rather than for the PR agency. Surely the basic principle here is no different from the one I underlined earlier in this chapter: in order to achieve a better reputation, as Socrates is said to have observed, we must endeavour to *be* as we desire to appear. In other words, it is necessary to provide people with *proof* of one's virtues. If the price of consumer respect is continuous and tangible evidence of corporate responsibility rather than pious statements, so much the better for everyone.

But, if one is cynical and believes that 75 per cent of organisations that preach the 'triple bottom line' are merely window-dressing, still, the fact that a quarter of all those companies have fundamentally reviewed the ways, means, causes and effects of doing business, and have cleaned up their act as a result, is revolutionary. What a revolution it would be if countries, cities and regions, nowadays as obsessed with the value of their reputations as companies are, were to follow the same principles. It is already clear from the Nation Brands Index data that more and more people in more and more countries feel unable to admire or respect countries or governments that pollute the planet, practise or permit corruption, trample human rights or flout the rule of law: in other words, it's the *same audience* starting to apply the *same standards* to countries as they apply to companies. In just a few decades, consumer power has changed the rules of business and transformed the behaviour of corporations almost beyond recognition. It doesn't seem unreasonable to hope that consumer power might achieve a similar transformation in the way that countries, cities and regions are run in the years to come.

# ITALY: PAYING THE PRICE

The potential gains from pursuing ethical policies are of course matched by the corresponding risks of failing to pursue them. Italy, for example, has the sixth best national image in the world, according to the Nation Brands Index, coming top for tourism and second for culture. Its ranking is only let down by rather poor scores for business and governance, as one might perhaps expect.

And yet there is a worrying undercurrent when one looks more closely at Italy's rankings over the last few years: not only is it the most volatile of any Top 10 country in the Index, but it is also in steady decline. Italy's rankings have dropped by 2.3 per cent since the questionnaire of the Nation Brands Index was stabilised in the last quarter of 2005 – which may not sound much, but at this rate Italy will have a weaker image than Mexico in 10 years' time.

It seems pretty clear that Italy's brand is not actually declining in absolute terms: the reason why Italy's NBI scores are falling so fast is because the world is changing its mind on a number of issues, and Italy is being very gradually 'squeezed out' of the new scenario. As the Nation Brands Index has abundantly proved over the years, country images are normally remarkably stable, and barely change from year to year. What Italy seems to be facing is not a loss of attraction in its image, but a decline in the relevance of that image for many people: in other words, Italy seems to be going out of fashion.

Tellingly, one of the areas where Italy is increasingly failing to make a connection with global public opinion is in the area of its environmental standards and commitment: worse than being perceived as just another country that isn't doing very much about climate change, it is perceived as a country with a hugely important natural and cultural heritage that isn't doing enough to look after it.

Italy isn't the only country whose image is suffering as a result of such a perception; a similar perception drags down China's and America's images too (and China's image is dragged down even more markedly by its weak scores for governance and human rights). America's scores in most areas have improved dramatically since President Obama took office, but it remains to be seen whether this 'blip of hope' will prove durable or not.

Are we observing the first victims of a 'consumer power' revolution? It is, of course, too early to say; but there is no doubt that international public opinion is beginning to emerge as a formidable new player in the complex equation of international relations and sovereign power.

## THE PARADOX OF SOVEREIGNTY

The fundamental problem of sovereignty is that national leaders, assuming they care about public opinion at all, care most about the opinions of their own populations; even if they aren't elected leaders, this is simple self-interest. And, when their national interest is at odds with the national interest of other states, governments will invariably focus on pleasing their electorates at the expense of pleasing foreign populations; indeed, populist politicians such as Mahmoud Ahmedinejad and Hugo Chávez sometimes rely on displeasing certain foreign publics in order to enhance their domestic appeal.

But it may not be too naive to hope that things are slowly changing, and the paradox may be starting to resolve itself. As more and more of the issues that governments face today cut across national sovereignty (of the long list of important topics which I mentioned earlier, from climate change to arms control, none are respecters of national boundaries), as national governments are held more and more to account by their own populations for these shared challenges, and as those populations feel more and more closely connected through shared issues with populations in other countries, it becomes harder for leaders to pursue radically different agendas from those of the 'international community'. The tragedy of the commons may not, after all, be destined to be a tragedy for ever.

A kind of common morality shapes the (very rough) boundaries of what is deemed acceptable behaviour in most parts of the world today, a morality characterised by human rights, environmentalism, the rule of law, anti-colonialism, democracy and free market economics; whilst the universality of these values is, quite rightly, under constant scrutiny and discussion, there is no denying a sense of basic consensus on at least some of the principal ones. The governments today that appear *not* to mind being regarded as moral outsiders by international public opinion, or who don't see the need to maintain a positive national image, can almost be counted on the fingers of two hands.

Acquiring the support, or at least avoiding the censure, of public opinion in other countries is also driven by the emergence of more and more regional and multilateral groupings. Most governments of EU member states, for example, would prefer to avoid incurring public disapproval elsewhere in the European Union if they can help it, since it reduces their ability to support their own country's interests, and similar effects occur within other multilateral 'clubs' such as NATO, ASEAN and MERCOSUR.

For developing countries that are dependent on foreign aid, being seen as worthy recipients of that aid is an essential precondition of their continuing to receive it: donor governments cannot long continue to donate their taxpayers' money to regimes or countries with very weak or very negative 'brand images'. The willingness of China to extend enormous amounts of aid without regard to such matters has considerably upset the delicate moral balance in this area, but there are signs that the same mechanisms are, gradually, having the effect of bringing China into line with the views of the 'moral majority' too – for, of course, China itself depends on the approval of international public opinion in order to maintain the health of its all-important exports. One way and another, it seems that governments find international public approval ever more worth their while to value, to seek and to retain; and the mechanism of shared values and reciprocal esteem appears to function better with each decade that passes. Just as in the corporate sphere, earning and maintaining a good reputation are becoming the cost of entry into the marketplace; survival outside that marketplace is no longer an option.

## RICH IS GOOD

So the last thing, it seems to me, most countries should want is a 'brand'. If a brand image is the catchy reduction of something rich and complex into a simple, naive, one-dimensional formula, then many of the countries which already have one would probably do better to get rid of it. Nation branding is surely the problem, not the solution: branding is what the media and public opinion do to countries, not what governments should try to do to their own states and populations. What countries need is for people around the world to have a richer, deeper, more complex, more nuanced, more democratic, more chaotic, more human view of their land, their population and their civilisation – not a fabricated stereotype to replace the inherited stereotype.

Why else did Egyptian respondents' scores for Denmark drop 36 places in the Nation Brands Index following the publication of a handful of cartoons, while their scores for America never fell further than 6, despite the invasion and military occupation of two Muslim countries? Because Denmark had a simple brand image, while America moved beyond a brand centuries ago. Most Egyptians knew only one thing about Denmark – that it was a Scandinavian country – so they admired it; then they learned one new thing – that it had insulted their Prophet – so 50 per cent of its image became negative, and they hated it. By contrast, Egyptians knew thousands of things about America, so one new negative fact only formed a small proportion of the whole, and inflicted only limited damage on this very large idea.

What most countries should be attempting is surely more like education than branding: to find ways of helping people in other countries to get to know them; and to increase and celebrate rather than reduce their own complexity. This is one reason why I have claimed that cultural relations is the only demonstrably effective form of 'nation branding' I have ever encountered. The experience of countries that have successfully practised cultural relations over many years shows that consistent, imaginative cultural exchange does eventually create an environment where respect and tolerance flourish, and this undoubtedly also favours increased trade in skills, knowledge, products, capital and people. People who understand each other tend to get on better, and people who get on better tend to trade with each other more frequently, more freely and with greater mutual profit.

I remember hearing about a study carried out in Iraq some years after the US–UK invasion, in which young Iraqis were questioned about their attitudes towards the presence of British soldiers in Baghdad: some 99 per cent of those interviewed expressed strong antipathy to their presence, but 1 per cent had much more favourable views. It turned out that this 1 per cent corresponded almost exactly to individuals who had used the British Council Library in Baghdad. If you know people through understanding and sharing their culture, it's hard to hate them. You can sometimes hate what they *do*, but that's infinitely easier to deal with and to recover from. Of course, extending the reach of the cultural relations effect beyond the unavoidably limited number of individuals that the country's cultural centres can engage with directly is a challenge. It's slow work, one individual at a time, and requires enormous numbers of highly trained and highly dedicated people to achieve.

One of the most important aspects of cultural relations is that 'cultural promotion' is never entirely satisfactory for either the sender or the receiver. Nobody likes having another nation's cultural habits or achievements thrust upon their attention: what the British Council has learned to stress over the last 80 years is the importance of mutuality.

This principle is based on the observation that people who like culture like to *engage* in culture, so rather than being expected to admire another nation's culture it is much more rewarding, much more exciting and much more effective for two nations to *do culture together*. Engagement is invariably more productive than promotion, listening an indispensable adjunct to talking, and if you want something from somebody it is only reasonable to ask what they want from you. Such groundwork is the essential, indispensable and irreplaceable means of resolving, avoiding and mitigating hatred and ignorance between peoples: where culture is the problem, culture is also the solution. This seems to me so much safer and more valuable a way of increasing understanding between nations than the rather risky game of reducing a country's history, culture and population to an infantile stereotype, and then discharging it at other nations as if from a gun.

You will have your differences with other cultures, of course, but against a background of ignorance those differences will find their expression in protectionism and isolation at best, and indoctrination, hatred and violence at worst. Against a background of understanding and respect, differences remain harmless mysteries at worst, and the source of highly fruitful relationships at best – the mingling of opposites and the chaos of cultural diversity being the most creative and productive power on earth. As I wrote in an article in 2006, 'if the world's governments placed even half the value which most wise corporations have learned to place on their good names, the world would be a safer and quieter place than it is today'. I think we have reason to feel hopeful that this dynamic, notwithstanding the almost chronic pessimism of the commentariat today, is starting to make things better.

# PART IV

# Conclusions

# 18. Creativity, brands, finance and beyond: Notes towards a theoretical perspective on city branding

**Adam Arvidsson**

## INTRODUCTION

City branding is by now a widespread practice. In the last few decades, a great number of cities across Europe and the US have attempted to brand themselves out of post-industrial decline with varying degrees of success or, as in the case of Asia, transform themselves into attractive destinations for tourism and corporate relocation (Braun and Lavagna 2007). Arguably city branding can be seen as part of the overall turn to 'entrepreneurial' urban governance, which David Harvey (1989) locates to the mid-1970s. As a response to the decline of traditional manufacturing economies and to the emerging new global economy, a number of city governments have abandoned an earlier 'managerial' approach, which was primarily focused on the local provision of services and facilities. Instead they have put an emphasis on fostering new ways of local development and growth and, not least, encouraging success in the 'zero sum competition' now emerging between global cities for jobs and corporate relocation (see Sassen 2007). In this phase the brand comes to stand for and symbolize the new image that local government wishes to construct around the city. For example, the city of Copenhagen embarked on a wave of architectural expansion and invested heavily in officializing the city's 'underground' cultural life through the support of a series of festivals and cultural events in order successfully to attract corporate head offices as an alternative to a declining industrial infrastructure (Hansen *et al.* 2001). However, in the most recent decade, the practice of city branding has proceeded one step further. As consumer branding has progressed from a mere matter of semiotic intervention, of creating an attractive symbol for a product, to more far-reaching attempts at producing particular affective attachments or even lifestyles around products (see Arvidsson 2006), so city branding now contains more ambitious aims than the fostering of a good business climate or the erection of significant monuments able to 'put the city on the map'. City branding now also includes the direct fostering of desirable forms of life (and the repression or containment of undesirable ones) through various forms of what Michel Foucault would have called 'biopolitical' intervention that directly address practices, lifestyles and subjectivities (Foucault 2004; Rose 1999).

This more invasive, biopolitical turn in city branding has been particularly evident in the emphasis on 'creativity'. Following the works of Charles Landry (2000) and even more crucially Richard Florida (2002, 2005) city governments worldwide – from Osaka in Japan to Lansing, Michigan – have embarked on a series of measures to foster a creative climate or creative lifestyles among their populations as the key to prosperity and development. Such interventions have focused on 'soft factors' like investments in or redeployment of cultural and educational institutions, the regeneration of inner city neighbourhoods, the selective use of licensing laws to create particular kinds of nightlife, or greater tolerance in relation to alternative or 'bohemian' lifestyles. Overall, it has been a matter of fostering particular styles of consumption that are thought to be able to foster particular outlooks and mentalities among significant parts of the urban populations (see Brooks 2000; Lloyd 2006). Generally, the promotion of such 'creative' lifestyles has been thought not only to be beneficial to economic growth, but also to be conducive to social and cultural modernization. As a UN report on the creative economy proclaims: 'The creative economy has the potential to generate income and jobs while promoting social inclusion, cultural diversity, and human development' (UN 2008: iii). The role of creativity as an important driver of economic growth has been subject to repeated critique, both conceptually (Lovink and Rossiter 2007; Arvidsson 2007) and empirically (Peck 2005; Oakley 2004). Taken together this critique suggests that the main function of creativity is different.

Interestingly, the focus on creativity as a significant aspect of city branding has coincided with the recent wave of financial expansion, which has built on an ever greater financialization of everyday life. After the crash of the dot.com boom in 2000 the new financial convention has focused in part on China and South-East Asia, but mainly on the financialization of mortgage and credit card debt. In turn this can be seen as the last step in a long-term drive towards the financialization of central aspects of welfare through, chiefly, the channelling of pension saving directly on to financial markets. This way the real estate market has established itself as perhaps the most significant mechanism for the distribution of rent. It is significant that creative city branding has been conducive to precisely the kinds of strategies of gentrification that have driven significant rises in inner city housing prices. For example, in the city of Milan, investments in gentrification and the associated promotion of the types of 'creative' lifestyles that are conducive to branding the city as a 'fashion city' have coincided with a fivefold increase in rents in the fashion retail street of Via Montenapoleone (Arvidsson *et al.*, 2010). This way the 'creative city' model establishes a direct link between the biopolitical intervention on practices, and the financial valorization of their results. In this chapter I would like to expand on this connection by arguing that the 'creative city' model represents an expression of a mature branding paradigm that centres precisely on this connection between life and finance. I will also suggest how current productive developments point beyond this paradigm. In order to start unwinding this admittedly rather complex argument it might be useful to go back to the famous 'I Love NY' campaign of 1977, which arguably inaugurated the promotion of 'creativity' as a desirable urban feature (although this precise term was, to my knowledge, never used).

## 'I LOVE NY'

Although urban boosterism has a long tradition in the case of New York, and although the city established a tourism and conventions bureau as early as 1934, the 1977 'I Love NY' campaign constituted a significant novelty (Greenberg 2008). This was because the campaign brought together a new configuration of three different factors that were to remain crucial to the contemporary 'creative city' branding model.

First, globalization and ensuing de-industrialization and economic restructuring had undermined the blue-collar working class that had acted as a fundamental component of the Fordist social compromise in the city, and generated a wave of unemployment and social unrest. This created a widespread perception, enforced by the media, that the older social order was breaking down. At the same time the growing power and mobility of multinational, now increasingly global, companies generated a new situation where the image of the city acquired a new importance in affecting decisions on corporate location. There was a perception that desirable, well-paid managerial jobs were fleeing the city as crime and social unrest grew.

Second, the financialization of the economy offered a new vehicle for economic redistribution. This process had been under way since the early 1970s when the combination of the end of the Bretton Woods accord and the OPEC crisis put an end to the relatively stable financial regime of the post-war years. The new salience of financial markets affected the branding of New York in two principal ways. The first way was that it gave the city the opportunity to issue city bonds as a way out of the fiscal crisis that had hit in 1975, as an effect of the processes of economic restructuring described above. Branding became crucial in this respect, as the image of the city now acquired a novel influence on investor perceptions of risk and hence on the cost of capital. The second way was that the New York real estate market began to move, as an effect of the gentrification of derelict post-industrial inner city neighbourhoods and the middle-class fashion for 'loft living' (Zukin 1982). This established housing prices as an increasingly central component of middle-class wealth and, consequently, gave real economic value to the image of a city or a neighbourhood.

Third and finally, processes of mediatization provided a vehicle through which a city branding process could be shaped and implemented. This process had generated new cadres of marketing and communication professionals, as well as other kinds of consultants, for whom branding and similar forms of cultural intervention appeared as a natural way to address overall problems of governance (Frank 1997; Boltanski and Chiapello 1999). In addition, the proliferation of television channels, films and lifestyle magazines had broadened the repertoire of the media and empowered its ability to create and maintain the spectacle of 'image'. With the onset of lifestyle consumerism the media had also penetrated deeper into the life-world of, at least, the middle classes, and thus achieved a greater power actually to affect everyday practices (Arvidsson 2006).

So in essence the New York branding campaign inaugurated a new strategy, to use the media to create an image that could attract the financial capital necessary to address the problems arising from the end of the Fordist, industrial urban order. But, and this is important to note, its scope went way beyond the creation of mere image. The financialization of the city economy effectively shifted power away from democratically elected institutions and to the banking and finance elites that had supplied the capital. These acquired popular support for their cause by convincing middle-class city workers' unions to invest their pension funds in city bonds. This move created a popular interest in the long-term economic performance of the city, and generated support for the kinds of governance that could promote practices and lifestyles that were conducive to such long-term economic performance. The results were twofold. On the one hand it resulted in the use of city funds to support the kinds of cultural policies that would generate a climate attractive to the cosmopolitan managerial elites. As David Harvey describes the process:

The ruling elites moved, often fractiously, to support the opening of the cultural field to all manner of diverse cosmopolitan currents. The narcissistic exploration of self, sexuality and identity became the *leitmotif* of bourgeois urban culture. Artistic freedom and artistic licence, promoted by the city's powerful cultural institutions, led, in effect, to the neoliberalization of culture. 'Delirious New York' (to use Rem Koolhaas's memorable phrase) erased the collective memory of democratic New York. The city's elites acceded, though not without struggle, to the demand of lifestyle diversification (including those attached to sexual preference or gender) and increasing consumer niche choices (in areas such as cultural production). New York became the epicentre of postmodern cultural and intellectual experimentation. (Harvey 2005: 47)

On the other hand this led to a policing and suppression of forms of life deemed not conducive to such a performative climate, like those of rebellious, often ethnic youth and the urban poor, leading up to mayor Rudolph Giuliani's famous zero-tolerance campaigns of the 1990s, which virtually cleansed the island of Manhattan of undesirable elements and lifestyles.

The branding of New York thus establishes the brand as something much more than the symbol or image of a city. It becomes a new assemblage of governance that effectively connects financial markets to biopolitical interventions that aim at shaping and forming not just image and symbols, but actual practices and forms of life. In the most recent decades this assemblage has spread not just to other cities, but far beyond cities to new kinds of consumer, corporate or even personal self-governance. In order to understand this, we need to take a closer look at the economic function of brands in relation to the new centrality of finance in the information economy.

## BRANDS AND FINANCE

Although the practice of marking or 'branding' is ancient, brands acquired a crucial economic function with the development of mass production and mass consumption in the late nineteenth century. With the new proliferation of aesthetically similar and functionally equivalent goods, it became crucial to construct artificial differences that could motivate price differentials and, more generally, enable market choice. This way brands can be understood as an early mechanism that established the kinds of artificial 'monopoly rents' that have become fundamental to the functioning of a highly symbolic information economy (Harvey 2001). But, in the post-war years, the commercial institution of the brand underwent a significant development. Marketing professionals now began to realize that the new mobility and symbolic productivity of an ever more mediatized consumer culture had a significant influence on the ability of a branded object to attract such monopoly rents: that what young people thought of and did with Coca-Cola affected the value of the Coca-Cola brand, simply put. While this might seem self-evident today, it triggered a major re-conceptualization of the brand in the 1950s, and led to the establishment of brand management as a central aspect of business administration. It is significant that the object of brand management was not only the brand itself, its design, advertising and media presence, but also, crucially, consumer practices around the brand. In other words, with the establishment of brand management, brands evolved from simple symbols of products able to set them off from others, to an institution that allowed the management of the kinds of productive practices that evolved outside of the corporate organization, among consumers and other actors, and that could, by definition, be neither rewarded nor directly commanded. To put this in more general and abstract terms, with the onset of a modern information economy where productive practices are highly socialized, brands have evolved from semiotic to biopolitical instruments.

This biopolitical dimension of branding practices has evolved further as globalization and the proliferation of new information and communication technologies have enabled a significant extension of global value chains. Brands like Apple or Nike have come to stand less for single products and more for a particular form of life that is embodied in a proliferation of different products (produced in outsourced factories) and media texts. Similarly, corporate branding has risen in importance as a means of giving coherence and direction to complex productive networks. Finally, personal branding has become an important means for freelance knowledge workers to provide an intelligible representation of their ability to draw on the general intellect embodied in the productive networks in which they move (Hearn 2008). It is possible to suggest that the transformation of brands from semiotic to biopolitcal instruments has been integral to the emergence of the institution of the brand as a key mechanism of value accumulation in contemporary, cognitive capitalism. In this respect, brands work by organizing highly socialized flows of value creation that move outside of direct corporate command. This can be a matter of consumers contributing to the value of a brand by making it 'matter' to them in their everyday life, of employees going beyond what is contained in their job description and offering their creativity and enthusiasm freely to their employer, or, crucially, of citizens adopting the kinds of lifestyles that are deemed successful to city branding policies. Seen this way, contemporary biopolitical brands are ways of managing the 'unmanageable' and of providing a context in which practices are organized from below and empowered to emerge in the right kind of directions. This function of the brand, its ability to organize formally free practices in ways that enable them to produce results that can be commoditized and enter corporate value flows, also contributes to explaining the diffusion of the brand as an organizational form, beyond product markets to corporate management and city governance. The brand has become a paradigmatic organizational form, because it provides an institutionalization of a modality of value capture that is central to the information economy.

At the same time there has been a significant increase both in the overall importance of financial markets and in the importance of brands as financial assets. This means that financial rents have become more important vis-à-vis direct profits as a means of corporate accumulation. In so-called shareholder-oriented corporate governance, the aim of the game is not primarily to deploy private capital in order to extract surplus value from a proprietary, internal production process, but to acquire as large a share as possible from the global surplus that circulates on financial markets (Lazonick and O'Sullivan 2000). But since the long-term performance of shares and other corporate assets now depends on a number of factors that lie beyond the direct command of the company, like consumer benevolence or even the sentiment of financial markets themselves, a large part of the value of shares is now attributed to so-called intangible assets – like brand or reputation – that represent a company's ability to attract such valuable externalities from the social context in which it moves. To put this shift in more general terms: in an earlier, Fordist model financial markets rewarded companies for their ability to put proprietary productive resources to work. In the present model, financial markets reward companies for their ability to attract productive externalities from their social environment (see Marazzi 2008).

However, since intangible assets are difficult to measure, partly because they lie outside of the domains of corporate control, and partly because of the complex and unpredictable nature of the value flows that they represent, their precise values are difficult to calculate (Lury and Moor 2010). Brands fill this void by supplying a convention that can legitimize the valuation of intangible corporate assets beyond the kinds of book values that can be arrived at by established accounting systems. This way, the brand is a kind of 'measure' of the ability of a company to attract free productive resources from its social environment.

If this model applies to the contemporary role of corporate brands, then how can it be applied to city branding? We need to consider that the shift towards more intensive, 'biopolitical' forms of city branding has happened in the last decade. This period has also been a period of intense financialization of the economy of cities, chiefly via the expanding importance of the real estate market. The real estate market has served two interconnected aims in relation to the economy of cities. First, the commercial real estate market has become an important growth engine of cities. Second, the private real estate market has become an important mechanism of economic redistribution that has by and large favoured the middle classes. This has led to a re-composition of the class structure of many cities, as gentrification has moved lower-class residents into the suburbs in favour of middle-class residents. Such gentrification has contributed to both broadening the tax base and lowering welfare expenditure, thus improving the finances of many urban governments. But, since the value dynamics of urban real estate, and in particular the relative values of central and more peripheral neighbourhoods, are very difficult to predict with any precision, investors need other kinds of support for their investment decisions. City branding, like corporate branding, fulfils this function by creating a convention that makes the risk related to real estate investments appear calculable and manageable. It is able to justify, in the eyes of investors as well as banks, why real estate prices in one city can be twice as high as in a neighbouring city, or why similar differences can apply between gentrified and non-gentrified neighbourhoods.

## CREATIVITY

So how is all this linked to the recent salience of the notion of 'creativity' within city branding? The discourse on 'creativity' goes back to the dot.com boom of the second half of the 1990s. It is worth remembering that the first explicit reference to 'creativity' as a policy term came with the first Blair government's UK Department for Culture, Media and Sport's *Creative Industries Mapping Document* in 1998 (DCMS 1998). While the definition was highly disparate at the time, the salience of 'creativity' as a new factor of production was mainly related to the boom of the new media sector. That sector represented the coming into the fold of corporate capitalism of what used to be expressions of the subcultural urban underground. With the commercial expansion of the Internet, corporate investments in online presence boomed, and hence a generation of formerly unemployed college gradates who had been educated in the hacker and new media art scenes in the preceding decades now were directly employed in the production of brandable content for corporate capital (Niessen 2009). This way, 'creativity' came to denote the commercial deployment of what had previously been referred to as subculture, counter-culture or 'underground'.

This suggestion deserves to be put in a wider sociological framework. The development of creativity as a productive force is due to two main factors. First, since the 1960s, the diffusion of media technologies and of new, less structured identities and lifestyles has massively increased the symbolic productivity or 'mass intellectuality' of everyday life, to use Paolo Virno's (2004) expression. This has effectively socialized the ability to engage in the kinds of symbolic production that used to be the privilege of the cultural industries. The diffusion of networked information and communication technologies has significantly boosted this development, radically enhancing both the productive potential and the access to information and knowledge of ordinary people. The result is massive socialized productivity that largely moves outside of the organizational boundaries of corporate capitalism.

Second, and very synthetically, the expansion of secondary education, particularly in the media, arts and business administration fields, has created a large pool of people who possess the skills and talents to engage in cultural production and, perhaps more importantly, to organize such processes of production. The result of this is a large pool of skilled labour that often exceeds market demand. Consequently many people in this sector are underemployed, but have the motivation to remain at the margins of the market and engage in self-organized forms of production. Some, like software engineers who possess less common skills, are able to move in and out between self-organized production and market production, sharing their time between paid employment and engagement in open source contexts. Indeed, in some sectors having acquired a reputation in an open source context becomes a precondition for employment.

Finally, sociologists have documented a secular shift over to post-materialistic values within the global middle class. This has translated into a number of social movements that have promoted creativity as an alternative to the oppressive rigours of mass society, as well as a massive 'Buddenbrooks effect' by means of which the children of the global middle class increasingly choose creative careers despite meagre economic prospects.

The comprehensive result of these three developments is the growth of a large and autonomous productive power, essentially motivated by values that are contrary to, or at least different from, those of mainstream consumer society. During the 1960s and 1970s this growing productive force fuelled social movements and anti-systemic counter-cultures. The concept of creativity can be understood to have developed as part of a neoliberal strategy to keep this autonomous productive force within the fold of corporate capitalism. In economic development the 'creative industries' discourse has signified a number of attempts to promote a climate in which such autonomous productivity is directed towards the production of the kinds of cultural content that can enter the corporate services market. In the 'creative city' discourse, the same resource is deployed in the generation of the kinds of lifestyles that can secure the brand image necessary to reduce risks for real estate investors.

## BEYOND CREATIVE CITIES?

As David Harvey (2005) suggests, the neoliberal paradigm can be seen as a result of a process of 'muddling through' in which established elites attempt to confront social change through a series of ad hoc measures without much of an overall strategic vision. In the field of city branding this has evolved to a model of the 'creative city', whereby the two chief structural aspects of the information economy are united: the ever more central mechanism of financial distribution is connected to the growing autonomy of social production. Through discourses on creativity with related forms of biopolitical intervention such autonomous forms of social production are put to work in the creation of the kinds of lifestyles and practices that can provide the basis for a convention, or a brand, that is able to reduce investor perceptions of risk.

It is important to underline this primarily financial function of the branding of creativity. While the promotion of production-based economic development has been one of the major ideological goals of the creative cities paradigm, research shows that, at least in the UK, effects on the 'real' economy have been negligible, while effects on housing prices have been significant (Oakley 2004). In any case the present financial crisis has dealt a severe, and possibly permanently destabilizing, blow to the brand-centric model of financial accumulation that was a central component of this model. As a consequence the creative industries have been hit hard. Even if policy measures should succeed in resolving the present crisis by jump-starting financial markets through massive injections of liquidity, this is most likely to remain a short-term solution. Phases of massive financial expansion like that of the last three decades are the expressions of a deep structural problem: the inability of the existing institutional order to create a match between available productive resources and unmet needs (see Arrighi 1994). Consequently the crisis can find a long-term resolution only through structural reform. The neoliberal model, the creative city paradigm included, is past its designated lifetime. What could a different model look like?

We can identify two structural tendencies that have been integral to the growing irrelevance of the creative cities model, and that point beyond it towards a possible alternative policy paradigm. Both have also been integral to the secular emergence of 'creativity' as a powerful economic and social phenomenon.

First is the value shift. The secular shift towards a post-materialistic value structure has served to attract ever more people to potentially precarious creative careers. This can be viewed as an over- supply of 'creative labour', the result of a systematic irrationality in young people's career decisions. However, the situation can also be understood to result from inadequate demand: that is, an inability of the present system to put available resources to productive use. Such a perspective is also strengthened by the fact that the very same value shift is generating a set of new needs and desires that the existing creative city model is not designed to meet. This new structure of needs can be observed in the growing demand for ethically produced or fairly traded consumer goods, for organic or locally produced foodstuffs, for craftsmanship and unique objects and for sustainably produced goods overall (Ray and Anderson 2000). These new configurations of demand all have to do with new and different forms of material production. The existing creative cities model, on the contrary, is principally geared to meet corporate need for immaterial production: brand image, advertising, events and mostly abstract works of art: in short, spectacle. This new needs structure is further supported by a growing ecological consciousness that suggests that different, more sustainable and ethical forms of production will be necessary in response to a combined energy, food and climate crisis. Again, the creative cities model is unable to deploy existing resources (an over-supply of creative labour) to address these needs in anything but a purely spectacular way (such as corporate 'green-washing'). Instead such new needs are beginning to be addressed by an emerging self-organization of social production.

This leads us to our second structural tendency: the growing strength and autonomy of creative production. This is driven by the declining costs of material production, and the increasing potential for self-organization. Both are the result of the diffusion of networked information and communication technologies. The result is a growing independence of creative production vis-à-vis corporate investments. This can be easily observed by looking at the new media sector. In the 1990s, most media production occurred in dot.com companies after they had attracted corporate investments. When the crisis hit in 2001, most people predicted that innovation and product development would stop, and that consequently the era of Internet-centred growth would be over for the foreseeable future. This was not the case, and in fact the opposite occurred: innovation did not stop but accelerated during the downturn. The next wave of Web 2.0-centred economic growth came out of innovations produced by people who had been left unemployed by the crisis and who had little access to capital, but who possessed the know-how and technological means to develop new products without it. A new wave of 'neo-nomads' created new ideas and new companies on their laptops, working out of Starbucks cafés with Internet access (Fost 2007). The example of Bram Cohen is famous. He developed BitTorrent, the most important software for exchanging multimedia content over the Internet, without access to capital, surviving on the creative use of credit cards. This tendency has continued with the development of free and open source software, which is essentially a self-organized production system, developing a functioning (and often superior) product with little or minimal capital investments, and driving a significant secondary economy in corporate services. Now we can see how such self-organized forms of production are moving offline to invest the production of material goods and services. This is happening through the rapid development of open design and open hardware initiatives, whereby designs of material objects are developed collaboratively in peer-to-peer projects and then made freely available online for everybody to use. More significantly today perhaps, it is happening through the boom of local service economies, LETS systems, time banks, community-supported agriculture, co-housing and other forms of social production that we have seen accelerating as a response to the current crisis (Carlsson 2008). These tendencies are likely to become even more powerful in the next decade. This likely development has three fundamental drivers.

First, technological development is likely to continue. This will further expand the potential for self-organization *and* reduce the cost of production. Two main directions are visible already today. We can see a further diffusion of existing technological platforms and a narrowing of the present digital divide through declining costs of computers and Internet connectivity and, in particular, through the spread of cell phones with mobile internet in the Global South. This will enable many more people to participate in online activities, from open productive networks to the generation of consumer-produced public opinion. Such further empowerment will also come from new technologies. Vertically expanded connectivity, the 'Internet of things', connecting objects, buildings and machinery to the net, will enable new and radical forms of mash-ups. RFID tagging and cell phones equipped with readers or bar-code scanners are already a reality. When these systems are generalized, one can imagine easy access to user-generated data on the ethical or social history of products. This will further enhance the potential for the alternative forms of economic organization that I will discuss below. Finally, new cheaper and more versatile tools for material production are on the horizon. One of the most important changes that we can expect from the coming decades is probably the diffusion of means of material production as consumer goods. In a sense this has already begun with printers. Most of us now have the material means to print a book or our photos in our homes. Today a 3D printer costs about as much as a laser printer did in 1985; 10 years from now we'll be able to buy them at Currys. While we won't be able to print solar panels or advanced machinery with 3D printers, they will undoubtedly transform the market for simpler things like plastic toys. We can also expect the diffusion of versatile multi-purpose machinery that a skilled craftsman could use to produce a wider range of objects. Indeed, the declining costs of machine tools is one of the main factors behind the globalization of material production. We can expect this tendency to continue.

Combined with the boom in open design, it is conceivable that we will be faced with a wider range of non-consumerist alternatives to material production in a decade or two. It is possible that, just as the launch of the laser printer in 1985 together with new software created a revolution in desktop publishing, the current combination of open design and cheap material production technologies will create a similar revolution in desktop manufacturing. Indeed, there are already a number of companies that offer on-demand, customized manufacturing, along with a number of communities dedicated to the open design of shared platforms.

Second, we can expect that the current crisis will generate a growing mismatch between needs and productive resources. Unemployment levels will probably grow, particularly among the kinds of knowledge sectors that are more sensitive to downturns. In the West we can predict a growing unemployment among the creative class of designers, event managers and architects, and perhaps within the managerial class generally. These people possess precisely the kinds of skills that are required to engage in self-organized forms of production (in particular in its more technological and less 'creative' forms), and it is likely that many will choose this option as an alternative to unemployment, particularly if it offers them other benefits. Indeed the government of the Indian state of Kerala is investing heavily in open source software development as a way to keep unemployed engineers occupied and at the same time generate a surrounding business ecology. The combined future impact of the energy, climate and food crisis will probably further widen the mismatch between emerging needs and what the existing system can supply, which will also increase the attraction of alternative production systems. The city of Detroit, one of the most crisis-ridden cities in the US, is becoming a hotbed for the development of urban agriculture systems (Finley 2005).

Third and finally, we can already see a growing trend towards alternative forms of economic self-organization. Alternative currencies are a booming reality. With the diffusion of networked computers it is an administrative possibility for a wider range of groups and organizations to issue their own currency, and with the diffusion of more sophisticated mobile computing devices we can envision distributed technological platforms that enable the convertibility of different such currencies and hence the tradability of products and services outside the capitalist economy proper. We are also seeing the emergence of a number of community shopping networks, or consumer-generated ratings systems, where ordinary people rate, discuss or otherwise generate aggregated value judgements as to the utility or social impact of products and services. Such systems have the potential to develop into a number of alternative value logics, which, combined with alternative currencies, can further strengthen the position of such an alternative, non-capitalist economy. Finally, innovative, peer-based systems for finance and lending are emerging (like Kiva), and new kinds of financial instruments that connect social production initiatives directly to financial markets are on the horizon.

These tendencies suggest that we are likely to see a development of new forms of creative production that reach beyond the neoliberal model. The production of knowledge and cultural content, of food and services and perhaps also of some material objects will increasingly proceed in self-organized bottom-up processes where generally or almost generally available resources – like cheap machinery, free labour and abundant shared knowledge – are put to work. It is important not to see these developments as simply complementary to the existing economy, as new forms of welfare or ways of putting the unemployed to work (see Leadbeater & Meadway 2008). While such bottom-up self-organization might very well provide new opportunities for the poor or new ways of organizing welfare, they will most probably also support a host of new business opportunities. We can identify two principal reasons for this.

First, we can already see how new kinds of social production are generating new business models and new hybrid formats where monetary and social value combine. The recent boom in social entrepreneurship is one indicator of this. But we are also seeing the emergence of new kinds of business models that are organized around the core logic of open production. Arduino, the Italian circuit-board company, freely shares designs and technical specifications for its products. The rationale for this is twofold: since the circuit-boards are produced in China, they are most likely to be copied anyway; and, more importantly, by freely sharing its product, Arduino creates a brand community with strong affective ties in which knowledge circulates freely. This allows the Arduino company to stay at the top of a continuous collective innovation process and to be at the centre of the knowledge economy generated around the product. In short, by providing designs for nothing, Arduino organizes a collective innovation process that allows it to stay way ahead of competitors. Similar logics apply to the business ecologies created around open source, and to Google's use of an open operating system for its Android cell phone.

Apple has also opened up aspects of the operating system for the iPhone, hoping to stimulate a collective innovation process around the product. This way, the business value of the iPhone becomes that of a platform on which collective intelligence can congregate and circulate: a sort of technological Facebook if you will. We are likely to see much more of these developments in the future, as small designers come together to form open brands where the surplus value of branding goes back to the producers, or where small producers find alternative ways of distributing their product, coming together in online communities, for example. A next step would be new kinds of bottom-up organized financial institutions. Arduino is presently launching an open hardware bank gathering investments to be directed to this booming sector.

It is significant that large companies are beginning to realize the potential of such new forms of production as well. Procter & Gamble has run an open innovation project for five years now, increasing the productivity of the R&D department by some 60 per cent. Many other companies, like Nokia, Heinz and Ducati, are pursuing similar models, actively involving consumers, suppliers and stakeholders in the production process. Energy companies are also considering the potential boom in local energy production systems (solar panels and small wind turbines, connected in P2P grids) as a potential market for a next generation of their business. Large consumer goods companies like Unilever and Procter & Gamble are actively focusing on the 'bottom of the pyramid', the potentially vast market of the global poor who are involved in co-producing goods and distribution channels (Prahalad 2004). Again, we are likely to see further developments in this direction as the monopoly of the means of production and distribution that has supported the ability on the part of large companies to control productive development is undermined by cheaper and more abundant productive resources.

Second, the strengthening of similar alternative production and distribution systems is also likely to generate new waves of technological development. We can already see this in the growing open design community, where technological innovation is accelerating. An alternative field could be the development of software platforms and tools to coordinate new alternative economic systems. Mobile phones could, for example, easily be transformed into devices that are able to locate individuals willing to perform particular services for 'credit' or function as carriers of alternative currencies able to communicate with each other and negotiate 'exchange rates'. In the Global South we are already seeing a substantial development of simple yet robust systems for sharing and generating information via SMS interfaces. Keralan fishermen can now get information on the market price for their catch on their mobiles; the Bangalore-based company Wikiocean is developing SMS-based systems for coordinated collective bargaining that can bring down the consumer price of basic goods like rice or oil. With the spread of RFID tags this could produce new and radical possibilities for managing value flows. This will force a substantial rethinking of the brand-model that companies are presently working with. It is likely that brands need to be thought of less as add-ons, to products and more as enduring communities that function as important sources of innovation and product development. Rather than the brand representing the product, the product becomes a temporary materialization of the brand.

## BEYOND THE CREATIVE CITY

Present developments allow us to envision the emergence of an entirely new economic paradigm. In this new paradigm the kinds of self-organized social production that fuelled the social movements and subcultures of the 1960s and 1970s and that fed the creative industries of the 1990s are moving beyond the 'creative city' paradigm presently deployed. Indeed, the present creative city paradigm risks becoming counterproductive in relation to this new economy. There are three main reasons for this. First, the creative industries or creative city paradigm relies on strong protection of intellectual property, and more generally postulates the market as the only legitimate avenue for the valorization of productive efforts. This restricts the overall productivity of an ever more socialized knowledge economy, where the ability for knowledge to circulate is what determines its productivity. The market has already proven itself to be a strong bottleneck for valorization of autonomous forms of production leading to a proliferation of underemployed or precarious creative producers. This mechanism of valorization needs to be rethought.

Second, the centrality of the real estate market to creative city-based strategies of financial accumulation and connected processes of gentrification has already been shown to create significant crowding-out effects whereby 'genuine' creative producers not only are deprived of the value that their lifestyles produce, but often find themselves unable to remain in the neighbourhoods that undergo such transformation (Oudenampsen 2007). In order to promote a more innovation-based strategy of urban growth, such gentrification processes need to be contained and countered by city-based provisions of access to space, both private and public. Indeed, studies of creative scenes in Malmö and Copenhagen, as well as many other similar studies, have stressed how access to production space and to lively and diverse social interaction is what determines the success of a creative scene (Arvidsson and Tjader 2008).

Third, instead of leaving such tasks entirely to the market, city governments could play an important role by helping smaller productive networks to get access to tools, capital and market networks. One could envision city-based workshops, like Manchester Fab Lab, that give access to cutting-edge technology, city-based marketing agencies that connect local innovation networks to global economic flows, and city-based bonds that are able to attract financial capital to small start-ups that would otherwise be deprived of such resources.

In short, the end of the financial expansion that enabled strategies of gentrification-driven urban growth has made it clear that the established 'creative city' paradigm is past its prime. Even Richard Florida concedes this (see Florida 2009). At the same time, productive developments within the real 'creative' economy are pointing to a different way of configuring urban economic development. To understand and find ways to support this will be an important policy challenge for cities in the decades to come.

# REFERENCES

Arrighi, G. (1994) *The Long Twentieth Century*, London: Verso.

Arvidsson, A. (2006) *Brands: Meaning and Value in Media Culture*, London: Routledge.

Arvidsson, A. (2007) 'Creative class or administrative class: On advertising and the "underground"', *Ephemera*, 7, 1, 8–23.

Arvidsson, A. and Tjader, D. (2008) *Slutrapport: Laboratorium for Spontankultur*, Malmoe: Malmoe Kulturforvaltning.

Arvidsson, A., Malossi, G. and Naro, S. (2010) 'Passionate work? Labour conditions in Italian fashion', *Journal for Cultural Research*, 14, 3, 295–309.

Boltanski, L. and Chiapello, E. (1999) *Le nouvel esprit du capitalisme*, Paris: Gallimard.

Braun, E. and Lavagna, M. (2007) *An International Comparative Quick Scan of National Policies for Creative Industries*, Rotterdam: EURICUR.

Brooks, D. (2000), *Bobos in Paradise: The New Upper Class and How They Got There*, New York: Simon & Schuster.

Carlsson, C. (2008) *Nowtopia: How Pirate Programmers, Outlaw Bicyclists and Vacant Lot Gardeners Are Inventing the Future Today*, Oakland, CA: AK Press.

Department for Culture, Media and Sport (DCMS) (1998) *Creative Industries Mapping Document*, London: DCMS.

Finley, N. (2005) 'Urban farming may well hold the key to Detroit's future', *Detroit News*, 15 March, http://www.cityfarmer.org/detroit.html, accessed 1 April 2009.

Florida, R. (2002) *The Rise of the Creative Class: And How It's Transforming Work, Leisure and Everyday Life*, New York: Basic Books.

Florida, R. (2005) *Cities and the Creative Class*, New York: Routledge.

Florida, R. (2009) 'How the Crash will reshape America', *Atlantic Online*, March, www.theatlantic.com/doc/print20093/metldown-georgaphy.html, accessed 15 February 2009.

Fost, D. (2007) 'Where neo-nomads' ideas percolate', *San Francisco Chronicle*, 11 March, http://www.sfgate.com/cgibin/article.cgi?file=/c/a/2007/03/11/MNG KKOCBA645.DTL, accessed 1 April 2009.

Foucault, M. (2004) *Sécurité, territoire, population: Cours au Collège de France, 1977–1978*, Paris: Gallimard.

Frank, T. (1997) *The Capture of Cool*, Chicago: University of Chicago Press.

Greenberg, M. (2008) *Branding New York: How a City in Crisis Was Sold to the World*, New York: Routledge.

Hansen, A., Andersen, H.T. and Clark, E. (2001) 'Creative Copenhagen: Globalization, urban governance and social change', *European Planning Studies*, 9, 7, 851–869.

Harvey, D. (1989) 'From managerialism to entrepreneurialism: The transformation in urban governance in late capitalism', *Geografiska Annaler*, 71 B, 1.

Harvey, D. (2001) 'The art of rent: Globalization, monopoly and cultural production', in L. Panitch and C. Leys (eds), *Socialist Register, 2002*, London: Merlin Press, 93–110.

Harvey, D. (2005) *A Brief History of Neoliberalism*, Oxford: Oxford University Press.

Hearn, A. (2008) 'Meat, mask and burden: Probing the contours of the branded self', *Journal of Consumer Culture*, 8, 2, 197–217.

Landry, C. (2000) *The Creative City: A Tool Kit for Urban Innovators*, London: Earthscan Publications.

Lazonick, W. and O'Sullivan, M. (2000) 'Maximizing shareholder value: A new ideology for corporate governance', *Economy and Society*, 29, 1, 13–35.

Leadbeater, C. and Meadway, J. (2008) 'Attacking the recession: How innovation can fight the downturn', NESTA, Discussion paper.

Lloyd, R. (2006) *Neo-Bohemia: Art and Commerce in the Post-Industrial City*, New York: Routledge.

Lovink, G. and Rossiter, N. (eds) (2007) *My Creativity Reader: A Critique of Creative Industries*, Amsterdam: Institute for Network Cultures.

Lury, C. and Moor, L. (2010) 'Brand valuation and topological culture', in M. Aronczyk and D. Powers (eds), *Blowing up the Brand: Critical Perspectives on Promotional Culture*, New York: Lang.

Marazzi, C. (2008) *Capital and Language: From the New Economy to the War Economy*, New York: Semiotext(e).

Niessen, B. (2009) 'Going commercial: L'integrazione degli artisti underground a Milano e a Berlino', Ph.D. thesis, Department of Sociology, University of Milano-Bicocca.

Oakley, K. (2004) 'Not so cool Britannia: The role of creative industries in economic development', *International Journal of Cultural Studies*, 7, 1, 67–77.

Oudenampsen, M. (2007) 'Back to the future of the creative city: Amsterdam's creative redevelopment and the art of deception', in G. Lovink and N. Rossiter (eds), *My Creativity Reader: A Critique of Creative Industries*, Amsterdam: Institute for Network Cultures.

Peck, J. (2005) 'Struggling with the creative class', *International Journal of Urban and Regional Research*, 29, 4, 740–770.

Prahalad, C.K. (2004) *Fortune at the Bottom of the Pyramid*, Pittsburgh, PA: Wharton School Publishing.

Ray, P. and Anderson, S. (2000) *The Cultural Creatives: How 50 Million people Are Changing the World*, New York: Three Rivers Press.

Rose, N. (1999) *The Powers of Freedom: Reframing Political Thought*, Cambridge: Cambridge University Press.

Sassen, S. (2007) *A Sociology of Globalization*, New York: Norton.

UN (2008) *Creative Economy Report, 2008*, Geneva: UNCTAD.

Virno, P. (2004) *A Grammar of the Multitude*, London: Verso.

Zukin, S. (1982) *Loft Living: Culture and Capital in Urban Change*, Baltimore, MD: Johns Hopkins University Press.

# 19. Conclusions: Brands and branding geographies

**Andy Pike**

## INTRODUCTION

Against the backdrop of uneven recognition and relatively limited research, this collection has sought to establish the importance of and provide a focus for brands and branding geographies in a multi-disciplinary and international context. It has, first, set out and engaged critically with emergent conceptual and theoretical literature and empirical analyses on brands and branding geographies. Second, it has connected and related multi-disciplinary and international work on the spatial dimensions of brands and branding, illuminating some aspects of the connections between goods, services, knowledges and space and place brands and branding. Third, it has raised and reflected upon the ways in which a geographical understanding can help in considering the politics and limits of brands and branding. Last, the collection has begun to map out potential future research directions in geographies of brands and branding. This concluding chapter reiterates the main contributions of the collection and distils some broader conclusions and reflections. It then outlines some methodological contributions and issues for researching brands and branding geographies. Reflections on how a geographical approach can contribute to the politics and limits of brands and branding are then discussed. Some future potential research agendas are then developed to close the collection.

## CONTRIBUTIONS, CONCLUSIONS AND REFLECTIONS

Dispelling any idea that brands and branding could be meaningfully understood as somehow 'spaceless concepts' (Lee 2002: 334), this collection has established the inescapable spatial associations and connotations that constitute the geographies of brands and branding. The seemingly unavoidable ways in which geographical connections intertwine goods, services, knowledges and especially spaces and places are written through many of the contributions. Celia Lury demonstrates the integral space-making activities of brands and branding as well as the ways in which they inhabit multiple spaces. Nicolas Papadopoulos explains the centrality of place in understandings and valuations of goods and services in consumer buying decisions. Bodo Kubartz situates knowledge and knowing in the context of proximity and distance in the creation and branding of perfumes in the fragrance industry. As ostensibly 'non-spatial' disciplines engaging the 'spatial' and 'spatial' disciplines engaging brands and branding geographies, each contribution has recognised the integral role of geography, even though the conceptualisation and theorisation of such geographical associations and the historical and geographical situatedness of their construction remain varied and shaped by disciplinary concerns. These concepts include, for example, 'place-based' brands and 'spatial attachments' (Power and Jansson, this volume, Chapter 9), 'geographical entanglements' (Pike, this volume, Chapter 1), 'present' and 'non-present' relational spaces (Lury, this volume, Chapter 3), 'placed-ness' (Moor, this volume, Chapter 5), 'place images' (Papadopoulos, this volume, Chapter 2) and the importance of space and place in the geographical and historical constitution of brands, articulated at a variety of geographical scales (Jackson *et al.*, this volume, Chapter 4).

Geographical differentiation in the manifestation and circulation of brands and branding too is evident throughout the volume. Celia Lury illustrated that, as boundary objects, brands frame movement and mark difference in space, making them capable of enclosing and opening up territories. Nicolas Papadopoulos showed the differential meanings and value associated with different kinds of brands associated with particular countries in different markets. Ngai-Ling Sum emphasised the negotiation and persuasion involved in the uneven geographical uptake of knowledge brands in circulation globally. Ulrich Ermann showed how the early and uneven penetration of western fashion brands was central in constructing markets and brand literacy in the transition economy of Bulgaria. Nick Lewis demonstrated the global articulation, representation and reach of Brand NZ through formal and informal spatial channels and networks. Crucially, many of the contributions demonstrated the importance of a geographically nuanced approach to territorial and relational notions of space and place, acknowledging tensions – relational *and* territorial, bounded *and* unbounded, fluid *and* fixed, territorialising *and* de-territorialising – that are fruitful in explaining their diverse, varied and often contingent development. As Lury (this volume, Chapter 3: 53) notes, the spaces brought into being by branded objects are 'not only the extensive, flat earth described by Levitt but also a dynamic, curved, multi-dimensional space'.

The uneven development of brands and branding geographies was a recurrent theme pronounced in several contributions. Liz Moor elucidated how powerful brand owners and regulators shape the place of brands, configuring how consumers experience them, and make place in much more narrow, exclusionary and instrumental ways. Guy Julier examined the contested branding of the city of Leeds in northern England between elite business and political interests and social organisations with alternative visions of local economy, culture, society and polity. Andrew Harris and Adam Arvidsson both highlighted the connection between 'creative city' branding and the financialisation and valorisation of its outcomes through spatially uneven asset inflation in urban property and housing markets. Anette Therkelsen and Henrik Halkier analysed the politics of branding provincial cities in Denmark and the unequal power dynamics around inclusion, strategy and commitment. Nick Lewis explained the explicitly political project underpinning the globalising aspirations of Brand NZ in the context of competitive national development.

In sum, the contributions in this collection demonstrate how more spatially aware readings of brands and branding offer a means of lifting their 'mystical veils' (Greenberg 2008: 31) to illuminate and explain their geographical associations and connotations. Taking a culturally sensitive political economy of brands and branding geographies, for example, demonstrates how the stories are not just about the business of making and constructing the brands and branding of goods, services, knowledges, spaces and places; they are about the 'manufacture of meaning' (Jackson *et al.* 2007) too. The distinctive essence of place – its 'spirit', 'personality' or 'state of mind' (Molotch 2002: 666) – is fluid and, to a degree, imaginary but can be appropriated in material, symbolic, discursive and visual forms by producers, circulators, consumers and regulators of brands and branding. A partial view results if the spatially uneven articulations, appropriations and differentiations of place in brands and branding geographies are considered only as cultural construction – what Edensor and Kothari (2006: 332) call the replacement of the use and exchange value of goods by sign value – without reference to the 'production of difference' (Dwyer and Jackson 2003) and political-economic dynamics of power and disciplines of 'costs and cash' (Sayer 1997: 22).

Once the inescapable spatial associations that constitute the geographies of brands and branding have been established, a next conceptual step is to go further in thinking through how and in what ways such geographical associations are (re)constructed by brand and branding agents. Reflecting the multi-disciplinary contributions in this volume, we can introduce the notion of 'origination', that is, the ways in which geographical associations are constructed for brands and branding that connote, suggest and/or appeal to specific and particular spatial referents that embody and mean certain things. Put simply, for goods, services and knowledges 'origination' is what brand owners do to show or try to suggest where something comes from or is associated with. For spaces and places, origination can be about the historically authentic and unique attributes in a place or associations with other places that it is similar to or aspires to be like. Papadopoulos (this volume, Chapter 2) demonstrates how place is becoming more important, and Moor (this volume, Chapter 5) notes that such forms of origination appear to use scale and networks in a fluid manner, fixing brands to particular territories or situating them in looser spatial entities. Origination seeks to construct and manage not just the material but the symbolic and perceived geographical associations in brands and branding.

Building upon 'country of origin of brand' (Phau and Prendergast 2000), it is significant that, for goods, services and knowledges, origination is being distinguished by brand producers and circulators for particular parts of their spatial circuits of value and meaning. The flight from cost-sensitive assembly and production in more advanced economies has witnessed the outsourcing of assembly, production and increasingly service delivery activities to lower-cost contractors and sub-contractors of comparable quality internationally (Smith *et al.* 2002; Dossani and Kenney 2007). Economic imperatives have compelled businesses in higher-cost and higher-wage economies to develop more sophisticated, productive and higher-value-added activities to establish defensible and distinctive market positions against lower-cost international imitation and replication (Storper 1995). The broader 'knowledge economy' narrative and emphasis upon innovation, design and styling have reinforced and enabled such processes (Rusten and Bryson 2009; Sunley *et al.* 2008).

While such developments in goods and services markets have not proceeded in a simple, linear and geographically uniform fashion towards a 'weightless economy' of 'brands not products' as Klein (2000) suggested, considering and reflecting upon the kind and nature of such origination in brands and branding presents a more geographically nuanced picture. The oft-quoted example is from the Apple brand with its 'Designed by Apple in California. Assembled in China' origination, reassuring consumers that the innovation and smart bits are undertaken at Apple's headquarters and R&D campus at Infinite Loop, Cupertino, California, while the product is actually put together in China to enable Apple to deliver a cost-competitive product. Elsewhere too, the Skunkfunk clothing brand emphasises 'Designed in the Basque Country. Assembled in China',

locating its roots in the culturally rich, meaningful and valuable traditions and style of an authentic place despite its international outsourcing.
Luxury fashion brand Burberry deploys a 'brand hierarchy' in retaining
manufacture of its iconic rainwear in the UK to secure its valuable and
meaningful version of 'Britishness', while its more commodifed branded
products lower down the brand hierarchy are outsourced internationally to central and eastern Europe, Turkey, Morocco and China (Pike
2011a). Social agents involved in brands and their branding, then, are
wrestling with the potentials and pitfalls of origination, treading the fine
line between strong geographical associations with valuable and meaningful places and seeking to obscure spatial connotations of anywhere more
commercially ambiguous or even damaging.

In considering the connections between the geographies of brands and
branding of goods and services and its migration into the realm of spaces
and places, several contributions return to the thorny problem of translation, that is, whether and how the concepts of 'brand' and 'branding' albeit
variously defined are able to engage with the objects and subjects of spaces
and places. As Warnaby *et al.* (this volume, Chapter 15), Therkelsen and
Halkier (this volume, Chapter 12) and Lewis (this volume, Chapter 16)
and others (Turok 2009) demonstrate, spaces and places are much more
complex, contested and fluid entities likely to resist codification, distillation and fixing into a single or even multiple set of brands subject to processes of branding. Places are not simply owned and controlled like a good
or service; they involve a mass citizenry of people, and they are variable
over time. They do not provide a consistent, quality-assured and standard
'product' or 'service' deliverable to each consumer – experience of places
can be different each time for each individual interaction. This critical
point appears sometimes to have been missed or deliberately overlooked
in the analysis and the business of selling commodified spaces and places
and their branding. Political issues about consent and permission from
citizens within places whose places are being branded and what kind of
brand and branding and for whom become important too (see Lewis, this
volume, Chapter 16). We return to this point below.

## METHODOLOGIES AND RESEARCHING BRANDS AND BRANDING GEOGRAPHIES

The collection's review of inter-disciplinary and international work highlights several issues for method in researching the geographies of brands
and branding. First, the desire to uncover detail and particularity to demonstrate the explanatory value of geography in understanding brands and

branding often results in the methodological dominance of case study. This is typically an in-depth examination of a particular brand of good, service, knowledge, space or place (e.g. Cook and Harrison 2003; Sum, this volume, Chapter 10; Harris, this volume, Chapter 11) or brands and branding within a particular industry or geographical context (e.g. Hauge, this volume, Chapter 6; Kubartz, this volume, Chapter 8; Power and Jansson, this volume, Chapter 9; Dwyer and Jackson 2003). Further, the breadth of empirical analysis is often relatively narrow, with the predominance of studies of consumer goods such clothing and food. Few studies undertake comparative analysis with some constants to contrast similarities and differences. Miller's (1998) material culture work on the hybridization of Coca-Cola in Trinidad, for example, explores the same brand in different places. Papadopoulos (this volume, Chapter 2) uses a range of survey and data analysis techniques to compare the role of place in international empirics across a range of goods and services over time. Therkelsen and Halkier's (this volume, Chapter 12) study compares the experience of two different cities in one national context. Lewis (this volume, Chapter 16) explores the family of brands and branding activities seeking to represent New Zealand.

Case studies and in-depth analysis have yielded rich insights. Further exploration of brands and branding geographies might use a more plural, diverse and varied set of mixed methods together with a wider empirical frame in material and geographical terms to provide opportunities rigorously to test our emerging understandings. Such endeavour could especially engage, first, the thorny issue of assessing and measuring the impact of brand and branding activities on goods, services, knowledges, spaces and places (Lury and Moor 2010; Turok 2009). Second, future work could explore instances of failure and counter-productive brands and branding geographies, for example where campaigns, slogans and logos change from year to year reinforcing the ephemeral feel of brands and branding or where such activities fix an identity and image in aspic, locking in a brand and its branding and inhibiting its evolution (see, for example, Hannigan 2004).

A further methodological issue concerns approaches that recognise and seek to interpret the selective valorization of history in the construction of geographical associations and narratives around brands and branding. Jackson *et al.* (this volume, Chapter 4) use an oral life history approach to understand the interweaving of personal and corporate narratives in the construction of new brands. Hauge (this volume, Chapter 6), Kubartz (this volume, Chapter 8) and Power and Jansson (this volume, Chapter 9) use historically literate and detailed analysis to situate the unfolding of their stories of brands and branding geographies. Lewis (this volume, Chapter

16) deploys participant observation to uncover the historical development
and articulation of the New Zealand brand. Elsewhere, Holt's (2004; 2006:
359) genealogies method is instructive for 'detailed analysis of the social
construction' of brands and branding. Situated in geographical context
and often undertaken to compare different kinds of cases, this approach
constructs socio-spatial biographies of the brand and branding of particular commodities to uncover their 'social and spatial histories' (Morgan
*et al.* 2006: 3). It draws from social lives and histories of commodities
(Appadurai 1986), commodity 'biographies' and 'careers' (Kopytoff 1986:
66) and material culture ethnographies (Miller 1998), as well as geographical approaches to 'biographies' and 'lives' (Watts 2005: 534), 'commodity stories' (Hughes and Reimer 2004: 1) and 'life stories' (Bridge and
Smith 2003: 259). Analytically, socio-spatial biography seeks to *place*
the geographical entanglements of brands and branding: tracing the particular ways in which place – with its multiple layers of meaning (Harvey
1990) and 'geographical imaginaries' (Jackson 2002: 3) – is appropriated,
articulated and represented by the webs of agents involved in production,
circulation, consumption and regulation (Pike, 2011b). Pasquinelli (this
volume, Chapter 14) and Warnaby *et al.* (this volume, Chapter 15) begin
to demonstrate the importance of tracing these historical origins and
development paths for space and place brands too as a means of explaining their selective construction of valuable and meaningful attributes and
characteristics. Echoing the aim of reflecting the tensions between territorial and relational understandings, the complex, even contested, nature
of the 'placeness of the brand' (Molotch 2002: 679) means identifying a
'whole host of specific interconnections . . . to be traced across a variety of
historical/geographical scales' (Cook and Harrison 2003: 311), as well as
spatially extensive flows, surfaces and networks (Bridge and Smith 2003;
Lury 2004).

Last, the methodological frameworks, research designs and strategies
deployed across the contributions to this collection suggest that securing access and cooperation from agents involved in brands and branding
can be challenging and even problematic. While numerous chapters have
secured direct cooperation from agents involved with the key brands in
question, others have had to rely upon more indirect routes in primary
and secondary research and source materials. The value and importance
of brand reputation, image and identity mean many brand owners of
goods, services, knowledges and even spaces and places are especially
concerned with safeguarding their key business and reputational assets
and cloak them in commercial and political confidentiality. Requests for
research materials or interviews can often be refused or redirected towards
external relations or public affairs functions or even external consultancies

that reproduce the corporate or institutional line or redirect researchers to publicly available websites and other materials. While useful, informative and often voluminous for the higher-profile brands and their branding, such empirical materials are not always sufficient to satisfy the needs of more independent and critical social science. What Huw Beynon (1988) described as the regulation and politics of research can prevent access to key interview subjects amongst the web of actors involved and empirical materials such as internal marketing analysis, rich historical archives of advertising campaigns and images, minutes of key meetings and decisions, and so on. As in other empirical contexts, ingenuity and serendipity are helpful, then, in researching brands and branding geographies.

## POLITICS AND THE LIMITS OF BRANDS AND BRANDING

As suggested at the outset to this collection, placing the geographies of brands and branding provides a 'non-abstract starting point' (Klein 2000: 356) to analyse their spatially uneven development and to reflect upon their politics and contestation and alternatives. Amidst the normalisation of brands and branding in consumer society (Bauman 2007), brand-based activism has mobilised around their visibility and value, targeting, resisting and subverting brands as symbols of capitalist globalisation and developing social critique (see, for example, Bollier 2005; Boorman 2007; Bové and Dufour 2002; Lawson 2009). But brands and branding are politically ambiguous. Echoing 'de-fetishisation' debates, brand-based activism is riddled with problems: a lack of reflexivity and uncertainty about such activism's meanings and 'anti-consumer' characteristics (Littler 2005); citizens' uneven political consciousness about brand provenance (Ross 2004); 'brand-based activism' as 'the ultimate achievement of branding' (Klein 2000: 428); the narrow focus upon 'designer injustices' (Klein 2000: 423); the marketing of resistance symbols back to brand-conscious dissenters; and the co-option of resistance movements by brands and branding concepts and language (Huish 2006).

Only offering up complexity, diversity and plurality in brands and branding geographies for delectation, deconstruction and reflection (see, for example, Cook *et al.* 2007), however, risks 'retreating into the discovery of fragments and contingencies' (Perrons 1999: 107). It is unclear how this response can address normative questions (Markusen 1999; Sayer 2001) and engage politically the economic, social and cultural dimensions of spatially uneven development (see also Castree 2004; Hartwick 2000). Analytically, the challenge is to hold together and articulate the 'singularity of economy' (Lee 2006) enabling social and material reproduction with greater sensitivity to complexity, diversity and variety (see also Pollard *et al.* 2009). The culturally sensitive political economy of geographical entanglements developed here seeks to contribute to this kind of reading of brands and branding. Disturbing and unsettling the constructed 'mystical veils' of brands and branding foregrounds their connections to geographically differentiated and unequal development – questioning the form, degree and character of spatial attachments, as Lewis (this volume, Chapter 16) manages in relation to the political project and aspirations of Brand NZ. Rather than 'dictating' meaning (see Cook *et al.* 2007), it provides ways of confronting what Marx called the 'vulgar commodity rabble' (cited in Watts 2005: 540) with geographical imaginaries that put brands and branding in their place – deflating the hype and reminding of their historical role as marks of identification and quality. In framing normative questions about 'what kind of brands and branding and for whom?', it can contribute to tackling the difficult questions about 'radical' and/or 'sustainable' politics of consumption (Cook *et al.* 2007) and scrutinise how brands might be entangled geographically in more progressive ways for people and places (see, for example, Arvidsson, this volume, Chapter 18; Julier, this volume, Chapter 13; and Lewis, this volume, Chapter 16).

A central challenge in reflecting upon the politics of brands and branding geographies is the dominance and usage of its language and concepts. Language is important in providing, even imposing, ordering devices that shape social thought and action in often powerful ways (O'Neill 2011). As the extension of its reach to people, places and things throughout economy, society, culture and polity demonstrates, the language and concepts of 'brand' and 'branding' have suffused public and policy discourse with resonant effects. Myriad aspects of the social world are conceived in terms of 'brands' that require distinctive 'branding'. As Ngai-Ling Sum (this volume, Chapter 10) demonstrates, 'knowledge brands' articulate commodified knowledges sold for commercial ends, and Adam Arvidsson (this volume, Chapter 18) explains how the 'creative city' has become a powerful branded discourse guiding action in city branding. Nick Lewis (this volume, Chapter 16) and Simon Anholt (this volume, Chapter 17) too show how the idea of the 'nation brand' has morphed into the practice and business of 'nation branding' above and beyond its original reach and meaning. Mobility and adoption of such techniques have generated homogenisation through mimicry of 'successful' strategies and deployment of a similar (if not the same) formula in different places, including: glass and steel signature buildings designed by international 'starchitects'; earthy, edgy and bohemian cultural quarters; waterfront redevelopment;

leisure- and retail-led regeneration; spectacle events such as the Olympics or World Cup football; and so on (Hannigan 2004; Turok 2009). Even contestation and resistance are framed in terms of subverting existing brands or constructing 'anti-brands' or 'counter-brands' (Julier, this volume, Chapter 13; Therkelsen and Halkier, this volume, Chapter 12; Klein 2000; Jensen 2007). As Heartfield (2004: 35) notes, 'both brand enthusiast and the anti-brand activist share the same belief in the superhuman power of brands', and the language of brand and branding risks narrowing the basis of the critique by 'reproducing the underlying prejudices of brand theory'.

Yet 'brand' and 'branding' may prove a reductionist, limiting and partial political discourse. The generic and translatable nature of brand and branding language and concepts encourages a distillation of 'good practice' and 'fast policy', with inevitably reductionist lessons, rendered mobile and uprooted from their often decisive spatial and historical contexts (Arvidsson, this volume, Chapter 18; Harris, this volume, Chapter 11; Sum, this volume, Chapter 10). Such an approach risks constraining political dialogue to pseudo-commercial musings about 'brand values', 'brand equity' and the basis for differentiating one particular good, service, knowledge, space or place in competition from the next. But how politically meaningful and worthwhile is challenging the dominant place brands constructed and serviced by elites with alternative citizens' brands or labour's brands or civil society's brands? What can such a strategy deliver for citizens, labour and civil society? A way of escaping being trapped by a brand they feel does not represent them and their place and substituting it for their own brand? A less unequal society and distribution of the value added generated by the brand? Rather than any (re)branding exercise, surely this would require a more thoroughgoing and radical shift in forms of social and political organisation.

The limits of 'brand' and 'branding' discourse raise the question of why social interests opt for a different and alternative brand to articulate the identity, meaning and aspiration of people and places. Such questioning can open up a set of possibilities by more critically reflecting upon or even abandoning the language and concepts of brand and branding. The challenge is finding another language to articulate and communicate social claims on place beyond the narrow and commercially framed optic of the brand and its branding. Some – such as Guy Julier (this volume, Chapter 13) – argue convincingly that brand and branding offer easily accessible and widely understood language and concepts that provide a way to engage citizens about what kinds of economy, society, culture and polity they aspire to or want. Critical to this politics is an understanding that brands, especially of place, are not essential entities waiting to be discovered and revealed and represented in particular ways to the world. There is no 'single originary moment' that can be established (Lury, this volume, Chapter 3). Places that lack a brand are not necessarily what Pasquinelli (this volume, Chapter 14) terms 'off the map': invisible, lacking in ambition and not players in the international place market (Julier, this volume, Chapter 13). As Nick Lewis (this volume, Chapter 16) demonstrates in his analysis of the political project of Brand NZ, brands and branding of goods, services, knowledges, spaces and places are – to varying degrees – socially and politically constructed, negotiated and contested. In the face of material challenges to existing ways of social organisation through climate change, financialisation and social inequality (Arvidsson, this volume, Chapter 18; Julier, this volume, Chapter 13), recognition of this openness may encourage such dialogue and deliberation.

## FUTURE POTENTIAL RESEARCH AGENDAS

A key area for future research concerns closer examinations of the limits of the economics and dislocations of brands and branding geographies. Spatial readings of brands and branding can begin to question and uncover the illusion of what brand owners fear most when it is no longer the case that 'The brand must seem to the consumer more than the thing itself' (Sennett 2006: 144). Sennett (2006: 145) goes on to crystallise this problem for brands of goods and services and their dilemma of producing cost-effective differentiation:

> The problem for the platform manufacturer is how to make differentiation profitable . . . The Volkswagen Corporation has to convince consumers that the differences between a modest Skoda and top-end Audi – which share about 90 percent of their industrial DNA – justify selling the top model for more than twice the low end model. How can a 10 percent difference in content be inflated into a 100 percent difference in price?

We know little about how brand owners, especially in goods, services and knowledges, are struggling with this problem of the artificial construction of difference, meaning and value and importantly how it relates to the geographies of their brands and branding. Questions of origination and the extent to which provenance matters in different goods and services markets appear a worthwhile avenue to explore, especially as

> Imaging difference thus becomes all-important in producing profits. If differences can be magnified in a certain way, the viewer will experience the consuming passion . . . The visual difference aims to destroy any association in the

buyer's mind between Skoda and Audi. By diminishing attention to what the object is, the manufacturer hopes to sell its associations. (Sennett 2006: 146)

In the context of a 'concentration on marketing' as largely a 'displacement activity for innovation', how what Heartfield (2004: 42) explains as 'brand loyalty beyond reason' is constructed and sustained is a critical research question.

Another potential research area in the economics of brands and branding geographies concerns the conventional wisdom about upgrading from sub-contractor to original equipment manufacturer (OEM) producing standard and simple goods for export markets through own design manufacturer (ODM) to own brand manufacturer (OBM) within commodity production systems, especially for producers in developing economies (Sum, this volume, Chapter 10; Gereffi *et al.* 2005). Little attention has been afforded to whether this linear model of movement up a ladder of ever more sophisticated and higher value-added activity is desirable. While the potential economic benefits in productivity, wage and innovation capacity are established for individual businesses and by at least some extension for their workers and locations, a fallacy of composition may be at work whereby it is not simultaneously possible for all producers to attempt market entry with their own branded goods and services. Markets may not be able to sustain such brand proliferation, and the strategy may prove self-defeating, risky and costly as multiple producers bid away each other's margins in competition and undermine longer-term business viability. This conundrum raises an important research question for territorial development strategies advocating versions of this linear model of upgrading.

Heeding the call to widen the range of methods and broaden the empirical focus to perhaps more difficult brands and branding geographies, interrogating Greenberg's (2008) thicker 'mystical veils' needs exploring for branded commodities whose geographical entanglements may appear, at first glance, to be less obvious, including goods, services and knowledges such as headache tablets, insurance, mobile communications, pet food, shampoo, supermarket own brands, transportation and so on. We can learn from Molotch (2005) and the commodity 'following' work here in their empirical ambition (Cook *et al.* 2006). Similarly, examination of space and place brands that have emerged with weak points of difference that have proved worthless and impossible to valorise in the place market would be interesting as cases where branding space and place doesn't work and/or yields disappointing results (see, for example, Hannigan 2004; Julier 2005). While this collection has emphasised the importance of the issue and made some worthwhile contributions, the connections between the brands and branding of goods, services, knowledges, spaces and places warrant much further investigation (Papadopoulos, this volume, Chapter 2; Power and Jansson, this volume, Chapter 9).

Again widening the empirical scope of future brands and branding geographies, further work on their uneven development would be welcome beyond the 'global' brands which have received significant attention to date amidst evidence of sharpening socio-spatial inequality and development. Returning to the Apple example, the uneven development amongst the brand's spatial circuit of value and meaning became especially apparent following an apparent worker suicide and labour unrest at its major Taiwanese-owned sub-contractor Foxconn in China in 2010. Foxconn was struggling to meet burgeoning international demand for Apple's latest iPhone and iPad products, and Apple sought to contain the pressures of increased wage costs by encouraging its lead sub-contractor to decentralise production from its Shenzhen hub to north and central China (Hille 2010). Yet such examples of inequality and social unrest amongst the highest-profile 'global' brands are often the only stories that attract media attention and are deemed newsworthy amongst rival, branded news businesses. Myriad everyday experiences of alienation, exploitation and inequity amongst people in places working to produce and deliver goods and services brands are undoubtedly more widespread internationally but seldom heard about (except Ross 2004). Important questions remain too concerning how brands and branding connect with local and regional development, for example in shaping economic structures, the quantity and quality of employment, and variations in consumption patterns, and providing relatively cheap but noisy initiatives in a fiscally austere era (Pike *et al.* 2011). Through the labour market, for example, deep inequalities appear evident as gurus such as Thomas Gad (2000: 164) argue that strong brands 'will enable you to have your pick of the best people from the universities or job market, and they will work for you for lower salaries, fewer fringe benefits, while making fewer demands for personal development'. Moreover, the ways in which '[c]itizens . . . complete the scenography' (Julier, this volume, Chapter 13: 218) through people experiencing their conscious or unknowing enrolment in the embodiment and performance of space and place brands have received little attention (but see Hannigan 2004).

Travelling further to engage with the politics of brands and branding geographies, the ownership of such brands and control of their branding warrant much further attention. While great insight has been gained from existing work on 'counter-branding' (Jensen 2007; Julier, this volume, Chapter 13), there is a tension between the logics of brands and branding and the complex nature of places. Narrowly conceived space and place brands and branding seek to distil, articulate, represent and sell singular understandings of what a space or place is about and to differentiate it in competition from other spaces and places. As Warnaby *et al.* (this volume, Chapter 15) suggest, places might be better understood as poly-phonic rather than monophonic brands that mean lots of different things to their different citizens and institutions. But if branded and projected in this multiple and plural way such a brand would confuse internal and external 'consumers' even though it would better reflect the diversity and variety of places. Questions of ownership and control, then, pervade the politics of such brands and branding geographies (Lewis, this volume, Chapter 16). They raise profound issues about whether places should have a degree of ownership of brands appropriating 'their' place as a source of differentiated value through branding practices. As Power and Jansson (this volume, Chapter 9) demonstrate, the ownership of the collective brand of Scandinavian design is rooted in an unbounded and evolving place. It provides a unifying and defining narrative that connects across different regions, products and sectors and is more distributed and fluid with no single controlling or owning structure behind its development. But, crucially, it remains highly valuable and meaningful by its reputa-tion. Arvidsson (this volume, Chapter 18) too introduces the idea of 'open brands' founded upon the sharing of open source principles in IT and wonders about the productive future of such socially rooted forms of pro-duction as brands become more meaningful as communities and sources of innovation rather than just private profit. These examples point to difficult political issues about 'Whose brand is it anyway?' and who has the author-ity to decide what brands and branding mean: a polyphonic multitude and variety of multiple voices or a single, monolithic and controlling owner?

Equipped with the conceptual and theoretical insights from across the disciplines internationally gathered in this collection, brands and branding geographies present a fruitful and challenging area for future research at the intersections of economy, society, culture and polity. The collection has reflected multi-disciplinary and international work as a means of demonstrating the diversity and variety of geographically literate ways of interpreting the spatial associations and implications of brands and brand-ing and their socio-spatial histories. The arguments here attempt to begin an engagement with the wider social science literatures to learn from their insights about the spatial dimensions of brands and branding and to dem-onstrate the importance of geography by projecting more clearly specified and sophisticated treatments of space and place into accounts of brands and branding. Worthwhile connections exist, then, between geography's sub-disciplines and beyond to the 'trading routes', 'bypasses' and 'risky intersections' (Grabher 2006) of cross-disciplinary dialogue.

# REFERENCES

Appadurai, A. (1986) 'Introduction: Commodities and the politics of value', in A. Apparadurai (ed.), *The Social Life of Things*, Cambridge: Cambridge University Press, 3–63.

Bauman, Z. (2007) *Consuming Life*, Cambridge: Polity.

Beynon, H. (1988) 'Regulating research: Politics and decision making in industrial organizations', in A. Bryman (ed.), *Doing Research in Organizations*, London: Routledge.

Bollier, D. (2005) *Brand Name Bullies: The Quest to Own and Control Culture*, Hoboken, NJ: Wiley.

Boorman, N. (2007) *Bonfire of the Brands: How I Learnt to Live Without Labels*, Edinburgh: Canongate.

Bové, J. and Dufour, F. (2002) *The World Is Not for Sale: Farmers against Junk Food*, London and New York: Verso.

Bridge, G. and Smith, A. (2003) 'Intimate encounters: Culture–economy–commodity', *Environment and Planning D: Society and Space*, 21, 257–268.

Castree, N. (2004) 'The geographical lives of commodities: Problems of analysis and critique', *Social and Cultural Geography*, 5, 1, 21–35.

Cook, I. and Harrison, M. (2003) 'Cross over food: Re-materializing postcolonial geographies', *Transactions of the Institute of British Geographers*, NS, 28, 296–317.

Cook, I. *et al.* (2006) 'Geographies of food: Following', *Progress in Human Geography*, 30, 5, 655–666.

Cook, I., Evans, J., Griffiths, H., Morris, R. and Wrathmell, S. (2007) '"It's more than just what it is": Defetishising commodities, expanding fields, mobilising change . . .', *Geoforum*, 38, 1113–1126.

Dossani, R. and Kenney, M. (2007) 'The next wave of globalization: Relocating service provision to India', *World Development*, 35, 5, 772–791.

Dwyer, C. and Jackson, P. (2003) 'Commodifying difference: Selling EASTern fashion', *Environment and Planning D*, 21, 269–291.

Edensor, T. and Kothari, U. (2006) 'Extending networks and mediating brands: Stallholder strategies in a Mauritian market', *Transactions of the Institute of British Geographers*, 31, 323–336.

Gad, T. (2000) *4D Branding: Cracking the Corporate Code of the Network Economy*, London: Financial Times/Prentice Hall.

Gereffi, G., Humphrey, J. and Sturgeon, T. (2005) 'The governance of global value chains', *Review of International Political Economy*, 12, 1, 78–104.

Grabher, G. (2006) 'Trading routes, bypasses, and risky intersections: Mapping the travels of "networks" between economic sociology and economic geography', *Progress in Human Geography*, 30, 2, 1–27.

Greenberg, M. (2008) *Branding New York: How a City in Crisis Was Sold to the World*, New York: Routledge.

Hannigan, J. (2004) 'Boom towns and cool cities: The perils and prospects of developing a distinctive urban brand in a global economy', Unpublished paper from Leverhulme International Symposium: The Resurgent City, 19–21 April, LSE, London.

Hartwick, E. (2000) 'Towards a geographical politics of consumption', *Environment and Planning A*, 32, 1177–1192.

Harvey, D. (1990) 'Between space and time: Reflections on the geographical imagination', *Annals of the Association of American Geographers*, 80, 3, 418–434.

Heartfield, J. (2004) 'Branding over the cracks', *Critique*, 32, 1, 31–64.

Hille, K. (2010) 'Foxconn to move some of its Apple production', *Financial Times*, 29 June.

Holt, D. (2004) *How Brands Become Icons: The Principles of Cultural Branding*, Boston, MA: Harvard Business School Press.

Holt, D. (2006) 'Jack Daniel's America: Iconic brands as ideological parasites and proselytizers', *Journal of Consumer Culture*, 6, 3, 355–377.

Hughes, A. and Reimer, S. (2004) 'Introduction', in A. Hughes and S. Reimer (eds), *Geographies of Commodity Chains*, London: Routledge, 1–16.

Huish, R. (2006) 'Logos a thing of the past? Not so fast, World Social Forum!', *Antipode*, 38, 1, 1–6.

Jackson, P. (2002) 'Commercial cultures: Transcending the cultural and the economic', *Progress in Human Geography*, 26, 3–18.

Jackson, P., Russell, P. and Ward, N. (2007) 'The appropriation of "alternative" discourses by "mainstream" food retailers', in D. Maye, L. Holloway and M. Kneafsey (eds), *Alternative Food Geographies: Representation and Practice*, Amsterdam: Elsevier, 309–330.

Jensen, O.B. (2007) 'Culture stories: Understanding cultural urban branding', *Planning Theory*, 6, 3, 211–236.

Julier, G. (2005) 'Urban designscapes and the production of aesthetic consent', *Urban Studies*, 42, 5/6, 869–887.

Klein, N. (2000) *No Logo*, London: Flamingo.

Kopytoff, I. (1986) 'The cultural biography of things: Commoditization as process', in A. Apparadurai (ed.), *The Social Life of Things*, Cambridge: Cambridge University Press, 64–91.

Lawson, N. (2009) *All Consuming*, London: Penguin.

Lee, R. (2002) '"Nice maps, shame about the theory"? Thinking geographically about the economic', *Progress in Human Geography*, 26, 3, 333–355.

Lee, R. (2006) 'The ordinary economy: Tangled up in values and geography', *Transactions of the Institute of British Geographers*, NS, 31, 413–432.

Littler, C. (2005) 'Beyond the boycott: Anti-consumerism, cultural change and the limits of reflexivity', *Cultural Studies*, 19, 2, 227–252.

Lury, C. (2004) *Brands: The Logos of the Global Economy*, London: Routledge.

Lury, C. and Moor, L. (2010) 'Brand valuation and topological culture', in M. Aronczyk and D. Powers (eds), *Blowing Up the Brand: Critical Perspectives on Promotional Culture*, New York: Peter Lang.

Markusen, A. (1999) 'Fuzzy concepts, scanty evidence and policy distance: The case for rigour and policy relevance in critical regional studies', *Regional Studies*, 33, 869–884.

Miller, D. (1998) 'Coca-Cola: A black sweet drink from Trinidad', in D. Miller (ed.), *Material Culture*, London: Routledge, 169–187.

Molotch, H. (2002) 'Place in product', *International Journal of Urban and Regional Research*, 26, 4, 665–688.

Molotch, H. (2005) *Where Stuff Comes From: How Toasters, Toilets, Cars, Computers and Many Other Things Come to Be as They Are*, New York: Routledge.

Morgan, K., Marsden, T. and Murdoch, J. (2006) *Worlds of Food*, Oxford: Oxford University Press.

O'Neill, P. (2011) 'The language of local and regional development', in A. Pike, A. Rodríguez-Pose and J. Tomaney (eds), *Handbook of Local and Regional Development*, London: Routledge, 551–568.

Perrons, D. (1999) 'Reintegrating production and consumption, or why political economy still matters', in R. Munck and D. O'Hearn (eds), *Critical Development Theory: Contributions to a New Paradigm*, London and New York: Zed Books, 91–112.

Phau, I. and Prendergast, G. (2000) 'Conceptualizing the country of origin of brand', *Journal of Marketing Communications*, 6, 159–170.

Pike, A. (2011a) 'Economic geographies of brands and branding: "Britishness" and Burberry in the luxury fashion business', Unpublished paper, CURDS, Newcastle University, Newcastle upon Tyne.

Pike, A. (2011b) 'Placing brands and branding: A socio-spatial biography of "Newcastle Brown Ale"', *Transactions of the Institute of British Geographers*, 36, 2, 206–222.

Pike, A., Rodríguez-Pose, A. and Tomaney, J. (2011) *Handbook of Local and Regional Development*, London: Routledge.

Pollard, J., McEwan, C., Laurie, N. and Stenning, A. (2009) 'Economic geography under postcolonial scrutiny', *Transactions of the Institute of British Geographers*, NS, 34, 137–142.

Ross, A. (2004) *Low Pay, High Profile: The Global Push for Fair Labor*, New York: New Press.

Rusten, G. and Bryson, J.R. (2009) *Industrial Design, Competition and Globalization*, Basingstoke: Palgrave Macmillan.

Sayer, A. (1997) 'The dialectic of culture and economy', in R. Lee and J. Wills (eds), *Geographies of Economies*, London: Arnold, 16–26.

Sayer, A. (2001) 'For a critical cultural political economy', *Antipode*, 33, 4, 687–708.

Sennett, R. (2006) *The Culture of the New Capitalism*, New Haven, CT: Yale University Press.

Smith, A., Rainnie, A., Dunford, M., Hardy, J., Hudson, R. and Sadler, D. (2002) 'Networks of value, commodities and regions: Reworking divisions of labour in macro-regional economies', *Progress in Human Geography*, 26, 1, 41–63.

Storper, M. (1995) *The Regional World*, New York: Guilford Press.

Sunley, P., Pinch, S., Reimer, S. and Macmillen, J. (2008) 'Innovation in a creative production system: The case of design', *Journal of Economic Geography*, 8, 5, 675–698.

Turok, I. (2009) 'The distinctive city: Pitfalls in the pursuit of differential advantage', *Environment and Planning A*, 41, 1, 13–30.

Watts, M. (2005) 'Commodities', in P. Cloke, P. Crang and M. Goodwin (eds), *Introducing Human Geographies*, 2nd edition, Abingdon: Hodder Arnold, 527–546.

# Index